THE ELECTION OF POPE FRANCIS

THE ELECTION OF POPE FRANCIS

An Inside Account of the Conclave That Changed History

Gerard O'Connell

ORBIS BOOKS
Maryknoll, New York 10545

ORBIS BOOKS
Maryknoll, New York 10545

Second Printing, April 2019

Founded in 1970, Orbis Books endeavors to publish works that enlighten the mind, nourish the spirit, and challenge the conscience. The publishing arm of the Maryknoll Fathers and Brothers, Orbis seeks to explore the global dimensions of the Christian faith and mission, to invite dialogue with diverse cultures and religious traditions, and to serve the cause of reconciliation and peace. The books published reflect the views of their authors and do not represent the official position of the Maryknoll Society. To learn more about Maryknoll and Orbis Books, please visit our website at www.maryknollsociety.org.

Library of Congress Cataloging-in-Publication Data

Names: O'Connell, Gerard, author.
Title: The election of Pope Francis : an inside account of the conclave that changed history / Gerard O'Connell.
Description: Maryknoll : Orbis Books, 2019. | Includes bibliographical references and index.
Identifiers: LCCN 2018045596 (print) | LCCN 2019004487 (ebook) | ISBN 9781608337811 (e-book) | ISBN 9781626983199 (print)
Subjects: LCSH: Francis, Pope, 1936– | Popes—Election. | Catholic Church—History—21st century.
Classification: LCC BX1378.7 (ebook) | LCC BX1378.7 .O26 2019 (print) | DDC 262/.13--dc23
LC record available at https://lccn.loc.gov/2018045596

For Elisabetta

CONTENTS

ACKNOWLEDGMENTS

I WISH TO THANK the many cardinals living and dead, not all of them mentioned in this book, who, before and/or after the conclave, graciously granted me interviews, offered comment, provided information, or gave other precious input that I have incorporated into this book.

I am deeply grateful to Matt Malone, SJ, president and editor-in-chief of *America* magazine, for giving me his backing. I also thank Tim Reidy, executive editor, and Kevin Clarke, chief correspondent of *America* for their understanding and patience, especially in the final phase of writing this work.

I cannot but express a very special word of gratitude to James Martin, SJ, editor-at-large of *America* magazine, for putting me in contact with Robert Ellsberg, the editor in chief and publisher of Orbis Books, who had the courage to accept my manuscript for publication. I had already experienced and greatly esteemed the highly professional, quality editing and careful attention with which Orbis published my previous book, *"Do Not Stifle the Spirit": Conversations with Jacques Dupuis* (2017), and I am delighted that this book too has received similar treatment.

In a special way, I want to thank those who at various times graced me with hospitality as I wrote this book:

Enrico Piqué, my brother-in-law, his wife Mercedes Recondo, and their daughters, Isabella and Paola, and son Lorenzo, at whose home in Bariloche, in the south of Argentina, I began writing this book in August 2017.

Claudio Rozencwaig, his wife Graziella Semino, and their daughter Costanza, in whose residence in Carthage, Tunis, I worked on this book.

Piero Piqué, my father-in-law, and his wife Ana Arduino, at whose home in San Isidro, Buenos Aires, I finished writing the manuscript in August 2018.

I want to express my gratitude also to:

Irene Hernández Velasco, former correspondent in Rome for *El Mundo* and one of the best friends of my wife, who kept prompting me to write this book.

Peter Coughlan, my friend of many years, for reading the draft text, and for his wise counsel, comment, and encouragement.

Frank Long, my cousin-in-law, who also read the draft text and whose positive comments and insightful suggestions helped me on the way.

Others too who read and commented on the draft text but wish to remain anonymous.

Teresa Justina Antelo, our housekeeper, for her practical support over all this period.

A special word of loving thanks to Juan Pablo and Carolina for their enthusiastic, youthful support and great patience throughout this year, to Edwin for his never-failing encouragement, and to my sister Fidelma for being close to me.

Finally, words are inadequate to express my gratitude to Elisabetta Piqué, my beloved wife, who first introduced me to Cardinal Bergoglio, and who accompanied me over these years in my research for this book and in my writing endeavor. Without her loving encouragement, backing, patience, rich input, and talented editorial assistance, this book would never have seen the light of day.

PREFACE

THIS BOOK TELLS THE STORY of what happened from the day Pope Benedict XVI announced his resignation, February 11, 2013, to when Cardinal Jorge Mario Bergoglio was elected pope on the evening of the second day of the conclave, March 13, 2013. It also reports on the words and actions of the new pope in the days from the election to the inauguration on March 19, which revealed a very new style of papacy.

Writing it has been like making a mosaic as I put together the countless pieces of information that I had gathered, not only in the thirty days between the announcement of the resignation and the election of the new pope but also in the five years since then. It has been a challenging and fascinating work that involved in-depth conversations with many people, investigative style research, verification, and then the delicate task of deciding which pieces to include in the final work.

I covered those days as an analyst for CTV, the most-watched television network in Canada, and as a journalist for Italy's *La Stampa*, a national daily, and its influential Vatican Insider website. I also gave interviews to other news outlets.

I kept personal notes on the main events that took place in that period and on the conversations I had with cardinals, Vatican officials, ambassadors, fellow journalists, and other persons who were either living in or visiting the eternal city during that time. By agreement with my interlocutors, much of the information that I gathered then could not be used because of its confidential or sensitive nature at that time of the papal election.

During that extraordinary period in the life of the Catholic Church I carefully monitored the Italian media, both secular and religious; throughout the last century their reports have tended to lead the conversation on the Vatican, the papacy, and conclaves. I knew their main reporters had close contacts with Italian cardinals, including many of the twenty-eight who would be electors in the 2013 conclave. I knew the reporters also had close relations with Italians and others working in the Roman Curia, from whom they sometimes receive confidential information. I was particularly attentive to the fact that, not infrequently, some prelates also tend to use the Italian media for their own agendas.

Having reported on the Vatican since 1985, I have come to realize that the Italian press relies mainly on Italian sources for its information on the Vatican and the papacy and has far fewer contacts outside Italy and Europe. While this may have worked well in the past when the papacy was an all-Italian affair, it is no longer the case. This was already conclusively demonstrated by the election of Pope John Paul II (Cardinal Karol Wojtyla) at the conclave of October 1978; it was obvious too with the election of Pope Benedict XVI (Cardinal Joseph Ratzinger), and was proven beyond doubt at the conclave of 2013 that elected Pope Francis.

I should mention also that in the period between February 11 and March 13 I not only tracked the Italian media but also monitored what was reported in some of the Brazilian, English, French, Spanish, and, to a lesser extent, German-language media; even though they too relied to a large extent on the Italian press for information regarding the papacy, they also had independent sources, both in the Vatican and in their home countries.

While I gathered some very important information in that pre- and post-conclave period, I continued my research over the past five years, talking with cardinals who participated in the conclave and with persons close to them. I also monitored what has since been published on the election of the Argentine pope.

This book is the result of that research and my understanding of what happened in the thirty days between the two revolutionary events in the Roman Catholic Church in 2013: the resignation of Pope Benedict XVI and the election of Pope Francis.

Written in the form of a diary—a journalist's diary—this book is divided into four chronological parts preceded by an introduction.

Part 1 offers an overview of what took place between February 11, when Benedict XVI announced his resignation, and February 28, when that resignation took effect.

Part 2 covers the happenings in the interregnum (*sede vacante*, in Italian) period from March 1 to 12, and especially in the ten secret pre-conclave assemblies of cardinals, known as General Congregations, that were held in the Vatican between March 4 and 11. More importantly, it provides hitherto unknown information on informal gatherings of cardinals that took place in that period at various locations in the eternal city, far from the public eye. Some of these gatherings proved decisive in moving the 115 cardinal electors in conclave to elect the first-ever Jesuit pope, and the first to come from the New World.

Part 3 provides an account of the voting that took place inside the Sistine Chapel on the evening of March 12, and on the morning and afternoon of March 13 that resulted in the election of Pope Francis.

Since the cardinal electors took an oath of secrecy regarding all matters relating to the conclave, I cannot disclose my sources. I can reveal, however, that several electors from different continents kept a record of the voting. Some of them shared memories of that historic event including, though perhaps unintentionally, confidential information discussed with persons close to them, which has in turn been made available to me. And, just as happened after the 2005 conclave when an anonymous cardinal elector, who had kept a secret diary of that papal election, later shared it with an Italian journalist who published[1] it the following November, so too one of the cardinal electors at the 2013 conclave, who kept a record of the voting in the Sistine Chapel, shared it with me for the historical record, on condition of total anonymity, but knowing that someday I would publish it.

Given that disclosure, and information that I have gathered from other sources over these years, I believe that what is presented in this book is a substantially accurate account of what happened in Santa Marta and in the Sistine Chapel during the 2013 conclave.

To avoid any misunderstanding, I want to state clearly that the anonymous cardinal elector is not any one of those whom I interviewed and named in this book.

Part 4 reports on what happened in the period between the election of Pope Francis and the inauguration ceremony for the beginning of his ministry as successor to Saint Peter. It highlights certain words and actions of the new pope that reveal what would be some of the main themes of his pontificate and herald the dawn of a new way of exercising the papal ministry.

The book ends with a brief personal reflection.

INTRODUCTION

THE ELECTION OF POPE FRANCIS on March 13, 2013, was a historic and momentous event for the Catholic Church. In becoming bishop of Rome, he also became the leader of the 1.2 billion church members around the world. He was elected in a secret ballot by 115 cardinals under the age of eighty who were kept incommunicado and isolated from the outside world during the conclave[1] in the Vatican's famous Sistine Chapel. He was elected for life, but can resign of his own free will.

His election marked a number of "firsts." He is the first pope from Latin America, home to the majority of the world's Catholics; the first non-European in almost thirteen hundred years;[2] the first Jesuit pope; and the first from one of the great metropolises of the southern hemisphere. He is also the first bishop of Rome ever to take the name of Francis, after Saint Francis of Assisi. In taking that name he sent a distinct signal to the world that he intended to be close to the poor, but at the same time the name recalled the mission given to Saint Francis by the Lord from the cross in the chapel of San Damiano: "Go, repair my house."

This book focuses on his election and tells the story of how this seventy-six-year-old cardinal from Argentina, Jorge Mario Bergoglio, archbishop of Buenos Aires, already on the threshold of retirement, came from the periphery and was elected leader of the Catholic Church in a conclave that lasted just over twenty-four hours. Even though he was runner-up in the 2005 conclave, his election as the 265th successor to Saint Peter took the world by surprise, as he was not ranked among the likely candidates to succeed Benedict XVI; at best, he was considered an outsider.

To understand how he became pope it is necessary to know the context in which his election took place. This introduction seeks to provide that context by recalling the situation of the Catholic Church when Benedict XVI stunned the world on February 11, 2013, by announcing that he would resign seventeen days later; he was the first pope in six hundred years to resign. The Church was then living through a period of great crisis—indeed, several crises.

The first was due to the scandal of the sexual abuse of minors by priests and religious, and its cover-up by cardinals, bishops, and religious superiors in several countries, mostly in the Western world. The scandal surfaced in the late 1980s / early 1990s and exploded with uncontrollable force in the early part of the twenty-first century, first in the United States, then in Ireland, the UK, Australia, Belgium, and Germany. It did incalculable damage to the credibility of the Catholic Church and its clergy. Seeking to respond to these scandals, the church in England and Wales first, in the year 2000, invited Lord Nolan, an esteemed UK judge, to investigate the abuse of minors by priests and the safeguarding of children in the Church. The 2001 Nolan Report report led to the drafting, and the approval a year later, of guidelines for safeguarding children and dealing with abusers in England and Wales. In the following year, 2002, the US bishops responded to the crisis that had exploded in Boston and elsewhere, and, at a meeting in Dallas, Texas, agreed to a charter for dealing with this grave problem. The Vatican too, starting under John Paul II but especially under Benedict XVI, moved to respond with strict new norms in church legislation for dealing with the crimes of the sexual abuse of minors by clergy.

Under pressure from the media and public opinion, some governments also took action. The Irish government established a commission in the year 2000 to inquire into child sexual abuse by clergy. Nine years later the commission published a devastating final report. The Australian government's newly established Royal Commission into Institutional Responses to Child Sexual Abuse began its work in January 2013, just before Benedict announced his resignation.

In 2005, the Vatican had to deal with the terrible scandal linked to Fr. Marcial Maciel Degollado, the charismatic, Mexican-born founder of the Legionaries of Christ, a religious institute composed of priests and seminarians and associated with a branch of lay men and women, now present in twenty countries. Maciel, who founded the institute in 1941 and led it until 2005, enjoyed the trust of John Paul II and senior Vatican officials because of his strong, orthodox positions on theological and moral issues, his success in attracting many young men to the priesthood, his founding of Catholic educational institutes in many countries, and his facility in raising money for papal projects—including in Poland. But an investigation ordered by Cardinal Joseph Ratzinger as John Paul II was on his deathbed and conducted by Monsignor Charles Scicluna, the Vatican's top prosecutor[3] of clergy who sexually abused minors, concluded that Maciel had abused minors and was guilty of other serious offenses. Benedict XVI sentenced the then more-than-eighty-year-old priest to a life of prayer and penance.[4]

Because of such scandals, many of which were first revealed by the media, bishops were accused of putting the good name of the church institution before the welfare of children, covering up the abuse, and protecting priest abusers. Many lost credibility in the countries affected. Catholic priests in these lands who had lived their lives with integrity were demoralized and were sometimes treated with suspicion or contempt. In some countries the Church was in a veritable free-fall.

The sexual abuse scandal, which had shaken the Church to its foundations, was still unfolding as the cardinals gathered in Rome to elect a new pope. It hovered like a dark cloud over their pre-conclave meetings as organizations representing victims of abuse, especially in the United States, called on several cardinals not to participate in the election because of their alleged failure to have dealt properly with abuse cases in their dioceses.

A second major crisis, known as "Vatileaks," erupted in May 2012 when an Italian investigative journalist, Gianluigi Nuzzi, published a three-hundred-page book, *His Holiness: The Secret Papers of Benedict XVI*,[5] based on confidential correspondence stolen from Pope Benedict's desk and given to the reporter by Paolo Gabriele, the pope's butler. An estimated 75 percent of it had crossed the desk of the pope's private secretary. The trove of leaked material fell into four categories: exchanges between senior Vatican officials and other persons with Benedict XVI or his private secretary; exchanges between Vatican officials and the cardinal secretary of state; communications between the head of the Vatican bank (the Institute for the Works of Religion) with the pope and senior Vatican officials; and encrypted reports to the Secretariat of State from the Holy See's nunciatures (embassies) in many countries, including the United States, Germany, Spain, Israel, and Japan.

The explosive documentation included letters from the number-two official in the Governorate of the Vatican City State, Archbishop Carlo Maria Vigano, to Benedict XVI and Cardinal Taricisio Bertone, his secretary of state, denouncing corruption, malpractice, internal fighting and the internal opposition he encountered when he tried to clean things up. The archbishop lost the internal battle and was subsequently reassigned, somewhat unwillingly, to Washington DC as the papal nuncio or ambassador to the United States, in a classic move of "promote so as to remove."[6]

The documentation also included correspondence relating to Benedict XVI's controversial rehabilitation of four excommunicated Lefebvrite bishops, including Richard Williamson, a British-born cleric who denied that six million Jews had died in the Nazi gas chambers and claimed that the US government had staged the September 11 attacks as a pretext to invade Afghanistan and Iraq. The four bishops were members of the Society of Saint Pius X, founded in 1970 by French archbishop Marcel Lefebvre, who rejected some of the Second Vatican Council's teachings. After Archbishop Lefebvre ordained the four in Switzerland in 1988, in defiance of John Paul II, all five were declared excommunicated. Archbishop Lefebvre died in 1991. Benedict's 2009 rehabilitation of the four remaining excommunicated bishops including Williamson caused a storm in the Jewish community, but it subsequently emerged that no one in the Vatican had informed the pope about Williamson's declarations.

The leaking of the confidential documents caused grave concern, not only among cardinals and bishops but also among government officials in some countries, who wondered whether their personal correspondence with Benedict or senior Vatican officials might also end up in the Italian press. Since confidentiality seemed no longer assured in the Vatican, many hesitated to write to Rome.

On May 24, 2012, after the publication of Nuzzi's book, the pope's butler, Paolo Gabriele, was arrested, charged with "aggravated theft" of confidential documents, and sent for trial. Pope Benedict was shocked and saddened by all of this. Moreover, the day before the arrest, Benedict suffered another grave blow when he was informed that the man he had tapped to head the Vatican bank, Professor Gotti Tedeschi, who had helped him write his 2009 encyclical *Caritas in Veritate* (Charity in Truth), had been sacked by the institute's board of directors for an alleged deterioration in standards of governance, though he insisted the reasons were linked to his push for transparency.[7]

A Vatican tribunal in October 2012 found Paolo Gabriele guilty of the theft of confidential documents and sentenced him to eighteen months in prison, but Benedict XVI visited him in prison before Christmas and pardoned him.

In the wake of Vatileaks, Benedict XVI set up a commission of three cardinals over the age of eighty—Julián Herranz (Spain), Salvatore De Giorgi (Italy), and Josef Tomko (Slovakia)—to investigate the wider background to the Vatileaks scandal. They handed him their confidential report on December 17, 2012. Soon after the pope announced his resignation, Italy's highest circulation daily, *La Repubblica*, ran a front-page story under the title "Sex and Career: The Blackmails in the Vatican behind Benedict XVI's Resignation"[8] that claimed to reveal key elements of the top-secret report. According to the article, the report revealed the existence of "lobbies" in the Vatican linked to religious orders and geographical areas, along with a "gay lobby." It alleged that Benedict decided to resign after reading the report.

These events in 2012 and 2013 left everyone in Rome and leaders worldwide wondering what was happening in the Vatican and what might come next. It was difficult for cardinals gathering for the conclave to distinguish fact from fiction and misinformation. The situation seemed out of control.

Cardinals, especially those from Europe, the Americas, and Australia who were more aware of what had happened, were concerned by the leaks, the alleged corruption, the infighting, and much else that had been revealed and that was damaging the Church's credibility. Before electing a new pope, they wanted to understand the real situation in the Vatican and what problems he would have to deal with.

Many foreign cardinals, but also several Italians, were looking to elect a pope who could govern, clean house, and bring order in the Roman Curia. They wanted a pope who would bring transparency to Vatican finances and ensure that the Vatican would incentivize rather than obstruct the preaching of the Gospel.

In addition to these two major crises, several other crises had emerged clearly during the eight-year pontificate of Benedict XVI, and these also weighed heavily on the minds of the cardinals as they gathered for the election.

The first related to the rapid decline of Christianity in Europe and the spread of secularization in what had once been the powerhouse of the Church. The number of Catholics going to church in Europe had decreased significantly over the preceding forty years (Poland was the exception); so too had the number of vocations to the priesthood and religious life. Five decades earlier, Europe had been sending missionaries all over the world, but by 2013 Africa and Asia were sending priests, and especially nuns, to help the struggling church in Europe. Paradoxically, as the Catholic Church in Europe declined (in spite of the emergence of new lay movements[9]), it was now flourishing in African and Asian countries where vocations were plentiful. Significantly, too, some 43 percent of the world's Catholics now lived in Latin America. The Church had ceased to be Eurocentric.

The decline of Christianity and Catholicism in Europe was a matter of grave concern to the cardinals, the majority of whom were European. They wondered what kind of pope might help revive the faith on the old continent. Did it have to be another European? What would it mean for the future of the Church in Europe to elect a non-European?

At the same time, the cardinals were aware that the Catholic Church in Latin America was also in crisis in several countries, as many faithful were abandoning Catholicism and moving to the evangelical or Pentecostal churches, which drew inspiration and often much funding from the purveyors of the "Prosperity Gospel" in the United States. The evangelicals were growing, especially among poor people on the outskirts of the great metropolises.

Brazil, the country with the largest Catholic population in the world, illustrated the problem most clearly. In 1940, some 95.2 percent of the population was Catholic, but this had decreased to 73.8 percent by the year 2000. The evangelicals, on the other hand, had grown from 2.7 percent of the population in 1940 to 9 percent in 1991, and their numbers were continuing to rise.

Cardinal Cláudio Hummes, prefect of the Congregation for Clergy and former archbishop of São Paulo, highlighted the gravity of the problem at the 2005 synod of bishops. He reported that while 83 percent of all Brazilians were Catholic in 1991, the number had declined to 67 percent by 2005. "The number of Brazilians who declare themselves Catholics has diminished rapidly, on an average of 1 percent a year," he stated, adding that "there are two Protestant pastors for each Catholic priest in Brazil, and the majority come from the Pentecostal churches." Noting that much the same seemed to be happening throughout Latin America, he asked: "We wonder, until when will Latin America remain a Catholic continent?" He called for the Catholic Church to "pay more attention to this serious situation." Less than two weeks later, Pope Benedict decided that the Conference of Latin American and Caribbean Bishops Conferences (CELAM) would hold its fifth plenary assembly at the Marian shrine of Aparecida, Brazil, in 2007, and that he would attend.[10]

This flight of Catholics from the Church to the evangelicals and Pentecostals across the Latin American continent was one of the main issues on the agenda of the fifth CELAM conference at Aparecida, which took place from May 13 to 31, 2007. Benedict XVI opened the conference, at which 162 cardinals and bishops (from Latin America and the Caribbean as well as the United States and Canada) and 110 other persons (including theological experts, religious men and women, and some laity) took part. Cardinal Bergoglio played a central and inspiring role at the conference as it sought to plot a course for the Catholic Church in Latin America and the Caribbean; he was elected, almost unanimously, to serve as editor in chief of the Aparecida final document, which called for the building of "a missionary church" in the continent.[11] Through his role at the assembly he emerged as the leader of the Latin American church, a fact that would impact the 2013 conclave.

Across the world from Latin America, the cardinals knew the Catholic Church was facing another major crisis, this time in the Middle East, due to the ever-diminishing Christian population there. Before World War I (1914–1918), Christians made up some 20 percent of the population in the Middle East, but by the time of the conclave it was estimated that they made up less than 5 percent. The decline had increased rapidly over the twenty years preceding the conclave and was exacerbated as a disastrous consequence of the war launched against Iraq in March 2003 by a coalition led by the United Sates and Great Britain. John Paul II and the Holy See had tried in every possible way to prevent that war; on the eve of the invasion of Iraq the pope had sent special envoys[12] to the Iraqi and US leaders, Saddam Hussein and George W. Bush, appealing to them to find a negotiated solution to the escalating crisis and insisting that a decision to use military force could be taken only within the framework of the United Nations. The pope and the Holy See warned the main political actors, as well as governments across the world, that such a war would bring immense suffering to the Iraqi people and all those involved in the military operations, impact negatively on Christian-Muslim relations, and likely provoke geo-strategic disorder in the region.[13] But their prophetic warnings fell on deaf ears. Seven years later, in 2010, in the wake of the Arab Spring, the civil war started in Syria, forcing many Christians to leave the land of their birth. That war was still being fought on the eve of the conclave.

The cardinals were gravely concerned at the failure of the international community to find a negotiated solution to the ongoing Israeli-Palestinian conflict that had started in 1948—a conflict that a former Vatican secretary for relations with states (that is, foreign minister)[14] once described as "the mother of all conflicts." This situation too contributed to the ever-decreasing Christian population in the Holy Land, as well as to an escalation in tensions between Jews, Muslims, and Christians there, and the failure to guarantee the right of access of all Muslim and Christian believers to their respective holy sites in Jerusalem. The specter of a Holy Land without Christians was looming on the horizon.

In addition to these crises, the cardinals—particularly those from Asia and Africa—were deeply concerned about interreligious relations, especially between Christians and Muslims. This was a matter of the utmost importance in Asia, where the majority of the world's Muslims live, and where Christians are a tiny minority in majority-Muslim states, including

Indonesia, Pakistan, Bangladesh, and Malaysia. Relations between Muslims and Christians were good under John Paul II but suffered a significant setback in September 2016 when Benedict XVI, in a lecture at Regensburg University in Germany, appeared to link Islam and the prophet Muhammad to violence; his words sparked protests across the Islamic world and—in some places—violence against Christians. While the German pope, with the assistance of the Pontifical Council for Interreligious Dialogue led by Cardinal Jean-Louis Tauran, succeeded in repairing relations with Muslim leaders and scholars in most countries by, among other things, visiting the Blue Mosque in Istanbul, Turkey, church and diplomatic sources in several countries[15] said he never regained the confidence of the Muslim people. Given this reality, the cardinals preparing for the conclave wanted to ensure that the next pope would able to dialogue well with Muslims and with the followers of the other religions too, including Hinduism and Buddhism. In a word, interreligious dialogue was a matter of fundamental importance for cardinals from Asia and Africa.

Yet another major concern of cardinals on the eve of the conclave was the difficult situation of an estimated twelve million Catholics in mainland China and the future of the Church in the most populous country in the world. For several years during Benedict XVI's pontificate, the Holy See had engaged in dialogue with the authorities in Beijing, seeking to reach agreement on the crucial question of the appointment of bishops, to ensure that it is the pope and not the communist authorities who have the last word on the nomination of bishops. On May 27, 2007, Pope Benedict wrote a letter of great importance to Catholics in the People's Republic of China in which he sought to offer a way forward.[16] In 2010, however, the negotiations floundered and then broke down. Beijing retaliated by ordaining several bishops without papal approval. The Holy See declared or considered them excommunicated. As the cardinals reviewed the possible candidates to be pope, they were hoping to find one who would be able to reach out to Beijing and obtain an accord with the Chinese authorities.

At the time of the conclave, conflicts, wars, and terrorism continued to plague the world. In his last speech to the diplomatic corps accredited to the Holy See on January 7, 2013,[17] Benedict XVI drew attention to conflicts in the Middle East and, in particular, in Syria. He spoke too about the violence in the Horn of Africa and the Democratic Republic of the Congo, as well as the hostilities in Mali, terrorist acts in Nigeria, and much else. He noted with sadness that, especially in the West, "one frequently encounters ambiguities about the meaning of human rights and their corresponding duties. Rights are often confused with exaggerated manifestations of the autonomy of the individual, who becomes self-referential, no longer open to encounter with God and with others, and absorbed only in seeking to satisfy his or her own needs. To be authentic, the defense of rights must instead consider human beings integrally, in their personal and communitarian dimensions."

In addition to all this, Benedict and the Holy See were concerned over the developing humanitarian crisis of refugees and migrants caused by the wars in Iraq, Syria, Libya, and other places. Problems such as these have been an area of constant attention for all the popes of the last century, as have issues related to the right to life from conception to natural death, the denial of religious liberty, and the persecution of believers. The cardinals expected the next pope to be sensitive to all such matters.

Above and beyond these many crises however, there was an overarching concern that all the cardinals agreed was an absolute priority: evangelization. How can the Church bring the Good News of Jesus Christ to all the peoples of the world? What does it need to do to preach the Gospel in this epoch-changing globalized world, where two out of every three inhabitants of planet Earth have never heard of Jesus Christ?

Many cardinals were profoundly conscious that the scandals mentioned earlier, especially the sexual abuse of minors by clergy, were undermining the Church's best efforts to evangelize, and thus compromising the Church's primary mission and the very reason for its existence: to enable all people to know and believe in Jesus. They understood that it would be necessary for the new pope to deal effectively with these scandals if the Church was to regain credibility and make progress in its mission to evangelize.

Several cardinals emphasized that evangelization and the future of the Church are closely linked to the family—now often in crisis—and to involving women and young people more fully in the Church's life.

The crises and questions discussed above were, in varying degrees, on the minds of the 150 or more cardinals from around the world who assembled in Rome two weeks before the conclave. They recognized that the next pope would have to face these issues. They talked among themselves, one-on-one or in small groups, reflected and prayed in the pre-conclave period as they sought to discern who among them was best suited to lead and govern the Church at this moment in history.

By the time they gathered in the Vatican on March 4 for their first plenary assembly, or "General Congregation," a significant number of cardinals seemed to be focusing on three potential successors to Benedict XVI: Cardinal Angelo Scola, 72, the theologian-archbishop of Milan, the foremost Italian and European candidate; Cardinal Odilo Scherer, 63, the archbishop of São Paulo, Brazil, who had worked for many years in the Vatican; and Cardinal Marc Ouellet, 68, the former archbishop of Quebec, Canada, who had worked for several years as a priest in Latin America and was now prefect of the Vatican's Congregation for Bishops.

There seemed to be a general consensus among journalists too, particularly those who specialized in Vatican affairs, that these three were the front-runners. This consensus was based on private conversations with cardinals, Vatican officials, and other insiders, as well as on the information they themselves had gathered over the preceding years.

In the thirty-day period between Benedict's resignation and the conclave, several other cardinals, including Cardinal Jorge Mario Bergoglio, 76, archbishop of Buenos Aires, were mentioned as possible candidates, but they were generally considered outsiders who would stand a chance only if the conclave failed to agree on electing one of the three front-runners. At the same time, even a week before the conclave, there was much uncertainty in the air; the search was still on for the next pope.

The 2013 papal election was being followed not just by Catholics but also by the rest of the world's 2.3 billion Christians, who count for 31 percent of the population of planet Earth.[18] Due to historical reasons, Christians are divided into many churches and communities, but now many were hoping for a pope who would inspire and somehow open new paths to Christian unity. John Paul II had made some significant contributions, especially with his encyclical *Ut Unum Sint* (On the Commitment to Ecumenism),[19] in which he opened discussion on the papacy, asking how it might be reformed in order to become more a "service of love recognized by all concerned."[20] Few responded to his call to dialogue.[21] His decision to hold an ecumenical celebration of the Christian martyrs of the various Christian churches at the Coliseum in Rome, on May 7, 2000, was welcomed and greatly appreciated by the other Christian churches. But his strong stance in 1994 against the ordination of women as priests,[22] following the teaching of Paul VI, was not well received in many Christian churches.[23]

His successor, Benedict XVI, also made a significant contribution in the ecumenical field and was much liked by the Russian Orthodox, but neither he nor John Paul II were able to meet the Orthodox Patriarch of Moscow and of All Russia, even though they both tried. Soon the Lutheran Church would be celebrating the five-hundredth anniversary of the Protestant Reformation. Many Christians hoped that the new pope would be able to open new horizons on both fronts and also find new and creative ways to relate to Anglicans, Evangelicals, and Pentecostals.

The election of a new pope was a matter of some interest to the leaders and followers of the other great world religions as well, beginning with Islam (with 1.8 billion followers) and including, among others, adherents of Hinduism, Buddhism, Traditional Religion, and Judaism. Their interest was based on the realization that harmonious relations between Christianity and these religions is a fundamental factor for peace not only in African and Asian countries but also at the international level, as we have seen clearly at the start of this century.

Governments across the globe also monitored the papal election; they had seen religion emerge again as a major force in the world, particularly in the twenty-first century. They were well aware of the moral authority of the pope and the role he and the Holy See can play as a force for stability and peace in a fragmented world with a globalized economy. Governments know the invaluable contribution that the Catholic Church makes in many lands, particularly in the developing world, in the fields of education, health, and care for the poorest and weakest members of society. Because of all this, some 180 states had already established diplomatic relations with the Holy See by the time of the conclave, and their ambassadors in Rome were tracking the process of electing a new pope.

For the media too, a papal election is a global news event, and never more so than in the modern era of social communications. The March 2013 conclave brought more than six thousand journalists, radio and television reporters, and photographers from all over the world to Rome to cover what has been described as "the world's most secretive election." They came to report on the conclave but, as this book demonstrates, they also to some degree influenced its outcome.

The following pages provide the reader with a day-by-day account of much of what happened in Rome from the time when Benedict XVI announced his resignation to the evening when Cardinal Bergoglio was elected pope. It presents the people and events that influenced the cardinals as they prepared for the papal election and explains what in the end moved them to vote for the first Latin American pope in the history of the Church. Few understand how this historic decision came about, and many wonder whether the cardinals truly knew the man they were electing to be pope. This book aims to shed light on all this.

PART I

FROM THE ANNOUNCEMENT
TO THE RESIGNATION
OF BENEDICT XVI

(February 11–28, 2013)

Benedict XVI Stuns the World

BENEDICT XVI TOOK THE WORLD BY SURPRISE on Monday morning, February 11, 2013, the feast of Our Lady of Lourdes, when at approximately 10:40 AM he announced his decision to resign from the papacy after having served for almost eight years as bishop of Rome. His resignation, he said, would take effect on February 28, at 8:00 PM (local time).[1]

The eighth German pope in the history of the Church, Benedict read the announcement in Latin, the official language of the Roman Catholic Church because, as he explains in *Last Testament*, the 2016 book based on interviews by Peter Seewald, "Latin is the language that I've so mastered that I can write in it properly." He did not trust his Italian to the same extent and did not want to make a mistake or allow for misinterpretation on such an important matter.[2]

I was at home, working at my computer, as Benedict made his announcement. I was not following what was happening at the Vatican because there had been no indication that anything significant was in the offing, apart from the consistory of cardinals called by the pope to give the green light to several causes for canonization. Those causes included eight hundred martyrs from Otranto, Italy, killed under Ottoman rule in 1480 for refusing to renounce their Christian faith; Colombia's first saint, Mother Laura Montoya, who championed the rights of the country's indigenous peoples and died in 1949; and María Guadalupe García Zavala, Mexico's famous "Mother Lupita," who dedicated her life to nursing the poor.

The ceremony had just finished when I received an urgent phone call from Elisabetta Piqué, my wife and a fellow Vatican correspondent, which immediately brought me to my feet. Calling from the Foreign Press Association, she told me, in an excited voice, that a news report from ANSA, Italy's state news agency, at 10:46 AM had announced: "*Papa lascia pontificato 28/2*" ("the pope will leave the papacy on February 28"). Benedict was going to abdicate. I checked the wires and saw this was breaking news everywhere. At that very moment, we both received a media alert from the Vatican Press Office informing us that a press conference would be held at midday, in just over one hour.

My immediate reaction was to phone Cardinal Jorge Mario Bergoglio, our friend in Buenos Aires for many years, to alert him to this historic development. I felt I had to tell him first; it was important that he should know. Even though it was still early morning in Buenos Aires, he answered the phone. As I told him what I knew, he listened in silence. I explained that I was going to the Vatican press conference scheduled for midday and would give him more information afterwards. He thanked me for the news and said he would call me in one hour.

I next phoned Cardinal Cormac Murphy-O'Connor,[3] the archbishop of Westminster and another good friend. He too was taken by surprise, even though he had heard a rumor a year earlier that this could happen.

Once I had made these two calls, I put down my mobile phone. Nevertheless, it started ringing like crazy as several media outlets contacted me for a comment or an interview. The first call was from CTV (Canada) for which I had reported on Vatican affairs during the last seven years of John Paul II's pontificate, his funeral, and the 2005 conclave that followed. Other calls came in from the BBC, ABC (Australia), Al Jazeera, and RTE (Ireland).

I phoned for a taxi to take me to the Vatican Press Office on Via della Conciliazione, and while en route gave brief phone interviews to some of those media outlets, starting with CTV, explaining the revolutionary and historical significance of Benedict's decision.

On entering the press office, I immediately got a sense of the awesome significance of what was happening. An unprecedented atmosphere of excitement and anticipation mixed with tension prevailed as we were all suddenly under pressure from our respective newsrooms, which were clamoring for more information.

Many colleagues had arrived before me at the press office. Elisabetta came in some minutes later. Giovanna Chirri, an Italian reporter on Vatican affairs for ANSA, was the star of the day. She had gained the biggest scoop from the Vatican in modern history when she broke the news of Benedict's resignation. A diligent reporter, she had been following on closed-circuit Vatican television the consistory of cardinals, presided over by the pope, for the approval of new saints. She was watching and listening when, at the end of the ceremony, Benedict stunned everyone present; instead of giving the usual blessing, he began to read a statement in Latin. Giovanna understood sufficient Latin to grasp what he was saying: he was announcing his resignation and plans for an imminent "conclave."

Next she listened as Cardinal Angelo Sodano, dean of the College of Cardinals, said that the news had flared like lightning in a calm sky.

Though her legs were trembling, her head remained clear. She immediately phoned various Vatican officials, including Fr. Federico Lombardi, SJ, director of the Vatican Press Office, to seek confirmation, but no one answered. She prepared her news flash, but had not yet sent it when, to her great relief, Fr. Lombardi returned her call and confirmed that she had understood correctly. Her news flash went viral in a matter of minutes as the major news agencies around the world picked it up. Overcome with emotion and tension, she broke down crying, but soon returned to fill out the story. As those in the press office offered their congratulations, it was clear that she was still somewhat in a daze.[4]

Shortly before midday, the Vatican Press Office released the text of Benedict's statement in Latin and Italian, which showed that he had signed it the previous day. An English translation provided later by the Vatican read as follows:

Dear Brothers,

I have convoked you to this Consistory, not only for the three canonizations, but also to communicate to you a decision of great importance for the life of the Church. After having repeatedly examined my conscience before God, I have come to the certainty that my strengths, due to an advanced age, are no longer suited to an adequate exercise of the Petrine ministry. I am well aware that this ministry, due to its essential spiritual nature, must be carried out not only with words and deeds, but no less with prayer and suffering. However, in today's world, subject to so many rapid changes and shaken by questions of deep relevance for the life of faith, in order to govern the barque of Saint Peter and proclaim the Gospel, both strength of mind and body are necessary, strength which in the last few months has deteriorated in me to the extent that I have had to recognize my incapacity to adequately fulfill the ministry entrusted to me. For this reason, and well aware of the seriousness of this act, with full freedom I declare that I renounce the ministry of Bishop of Rome, Successor of Saint Peter, entrusted to me by the Cardinals on 19 April 2005, in such a way that, as from 28 February 2013, at 20:00 hours, the See of Rome, the See of Saint Peter, will be vacant and a Conclave to elect the new Supreme Pontiff will have to be convoked by those whose competence it is.

Dear Brothers, I thank you most sincerely for all the love and work with which you have supported me in my ministry and I ask pardon for all my defects. And now, let us entrust the Holy Church to the care of Our Supreme Pastor, Our Lord Jesus Christ, and implore his holy Mother Mary, so that she may assist the Cardinal Fathers with her maternal solicitude, in electing a new Supreme Pontiff. With regard to myself, I wish to also devotedly serve the Holy Church of God in the future through a life dedicated to prayer.

From the Vatican, 10 February 2013
BENEDICTUS PP XVI

I had just finished reading the statement in the foyer of the press office when Cardinal Bergoglio phoned, seeking more news. I moved away from colleagues standing close to me and briefed him rapidly, promising that I would give further information after the press conference that was about to start. Again, he listened without commenting and thanked me for sharing the news.

Fr. Federico Lombardi, SJ, director of the Holy See's press office, stepped up to the podium. "The pope took us by surprise!" he told the crowded room of some 150 reporters representing media organizations from around the world. He recounted what had happened at the consistory just over one hour earlier, and he noted that the pope had read his statement of resignation in Latin. Since this had been translated into Italian and distributed to the press just prior to this conference, he presumed everyone had read it.

Notwithstanding the heightened tension and a tsunami of questions, Lombardi remained calm, courteous, and patient, as he would throughout the next thirty days. He explained that Benedict would use his last public audience in Saint Peter's Square on February 27—"the last great celebration," as he called it—to bid farewell to the faithful. He confirmed that until then Benedict would conduct the audiences that had already been scheduled with the heads of state of Romania and Guatemala and that he would continue to carry out his other previously planned duties.

Finally, he announced that Benedict would meet the College of Cardinals for the last time as pope on the morning of February 28, and that evening he would leave the Vatican and travel to Castel Gandolfo, the papal summer residence, where at 8:00 PM (local time) he would cease to be pope. From that hour the See of Peter would be vacant—*sede vacante*—as they say in Italian, and a conclave would be called to elect a new pope.

Responding to questions, Fr. Lombardi denied suggestions that Benedict XVI was ill; he had taken the decision to resign because of his declining strength due to old age. He confirmed that Benedict had visited a private clinic in Rome three months earlier, to replace his pacemaker, but insisted that this was a routine procedure and had not influenced his decision to abdicate. The press office director speculated that after Benedict's resignation he could be known as "the emeritus bishop of Rome."

A MEDIA FRENZY FOLLOWED Lombardi's briefing as journalists contacted their news desks and began to discuss with one another who might be the possible successors, the *papabili*, as they are known in Italian, to Benedict XVI.

Identifying the *papabili*, the candidates who could be pope, is a challenging task—even for the most experienced journalists. The process takes into account several factors, starting with information gleaned from personal knowledge of the individual cardinals, their character, lifestyle, and pastoral accomplishments. Information can be obtained from private conversations with cardinals who are friends, or at least trust you enough to be willing to share their opinions on brother cardinals. Also involved are insights gained from what Vatican officials have to say about the various cardinals. Some valuable information can come from ambassadors who know cardinals, and from fellow journalists whose knowledge and judgment one trusts. Armed with all this input, and assisted by one's own intuition, one arrives at names.

Nevertheless, it is easier to identify the *papabili* than to predict who will be the next pope, as my friend John L. Allen made clear on the eve of the eve of the 2005 conclave. Writing for the *National Catholic Reporter*, he noted, "Prognostication is a notoriously hazardous business, and the trash heaps of church history are littered with the carcasses of journalists who have tried to predict the next pope. Almost no one, for example, correctly anticipated that the archbishop of Kraków, Karol Wojtyla, would emerge from the second conclave of 1978 as Pope John Paul II."

SOON AFTER THE VATICAN PRESS CONFERENCE ENDED, Mario Calabresi, editor in chief of the Turin-based national daily *La Stampa*, contacted the four main reporters who worked for Vatican Insider, a website run by the newspaper. These were Andrea Tornielli (its coordinator), Andrés

Beltramo (from Argentina, who also works for Notimex, a Mexican news agency), Giacomo Galeazzi (the paper's staff reporter), and me. He asked each of us to draw up a short list of the *papabili* by four o'clock that same afternoon. He wanted a list of four to six names for publication in the following day's print edition of the paper.

I included Cardinal Bergoglio on my short list, as did my friend, Andrea Tornielli. Few other news outlets included him on their initial short lists. The exceptions were Agence France-Presse (AFP), an international news agency headquartered in Paris; *La Nación*, the paper of record in Argentina, for which Elisabetta Piqué is the Rome correspondent;[5] and *El País*, the Spanish daily.

It soon became clear that the Italian cardinal, Angelo Scola, archbishop of Milan, was the number-one pick of most media outlets, including ours. Brazil's cardinal, Odilo Scherer, archbishop of São Paulo, was ranked second, while the third slot was assigned to the Canadian cardinal Marc Ouellet, former archbishop of Quebec and then head of the powerful Vatican Congregation for Bishops. There was general consensus in the media that these three were the front-runners, with Scola in lead position.

"There's a very strong likelihood that it will be someone from Europe." This was the opinion of Fr. Thomas J. Reese, SJ, former editor in chief of *America* magazine and now senior fellow at the Woodstock Theological Center at Georgetown University, speaking to the *New York Times*. Interestingly however, in the same article, Philip Jenkins, distinguished professor of history at the Institute for Studies of Religion at Baylor University, in Waco, Texas, had a different opinion. In light of the decline of Christianity on the old continent and the rise of such in Latin America, he remarked, "If I were investing the church's efforts, I would put Latin America high, to avoid a second Europe."[6]

During the following days, national and international news outlets added other *papabili* to the original three, including Claudio Hummes (Brazil), Óscar Andrés Rodríguez Maradiaga (Honduras), Norberto Rivera Carrera (Mexico), João Braz de Aviz (Brazil), Leonardo Sandri (Argentina), Luis Antonio Tagle (Philippines), Peter Turkson (Ghana), Christoph Schönborn (Austria), Peter Erdo (Hungary), Francis Arinze (of Nigeria, though now over eighty years old), John Onaiyekan (Nigeria), Timothy Dolan (United States), and Laurent Monsengwo Pasinya (Democratic Republic of the Congo). It was a wide field, and still more names would be added.

Having identified potential candidates, reporters in Rome began to search for "the real reasons" behind Benedict's decision. Many quizzed

Vatican cardinals and Roman Curia officials, but, as they quickly discovered, these too were in a state of shock; they knew little, though hypotheses abounded.

Benedict XVI had kept the cardinals and other officials of the Roman Curia, the Vatican's civil service, totally in the dark regarding his decision. It was the best-kept secret in a pontificate marked by leaks. No one had seen the resignation coming, at least not at the time. Most had forgotten or were unaware that some ten years earlier, Cardinal Joseph Ratzinger, then prefect of the Congregation for the Doctrine of the Faith, had spoken of the resignation of a pope as a distinct possibility. Asked by a journalist in 2002 whether he thought the visibly ailing John Paul II should resign, Ratzinger replied: "Not him, but given that we live longer nowadays I can foresee that a future pope could resign." They had also forgotten that Benedict had sparked much speculation on April 29, 2009, when, on a visit to the city of Aquila, in the Abruzzi region of Italy, he had prayed at the tomb of Celestine V (1209–1296), the last pope to resign, and had left his own pallium, the symbol of his episcopal authority, on the tomb. As it turned out, it was a prophetic gesture.

We knew of course that the question of resignation had come up in *Light of the World: The Pope, the Church and the Signs of the Times*, the book-length interview Benedict did with Peter Seewald, a German journalist, in 2010.[7] That was at a time when reports of sexual abuse of minors by clergy in Germany were being reported, and Seewald asked whether, in light of all this, he had ever considered resigning. Benedict answered, "When the danger is great, one must not run away. For that reason, now is certainly not the time to resign." But he added, "One can resign at a peaceful moment or when one simply cannot go on. But one must not run away from danger and say that someone else should do it." Later in the book Benedict stated, "If a pope clearly realizes that he is no longer physically, psychologically, and spiritually capable of handling the duties of his office, then he has a right and, under some circumstances, also an obligation to resign."[8]

Clearly, Benedict always saw resignation as a possibility for a pope. He knew that Pius XII, Paul VI, and John Paul II had, for different reasons, mulled over the possibility. John Paul II rejected it because, as his secretary, then Archbishop (now Cardinal) Stanislaw Dziwisz reported at the time, "One does not come off the cross." But for Benedict it was always a viable option, and it did not mean coming off the cross. He described it instead as "another way to be connected to the suffering Lord, in the stillness of silence, in the grandeur and intensity of praying for the entire church," adding, "so this step is not flight, not an attempt to es-cape, but in fact another way of remaining faithful in my service."[9]

We now know from Benedict's own revelation in *Last Testament*, which was completed on May 16, 2016, that after his visit to Mexico and Cuba (March 2012) he realized, and his doctor confirmed, that he could not undertake another transatlantic flight, and so would be unable to at-tend World Youth Day in Rio in 2014. "It was clear to me that I must step down in plenty of time for the new Pope to plan for Rio...I knew that I could no longer manage it," he said. He revealed that "the decision matured gradually after the Mexico-Cuba trip," and so, "after talking about it extensively with the loving God," he made up his mind "during the summer holidays of 2012," around the month of August.[10]

Cardinal Tarcisio Bertone, the Vatican secretary of state, revealed that Benedict first mentioned the possibility of resignation to him on April 30, 2012, and that he had tried to dissuade him from this over the following months.[11]

Soon after he had finally made up his mind Benedict confided his de-cision first to Georg, his elder brother and only surviving sibling, and later to his private secretary, Msgr. Georg Ganswein. Then on February 5, a week before he announced it to the world, he shared the secret with his second secretary, the Maltese monsignor Alfred Xuereb.

Only these people—and probably also his confessor—knew about his decision until shortly before the announcement, when he informed Car-dinal Angelo Sodano, the dean of the College of Cardinals, to alert and prepare him for what was about to happen. The other cardinals were not informed.

In *Last Testament*, Benedict revealed that he had written the letter of resignation "at the most fourteen days beforehand." He had originally wanted to resign in December 2012, but then opted for February 11, 2013, the feast of Our Lady of Lourdes.[12]

The Nigerian cardinal, Francis Arinze, who had served as president of the Pontifical Council for Interreligious Dialogue for eighteen years and after that for another six as prefect of the Congregation for Divine Wor-ship, was one of the forty or more cardinals present in the Hall of the Con-sistory on February 11 when Benedict announced his resignation. He de-scribed the scene to me, in an interview soon after:[13] "It was like thunder; the announcement came without advance warning. It came at the end of the ceremony for voting for canonization. We were expecting to receive the Holy Father's blessing, but he told us to sit down as he had something important to say. Then he began reading a text in Latin. When he had read a few sentences, I began to suspect where he was going, because he started by telling us that after having repeatedly examined his conscience before God, he had come to the certainty that due to advanced age he no longer had the strength of mind and body to answer the demands of the Petrine ministry. It was clear to everyone that he was going to resign."

Arinze, who was the youngest bishop in the world at the final session of the Second Vatican Council, described the reaction of his fellow cardinals to the announcement of resignation: "Silence! We cardinals looked at each other. We didn't have words to say. We were still digesting the import of what he had said when, as if to save us from that embarrassing moment, Cardinal Angelo Sodano, the dean of the College of Cardinals, stood up and spoke. Obviously, he had been tipped off in advance, because he had written what he was going to say. He expressed the incredulity of all present, and the sense of feeling lost. He said the Holy Father's words conveyed yet again his great love for the Church. He summed up the feelings of everyone when he said, 'We are closer than ever to you in these days' and 'will remain close to you.'"

Arinze continued to describe how, after Cardinal Sodano finished speaking, Benedict imparted his blessing and then simply walked out of the hall, head bowed. (Four years later, Msgr. Alfred Xuereb revealed in a talk that when Benedict returned to his study he broke down crying and those present were moved.[14] The Maltese monsignor said to him, "Holy Father, but you looked so tranquil while you were reading [the letter of resignation]." Benedict simply responded, "Yes!")

Cardinal Arinze told me that after the pope left the hall, "all the cardinals stayed on. Nobody told us to stay, we just stayed. We gathered in little groups, each one asking the other, 'What do you make of all this?' We were there for quite some time. Then we began to walk away, slowly, each one reflecting, not saying much."

The American cardinal James Francis Stafford, the emeritus president of the Pontifical Council for the Laity and former Major Penitentiary, was the last to leave the hall. He just sat there reflecting, and left only when he was told that the lights were going to be switched off and the hall was going to be closed.

As he walked back to his residence just across the road from Saint Peter's Square that morning, Cardinal Arinze said he was "still trying to digest" what it all meant. "It was clear to me that the pope had arrived at that decision over a long period, he hadn't rushed it. He's not a person who rushes things," he remarked. "It was also clear that he took a courageous decision, because something like this has not happened in the Church for about six hundred years. It was clear too that he loves the Church. He didn't put himself at the center; he was concerned only with what is good for the Church. That was his only preoccupation; he was not concerned about his personal convenience, nor the honor or praise that he gets as pope. So, I said to myself, the pope is teaching us all something very important by this act. One of the titles of the pope is 'Servant of the servants of God.' We come and go. Any of us can go, only Christ does not go. Without Christ, the Church loses its foundation, its direction, its harmony. Popes come and go, bishops come and go, and so do politicians. The pope is teaching us all that the most important consideration for anyone in public office is not 'Do I like this seat?' No! The most important consideration is this: 'Does the community I serve profit by my service?'"

Cardinal Arinze admitted that he was at first "shocked, and surprised" at the news, but he soon regained his calm because "I was reassured by his courage and by the knowledge that the Church lives because Christ lives, and I was therefore strengthened in my faith." By his decision, he said, "Benedict was reminding us of that central truth that Christ is at the center; and that we preach not ourselves, but Christ, and him crucified."

He emphasized that Benedict's decision "doesn't change the nature of the papacy, but it can help us in reflecting on the faith, and how we look at the pope." Indeed, he said, "it can also help any of us who are in a position of authority to ask ourselves some questions, because sometimes an objective assessment could lead a person in a position of authority to conclude that it may be better that somebody else should take up this office and that I should step aside for the sake of the community that I serve. That is the lesson the pope is teaching us."

The Nigerian cardinal agreed with the archbishop of Canterbury, Dr. Rowan Williams, who declared that Benedict XVI has "demystified the papacy" by his decision to resign. "He's right. You know there's always a danger of personality cult, because some people believe that the person who is in authority now is the best person ever in that position. They think there's nothing to be changed in anything this person in authority decides, even though some decisions may be administrative, not dogmatic, and there can be different opinions. So, I think each of us should be humble, beginning with the person in authority, and extending also to those who have to obey authority."

The Italian cardinal Francesco Coccopalmerio, president of the Pontifical Council for Legislative Texts, was at the Marian shrine in Lourdes, France, that same morning for the anniversary of the first apparitions of Our Lady to Bernadette, as he had been in previous years. He recalled that "when we came out from the basilica after the solemn celebration it was snowing, and we began to hear the first rumors that something had happened in Rome. People started asking me, 'What has the pope done?' but I didn't know." However, he adds, after arriving at the Grotto of the Apparitions, "reliable news reached me, and I felt reasonably sure that the pope had given his resignation. I was surprised; I had no idea this was coming."[15]

For the archbishop of Madrid, Cardinal Antonio Maria Rouco Varela, to say that he was surprised would be a gross understatement. He was incredulous. He simply could not believe the news. He had just returned from Rome after having had a private audience with Benedict two days earlier. They had been friends for more than thirty years, ever since Rouco studied in Munich with Ratzinger as his professor. In that last conversation, they had spoken freely together in German, as was their wont, but Benedict never gave any indication by word or gesture that would lead Rouco to suspect his planned abdication. Thus, when Paloma García Ovejero, the Madrid-born correspondent of COPE (the radio station of the Spanish bishops' conference), phoned Fr. Juan Pedro Ortuno, Rouco's secretary, with the news at 11:50 AM, the cardinal flatly denied it. Calling from Rome, she could overhear the cardinal respond to his secretary: "What are you saying? It's impossible. I was with him the day before yesterday and he said nothing to me. Impossible! Pay no attention!"[16]

WHILE A CARDINAL MAY HAVE many responsibilities in the Church, his primary one is to vote in the election of a new pope after a pope dies or resigns from the papacy. At the time of Benedict's shock announcement, the College of Cardinals had 209 members, but only 117 were under the age of eighty, the cut-off age for electors eligible to vote in the conclave.[17] Off these electors, 50 had been created cardinal by John Paul II, 67 by Benedict XVI.

In the seventeen days between the announcement and the hour the resignation would take effect, cardinals from more than sixty countries prepared to travel to Rome. They had to suddenly change their plans, cancel long-standing engagements, book air tickets and accommodations. Many spoke by phone with brother cardinals during those days. Many too spoke with Vatican officials they knew, and with other people, including journalists, seeking to understand if there might be other reasons, besides failing health, behind Benedict XVI's decision. They were, of course, also discussing who could be the next pope.

Not a few wondered whether Benedict's resignation was due to the fierce opposition he had encountered many times during his papacy. Others attributed it to the Vatileaks scandal that first came to light in January 2012, but had become known worldwide in May of that year with the publication of the book written by investigative Italian reporter Gianluigi Nuzzi, based on confidential documentation leaked to him by the pope's butler, Paolo Gabriele.

Some cardinals told me they wondered whether the pope's dramatic decision could simply be attributed to his inability to govern. Benedict had seemed trapped in a quagmire, hit by myriad problems, which had begun with his lecture at Regensburg University on September 12, 2006.[18] His remarks in that lecture had linked Islam to violence and created an uproar in the Muslim world, even leading to violence against Christians in some places. His July 2007 decision to restore elements of the pre–Second Vatican Council liturgy and, in particular, the Tridentine Latin Mass as an "extraordinary rite" alongside the "ordinary" one that had resulted from the Second Vatican Council,[19] added to his problems by upsetting many bishops, priests, and faithful in various countries.

Another major problem arose in January 2009 when, in an effort to promote reconciliation with the Society of Saint Pius X, founded in 1970 by the French Roman Catholic Archbishop Marcel Lefebvre, he lifted the excommunication on the four Lefebvrist bishops illicitly ordained by the archbishop in 1988, including Richard Williamson, who had made statements about the Holocaust that questioned the use of the gas chambers and whether six million Jews had been murdered by the Nazis. No one in the Vatican had warned the pope about this.

Benedict compounded his difficulties in November 2009 with his decision to establish an ordinariate for groups of Anglican clergy who wished to join the Catholic Church,[20] a decision that greatly upset the leadership of the seventy-million strong Anglican Communion, and in particular the archbishop of Canterbury, Rowan Williams, who had not been consulted in advance.

Further problems arose in 2010, when Benedict had to deal not only with the ongoing scandal of sexual abuse of minors by priests in Ireland but also a new one that broke out in his homeland, Germany. This one risked involving him in a personal way, because it related to how he had handled the case of a priest-abuser in the archdiocese of Munich during his time there as archbishop from 1977 to 1982. Referring to this scenario, *Time* magazine ran a cover story on March 10, 2010, with Benedict's photo and the title "The Pope's Nightmare." The subtitle read: "From Ireland to Germany, the Catholic Church is under fire over the sexual abuse of priests. Will Benedict act?"

As they struggled to understand the real reasons behind Benedict's decision, it was clear to most of the cardinals that the barque of Peter, as the Church is often called, was being tossed violently on the high seas, and was suffering great loss of credibility in the eyes of the world, particularly because of the abuse scandals.

NEWS OF BENEDICT'S RESIGNATION hit the Catholic Church and the Vatican like a thunderbolt. By an extraordinary coincidence, which some interpreted as a mysterious sign, lightning struck the dome of Saint Peter's twice, accompanied by thunder, on that cold and icy night after Benedict had announced his resignation. Filippo Monteforte, an AFP photographer, captured the image and posted it on the Internet. It went viral.

News of the resignation impacted the secular world as well, and political leaders in many countries hastened to react. Benedict was the eighth German pope in the history of the Church and, not surprisingly, the German chancellor Angela Merkel was one of the first to comment. She expressed her "utmost respect" for Pope Benedict XVI and his decision and added, "the pope's words will accompany me for a long time to come." She praised him as one who is "deeply educated, with a sense of history's great correlations and a lively interest in the processes of European unification."

The White House responded with a statement from President Barack Obama that said: "On behalf of Americans everywhere, Michelle and I wish to extend our appreciation and prayers to His Holiness Pope Benedict XVI. Michelle and I warmly remember our meeting with the Holy Father in 2009, and I have appreciated our work together over these last four years. The Church plays a critical role in the United States and the world, and I wish the best to those who will soon gather to choose His Holiness Pope Benedict XVI's successor."

FEBRUARY 12 (TUESDAY)

Cardinals Unprepared for the Conclave

BENEDICT'S DECISION made front-page news worldwide today; it was the top story on the television and the radio. The Reuters news agency captured the widespread feeling: "Pope's sudden resignation sends shockwaves through the Church." *The New York Times* carried it as its main story under the headline: "Pope Resigns, with Church at Crossroads." Britain's *Daily Telegraph* featured a photo and a headline-quote from the pope: "I am too frail in mind and body to carry on." The *Times* of London printed a similar line on its front page: "I am too frail to go on." Germany's best-selling tabloid *Bild* posted a photo of the pope, taken from behind, on its front page under the title "*Keine Kraft Mehr*" ("I don't have any more strength"). Italy's *Corriere della Sera*'s headline said much the same: "*Non ho piu le forze, perdonatemi*" ("I don't have the strength any more, forgive me"). France's *Le Monde* title was different: "*Le geste qui change l'Eglise*" ("The gesture that changes the Church"), while *Libération* opted for the headline, "*Papus Interruptus.*" The headline in Spain's *El País* said: "*Benedicto XVI, solo y sin fuerza, renuncia por sorpresa su pontificado*" ("Benedict XVI, alone and without strength, renounces by surprise his pontificate"), while ABC chose "*El Papa Libre*" ("The free pope").

Benedict's decision was universally recognized as a historic act that opened a whole new horizon for the Church and the papacy in the twenty-first century. Many predicted it would impact powerfully on the conclave in ways not seen for centuries, as there would be no funeral or mourning for a dead pontiff, and no emotional impact on the conclave as happened in 2005 after John Paul II went to "the house of the Father"—as Cardinal Ratzinger stated so powerfully in his homily at the funeral Mass.

For the first time in more than seven hundred years, the College of Cardinals would enter the pre-conclave meetings, known as General Congregations, free to focus entirely on the current situation in the Church and the world and to identify the priority issues that the next pope would have to address. Benedict's resignation opened the way to a frank and unrestrained pre-conclave discussion.

It did much more than that, however. It took the College of Cardinals totally by surprise and radically reduced the time for advance canvassing for one or another candidate such as had happened in the final years of John Paul II's pontificate when some cardinals worked for a long time to ensure that Cardinal Ratzinger would succeed the Polish pope.

Sources told me that in the three years prior to the 2005 conclave some cardinals of a more conservative political and theological bent, particularly from Latin America, actively engaged in lobbying for Ratzinger. One was Cardinal López Trujillo (Colombia), president of the Pontifical Council for the Family, who, according to sources in the College of Cardinals, hosted lunches or dinners in his Vatican apartment—some suggest perhaps as many as a hundred—to which he invited his fellow cardinals, individually or in small groups, for this very purpose. He worked hand in hand with the Chilean cardinal, Jorge Medina Estévez, to get Ratzinger elected, according to an anonymous Brazilian cardinal, who told journalist Gerson Camarotti that the Colombian and Chilean cardinals "made clear" to electors when they arrived in Rome "that they had consulted Ratzinger and that the German cardinal would accept becoming pope and had given the green light for the campaign."[21] But they were not the only ones pushing for Ratzinger; others, like Cardinals Law, Pell, and Schönborn, were also doing so in different ways.

The more progressive bloc too were thinking about the papal succession, especially the Sankt Gallen[22] group of European cardinals and bishops, which met periodically from 1995 to 2006 to discuss how best to carry out the new evangelization and address a range of other pastoral issues in the cities and lands of the old continent where Christianity was on the decline. As they watched John Paul II's health visibly decline, they discussed the situation in the Church and what kind of pope might best respond to their hopes and dreams. But they had not opted for any one candidate by the time John Paul II died on April 2, 2005, and so found themselves surprisingly unprepared on the eve of the conclave later that month.

The Sankt Gallen group included, at various times, Cardinals Godfried Danneels (Belgium), Karl Lehmann and Walter Kasper (Germany) José da Cruz Policarpo (Portugal), Basil Hume and Cormac Murphy-O'Connor (UK), Carlo-Maria Martini and Achille Silvestrini (Italy), and Lubomyr Husar (Ukraine), as well as several bishops from Holland and Belgium. Like many cardinals on different continents they had originally thought the Jesuit cardinal-archbishop of Milan, Carlo-Maria Martini, was the one best qualified to succeed John Paul II, but when he confirmed that he too, like the Polish pope, was suffering from Parkinson's disease, it became clear that he could not be elected.

Aware that Ratzinger was the front-runner, these cardinals along with others discussed among themselves who might be an alternative candidate. They talked about this at coffee breaks during the General Congregations and in private meetings at different locations across the city. On the eve of the 2005 conclave several of them came together in Cardinal Achille Silvestrini's apartment in the Vatican to take stock of the situation. They knew many cardinals were not convinced that Ratzinger was the right man to succeed John Paul II, given that the two had worked so closely together for almost a quarter of a century. They felt the need for a new vision, a different style of leadership in the Church.

One of the names being mentioned everywhere as *papabile* was that of Cardinal Jorge Mario Bergoglio, notwithstanding the determined effort by certain groups in Argentina, especially in the political world, to torpedo his candidacy. In the pre-conclave period, these forces sent cardinals articles by Horacio Verbitsky, a left-wing political activist and author, that accused Bergoglio (falsely) of having colluded with the country's military dictatorship in the 1970s. But Fr. Guillermo Marcó, a priest of the Buenos Aires archdiocese who acted as the cardinal's communications officer and was in Rome in the pre-conclave period, ably defended him against such calumnies, particularly in an interview with the Italian newspaper *Corriere della Sera*.

At that eve-of-the-conclave meeting in Cardinal Silvestrini's apartment, the cardinals linked to the Sankt Gallen group and others too concluded that Bergoglio was the candidate best suited to be the next pope, given his pastoral experience and vision, his humble and austere lifestyle, and his concern for the poor. They believed that, in a pastoral sense, he represented a change from the previous pontificate, and so they decided to support him in the election.

In doing this, they were fully aware that it would be an uphill struggle against the much better known Ratzinger, cardinal-prefect of the Congregation for the Doctrine of the Faith (CDF). Furthermore, Cardinal Ratzinger had greatly impressed electors from all continents with his chairing of the pre-conclave assemblies of cardinals. Having been head of the CDF since 1981, he knew most cardinals by name, spoke several languages, and showed immense respect for those from distant lands, as several electors told me after his election. His closeness to John Paul II was a distinct advantage in the deeply emotional climate following the pope's death, and Ratzinger's powerful, heart-rending homily at the funeral Mass had a big impact. His magisterial denunciation of "the dictatorship of relativism" at the Mass *Pro Eligendo Romano Pontifice* (For the Election of the Roman Pontiff) in Saint Peter's Basilica before the cardinals entered the conclave had caused many electors to see him as the ideal successor to the pope they had called "the athlete of God." Consequently, Ratzinger entered the 2005 conclave with a very large package of votes, more than forty, as I and others discovered on the eve of the conclave. He was definitely in the best position entering the conclave.

We know much about what happened in the 2005 conclave thanks to an anonymous cardinal elector who kept a "secret diary of the conclave" and soon after the election shared it with an Italian journalist, Lucio Brunelli, who published it some months later in the autumn edition of *Limes*, an Italian geopolitical review.[23] He revealed that although the votes were widely scattered on the first ballot—"around 30" of the 115 electors received votes—the cardinal reported only the names of the 7 who got a significant number of votes.

According to his account, Cardinal Ratzinger received forty-seven votes and appeared almost unstoppable from the first ballot. Nevertheless, a sizable group of cardinals was against him and voted for other candidates—first of all Bergoglio, who received ten votes in that ballot, followed by Martini with nine, Ruini with six, Sodano with four, Rodríguez Maradiaga with three, and Tettamanzi with two. The situation changed significantly on the second ballot: Ratzinger got sixty-five, Bergoglio thirty-five, Sodano four, and Tettamanzi two. By the third ballot, Ratzinger's tally had increased to seventy-two, just five short of the seventy-seven needed to be elected pope, while Bergoglio obtained forty, sufficient to block the German's election. Castrillón Hoyos got one vote. The author of the secret diary did not say who the other two votes went to. It was a crucial moment.

Subsequently, over lunch at Santa Marta, Ratzinger's supporters, especially López Trujillo, sought in every way to convince the Latin Americans to vote for the German, while Cardinal Martini hinted that if the anti-Ratzinger vote held for the fourth and fifth ballots and resulted in a stalemate, they could then look for a compromise candidate.[24] The author of the secret diary reported that Martini began to carry out informal surveys on possible alternative candidates, and noted a distinct atmosphere of tension in Santa Marta that lunchtime, marked by a variety of "moods, comments, and contacts." The big question: Would the opposition to Ratzinger hold out?

Although the diarist does not say so, some electors told me that Cardinal Bergoglio realized that if the opposition to Ratzinger succeeded in blocking his election then the conclave could go on for a long time and thus reveal disunity in the Church. They said he understood that it would most likely result in the election of a third candidate, a compromise candidate, perhaps with less stature and ability than the German. Bergoglio made it clear that he didn't want to contest Ratzinger. He withdrew for the unity of the Church, they said.

According to the anonymous cardinal, during the fourth ballot Ratzinger was taking notes all the while the votes were being cast. Then, at 5:30 PM, he was elected. He had received eighty-four votes, and Bergoglio had received twenty-six. Cardinals Schönborn, Biffi, and—surprisingly—Law from Boston received one vote each, but the other two cardinals who also received one vote were not recorded in the diary.

When Ratzinger reached the seventy-seven votes needed for election, the diarist said, "there was a moment of silence, following by a long cordial applause." He added that Cardinal Danneels commented laconically, "This conclave tells us that the Church is not yet ready for a Latin American pope!"

The diarist suggested that several electors may have switched their votes from Bergoglio to Ratzinger in this ballot because they foresaw that a prolonged stalemate risked provoking a great split among the electors, especially in the absence of a real and convincing alternative to Ratzinger.

He also sought to offer a rationale as to why the majority chose Ratzinger. He suggested that they did so because of his unquestionable intellectual and moral authority, and because he would ensure continuity with the pontificate of John Paul II. Moreover, they liked his great sobriety of lifestyle and doctrine and, importantly, his age was a guarantee that his pontificate would not be a long one. But the anonymous cardinal also noted that several cardinals questioned whether it was right and proper that the dean of the College of Cardinals should also be the one to preside over the conclave; they saw a conflict of interest here and some proposed that the role of dean, in the future, should be given to one who is over the age of eighty, and so not an elector.

IN CONTRAST TO the long-anticipated conclave of 2005, the 2013 conclave took the cardinals by surprise. There was no time for advance canvassing, and there was not even the semblance of a campaign.

In the first edition of his acclaimed book, *The Great Reformer: Francis and the Making of a Radical Pope*, Austen Ivereigh suggested otherwise.[25] He said that Cardinal Murphy-O'Connor, together with three other members of the Sankt Gallen group—Cardinals Danneels, Kasper, and Lehmann—helped to orchestrate a behind-the-scenes, discreet lobbying campaign to get Bergoglio elected. Even though the group had disbanded in 2006, he claimed that this "Team Bergoglio," whose members had supported him in the 2005 conclave, now "spotted their moment" with Benedict's resignation and organized the campaign. He made the incredible claim (incredible to those who know the Argentinian) that the four cardinals had obtained Bergoglio's prior consent for this. This version of pre-conclave events was quickly picked up by media outlets and the blogosphere in the United States, the UK, Italy, and other countries too, and has been used since in attempts to delegitimize Pope Francis.

That version is simply without foundation. I can state this unequivocally, having spoken to two of the four cardinals Ivereigh named and having learned from a reliable source that the other two have also categorically denied it.

Cardinal Murphy-O'Connor's spokesperson issued a denial in a letter to *The Telegraph*, a UK daily, soon after the story broke. Moreover, following the publication of Ivereigh's book, the English cardinal (who died in August 2017) told me he was "quite upset" by this story. He said that while he had spoken with Kasper in the pre-conclave period—they were longtime friends, having worked closely together in the ecumenical field—he had not spoken with either Lehmann or Danneels between the time of Benedict's resignation and Bergoglio's election. He insisted that the four had not joined together in a campaign to get the Argentinian elected: "There was no such campaign."[26]

Indeed, these four European cardinals were so disturbed by what Ivereigh had written that they asked Fr. Lombardi, the director of the Holy See's press office, to issue a formal denial on their behalf and to communicate this to the book's publisher, demanding that any future edition of the book be revised to remove these errors.

Subsequently, December 1, 2014, Fr. Lombardi issued the following statement in Italian on the widely read, influential Vatican affairs blog-site, "Il Sismografo":

> In a recently published book on Pope Francis, written by Austen Ivereigh and issued in English with the title *The Great Reformer: Francis and the Making of a Radical Pope* (Henry Holt and Company), and in Italian, *Tempo di Misericordia. Vita di Jorge Mario Bergoglio* (Mondadori), it is affirmed that in the days preceding the conclave four cardinals—Murphy-O'Connor, Kasper, Danneels, and Lehmann—"first secured Bergoglio's assent" to his eventual election and "then they got to work" with a campaign to promote his election.
>
> I can declare that all the above-named four cardinals explicitly deny this description of the facts, both with regard to the request for the prior consent on the part of Cardinal Bergoglio, and with regard to conducting a campaign for his election. And they desire [to say] that they are astounded and upset (*stupiti e contrariati*) at what has been published.[27]

In a follow-up to Lombardi's statement, Ivereigh acknowledged his error "concerning a passage in my account of the 2013 papal election," and stated publicly:

1. What I wrote ("They first secured Bergoglio's assent") on the top of p. 355 in the English-language edition could be interpreted as implying some kind of agreement between a group of cardinals and Cardinal Bergoglio in respect of his election.

I never meant to suggest this, only that (unlike 2005) the cardinals believed that this time Cardinal Bergoglio would not resist his election. As Fr. Lombardi says, no such agreement existed. I am sorry for any misunderstanding arising from my choice of words.

2. As the spokesperson for Cardinal Cormac Murphy-O'Connor pointed out in a letter to the *Daily Telegraph* on November 24, "no approach to the then- Cardinal Bergoglio in the days before the conclave was made by him or, as far as he knows, by any other cardinal to seek his assent to becoming a candidate for the papacy." Indeed, in the course of my research, I found no evidence of any such approach, or of any violation of the conclave rules.

3. In the line after the above I also write (also p. 355): "Asked if he was willing, he said he believed that at this time of crisis for the Church no cardinal could refuse if asked." Although this is accurate, for the avoidance of doubt: this question was not to my knowledge asked of him by the group of cardinals who urged his election.

4. As a reading of the whole chapter on the 2013 conclave makes clear, Cardinal Bergoglio played no role whatsoever in the bid for his election.

5. In future reprints, the top of p. 355 will be amended as follows:

[EXISTING]
They had learned their lessons from 2005. They first secured Bergoglio's assent. Asked if he was willing, he said that he believed that at this time of crisis for the Church no cardinal could refuse if asked.

[NEW]
In keeping with conclave rules, they did not ask Bergoglio if he would be willing to be a candidate. But they believed this time that the crisis in the Church would make it hard for him to refuse if elected.

WHILE BENEDICT'S ANNOUNCEMENT of resignation took the College of Cardinals by surprise, it is worth mentioning that already for some years the names of a small number of cardinals were being mentioned as *papabili* in the media and by cardinals and Vatican officials in private conversations. On this list, the archbishop of Milan, Angelo Scola, was number one. The tall, heavily built, bespectacled, grey-haired Italian cardinal-theologian was clearly in the top position and widely considered to be the one Benedict wanted to succeed him.

Elisabetta and I knew Cardinal Scola. We had interviewed him in the Patriarchate of Venice, on February 2, 2011.[28] We liked this passionate, friendly pastor who is not afraid to show his feelings, but we found his discourse quite difficult to present in a way that could be easily understood by ordinary readers.

His biography is impressive. Angelo Scola was born in Malgrate, forty-five kilometers from Milan, on November 7, 1941, the son of a truck driver who was a convinced socialist and a Catholic mother. As a young man he was for many years an active member of the Communion and Liberation movement, which he credits with fostering his priestly vocation. A brilliant student, he earned doctorates in philosophy from the Catholic University of Milan and in theology from Fribourg University, Switzerland, where he also taught. In the early 1990s he collaborated with Henri de Lubac, SJ, Hans Urs von Balthasar, Jean Daniélou, SJ, and Joseph Ratzinger on the prestigious international Catholic journal *Communio*, which he also edited in Italian for many years. Along with Cardinal Martini, this polyglot author of many books and articles was then considered the foremost intellectual in the Italian hierarchy. But while the Jesuit Martini was considered progressive on many controversial theological and moral issues, Scola was considered as moderately—or even strongly—conservative. In the view of many cardinals, they represented very different visions of the Church—and of what should be changed in it.

After serving as bishop of the Grossetto diocese for four years, Scola was appointed by John Paul II rector of the Pontifical Lateran University in 1995. Seven years later he was named patriarch of Venice, where he made great efforts to build bridges with the Orthodox churches and the Muslim world. On June 28, 2011, however, Benedict XVI surprised the church in Italy with an unprecedented decision: he transferred the cardinal from Venice to Milan, in what was widely interpreted as a signal that he would like Scola to succeed him as pope.

In our hour-long conversation with Scola in February 2011, he told us how deeply impressed he was by the vitality of the churches in Africa, Asia, and Latin America. But when I noted that there are few cardinals from these regions in comparison with Europeans in the College of Cardinals, he responded, "There are some, and it seems to me that the process of the internationalization of the truly Catholic nature of the College of Cardinals, of the bishops and of the Roman Curia is an unstoppable process; it is irreversible" and has been "accentuated" from Paul VI onwards. He asserted that "as the election of the last two popes showed clearly, there no longer exists the problem of the automatic choice of an Italian pope." He said he was convinced that in "the government of the Church all the doors are open."

When I mentioned that many inside and outside the Vatican are saying that after Polish and German popes, and the many crises of this pontificate, we need an Italian pope once again to put order in the Church, Scola replied, "Well, we'll see!" He insisted that Benedict XVI "is very well and is doing his task in a formidable way, giving us a teaching of the highest level that is arousing enormous and passionate confrontation throughout the whole world." He said, "Benedict is also renewing the pastoral work of the Church through rooting it in the liturgy and the sacraments" and "is portraying the profound nature of Christianity as an event and he is giving the lead here, he is testifying to this."

Cardinal Scola told us, "I do not at all agree with those who say that this is a papacy which has generated crises. There have been moments when the pope has had to take on his own shoulders great problems of men of the Church, and he did so by taking the lead, without ever pulling back. In any case I don't know when, or who could be the next pope, but I believe that the Italians have the same probability as the others and, in my view, perhaps even less." With hindsight, his last remark may be considered as both shrewd and prophetic. He had few illusions.

Since he had introduced the subject of the next pope, I mentioned that we were both struck when we entered the curial offices of the patriarchate and saw the large portraits of his predecessors who were popes in the twentieth century: Pius X, John XXIII, John Paul I. Moreover, I remarked, we could not help thinking that maybe he could be the next pope, as many were predicting. Scola, who had participated in the 2005 conclave, smiled kindly and responded calmly. "I understand," he said. "These are coincidences. Anyone who has inside experience of a conclave, which is secret, will realize that all these predictions melt into thin air when you are actually in there. It's true that the pope is chosen by the Holy Spirit, and I believe that the Holy Spirit guides the Church and makes use of everything, including the poverty of men—I mean the factions (*cordate*) and counter-factions (*contracordate*). But so many different factors go into the selection of a candidate to be pope that no one is able to dominate them all in advance. And it's there that the Holy Spirit intervenes and makes his choice."

He laughed heartily when I told him that Irish bookmakers were already offering odds on likely candidates to be the next pope. But neither he nor we imagined then that in less than two years there would be a conclave and he would be the front-runner.

FEBRUARY 13 (ASH WEDNESDAY) _____

Emotional Last Public Liturgy as Pope

WHEN BENEDICT XVI ARRIVED for his usual Wednesday public audience in the Paul VI Hall, he was given an emotional welcome and warmly applauded by the eight thousand pilgrims and Romans present. Although he focused his talk on the gospel story about the temptations of Christ and the need for conversion, he clearly sensed that people were waiting for him to say something about why he had decided to resign, and so he told them:

> Dear brothers and sisters, as you know, I have decided to renounce the ministry which the Lord entrusted to me on 19 April 2005. I have done this in full freedom for the good of the Church, after much prayer and having examined my conscience before God, knowing full well the seriousness of this act, but also realizing that I am no longer able to carry out the Petrine ministry with the strength which it demands. I am strengthened and reassured by the certainty that the Church is Christ's, who will never leave her without his guidance and care. I thank all of you for the love and for the prayers with which you have accompanied me. Thank you! In these days which have not been easy for me, I have felt almost physically the power of prayer—your prayers—which the love of the Church has given me. Continue to pray for me, for the Church and for the future Pope. The Lord will guide us."[29]

His words electrified the thousands of faithful at the audience; they gave him a standing ovation. Many shouted "*Viva il Papa!*"

Later that day, Benedict presided at his last public liturgy as pope: the Ash Wednesday celebration in Saint Peter's Basilica. He began his homily[30] by recalling that traditionally this first station of the Lenten period is held in the Basilica of Santa Sabina on the Aventine Hill, but, he said, alluding to the unusually high numbers of faithful who wanted to attend and had sought tickets, "Circumstances have suggested that we gather in the Vatican Basilica. This evening we meet in great numbers around the tomb of the Apostle Peter, also to beg his intercession for the Church's path forward at this particular moment, renewing our faith in the Chief Pastor, Christ the Lord."

On a more personal note, he added: "For me it is a fitting occasion to thank everyone, especially the faithful of the Diocese of Rome, as I prepare to conclude my Petrine ministry, and to ask for a special remembrance in your prayers."

At the ceremony's end, Cardinal Tarcisio Bertone, his secretary of state and friend of many years, spoke in a voice overflowing with emotion: "We wouldn't be sincere, Your Holiness, if we didn't say there's a veil of sadness over our hearts." He thanked Benedict for his eight years of service as bishop of Rome, and "for giving us the luminous example of a simple and humble laborer in the vineyard of the Lord." His choice of words recalled those Benedict had spoken at his first public appearance as pope. When Bertone finished speaking, the congregation responded by giving Benedict a highly emotional, standing ovation that lasted for over a minute.

THAT SAME MORNING, Argentina's *La Nación* newspaper carried Cardinal Bergoglio's comments on Benedict's resignation. After recalling that Benedict XVI had been referred to as "a conservative pope," he hailed his announcement of resignation as "a revolutionary act, a change in six hundred years of history." Indeed, he said, "I believe it was a decision much thought out before God and very responsible on the part of a man who did not want to make a mistake, or to leave the decision in the hands of others." Benedict XVI, he said, "is a man who decides things in the presence of God: he shows his greatness." He added, "The pope is a peaceful and humble man. His search for meekness is proverbial. He defines the principles but never attacks persons" and his pontificate "had a great desire for the search for unity which he believed was superior to conflict. He always held his hand out." Bergoglio praised his "magisterium," which expressed itself "through his homilies and his angeluses with great beauty, sensitivity and depth."

La Nación also carried Elisabetta Piqué's interview with another of Argentina's three cardinals, Jorge Mejia, 90, an intellectual and biblical scholar and a friend of John Paul II since their days together in the Pontifical University of Saint Thomas ("the Angelicum"), as well as former secretary of the Congregation for Bishops and subsequently the Vatican's chief archivist. "The papacy has become an enormous weight for any human being, including a young man with strength," he declared, as he listed the challenges facing the Church today. When Elisabetta noted that the two Argentine cardinal electors (Bergoglio and Sandri) were being mentioned as *papabili* and asked, "Has the time come for an Argentine pope?" Mejia, who received the red hat with Bergoglio in 2001, paused a little, and then responded diplomatically, "I cannot pronounce on that. I don't know. The two are very good."

La Nación today also carried an Associated Press story saying that when Cardinal Théodore-Adrien Sarr, from Senegal, one of the eleven African electors, was asked if the time had come for an African pope given that the continent now has 176 million Catholics, he responded: "I have asked myself this for many years. But, I ask, is the Church ready for an African pope? Is the whole world ready to accept an African pope?"

His words brought back to my mind the comment of a senior African cardinal who told me after the 2005 conclave in which he participated, "I think it will be a hundred years before we will have an African pope, but I think we could have one from Latin America within twenty-five years." Bergoglio had been runner-up in that conclave, and his fellow elector from Africa interpreted that as a sign that the day was not far off when a conclave would look to Latin America for the Successor of Peter.

SPAIN'S LEADING DAILY, *El País*, carried an article today by Lola Galan, who has good contacts not only with the Spanish cardinals but also with many in the Vatican from her years as a reporter here. "Betting on who could be the next pope is the principal journalistic distraction on the eve of a conclave, but it is also a discreet way of putting a name into circulation or definitely burning another one," she remarked. Still, "beyond the questionable matter of bets," she said, "one thing seems clear: after the pontificate of Benedict XVI, marked by a certain lack of communication with the masses of the faithful, especially those in Latin America, and a decadent air (one cannot forget his passion for the old liturgy and ancient religious vestments), the universal Church needs a young pope."

But what does "young" mean in terms of the conclave? "If by young you mean someone in their sixties, better late sixties," she remarked, then forty of the electors are in the sixty-to-seventy age-bracket, while another five are between fifty and sixty. Indeed, 72 of the 115 cardinals who will vote in the conclave are in the upper age bracket of seventy-one to seventy-nine. She concluded her analysis by presenting her own list of *papabili*: Scola, Ouellet, Scherer, Maradiaga, Turkson, and Tagle.

Cardinal Maradiaga, however, quickly made clear that he was not the right man to be pope: "It's an implacable job, without rest, in which one has no time for oneself, because everything is concentrated on the good of the Church. I am not suited." Moreover, he added, "It's something that one should not humanly desire; it's something that comes from the will of God expressed through the College of Cardinals, and even to aspire to it would be to disqualify oneself."[31]

La Stampa carried an interview by Andrea Tornielli with the Spanish cardinal Julián Herranz, a top expert on canon law, who revealed that John Paul II had consulted him in secret between 2001 and 2004 about resignation. But he said the Polish pope had decided against it, according to his secretary Msgr. Stanislaw Dziwisz, "because he entrusted himself to Divine Providence" and, moreover, "he feared creating a dangerous precedent for his successors, because one could remain exposed to maneuverers and subtle pressures to depose him."[32]

On the other hand, the Portuguese cardinal, José Saraiva Martins, 80, former head of the Congregation for Saints who was among the *papabili* in 2005, told Tornielli that he considered Benedict's resignation as "a gesture of Christian realism."[33]

In articles such as these, the media were flagging names and issues that would feature in discussions among cardinals during the lead-up to the conclave.

FEBRUARY 14 (THURSDAY) ⸻⸻⸻⸻⸻⸻⸻
Reminiscing on Vatican II

KEEPING TO HIS ALREADY FIXED AGENDA, Benedict XVI this morning held his traditional meeting with the parish priests and clergy of the Rome diocese for the beginning of Lent. I went to the Paul VI Hall to listen to what he had to say and to get a feel for the mood among the five hundred priests that attended. They gave him a standing ovation as he entered; many shouted "*Viva il Papa!*" It was a scene we had seen in previous days, and one that would be repeated over the next two weeks.

The serene, eighty-five-year-old pontiff gave a remarkable talk,[34] without a script, recalling his experiences as a theological expert (*peritus*) at the Second Vatican Council (1962–1965). He recalled its major achievements but lamented the subsequent distortion of some of its teachings, for which he partly blamed the media and what he called the "Council of the Media," as distinct from the Vatican Council he had attended. Benedict spoke for almost one hour. I marveled at his mental stamina and clarity and could not help wondering why he had decided to resign, given that he could hold forth like this in such a brilliant and engaging manner. I heard priests near me asking the same question.

When he finished his magisterial talk, Cardinal Agostino Vallini, his vicar for the Rome diocese, thanked him in an emotional and tearful but brief farewell. He assured him that the priests, religious, and faithful of the diocese would continue to pray for him in the days and years ahead. His words provoked thunderous applause, followed by yet another standing ovation.

An hour later, at the daily press briefing for the international media, Fr. Lombardi announced that Archbishop Georg Gänswein, whom Benedict had promoted to be head of the Papal Household and made an archbishop on December 7, 2012, would go to stay with him at Castel Gandolfo, together with the four consecrated lay women of the Memores Domini branch of the Communion and Liberation movement who have served the pope in these years. Moreover, they would all go to live with Benedict at the Mater Ecclesiae monastery in the Vatican Gardens, behind Saint Peter's Basilica, once its restructuring and refurbishing was completed.

It soon became clear, however, that a number of cardinals were not in accord with Benedict's decision to continue living inside the Vatican; they are concerned that his presence there could create serious problems for his successor, as the emeritus bishop of Rome could become, willynilly, a potent magnet for those who might disagree with the direction taken by the new pope.

LATER THAT AFTERNOON, I visited Cardinal Arinze, the senior African cardinal in the Roman Curia. More than a decade ago, I did an interviewstyle book with him, *God's Invisible Hand*, that was first published in

Nairobi and later in the United States.[35] Before the 2005 conclave he had been widely touted in the media as *papabile*, but now that he is over the age of eighty he is no longer an elector. Nevertheless, he will participate in the important pre-conclave assemblies of cardinals, known as General Congregations, and is sure to be consulted by African cardinals and others who hold this wise and humble man in high esteem.

We talked freely for more than an hour. Speaking on the record about the qualities he was looking for in a candidate to be the next pope, he emphasized the need for pastoral experience in running a diocese and managerial ability. Moreover, the new pope must be committed to "evangelization—to preach the Gospel to the world," and have "a spirit of openness to the world, like that of the Second Vatican Council's *Gaudium et Spes* constitution." In his view, the new pope "should not be under sixty-five, but he could be up to eighty. The ideal age would be between seventy and seventy-five." While he thinks there are "some excellent" African candidates, Arinze said he was under no illusion: this conclave would not elect an African pope.

FEBRUARY 15 (FRIDAY) _____

Soundings on the Front-runners

IT HAS BEEN ONLY FOUR DAYS since Benedict announced his resignation, but I have already picked up the views of several cardinals from different continents on some of the front-runners mentioned in the media.

It's already clear that there are mixed feelings about Scola, the strongest and perhaps the only Italian with a real chance at this conclave. One senior Vatican cardinal told me that he "has long considered Scola *papabile*" because he has pastoral experience in three dioceses and was a good rector of the Lateran University. He expected him to be elected. A non-European elector known for his conservative theological positions said he would like to see the papacy return to Italy after thirty-five years and is convinced that Scola is "the best prepared to succeed Benedict." A cardinal from Europe who likes Scola a lot as a person said he would not vote for him because "he is too complicated in his thinking and in his way of communicating." This problem of communication is often mentioned in conversations. A fourth, non-European, elector asked, "Do we really want another theologian as pope? Do we really want another Italian pope?"

An Italian friend who has been close to Scola for many decades but preferred not to be identified told me, "He is a good theologian on the lines of Ratzinger but without the latter's mental openness on theological questions." He recalled with praise the fact that after becoming archbishop of Milan, Scola consulted two hundred priests in the archdiocese before making any major appointments and then surprised everyone by choosing men who had been in key positions under Martini. Several sources told me that while Scola can count on support from cardinals in Central and Eastern Europe, and some in Spain, the Italian electors are deeply divided about him; while some support him, others are strongly opposed to his election as pope.

The only other Italian cardinal being mentioned is Gianfranco Ravasi, 70, a biblical scholar who spent summers working as an archeologist in Syria, Iraq, Jordan, and Turkey and was close to Cardinal Martini and shares much of his vision. A tall man of broad culture, well known in academic circles, he was appointed by Benedict XVI as president of the Pontifical Council for Culture in 2007. and in that role he has developed some very original initiatives in reaching out to the frontiers of society and culture and in dialogues with non-believers,. Benedict XVI made him a cardinal in 2010 and had him preach the retreat to the Roman Curia in February 2013. A fellow European cardinal who thinks highly of Ravasi told me he considers him "too young, and not yet ready" to be pope.

Hungary's Cardinal Peter Erdo, 60, has been mentioned as a candidate to succeed Benedict. After obtaining doctoral degrees in theology and canon law from the Lateran University in Rome, he taught in seminaries and a university in his native land. John Paul II named him bishop in 1999, appointed him archbishop of Estergom-Budapest in 2002, and gave him the red hat the following year, making him the youngest member of the College of Cardinals. He has served as president of the Hungarian bishops' conference and, since 2007, as president of the Episcopal Conferences of Europe. But some cardinals with whom I have spoken dismiss him as a *papabile* because of his lack of vision and inspiration. Another remarked, "We don't want a second pope from Eastern Europe."

THE CONCLAVE IS STILL roughly three weeks away, but I consider it quite significant that so few European cardinals are even being mentioned as *papabili*, in spite of the fact that more than half of the electors are European.

On the other hand, several cardinals from the Americas (North and South) are being talked about as *papabili*. Two are under close scrutiny: Scherer and Ouellet.

Cardinal Odilo Scherer, 63, a descendant of German migrants, earned a doctorate in theology from the Gregorian University in Rome and worked in the Vatican's Congregation for Bishops from 1994 to 2001 alongside the influential Italian Cardinal Giovanni Battista Re, who will preside over the conclave. Most of Scherer's priestly life has been spent in the field of education and formation. He was the rector of several diocesan seminaries and received a doctorate in theology from the Gregorian University in 1991. John Paul II appointed him auxiliary bishop of São Paulo in 2001, and he served as secretary general of the Brazilian bishops' conference from 2003 to 2007. Benedict XVI appointed him archbishop of São Paulo in March 2007, as successor to Cardinal Claudio Hummes, a member of the Franciscan order, whom he called to Rome to head the Congregation for the Clergy. This move was interpreted by some as a way to remove a theologically moderate and socially progressive bishop who was close to the president of the country— Luiz Inácio Lula da Silva—and replace him with a more theologically conservative bishop. In actual fact, however, Scherer too gave much attention to the poverty in his diocese, to young people, and to the family.

An Italian cardinal elector who knows Scherer well described him as "pastoral but not inspiring" and claimed that "he is 'domesticated' by a bloc in the Roman Curia (including Sodano and Re) who are supporting him, and so risks being their puppet." Nevertheless, most sources agree: he is certainly one to watch.

So too is Cardinal Marc Ouellet, 68, head of the powerful Congregation for Bishops and former archbishop of Quebec, who worked for several years in Latin America. Born in the small town of La Motte, Canada, he was ordained a priest for the diocese of Amos but later joined the Society of Priests of San Sulpice, which was founded in France in 1641 and focuses especially on the education of priests and to some extent on parish work; it has branches in the United States and Canada.

Ouellet also spent many years in academic life. After earning a doctorate in dogmatic theology from the Gregorian University in Rome, he taught in seminaries in Colombia for about seven years before returning to Montreal to teach and serve as rector of the seminary there. He later taught at the John Paul II Institute of the Pontifical Lateran University in Rome, and, in 1997, was appointed to the chair of dogmatic theology.

In 2001 John Paul II appointed him secretary of the Pontifical Council for Christian Unity, then headed by Cardinal Walter Kasper, and made him a bishop. It was during his time there that I first came to know him, and I subsequently interviewed him many times. In 2002 the Polish pope surprised everyone by appointing him archbishop of Quebec, a post he held until 2010 when Benedict XVI recalled him to Rome as prefect of the Congregation for Bishops. Ouellet participated in the 2005 conclave and was considered *papabile* then.[36]

The Canadian cardinal was strongly influenced by the Swiss theologian Hans Urs von Balthasar, whom he knew and on whom he wrote his doctoral thesis. Ouellet was closely associated with *Communio*, the international theological review founded in 1972 by von Balthasar, who described its purpose as "negatively: to resist at all costs the deadly polarization brought on by the fervor of traditionalists and modernists alike; positively: to perceive the Church as a central communio, a community originating from communion with Christ ('given from above'); as a communio enabling us to share our hearts, thoughts and blessings." Among the theologians linked to this journal were Henri de Lubac, Joseph Ratzinger (before becoming pope), Christoph Schönborn, and Angelo Scola.

As pope, Benedict XVI has shown his esteem for Ouellet in various ways, including by appointing him to head the Congregation for Bishops and by choosing him to present his new book *Jesus of Nazareth: From the Entrance to Jerusalem to the Resurrection*, at a Vatican press conference on March 10, 2011.

It is clear that Ouellet has backers at this conclave. Because of his experience in Latin America, his role as head of the Congregation for Bishops and president of the Pontifical Commission for Latin America, his linguistic skills and ability to work hard, many cardinals are viewing Ouellet as a possible bridge between the Western world and Latin America. Moreover, Ouellet is seen as a kind person, and that has been my experience too in my encounters with him.

On the other hand, several electors I have spoken with said they have three main concerns about him. The first is that "he doesn't listen to what other people say." A Canadian source who knows him well described this as "his big problem," and said it was evident in his clash with priests in Quebec when he was archbishop. Second, they consider him intransigent in his theological positions, as was shown, for example, at the last synod of bishops with regard to the question of whether confirmation should be given with baptism before communion. Their third major concern relates to his "managing skills" and whether he is "strong enough to withstand pressures." It seems that priests working in the Congregation for Bishops have told cardinals that Ouellet is weak on both counts

Like every *papabile*, Ouellet has his pluses and minuses, but there is no doubt he is a candidate to watch.

CARDINAL BERGOGLIO'S NAME has surfaced too, but not much. Many cardinals knew him from the 2005 conclave, where he was the runner-up, but most consider him now too old to be pope; he is seventy-six and on the verge of retirement. Nor does he see himself as a candidate.

Nevertheless, this son of Italian migrants is highly esteemed and respected by many cardinals. He is known to be a deeply holy and humble man, with a great love for the poor. Many know that he responded to his call to the priesthood after a particularly strong religious experience at the age of seventeen and entered the diocesan seminary in Buenos Aires. But in 1958, after hospitalization for the removal of the upper lobe of one lung and some months of prayerful convalescence, he decided to join the Jesuits.

After taking his first vows, he studied in Chile for two years, then returned to Buenos Aires in 1962 and earned a degree in philosophy. From 1964 to 1965, he taught literature and psychology at the Institute of the Immaculate Conception of Santa Fé in Cordoba, a top-ranking school sometimes referred to as the Oxford of Latin America. There he got to know Jorge Luis Borges, the famous Argentinian writer, and involved him in his literature classes. Bergoglio began studying theology in 1967 and was strongly influenced by the teachings of the Second Vatican Council. Ordained a priest on December 13, 1969, he was then sent to Spain in 1970 for the final part of his Jesuit training and studied at the University of Alcalá de Henares. After making his final profession as a Jesuit on April 22, 1973, he was assigned posts of responsibility: novice master, theology professor, and later rector of the faculty of philosophy and theology at the Colegio Maximo in Buenos Aires.

On July 31, 1973, Fr. Pedro Arrupe, superior general of the Jesuits, appointed Bergoglio—at the young age of thirty-six—provincial of the Jesuits in Argentina, a post he held for six years. A natural and strong leader with clear ideas, he introduced many reforms but also encountered opposition. In March 1976 the military took power in Argentina and his task became even more difficult as he sought to keep the Jesuits united and protect them and others from the pervasive violence and political polarization. Few cardinals at the conclave knew that he had opposed the military dictatorship and saved many lives in that period, including those of two Jesuits whom some in the Jesuit order and in the media still wrongly accused him of betraying, but all this became known only after his election.[37]

Having completed his time as provincial, he went to Dublin briefly in 1980 to study English. On returning to Buenos Aires, he became rector of the Colegio Maximo and parish priest at San Miguel, where he first revealed his pastoral skills.[38]

In 1986, Bergoglio went to Germany preparing to write a doctoral thesis on Romano Guardini, but some months later he decided to return home because he had concerns regarding the situation in the Jesuit province, fearing that the new leadership was dismantling many of the reforms he had put in place.

Back in Buenos Aires, he taught at the Colegio del Salvador. His standing was high, especially among the young Jesuits, and in 1987 he was elected procurator for the Jesuit province of Argentina. That September he went to Rome for an international meeting of Jesuit procurators, and from Italy he traveled to Japan to meet with Argentinian confreres working there. He then returned to his teaching post in Buenos Aires. To his surprise, on July 16, 1990, he was sent by his superiors into exile in Cordoba, a city about 430 miles from Buenos Aires, to serve as a spiritual director and confessor.

Though it was a difficult period in his life, it lasted only twenty-two months. On May 20, 1992, John Paul II surprised everyone by appointing him auxiliary bishop of Buenos Aires, and then, on June 3, 1997, he named him coadjutor there with the right of succession. Less than a year later, on February 28, 1998, following the death of Cardinal Antonio Quarracino, who used to call him "the little saint," Bergoglio became archbishop of Buenos Aires.

As archbishop, Bergoglio had to deal almost immediately with a major financial scandal in the archdiocese; he moved with decisiveness, brought in top external auditors, and resolved the matter. As he carried out his pastoral ministry in the years that followed, he identified several priority areas. He paid particular attention to his priests and opened a telephone hotline so that they could contact him at any time of day or night. He gave priority attention to the poor in the shantytowns and sent more priests to work there. His other priorities included the education of young people, combatting corruption in public life, and dealing with the problem of human trafficking. He traveled on public transport.

John Paul II made him a cardinal in February 2001. That October he attended the synod of bishops in Rome, which discussed the episcopal ministry, and had to take over as general-rapporteur when Cardinal

Edward Egan of New York needed to return home following the 9/11 terrorist attack. Bergoglio carried out his role in such an impressive way that many cardinals began to take notice of him.

He became known as a man of prayer, a humble, courageous pastor with a simple lifestyle, a powerful preacher who shuns the limelight, has great love for the poor, and is a frequent visitor to the shantytowns. He publicly defended a priest working there who had received death threats from the drug barons. He was never afraid to speak truth to power. He has good political antennae, and he has shown he is able to govern.

Runner-up at the last conclave, he played a central role in the plenary assembly of the Conference of Latin American Bishops (CELAM) at Aparecida, Brazil, in September 2007, was elected editor in chief of its final document, and emerged as the leading figure of the Latin American church.

In spite of this impressive biography, Bergoglio was not listed among the front-runners to succeed Benedict because of his age. "He would be good, but he may be too old," a cardinal who esteemed him told me, expressing a widespread view. "He had his chance in 2005, but didn't take it," a theologically conservative elector from the Anglophone world who participated in that conclave remarked. By the time Benedict XVI resigned, Bergoglio was not on the radar of most cardinals.

IF THE NEXT POPE WERE NOT TO COME from Europe, could he come from Asia? Several cardinals in Europe and Asia did not exclude this possibility and mentioned Luis Antonio Tagle, the youthful and dynamic archbishop of Manila since 2011, as *papabile*. He earned degrees in philosophy at the Ateneo de Manila University and theology at Loyola School of Theology. After being ordained a priest in 1982, he worked for three years in a parish and then became rector of a seminary. He was sent to study theology at the Catholic University of America in Washington, DC, and earned his doctorate in 1992. After returning to the Philippines, he first taught in a seminary for six years and was then assigned as a parish priest before John Paul II appointed him bishop of Imus in 2001. Benedict named him archbishop of Manila in October 2011 and made him a cardinal in his last consistory in November 2012.

Son of a Filipino-Chinese mother, Tagle lives a simple life and has great love for the poor. He is a brilliant communicator, at ease on television and with the media, who easily connects with the young and attracts people to Christ. I have interviewed him on various occasions and always found him inspiring; he exudes the joy and the hope of the Gospel. But age seems to be the major obstacle to his becoming pope this time around: he is just fifty-five, and if elected he could be pope for a very long time. Thinking of John Paul II, many cardinals told me they do not want another long pontificate.

SOME ASK WHETHER IT IS POSSIBLE that the cardinals might elect an African pope. Three cardinals told me they consider Cardinal Laurent Monsengwo from the Democratic Republic of the Congo as the best-qualified African candidate because of his theological, pastoral, and political skills. He studied in Rome under Cardinal Carlo Maria Martini and became the first African to earn a doctorate in biblical studies from the prestigious École Biblique in Jerusalem. Since his appointment by John Paul II as bishop in 1980, he has gained broad pastoral experience; he served first as secretary general and then as president of the Congolese bishops' conference. Widely recognized as a man of unimpeachable integrity and a courageous champion of human rights, he was called upon by his country to help the transition from the dictatorship of president Mobutu Sese Seko to democratic rule. He was appointed president of the Sovereign National Council in 1991, President of the High Council of the Republic in 1992, and speaker of a Transitional Parliament in 1994. He knows how to govern. Benedict XVI asked him to preach the Lenten retreat to the Roman Curia in February 2012. I have known him for twenty years and think he is certainly *papabile*, but several cardinals who admire and esteem him tell me that they think that the time has not yet come for an African pope.

Reviewing the biographies of the cardinal electors, one can see that there are indeed many plausible candidates to succeed Benedict XVI, but as yet there is no clear indication of whom the conclave might choose.

FEBRUARY 16 (SATURDAY) ———————————————————
Cardinals Have Many Questions, Few Answers

POPE BENEDICT RECEIVED the president of Guatemala today and also greeted the bishops from Lombardy, northern Italy, led by Cardinal Scola, his friend and now widely considered his likely successor. Scola later told Vatican Radio that the pope was "the most serene" of all the bishops in the room. "We were all deeply moved," he said, as they realized they were the last group of Italian bishops to meet Benedict as pope.

CARDINALS AND MANY JOURNALISTS have begun to arrive in Rome from across the globe and are looking to the post-Benedict era. Everyone has questions, few have answers.

CARDINAL BERGOGLIO PHONED this afternoon. We had just finished lunch. I was completely taken aback when he said he didn't think he could arrive in time for Benedict XVI's farewell to the cardinals on February 28. He had already committed himself to several important engagements in that period and said he felt he could not cancel them, and so he planned to arrive in Rome on March 3 or 4. I reacted strongly and, speaking frankly as a friend, I told him that I thought he should not miss that final meeting of Benedict with the cardinals, as many would interpret his absence in a political sense, as a negative judgment on Benedict's decision—especially since everyone was aware that Bergoglio had been the runner-up in the 2005 conclave. Moreover, I said I believed that it was of the utmost importance for him to be present also for the start of the pre-conclave meetings and discussions on the present situation in the Vatican and in the Church and the challenges the new pope would have to face. After listening calmly to my outburst, he responded by saying that, although he had made up his mind to arrive on March 3 or 4, he would nonetheless pray and reflect on what I had said to him.

When I put down the phone at the end of our conversation I felt very bad at the way I had treated him—so much so that I phoned him again fifteen minutes later to apologize and ask pardon for the way I had spoken and to explain a little better the rationale for what I had said. He was, as ever, kind and understanding, and he said, "It does me good to have someone scold me (*sgridarmi*)!" He reaffirmed that he would pray and reflect on the matter over the weekend.

THESE DAYS, journalists are busy attempting to contact cardinals in different countries. Several granted interviews. A few gave press conferences, like Peru's Cardinal Juan Luis Cipriani Thorne, a former national basketball player and industrial engineer before joining Opus Dei and going on to the priesthood.

"I think that the Pope's resignation is a very loud bell," he said, "and I hope that we cardinals will now be able to respond also to that God whom we ask to enlighten us so that we know what way we must go."[39]

Cipriani was an elector at the 2005 conclave and was recognized as a supporter of Ratzinger. At his press conference he recalled the atmosphere in the Sistine Chapel then as one of "great seriousness. A series of oaths are taken that give one the sense that at that moment one is doing what God wants one to do." In the conclave, he added, "there is much reflection, with great cordiality and fraternity, but at the same time we really feel the weight."

Cardinal Cipriani is the only Opus Dei elector at this conclave and he is known as a strong opponent of his fellow Peruvian, Fr. Gustavo Gutiérrez, the famous founder of liberation theology. Asked what he considers to be the main challenges facing the new pope, he answers, "It's very difficult to answer this hastily. Pope Benedict has been telling us that the world doesn't believe. There is too much self-sufficiency, as though God isn't needed. One is not interested in Him, and I'm speaking of the powerful. They have structured society in such a way that it is very difficult to live humanly with respect for life, respect for the family and respect for the truth. A plan has been put into place that is extremely contrary to the human being, notwithstanding the fact that there's much talk about human rights." The outspoken cardinal said he believed the Church has to respond "with her way of evangelizing. She doesn't have structures of power; she has prayer, the election of her bishops, the teaching of the faith by example, and she must have every baptized person believe that Christ is with him or her, because when we look at today's society, there seems to be a doubt: is God in these persons?"

Questioned about the possibility of a Latin American pope, Cardinal Cipriani responds: "I think geography has nothing to do with it. The person must be found with the help of God; no matter where he comes from, he will be the one. I think that geographical or political considerations won't have a place in the conclave." When asked if would like to be pope, he responded, "No! I think it's truly hard work which requires preparation. I think there are persons who are far more prepared."

THE *NEW YORK TIMES* has produced an interactive info-graph titled "The 115 Men Who Will Choose the Next Pope." I feel sure media outlets will follow suit.

FEBRUARY 17, SUNDAY _____

Benedict and Senior Vatican Officials Begin Weeklong Retreat

SOME FORTY THOUSAND ROMANS and pilgrims from many countries gathered in Saint Peter's Square at noon today to hear what Pope Benedict had to say and to pray the Angelus with him.

There was a palpable atmosphere of expectation. The crowd erupted in loud applause when he appeared at the study window of the papal apartment on the third floor of the Apostolic Palace. Ever gracious, he thanked people for their prayers and, without mentioning the word resignation, he described this as "an unusual time" for him and for the Church and asked everyone to continue praying for him.

That evening, respecting the annual program in the Vatican, Benedict and the senior officials of the Roman Curia began a weeklong retreat, from Sunday, February 17, to Saturday, February 23. He had invited the Italian cardinal, Gianfranco Ravasi, a biblical scholar and president of the Pontifical Council for Culture, to give the meditations, usually two a day. This will also give the curial cardinals the possibility to evaluate if Ravasi could be the next pope.

In his book, *Last Testament*, Benedict XVI throws an interesting light on the retreat when he says, "retreats are places of silence, prayer and listening," and this one "was part of the whole plan of the resignation for it to be followed by a week of silence, where everyone is able to work it out inwardly, the bishops, cardinals and staff of the curia at least. Because then everyone is taken away from external things and they interiorly face the Lord together." As he observes, "It was good for me that, on the one hand there was seclusion and silence and no one could disturb me...But, on the other hand, everyone stood in his own personal responsibility before the Lord. So, I have to say, the planning was very good. In retrospect, I think it was better even than I was aware of at first."[40]

The retreat meant that none of the twenty-two cardinals working in the Roman Curia would be available for conversations with journalists during this period. It is worth mentioning that about 35 percent, that is, almost 1 in 3 of the 117 cardinal electors in the forthcoming conclave are either working in the Roman Curia or have worked there. This is a higher percentage than at the 2005 conclave.

FEBRUARY 18 (MONDAY) ———————————————————
No Clear Favorite

GIVEN THAT THE VATICAN CARDINALS are on retreat, there is less news in the press regarding the conclave. But we got good news from Buenos Aires. Just after lunch the phone rang in our home. Elisabetta responded and found Cardinal Bergoglio on the other end of the line. He wanted to tell us that he would, after all, arrive in Rome on February 27, in time for Benedict's farewell to the cardinals. We were delighted and invited him for dinner on the following night.

Looking back now, I realize it was no accident that I had phoned Bergoglio first, immediately after learning of Benedict XVI's resignation. As Elisabetta recounts in her best-selling papal biography,[41] I first briefly met the archbishop of Buenos Aires in February 2001 during the traditional afternoon visit (*visita di calore*), when the Romans and others greeted the new cardinals after they had received the red hat from John Paul II. From that moment I had the sensation—in a way that I cannot even today explain—that there was "something very different" about Bergoglio; I had the inner feeling that he could become pope. I took a photo of him, along with his sister Elena and her husband and Fr. Guillermo Marco, his press officer, standing in a corner of a Renaissance hall in the Vatican's Apostolic Palace. He had been assigned this location to receive congratulations and good wishes from people. On that first occasion I merely greeted him and expressed my congratulations, nothing more.

In October of that year, I met him by accident on the Via della Conciliazione as he was walking to an afternoon session of the synod of bishops. Again it was just a fleeting encounter, but he took me by surprise when he asked me to pray for him.

As the historical record shows, that synod, which focused on the theme "The Bishop: Servant of the Gospel of Jesus Christ for the Hope of the World," catapulted the cardinal archbishop of Buenos Aires onto the radar screen of fellow cardinals. This came about by chance. As mentioned earlier, soon after the opening of the synod, Cardinal Edward Egan, the assigned chief rapporteur, had to return to New York in the aftermath of the 9/11 terrorist attack on the Twin Towers.

In hindsight, one could say that the 9/11 attack not only changed world history but also impacted the future of the Catholic Church. It led to Bergoglio having to substitute for Egan in the key role of chief rapporteur at that synod. While Egan had already given the initial keynote presentation, Bergoglio had to do everything else with the help of a team of theologians. His task involved synthesizing the interventions of the participants, presenting them in a way that would assist the synod fathers in their group discussions, and then coordinating the presentation of the resolutions from those discussions. It was his sterling performance on this occasion that suddenly caused the Argentinian archbishop to be seen by many cardinals as a plausible successor to John Paul II. At the end of each synod, participants elect a twelve-member council to oversee the concluding work of that synod and to prepare for the next one. Bergoglio came in at the top of the list with the most votes because of his outstanding work at the synod.

Immediately after the conclusion of the synod, Cardinal Cormac Murphy-O'Connor told me, "You should watch that man!" It was clear that he had put the archbishop of Buenos Aires on his short list of *papabili* to succeed the Polish pope.

Sandro Magister, the veteran Italian journalist and astute Vatican watcher who writes on religious affairs for the left-wing Italian weekly *L'Espresso*, is known to have good sources in the conservative wing of the Roman Curia and of the Italian bishops' conference. He also came to know that Bergoglio was on the radar screen of many cardinals as *papabile*. He was the first to report this. He did so in in a piece published late in 2002 that was subsequently picked up by international media outlets. He began the article as follows:

> Midway through November (2002), his colleagues wanted to elect him president of the Argentine bishops' conference. He refused. But if there had been a conclave, it would have been difficult for him to refuse the election to the papacy, because he is the one the cardinals would vote for resoundingly, if they were called together immediately to choose the successor to John Paul II.

He's Jorge Mario Bergoglio, archbishop of Buenos Aires. Born in Argentina (with an Italian surname), he has leapt to the top of the list of *papabili*, given the ever-increasing likelihood that the next pope could be Latin American. Reserved, timid, and laconic, he won't lift a finger to advance his own campaign—but even this is counted among his strong points.[42]

Magister reported that at the 2001 synod of bishops "Bergoglio managed the meeting so well that, at the time for electing the twelve members of the secretary's council, his brother bishops chose him with the highest possible vote."

He revealed that "someone in the Vatican had the idea to call him to direct an important dicastery," but Bergoglio was not keen on it. "Please, I would die in the Curia," the Argentinian implored, and so "they spared him."

Magister concluded his prophetic article saying: "Since that time, the thought of having him return to Rome as successor of Peter has begun to spread with growing intensity. The Latin-American cardinals are increasingly focused on him, as is Joseph Cardinal Ratzinger. The only key figure among the Curia who hesitates when he hears his name is Secretary of State Angelo Cardinal Sodano—the very man known for supporting the idea of a Latin-American pope."

Magister's article attracted attention in the Vatican, in the media, and among the ambassadors accredited to the Holy See. After Bergoglio's election as pope, it was reprinted in *Inside the Vatican*, the Catholic monthly magazine published in the United States, and picked up by other media too.

WHILE MY EARLIER ENCOUNTERS with Bergoglio were fleeting ones, my first real conversation with him took place some days before the 2005 conclave. Elisabetta set up the meeting at the Via della Scrofa 70, the Paul VI International Residence for Clergy known as Domus Paulus VI, where he always stayed when he came to Rome. She was the correspondent from Italy and the Vatican for *La Nación*, the Argentine paper of record, which he read, but for the conclave she was also reporting for CNN's Spanish service. Despite her heavy workload, she found time to accompany me to the meeting with him. He graciously welcomed us and took us to the room where he was staying. We spent an hour with him, talking about the upcoming conclave and much else. It was a truly enjoyable encounter. We got on well and have remained in contact ever since.

Whenever we went to Argentina—at least once a year—he would invite us for lunch at the diocesan curia where he lived. This was next to the cathedral, across the Plaza de Mayo from the Casa Rosada, the presidential palace. And when he came to Rome for meetings in the Vatican, he would always come to our home for dinner. In 2005 he baptized Juan Pablo, our first child, in the church of San Ignacio, the oldest Catholic church in Buenos Aires, and did likewise for Carolina, our second, in 2007.

At the end of one of our lunches with him in Buenos Aires, Elisabetta asked what his apartment was like. With a twinkle in his eye, he looked at me and commented, "Women like to see such things." He then invited us to "come and see!" First he showed us his small bedroom and study on the third floor of the curia building, and then he took us to visit his private chapel, on the second floor, where he prayed every morning and evening and sometimes said Mass.

Two things struck me on that visit to the chapel. On the right-hand side of the altar there was a small wooden statue of Jesus sitting on a chair, which he called "the patient Jesus." And outside, on the left-hand side of the entrance to the chapel, there was a slim wooden stand on which a white papal skullcap, known as a *zucchetto*, sat under a glass cover. When I asked how it had come to be there, he told me he didn't exactly know; it had been there before he took up residence. He presumed his predecessor, Cardinal Antonio Quarracino, must have been given it by John Paul II, the only pope to visit Argentina. The Polish pope visited Buenos Aires twice: first, in June 1982, during the Guerra de las Malvinas (the Falklands war) between Britain and Argentina, after having appealed in vain for a peaceful solution to the conflict; and a second time in April 1987 for World Youth Day. As I gazed at the *zucchetto*, I could not help wondering: Could it be a sign of things to come?

Apart from the white papal skullcap, I was also impressed by another thing on that visit. I noticed that while Bergoglio used a small room for his own office, he had turned his predecessor's stately office, where Archbishop Quarracino had received distinguished guests, into a storeroom for food, clothes, and other items that he would have distributed to the poor.

FROM FEBRUARY 18 ONWARDS, cardinals began to arrive in Rome from all over the world. Having covered the Vatican since 1985, I have come to know many of them at a personal level, and most were happy to talk about the upcoming conclave. They were willing to speak both on and off the record, and this was invaluable to me as a reporter in trying to understand where the conclave was heading and the qualities they were looking for in the man to be the next pope.

One of them was the Shanghai-born cardinal, Joseph Zen Ze-kiun, emeritus bishop of Hong Kong, whom I have known for more than fifteen years. As part of his training to become a Salesian priest, he had studied in Turin, Italy, and after serving as his order's provincial for the region, which covered mainland China, Hong Kong, Taiwan, and Macau, he went on to become a pioneer in seeking to build bridges with the state-recognized "open" church community in mainland China. Shortly before the massacre in Tiananmen Square in 1989 he was given the permission he had asked for earlier[43] to teach in the "open church" seminary at Sheshan, near Shanghai, where the legendary Jesuit Aloysius Jin Luxian, having spent many years in prison, was then bishop, recognized by Beijing but only much later by Rome. In the following years, Zen was also given permission to teach in seven other government-approved seminaries until 1996, when John Paul II nominated him coadjutor bishop of Hong Kong on the eve of its handover by Britain to China. He has been an inspiring force there ever since and has taken many courageous stances. Benedict XVI admired him and made him a cardinal on March 24, 2006. Zen became one of the pope's closest advisors on all matters relating to the Church in China.

Zen was one of two Chinese in the College of Cardinals, the other being John Tong Hon, his successor in Hong Kong. Now over eighty years old, he was no longer an elector but would be participating in the General Congregations. One evening during the General Congregations he invited me for dinner at a Chinese restaurant owned by a Catholic couple from the mainland, but even though we talked about the conclave, he declined to give an interview. After the conclave, he invited me again for another dinner to celebrate the election of Francis, whom he had on his short list of *papabili*.

IN THE ABSENCE OF HARD NEWS, *Der Spiegel*, a German weekly newsmagazine published in Hamburg, offered its analysis today: "A shift is taking place in the otherwise immovable Catholic Church. A global struggle has begun over the prerogative of interpretation, opportunities, legacy and positions—a silent battle for Rome." It asserted that "the ultimate effects of the pope's resignation are thus far impossible to predict. But it is clear that previous certainties will now be up for debate —certainties that were once just as firm as the understanding that the position of pope was for life."

The German magazine noted that "in the modern age, a pope has never resigned from the office, one that some believe is the most important on earth." It asserted that "never before has the decision of a single pope presented such a challenge to the Catholic Church as this one. Zero hour has begun at the Vatican. The pope's resignation was certainly 'great' within Dante's meaning. But it was not made through cowardice. On the contrary, it was probably the most courageous step in a long-drifting papacy marred by scandals and misunderstandings. With his revolt against tradition and the church machinery, Benedict XVI may have brought more change to the church than he did in the seven years and ten months of his papal reign."

Today, also, Spain's *El País* published an interesting interview by my friend Lola Galan with the Spanish cardinal, Julián Herranz, under the title: "Corruption in the Vatican is Limited."

The eighty-two-year old cardinal from Córdoba, the only other member of Opus Dei in the College of Cardinals besides Cipriani, is still a big-hitter, having spent half of his life in the Roman Curia, including thirteen years as head of the Pontifical Council for the Interpretation of Legislative Texts. Benedict chose this expert in canon law, who was once a doctor and psychiatrist, to serve as president of the committee of three cardinals that he established in March 2012 to investigate the Vatileaks scandal and the situation in the Roman Curia that led to it.

Cardinal Herranz began by commenting on Benedict's resignation. He was present in the Hall of Consistories when the pope announced his resignation and confessed, "I was moved. As an expert in canon law, I must say the resignation conformed perfectly to Canon 332, paragraph two. At the same time, I felt sad because of all the years I have worked with him." He described Benedict as "an exceptional theologian" and "a man with extraordinary innate qualities, with a love of Jesus Christ that he has demonstrated in the three books he wrote on Jesus of Nazareth." He said he "felt inner joy at the humility and love of the Church that he demonstrated: humility because abandoning power is not something you see every day, not even in civilian life. The pope had done some soul-searching regarding his psychological and physical limitations, which have gotten worse in the last few months, and concluded: 'I cannot go on, there is need for another to guide the barque of Peter.'"

On December 17 of last year, Cardinal Herranz, together with the other two cardinal investigators of the Vatileaks scandal—Jozef Tomko (Slovakia) and Salvatore De Giorgi (Italy)—submitted their final report to Benedict XVI. Now, on the eve of the conclave, many cardinals believed that the trio's analysis of the internal turmoil in the Vatican, coming on top of the Vatican bank's opaque monetary transactions and the sexual abuse of minors by priests in many countries including Germany, may have provoked the pope's resignation. Herranz rejected that interpretation. "This issue has been blown out of all proportion," he stated. "As chair of that committee, I can assure you that a bubble was created that has burst all by itself."

He noted that it is quite frequent in the Vatican to create this sort of committee, "to examine how things are going in a specific area." He claimed the Vatican sets a world example as far as governments go. Then, perhaps in reaction to stories that had appeared in the Italian and international media, Herranz declared, "This desire to see vipers' nests everywhere, mafias fighting one another, internal hatreds...it is all absolutely false." Speaking as one who has worked in the Vatican for over half a century he declared, "I can say that I admire many of my colleagues for their devotion and sacrifice. There might be some black sheep, like in all families, but it is the least corrupt, most transparent government that I know of, more than any international organization or civilian government." Moreover, "I follow the news a lot, I am not a hermit, and I read about what is going on in the world, and I see that it (the Vatican) is the least corrupt and a role model in many ways."

Looking ahead to the conclave, Herranz said the best candidate to be the new pope "must be a man who is in love with Christ" and "able to explain his love of God." He should be a good communicator, but other factors should be taken into account too, such as "age, health, language skills, ability to travel, and perhaps also his nationality."

THAT SAME DAY, John Allen, a good friend and Vatican correspondent for the *National Catholic Reporter* in the United States, began publishing what would be a closely watched series of profiles of candidates to succeed Benedict, under the title "The *Papabile* of the Day." But he opened with a word of caution by recalling the Roman saying: "*He who enters a conclave as pope exits as a cardinal, meaning there's no guarantee one of these men actually will be chosen.*"

Claiming that his list contained "the leading names drawing buzz in Rome these days, ensuring they will be in the spotlight as the conclave draws near," he said, "the profiles of these men also suggest the issues and the qualities other cardinals see as desirable heading into the election." By the time the conclave opened on March 12 he had identified twenty-four *papabili*, among them three Americans: Dolan from New York, O'Malley from Boston, and Donald Wuerl from Washington, DC.

He acknowledged that "by consensus, there's no slam-dunk, take-it-to-the-bank favorite heading into the next papal election" but "the closest thing to someone in pole position is probably 71-year-old Cardinal Angelo Scola of Milan."

He noted that in *La Stampa* today, Andrea Tornielli reminded readers that "one way to judge how serious a papal candidate may be is by how much whispering, rumor and character assassination that person generates." By that standard alone, Allen concluded, "one probably ought to take Cardinal Marc Ouellet seriously indeed."

Thirteen days later, on March 3, Allen offered a profile of Bergoglio. He recalled that while the archbishop of Buenos Aires was "definitely on the radar screen" in 2005, "he's eight years older now, and at seventy-six is probably outside the age window many cardinals would see as ideal." Moreover, "the fact he couldn't get over the hump last time may convince some cardinals there's no point going back to the well." At the same time, he noted that on the previous day an Italian writer quoted an anonymous cardinal as saying that "four years of Bergoglio would be enough to change things." Allen's conclusion: "Whether Bergoglio catches fire again as a candidate remains to be seen." In any case, "he seems destined to play an important role in this conclave—if not as king, then as a kingmaker."

OTHER NEWS REPORTS from the United States today say Cardinal Roger Mahony's participation in the conclave is being challenged by a group of US Catholics over his handling of abuse cases when he was archbishop of Los Angeles.

EVER ANXIOUS FOR A SCOOP, *La Repubblica* today published an article under the eye-catching headline: "The dossier that shocked the pope." Its subtitle spoke about "struggles for power and money" and "a gay lobby" in the Vatican. Signed by the Italian journalist Concita De Gregorio, the article asserted that high-ranking prelates in the Roman Curia are being subjected to "external pressure" from lay people. It alleged that all this was in the top-secret three-hundred-page report from the commission of three cardinals that Benedict had set up last April to investigate Vatileaks. The author recalled that the cardinals had handed their report to Benedict on December 17 and suggested that this had caused him to resign. A similar story by Ignazio Ingrao appeared yesterday in the Italian weekly, *Panorama*.

While I was skeptical about such reports,[44] I could see that they were feeding the rumor mill in the run-up to the conclave. I would later confirm that these articles were read by not a few cardinals trying to understand what was in that secret report and whether it really had contributed to Benedict's resignation.

FEBRUARY 19 (TUESDAY) _____

Italian Cardinals Have a Head Start in the Conclave

AUSTRALIA'S CARDINAL GEORGE PELL, 71, the archbishop of Sydney, who participated in the 2005 conclave that elected Benedict XVI, arrived in Rome a few days ago. I have known him for almost two decades, and so phoned to request a meeting and interview. He invited me to the Domus Australia, a boutique four-star guesthouse for Australian pilgrims, refurbished on the site of a former monastery near the Porta Pia, about a thirty-minute car ride from the Vatican. He was mainly responsible for establishing this guesthouse in 2010. At his request, Benedict XVI came to bless it. Pell resided here before the conclave.

I arrived at Australia House at 10:30 AM and was immediately received by the very tall, robust, former football-player cardinal. We spoke together for almost an hour, mostly off-the-record, and at the end he granted me an interview that was published both in *La Stampa* and Vatican Insider on March 5.

He told me he "was surprised by the timing" rather than the fact of Benedict's resignation. "I was aware that he was open to the possibility of retirement if he felt he wasn't up to it. He had said as much in Seewald's book. I was also aware that he had visited the tomb of Celestine V, and I think he left his pallium there. So, all those were signs that resignation was a live option for him, but I certainly didn't expect it at that time."

He admitted to having "mixed feelings" about the resignation, saying that "the whole business is tinged with sadness." But he understood that

Benedict "has done it for the good of the Church" and he considered it "a courageous decision." He felt sure Benedict "was delighted that he would be able to announce it with almost nobody realizing that it was about to come. It was a genuine secret in the Vatican, which is quite something."

The Australian cardinal, who had studied at Oxford University, recognized nonetheless that the resignation "puts a bit of question mark over the future," even if we know that, for example, while the Eastern Catholic patriarchs are appointed for life some of them have stood down, as did Fr. Peter Hans Kolvenbach, the superior general of the Jesuits, who had also been elected for life. Benedict's decision had changed the nature of the papacy "to some extent," he said, though some folk back in Australia told him the pope was bringing the Church into the twenty-first century. He broadly agreed with them, because "in the days when there was no intercontinental media an incapacitated pope could limp along, but the twenty-four-hour news cycle puts all these matters in a different perspective." Moreover, the Church is facing some very significant challenges today and Benedict "might have felt that it needed a younger man to face up to these." He believed Benedict "has been grieved" by Vatileaks, the betrayal by his butler, and the problems linked to governance of the Church in these years, but he wasn't sure how much this impacted his decision.

Looking to the upcoming conclave, Cardinal Pell said, "it's unlikely that we will choose somebody who's seventy-seven or seventy-eight . . . or somebody who is too young." He believed "there's virtue in the papacy changing every ten, fifteen, or twenty years."

As an elector, he's looking for "a man of faith and prayer" with "pastoral experience and a good record" and the "capacity to lead the Church." Right now, he said, "we need somebody who is a strategist, a decision-maker, a planner, somebody who has got strong pastoral capacities already demonstrated so that he can take a grip of the situation and take the Church forward." He thought it should also be a person who will try "to open up to China" and "reform and give leadership" to the Roman Curia and "improve its morale." He insisted that "the ability to govern is very important," given the substantial problems that emerged with Vatileaks.

Aware that many non-Italian cardinals are saying "the Italians created this mess, so we should look for a non-Italian pope who can clean it up, and put order in the house," Pell rated nationality "a secondary question." But, he said, "since the pope is the bishop of Rome, I don't think it would be good for the Church in Italy to have hundreds of years without an Italian pope." He believed that "good" Italian candidates "have a bit of a head start in the conclave" and he saw "a few" such in this conclave. But he remarked, "I'd be very surprised if within the next fifty or a hundred years we don't have quite a number of popes from South America."

Speaking of the main challenges facing the Church and the new pope, Pell mentioned "the secularization of Europe and demographic decline there and in Catholic countries too" and "the problems of growth in [the churches of] Africa and Asia." He noted however that in South America, despite the progress of the evangelicals [the "sects"], secularization "is not nearly as far advanced." He believed that "Europe is very important for the Church because most of the new movements and ideas have come from Europe. America is proving to be a great engine for the Church today, especially in the English-speaking world, but I can't see any alternative to European vitality, so that remains a vital concern." Another major challenge is "working with the Muslims in Europe to produce a tolerant and peaceful society," he said; it's "a very difficult" challenge "given the violence occurring in the Middle East, Pakistan, and places like that." This is "a very important struggle," he said, and it underlines the vital need "to continue to dialogue and cooperate in every way we can."

Cardinal Pell is convinced that "this century will be an Asian century" and noted that "we have to remain faithful to those who are faithful to the pope in China, to the Catholics there, but we have also to work constructively to try to open China up." He said, "Catholics there would be no threat at all to government, and I think they'd actually be a useful antidote to the corruption which allegedly is quite widespread there, by giving people meaning in their lives."

The Australian cardinal concluded by saying he doesn't expect the conclave to last long.

THE *NEW YORK TIMES* REPORTED today that Cardinal Dolan, 63, speaking on Sirius XM satellite radio, declared that it's "highly possible" that the next pope could be non-European. He recalled that when he was growing up "it was presumed" the pope would be an Italian but then the Polish cardinal, Karol Wojtyla, was elected pope in 1978 and that was considered "an earthquake." But, "we don't even think that anymore, do we?" Dolan remarked. "The pope is the earthly, universal pastor of the Church. To think that there might be a pope from North America, to think that there might be a pope from Latin America, a pope from Asia, a pope from Africa, I think that's highly possible, don't you?" But he dismissed the idea that he might himself be chosen as the next pope. "I could be the next shortstop of the Yankees too. Everything is possible!" he quipped.

CARDINAL STANISŁAW DZIWISZ, the long-serving private secretary of John Paul II and now archbishop of Krakow, knows most, if not all the cardinals. He also spoke about Benedict's resignation and the future conclave in an interview with the Polish Catholic weekly *Niedziela*, which the Zenit news agency translated and published today in English. He recalled that John Paul II was very close to Cardinal Ratzinger and consulted him "also in the last days of his life." He described Benedict XVI as "a great pope" who "influenced the renewal and deepening religious life of the Church through his intellectual and theological preparation and spirituality."

Referring to Benedict's decision to resign, he said, "we must absolutely accept it as God's will. The decision was full of prayer, reflection, and the Holy Father can't surely have made it easily. Being for so many years near John Paul II, I know that such decisions cost a lot. And this decision was difficult but brave."

He admitted that "Benedict XVI surprised all of us very deeply. We did not expect it, but we accept it with faith and we thank the Holy Father for everything that he did and is still going to do for us."

He asserted that the Church has had "really great popes" in the twentieth century—from Leo XIII to Benedict XVI. Each had "his charism" and "personality" but "they complemented one another" and in this way "the Church was directed, with pastors who knew how to be a support at a particular moment [in history], pastors on whom the Church relied as well as the whole of humankind." The new pope too will bring his own personality, and "will enrich the Church with a new charism."

While it will be his first time in a conclave, he said, "I have heard from other cardinals, one can feel the presence of the Holy Spirit in a conclave. One has to be open to His inspiration and choose the man whom God wants."

THE VATICAN ANNOUNCED TODAY that the Sistine Chapel will be closed from February 28 until the conclave has ended.

On a more mundane level, the director of the Vatican Museums, Antonio Paolucci, is quite optimistic that the closure will benefit the museums because it will draw even greater worldwide attention to that "priceless jewel"—the Sistine Chapel—in which the election of the pope is held.

FEBRUARY 20 (WEDNESDAY) ──────────────────────────
New Pope Must Be Able to Govern

THE BREAKING NEWS TODAY came from Fr. Federico Lombardi. He announced at the press briefing that Benedict XVI "was considering issuing" a motu proprio, or edict, to modify some norms of the apostolic constitution, *Universi Dominici Gregis*,[45] which was promulgated by John Paul II on February 22, 1996, and governs the period of the vacancy of the See of Peter and the election of the new pope.

He said that Benedict "will make precise some particular points of the apostolic constitution that have been raised in these years," but he didn't know if he would also address the question of the time for the start of the conclave, nor when the motu proprio would be published.

Il Sole 24, the highest-circulation Italian financial daily, quoted Dr. Ambrogio Piazzoni, the vice prefect of the Vatican's Apostolic Library and an expert on such matters, who said, "The Holy Father is the only one who can intervene in the legislation relating to the conclave." *Il Fatto Quotidiano*, another Italian paper, underlined that the edict "will be the last act of government" of Benedict XVI.

VARIOUS ANGLOPHONE MEDIA are reporting that, in addition to the contestation of Cardinal Mahony's participation in the conclave, questions are also being raised for similar reasons about whether Ireland's Cardinal Sean Brady should attend. The scandal surrounding the sexual abuse of minors by clergy appears to be hounding the conclave through the media. It remains to be seen how much this will impact the cardinals in their pre-conclave meetings.

TODAY, I interviewed the English cardinal, Cormac Murphy-O'Connor, emeritus archbishop of Westminster and well known as a leader in the ecumenical field. A former rugby-player and good pianist, he is a joyful, humble pastor with a great sense of humor. I have known him for many years and consider him a friend. He participated in the 2005 conclave but last August turned eighty and is therefore excluded from participating in this conclave. Nevertheless, he will attend the important pre-conclave meetings of cardinals at which they discuss the situation in the Church today, the challenges it faces in the world, and the qualities the next pope should possess.

In the interview, he said he "was surprised" by Benedict's resignation, but considered it "a humble, brave, and good decision." It was clear that "he had thought about it for some time and was aware that at some point in history a pope might have to resign" and so "he was brave enough to say that given my ill-health and my age, it would be good if I took that step."

Since Benedict had resigned for reasons of age and waning mental and physical strength, I asked the cardinal if he thought age would be an important factor in choosing the next pope. "I think it will be a factor, but not a hugely important one," he stated. He believed Benedict's resignation "gives a greater freedom to the cardinals to choose a man as pope whatever his age, provided he has the strength and ability to do that task." Nevertheless, he thought it "unlikely" they "would choose somebody of the same age as Benedict was, but I wouldn't rule it out because of the possibility of resignation if his health doesn't permit him to continue." Benedict was elected pope at the age of seventy-eight.

He believes Benedict's successor will face two kinds of challenges: challenges within the Church and challenges regarding the Church in the world. Within the Church there is always the challenge for every pope to do what is his main task: to hold together the Church in unity and truth, and to do what the Lord said to Peter, 'Confirm your brethren.' He believed the next pope "will have to do that too and even more evidently and in new ways."

Referring to the challenges from the world, the cardinal whose motto was "*Gaudium et Spes*" ("Joy and Hope"),[46] said, "I hope for a pope who will be able to understand our strange world of today, with all its advances in science and technology, which is still a world that is somehow searching for hope and for meaning. I hope the pope will be able, through what he says and what he does, to give expression to the Gospel of the love and mercy of God to this world, and to articulate the joy and hope of the Gospel to the many poor people in the world, and to the many in the Western world who are searching for meaning and hope."

Speaking about the characteristics cardinals are looking for in the man to be the next pope, he said he must be "a man who is strong enough to govern the Church." He recalled that Celestine V resigned after five months in 1294 "because he just wasn't able to govern the Church." So, he said, there's "an element of strength of character, as well as the obvious elements of intelligence, spirituality, and the capacity to speak clearly and to encourage dialogue with other Christians and with the other religions." Nationality isn't an issue, he said. "What we want is a man with the qualities to be able to do this particular daunting task."

He believed the new pope will have to address problems related to the central government of the Church. He recalled the Latin adage *ecclesia semper reformanda* ("the Church must always be reformed"), and said "this applies today not only to the Roman Curia but also to the Church at large."

Cardinal Cormac—as he is popularly known—may not be an elector at this conclave but, given his network of contacts in the Vatican and worldwide, he could be one of the kingmakers.

FEBRUARY 21 (THURSDAY) _____

A Mystery Man Called Dolan

THE ITALIAN MEDIA reported that some cardinals in the Roman Curia want the conclave to start early, and claim this might favor an Italian candidate, but Cardinal Dolan assured the press there's no rush. According to John Paul II's constitution, the conclave should start between fifteen and twenty days after the see is declared vacant (*sede vacante*), which, in this case, would be between March 15 and 20.

At the press briefing today, Fr. Lombardi stated that the date of the conclave will be decided by the cardinals during the General Congregations. All else is speculation. He then read a communication from the Prefecture of the Papal Household announcing that Benedict XVI would individually greet all the cardinals present in Rome at a meeting in the Vatican, February 28, at 11:00 AM. It would be his final farewell.

IN THIS CITY OF RUMORS, one rumor making the rounds is that all the cardinals will be enclosed in Santa Marta from March 1 so as to avoid their getting together for private meetings and planning for the conclave.

This turns out to be fake news. What is sure, however, is that preparations are under way in the Vatican to ensure that there are no communications or leaks from the conclave by smartphones, Twitter, Facebook, or other means, and to prevent electronic interception or recording of the proceedings in the Sistine Chapel.

ASIANEWS, the official news agency of the Pontifical Institute for Foreign Missions (PIME), reported that the Indonesian cardinal, Julius Riyadi Darmaatmadja, 78, emeritus archbishop of Jakarta and a Jesuit, decided by "a free and personal choice" not to attend the conclave because of serious health problems. This would mean the number of electors has been reduced to 116. The Vatican has yet to confirm the news.

LUIGI ACCATTOLI, once *Corriere della Sera*'s best reporter on the Vatican and the papacy but now retired, posted an interesting comment in his blog today. He wrote that after ten days he had finally come to understand that "Benedict took his decision not only to give peace to himself but above all to give a shock to Christians. Not just to Catholics but to Christians."[47]

A MYSTERY MAN, who identified himself under the name "Dolan" and said he was working in the Vatican, started communicating with Irene Hernandez Velasco, the correspondent in Rome for *El Mundo*, the second largest daily in Spain. Irene, a talented journalist and friend of Elisabetta and mine, shared this story. She has been in Rome for many years and was set to cover the 2005 conclave but gave birth to her son Manuel on the very day that John Paul II died, April 2, and thus could not do so. This time, however, she was excited to be able to cover the 2013 conclave, as Manuel's father, Juan Galdeano, a recognized artist, was able to stay home and care for him.

Irene told me that the communications from "Dolan" had begun some days after Benedict announced his resignation. She was surprised to receive a direct message via Twitter from this mystery man who presented himself as "Dolan" and expressed great admiration for her articles and writing style. They began to communicate late every evening via Twitter's direct messaging system, but never once saw each other face-to-face or spoke to each other by phone. He insisted on concealing his identity and explained that he had chosen the pen name "Dolan" because he esteemed the homonymous archbishop of New York. He confided that he was deeply concerned about the situation in the Vatican and the future of the Church and felt there was an urgent need for change, for major reform. He fervently hoped the new pope would bring this about and believed Cardinal Ouellet was the only one who could do it. "Dolan" spoke in Spanish, with the idioms of Spain, and expressed great love for the Church, she said. He was very knowledgeable about the situation in the Vatican and the *papabili*, and briefed her on many of them, but he constantly pushed Ouellet as the best man to clean up the Roman Curia.

Theirs was a curious relationship, and it was but one of many strange things that happened here in the interregnum period. After the papal election, "Dolan" told Irene of his immense happiness that the conclave had chosen the first Latin American pope and said he considered Francis "a miracle," far beyond his wildest dreams. Some weeks later, "Dolan" suddenly stopped communicating. Their relationship ended.

FEBRUARY 22 (FRIDAY) _____
Bookmakers Give Odds on Papal Election

THE BOOKMAKERS clearly see money in the papal election. Paddy Power, Ireland's leading bookmaker, is giving the following odds on the cardinals who are rated as likely to succeed Benedict XVI.

1. Peter Turkson (Ghana),11/4
2. Angelo Scola (Italy), 3/1
3. Tarcisio Bertone (Italy), 4/1
4. Marc Ouellet (Canada), 6/1
5. Angelo Bagnasco (Italy), 12/1
6. Leonardo Sandri (Argentina), 12/1

I was surprised to see Bertone's name on this list. I've not heard anybody else mention him as *papabile*, but it seems someone thinks he has a chance!

THIS AFTERNOON, as I was preparing to be interviewed by Associated Press TV in front of the Basilica of Santa Maria Sopra Minerva, near the Pantheon, I spotted Cardinal Donald Wuerl, archbishop of Washington, walking past. He had just been to Barbiconi, the nearby clerical outfitter, to buy a new white miter for the conclave. Since I have known him for several years, I went to greet him and asked if I could come and talk with him and perhaps get an interview sometime before the General Congregations began. He proposed we meet the very next day, Saturday afternoon, at the North American College, where he and seven of the eleven American cardinal electors are residing before the conclave.

FEBRUARY 23 (SATURDAY)_____

Vatican Denounces Pressure on Cardinals

THE LENTEN RETREAT has ended. Vatican cardinals are now free to give interviews. Some are at ease with journalists and are happy to do so; others decidedly not.

At noon today, the Vatican press office published a communiqué from the Secretariat of State denouncing attempts to influence the papal election. It "deplored" the attempts to condition the freedom of cardinals in the upcoming conclave "by publishing news, often not verified, or not verifiable, or even false, also with grave damage to persons and institutions."

Vatican Radio provided the following English translation of the communiqué:

> The freedom of the College of Cardinals, which alone, under the law, is responsible for the election of the Roman Pontiff, has always been strongly defended by the Holy See, as a guarantee of a choice based on evaluations solely for the good of the Church.
>
> Over the centuries, the Cardinals have faced multiple forms of pressure exerted on the individual voters and the same College, with the aim of conditioning decisions, to bend them to a political or worldly logic.

If in the past it was the so-called superpowers, namely States, who sought to condition the election of the Pope in their favor, today there is an attempt to apply the weight of public opinion, often on the basis of assessments that fail to capture the spiritual aspect of this moment in the life of the Church.

It is regrettable that, as we draw near to the beginning of the Conclave when Cardinal electors shall be bound in conscience and before God, to freely express their choice, news reports abound which are often unverified or not verifiable, or even false, and cause subsequent damage to people and institutions.

It is in moments such as these that Catholics are called to focus on what is essential: to pray for Pope Benedict, to pray that the Holy Spirit enlighten the College of Cardinals, to pray for the future Pope, trusting that the fate of the barque of St. Peter is in the hands of God.

It was clear to Vatican watchers that the communiqué had been issued in response to calls from victims' organizations, including the Survivors Network of those Abused by Priests (SNAP) which was founded in the USA in 1989, to exclude from the conclave any cardinals who are alleged to have mishandled or covered up of cases of abuse. Cardinals Mahony (archbishop emeritus of Los Angeles) and O'Brien (St. Andrews and Edinburgh) are the main targets of these calls, but not the only ones.[48] Cardinal Roger Mahony decided to come, notwithstanding the media storm, and his successor, the Mexican-born archbishop José H. Gómez, a member of Opus Dei, defended his right to do so.

In the light of all that was happening, Fr. Lombardi, who is greatly respected by journalists, sought to provide some perspective in his weekly editorial on Vatican Radio by addressing the challenges facing the mainstream media as they cover this important moment in the Church's life.

He wrote: "The journey of the Church in these last weeks of Pope Benedict XVI's pontificate and up until the election of the new Pope—passing through the '*sede vacante*' and the conclave—is very demanding, given the newness of the situation. We rejoice that we do not have to carry the pain of the death of a much-loved Pope, but we have not been spared another test: that of the multiplication of the pressures and considerations that are foreign to the spirit with which the Church would like to live this period of waiting and preparation."

He noted that "there is no lack, in fact, of those who seek to profit from the moment of surprise and disorientation of the spiritually naive to sow confusion and to discredit the Church and its governance, making recourse to old tools, such as gossip, misinformation and sometimes slander, or exercising unacceptable pressures to condition the exercise of the voting duty on the part of one or another member of the College of Cardinals, who they consider to be objectionable for one reason or another."

Hitting hard, he declared, "In the majority of cases, those who present themselves as judges, making heavy moral judgments, do not, in truth, have any authority to do so. Those who consider money, sex, and power before all else and are used to reading diverse realities from these perspectives, are unable to see anything else, even in the Church, because they are unable to gaze toward the heights or descend to the depths in order to grasp the spiritual dimensions and reasons of existence. This results in a description of the Church and of many of its members that is profoundly unjust."

But, he added, "all of this will not change the attitude of believers; it will not erode the faith and the hope with which they see the Lord, who promised to accompany his Church. According to the indications of Church law and tradition, we want this to be a time of sincere reflection on the spiritual expectations of the world and on the faithfulness of the Church to the Gospel, of prayer for the assistance of the Spirit, of closeness to the College of Cardinals that is preparing for the demanding service of discernment and choice that is asked of it and for which it principally exists."

He concluded: "In this, we are accompanied first and foremost by the example and spiritual integrity of Pope Benedict, who wanted to dedicate to prayer, from the start of Lent, this final stretch of his pontificate —a penitential journey of conversion toward the joy of Easter. This is how we are living it and how we will live it: in conversion and hope."

THIS AFTERNOON, I went to the North American College to talk with Cardinal Wuerl. The college is located on the Janiculum hill, next to the Bambino Gesù' Hospital, a mere ten minutes' walk from the Vatican. Its construction began in 1946, following the Second World War, and was completed in 1953. It was dedicated in October of that year by Pius XII. Today it is home to three hundred or more students for the priesthood from the United States and some other countries, including Australia. The American cardinals and bishops usually stay here when they visit Rome; many are ex-alumni, like Wuerl.

Ever gracious, the cardinal took me upstairs to "the red room" (thus called because of the red door that opens into a very large room). Over the past half-century, many important meetings of American cardinals and bishops have been held here. He drew my attention to the grandfather clock that stands on the right-hand side as one enters the room, and said it was a gift to the college from Cardinal John Wright, once the highest ranking American prelate in the Roman Curia when he was prefect of the Congregation for Clergy. Wuerl was his secretary then and accompanied the cardinal to the October 1978 conclave that elected John Paul II. Because Wright, following surgery, was in a wheelchair and in need of assistance, Wuerl was allowed to accompany him inside the conclave—one of only three non-cardinals present for the election of the first non-Italian pope in 455 years. This time he will enter the conclave as an elector, having been made a cardinal by Benedict XVI in November 2010. He is one of the eleven electors from the United States.

We chatted for about forty-five minutes, and in the course of the interview he spoke about Benedict XVI's resignation. He said that after "the initial shock," when "the dust has settled, people are saying yes, this is something that should be able to happen, especially since Pope Benedict put it in such reasonable terms. He clearly loves the Church. He served well as pope, and when he said 'I just don't have the energy to do the job as well as I know I should,' I think that resonated with a lot of people."

Given that resignation is now a real possibility, he believes that when it comes to the election of the next pope, "age will not be as important as two other factors: first, the perception that the person has the vision to carry us into the future and, second, the perception that the person has energy to do this. But I'm not certain that I'm necessarily talking about physical stamina."

"Vision," not "nationality," was the all-important factor for Wuerl in choosing the next pope: "I think the person who will now fill the Chair of Peter has to carry on the vision of Blessed John Paul and of Benedict that the New Evangelization is where we have to be focused... Submerged as we are in secularism and engulfed in this vision of the world that has limited the horizon to the here and now," Wuerl said, "we have to be able to look to the young people coming along in the future and invite them to an experience of God. I think that has to be the overriding vision of the next pope."

In his view, the next pope "has to have a ministry of presence, but that ministry today does not require travel," as it did for John Paul and Benedict. "Since we live in a world of instantaneous electronic communication," he said, "I think the pope has to have the vision to see this as the way to exercise the Petrine Office around the world, and the energy to devote a substantial proportion of his ministry to this virtual presence, an electronic presence. That will take energy, not necessarily physical stamina."

Cardinal Wuerl identified three challenges facing the new pope. The first is "on the level of the academic, intellectual, elitist world, and that is to re-introduce into that discussion—something that Benedict has done well—the compatibility of faith and reason, the complementarity of faith and reason." The second is "on the pastoral level, we have to be focused on the need to be proclaiming the basic kerygma of the Gospel." The third is "the re-appraisal of how the Petrine Office is exercised, and I think that is going to require an enormous concentration on communications."

While many are calling for a reform of the Roman Curia, Wuerl felt he didn't have sufficient information to comment on that but declared that one thing was already clear: "The pope has to govern the Church." Speaking from twenty-seven years' experience as a diocesan bishop, he said, "It's very important that there be a central direction in any central office, whether it's a local curia and certainly where it's a curia for the whole universal Church, there has to be a clearly identified chain of command."

He said he had no idea of how long the conclave might last. "I think a lot is going to depend on the unfolding in the first days in the conclave. I read the papers. I tried to be as informed as anybody. There doesn't seem to be a cardinal going into the conclave that everybody says is clearly going to be the pope. Of course, they often say, he who enters as pope comes out as cardinal. So, I think it is going to take a little while. How little or how long, that's all in the hands of God." Nevertheless, he hoped to be back in Washington, DC, for Holy Week, which starts on March 24.

FEBRUARY 24 (SUNDAY) _____

"The Lord Is Calling Me to Climb the Mountain"

BENEDICT XVI gave his last Sunday address at midday, from his study window in the Vatican's Apostolic Palace, before reciting the Angelus. Thousands of Romans and pilgrims from many lands had gathered in Saint Peter's Square to express their closeness and solidarity with him. Elisabetta and I brought Juan Pablo and Carolina, our children, to receive his blessing. The sky was overcast, and one could sense an air of great sadness.

The crowd greeted the pope with emotional applause when he appeared at the window. They were moved and applauded with warm affection when he told them: "The Lord is calling me 'to climb the mountain,' to devote myself even more to prayer and meditation. But this does not mean abandoning the Church; indeed, if God asks me this it is precisely so that I may continue to serve her with the same dedication and the same love with which I have tried to do so until now, but in a way more suited to my age and strength."

He concluded with a heartfelt greeting to the Italians in the square, saying he knew "many dioceses are present" together with "representatives of parishes, associations and movements, institutions, as well as many youth, elderly people and families. I thank you for your affection and for your sharing, especially in prayer, at this special moment, for me myself and for the Church...Thank you! In prayer we are always close. I thank you all!"

His last words provoked another emotional outburst of applause but also many tears. People clung to each other, and many wept openly. Carolina, not yet six years old, observed all this and when she saw the curtains close in the papal study as Benedict went back into the study, she asked Elisabetta, "Has the pope died?"[49]

Afterwards, as we walked down the Via della Conciliazione, we happened to meet Juan Pablo Cafiero, the Argentinian ambassador to the Holy See, whom we know well. We talked about the conclave and possible candidates, but neither he, nor the journalists who had just arrived from Argentina and whom we met later, thought that Cardinal Bergoglio had a chance.

FEBRUARY 25 (MONDAY)

Scandal in Scotland

THE VATICAN ISSUED Benedict XVI's new motu proprio introducing several modifications to the norms governing the process for the election of the pope that John Paul II had promulgated in the apostolic constitution *Universi Dominici Gregis* on February 22, 1996.

Benedict had already amended it in a significant way on June 11, 2007,[50] by reinstating the norm that a majority of two-thirds of the cardinal electors present in the conclave is always necessary for the election of the new pope, however long it goes on. This had always been the norm since 1179, but John Paul II had changed it, opening the possibility for a simple majority to elect the pope. Benedict removed that possibility.

In his new edict, called in Latin "*Normas Nonnullas*" meaning "certain modifications,"[51] Benedict decreed, among other things, that "no cardinal elector can be excluded from active or passive voice in the election of the Supreme Pontiff, for any reason or pretext."[52] As mentioned earlier, there has been much pressure from survivors' groups, through the media, for the exclusion of several cardinals because of their alleged mishandling of cases of the abuse of children by clergy. This norm was a response to such pressure.

Since Benedict announced his resignation, there has been considerable discussion regarding the date when the conclave could start, given that there is no funeral. Aware that this could become an even bigger issue when the cardinals gathered in plenary assembly at the General Congregations before the conclave, he set out to resolve this problem too.[53] While reconfirming the earlier norm that "from the moment when the Apostolic See is lawfully vacant, fifteen full days must elapse before the conclave begins, in order to await those who are absent," he nevertheless granted the College of Cardinals "the faculty to move forward the start of the conclave if it is clear that all the cardinal electors are present," or to "defer, for serious reasons, the beginning of the election for a few days more." He decreed, however, that "when a maximum of twenty days have elapsed from the beginning of the vacancy of the See, all the cardinal electors present are obliged to proceed to the election." In other words, he gave the College of Cardinals considerable flexibility in setting the date for entry into the conclave.

Benedict's next concern related to the protection of cardinals from outside disturbance of any kind. He decreed[54] that from the beginning of the electoral process until the announcement that a new pope has been elected "the rooms" of Santa Marta and especially the Sistine Chapel and areas reserved for liturgical celebrations "are to be closed to unauthorized persons." During the election period "the entire territory" and "the ordinary activity of the offices located therein" shall be regulated in a way that ensures the papal election can take place "with due privacy and freedom." He ordered that provision be made "to ensure that no one approaches the cardinal electors" as they go from Santa Marta to the Apostolic Vatican

Palace. Having participated in three conclaves as a cardinal,[55] Benedict knew that some cardinals like to walk from Santa Marta to the Sistine Chapel, and he wanted to ensure that nobody would disturb them.

Well aware that many people—around ninety, including the clerics directly involved in the conclave,[56] as well as the cooks and service staff at Santa Marta—are needed to ensure the smooth running of the conclave, he made provision for this,[57] ensuring their lodgings within the protected territory of Vatican City.

Benedict was particularly concerned about confidentiality at the conclave. He was perhaps even more sensitive to this than his predecessors because of the painful experience of Vatileaks. Moreover, he knew there had been a breach of confidentiality at the 2005 conclave when a cardinal sent a text message to a German television station from inside the Sistine Chapel informing them of Ratzinger's election even before the senior cardinal-deacon, Jorge Medina Estévez,[58] had announced it to the world.

In this new edict, he set out to ensure that everything related to the election of the pope is to be conducted in "strict secrecy," especially in these times of electronic interceptions. Consequently, he decreed[59] that all involved in the conclave "who in any way or at any time should come to learn anything from any source, directly or indirectly, regarding the election process, and in particular regarding the voting which took place in the election itself, are obliged to maintain strict secrecy with all persons extraneous to the College of Cardinal electors."[59] He reaffirmed the legislation that before the conclave begins the cardinal electors "shall take an oath" to this effect, and refrain from using any electronic equipment capable of recording anything related to the papal election. Failure to do so incurs automatic excommunication reserved to the Holy See.

The modifications in *Normas Nonnullas* did not affect the three-phase format of the election process itself as laid out in *Universi Dominici Gregis*.[60] In Phase I, the pre-scrutiny, the masters of ceremonies prepare and distribute to each of the cardinal electors at least two ballot papers. The junior cardinal-deacon draws by lot nine names from among the electors: three to be "scrutineers," three "*infirmarii*" to collect votes of the sick (if any), and three "revisers." The voting process then takes place in accordance with *Universi Dominici Gregis* (65–66). This requires, first, that "the ballot paper must be rectangular in shape and must bear in the upper half, in print if possible, the words *Eligo in Summum Pontificem* (*I elect as Supreme Pontiff*); on the lower half there must be a space left for writing the name of the person chosen; thus the ballot is made in such a way that it can be folded in two." Second, "the completion of the ballot must be done in secret by each Cardinal elector, who will write down legibly, as far as possible in handwriting that cannot be identified as his, the name of the person he chooses, taking care not to write other names as well, since this would make the ballot null; he will then fold the ballot twice." Third, "during the voting, the Cardinal electors are to remain alone..." Phase II, the *scrutiny* proper begins with the placing of the ballots in the appropriate receptacle: "each Cardinal elector, in order of precedence, having completed and folded his ballot, holds it up so that it can be seen and carries it to the altar at which the Scrutineers stand and upon which there is placed a receptacle, covered by a plate, for receiving the ballots. Having reached the altar, the Cardinal elector says aloud the words of the following oath: *I call as my witness Christ the Lord who will be my judge, that my vote is given to the one who before God I think should be elected.* He then places the ballot on the plate with which he drops it into the receptacle. Having done this, he bows to the altar and returns to his place." This is followed by the mixing and counting of the ballots, and the opening of the votes by the three scrutineers. Finally, in Phase III the votes are counted and checked by the three revisers, and when they confirm the accuracy of the counting, the ballot sheets and report cards are burned in the stove specially installed in the Sistine Chapel. If no one has obtained at least two thirds of the votes on that ballot, the pope has not been elected, but if someone has obtained at least two thirds, then the "canonically valid election" of the Roman Pontiff has taken place.

Benedict refined the process for voting[61] and for taking time out for prayer, reflection, and dialogue, as laid down by John Paul II if the voting has not resulted in an election after several days. If after at least thirty ballots there is still no result, then the electors will vote for one of the two candidates who have received most votes (although these two cannot vote), but he insisted that a two-thirds majority of the votes of the electors present is always necessary for the valid election of the pope.

He reaffirmed[62] that when the valid election has taken place, the junior cardinal-deacon summons into the election hall the secretary of the College of Cardinals, the master of Papal Liturgical Celebrations and two masters of ceremonies. Then the cardinal who is presiding at the conclave asks the one elected: *Do you accept your canonical election as Supreme Pontiff?* And once he has received the consent, he asks him: *By what name do you wish to be called?* Then the master of Papal Liturgical Celebrations, "acting as notary and having as witnesses the two masters of ceremonies, draws up a document certifying acceptance by the new Pope and the name taken by him."

WHILE BENEDICT'S MOTU PROPRIO gave the electors the possibility, within limits, to anticipate or delay the date of conclave, the breaking news today, however, was of another kind.

It came around midday when the Vatican spokesman, Fr. Lombardi, announced that Benedict XVI has accepted the resignation of Scotland's cardinal, Keith O'Brien, from his post as archbishop of St. Andrews and Edinburgh. The cardinal, who will celebrate his seventy-fifth birthday on March 17, had presented his letter of resignation last November, but it was accepted now, on the eve of the conclave. The reason for this was no secret: the previous day, *The Observer*, a British Sunday newspaper, had reported that the popular Scottish cardinal was embroiled in an unfolding sex-scandal back home over what was described, in a statement issued by the cardinal later today, as "unbecoming conduct" with three priests and a former seminarian. None were minors.

The scandal reverberated not only through the Catholic Church in Scotland with its 750,000 faithful, but also the churches in England, Wales, and Ireland as well as the wider society in the United Kingdom and Ireland. The Northern Ireland–born cardinal was well known and very popular. I had known him for many years, and the news came as a shock to me too.

Asked whether the pope had given him any instruction regarding his participation in the conclave, Fr. Lombardi said no.

Some hours later, however, O'Brien issued a statement in which he apologized to those he had offended and announced he would not participate in the conclave. He said: "Looking back over my years of ministry: For any good I have been able to do, I thank God. For any failures, I apologize to all whom I have offended. I also ask God's blessing on my brother cardinals who will soon gather in Rome, but I will not join them for this conclave in person. I do not wish media attention in Rome to be focused on me—but rather on Pope Benedict XVI and on his successor."

His decision not to participate in the conclave appeared to be without precedent, according to Dr. Ambrogio Piazzoni, the Vatican's main authority on conclaves; the only reason a cardinal did not do so in the past was for reasons of health. Nevertheless, Cardinal O'Brien's decision was greeted with much relief in the Vatican, though no one said so publicly. His self-exclusion meant the number of electors was now reduced to 115.

The O'Brien affair had been rumbling for several days, and as a journalist often contacted by the British, Scottish, and Irish media for comments about the Vatican or the pope, this case gave me lots of extra work that I happily would have done without.

The Scottish cardinal's decision had another effect, too. According to a report published in the *New York Times*, Terence McKiernan, president of BishopAccountability.org, a nonprofit website based in Massachusetts that seeks to collate documentation relating to the sexual abuse crisis in the Catholic Church, underlined the fact that this decision had set a precedent. He noted that "many cardinals scheduled to join the conclave have been involved as bishops in handling cases of clergy sexual abuse" and added that "some of them have done such a bad job that they, too, should recuse themselves from the conclave." He mentioned three in particular: Mahony (USA), Brady (Ireland), and Danneels (Belgium). He declared that if they participate in the conclave "they will taint the outcome, damaging the legitimacy of whoever is ultimately chosen."

FEBRUARY 26 (TUESDAY) _____

Emeritus Pope Will Wear White

THE HOUR FOR BENEDICT XVI'S RESIGNATION is on the near horizon and drawing most of the media attention. At the press briefing, Fr. Lombardi announced that after Benedict's resignation he will continue to wear a white cassock, but without the *mozzetta*, or short white cape worn over the shoulders, and instead of the red shoes that had attracted so much media comment, he will wear brown ones. Moreover, he will continue to be known as Pope Benedict, and addressed as "His Holiness," and after his resignation he will be referred to in two acceptable ways: "Pope Emeritus" or "Roman Pontiff Emeritus."

The Vatican spokesman said Benedict will give "the ring of the fisherman" to the College of Cardinals and the seal will subsequently be broken, as happens on the death of a pope. From then, he will wear the ring that he used as a cardinal. Furthermore, his twitter account @pontifex will be frozen immediately after he resigns, but it will be available again for use by his successor, once elected, if he so wishes. Lombardi confirmed that Vatican security, not the Swiss Guards, will have the reponsibility of ensuring Benedict XVI's safety after his resignation.

BRAZIL HAD FIVE ELECTORS out of the nineteen Latin American cardinals who will vote in the conclave: Agnelo, Damasceno Assis, Braz de Aviz, Hummes, and Scherer. As usual, with the exception of Braz de Aviz, who has a Vatican apartment, they stayed at the Brazilian College in Rome, on the Via Aurelia. Before departing from Brazil for the conclave, three of them gave exclusive interviews to *Jornal das Dez*, of Globo News, as Gerson Camarotti reported in his blog today.[63]

The first interview was with Dom Geraldo Majella Agnelo, emeritus cardinal-archbishop of Salvador and former president of the CNNB—the Brazilian bishops' conference (2003–2007). He served as secretary of the Congregation for Divine Worship and the Discipline of the Sacraments from 1991 to 1999. I have known him for many years, and have also interviewed him.

He put down a significant marker regarding the candidate to be the next pope when he stated: "To be a member of a [political] party would already separate him from [gaining] the necessary consensus" and, likewise, "to be part of a group [in the Church] would be a barrier too." In other words, a future pope could not be a member of an ecclesial group such as Communion and Liberation or Opus Dei, as Camarotti had noted in his book *Segredos do Conclave*.[64] It was an interesting comment given that in the second half of the twentieth century the Brazilian bishops' conference had had major problems with the Communion and Liberation movement.[65]

At the same time, Dom Geraldo affirmed that the next pope could come from any part of the world, given that after four hundred years of Italian popes the Church had no difficulty in accepting first a Polish pope and then a German, so "there would be no impediment in accepting a non-European pope."

The *Jornal das Dez*'s next interview was with Dom Claudio Hummes, OFM, archbishop emeritus of São Paulo (1988–2006) and former prefect of the Congregation for Clergy (2006–2010). I knew him, having, together with Elisabetta, interviewed him in 2002. He had clear ideas about the qualities he was looking for in the man to be next pope: "He must be a man of faith, a man of God. A holy man in whom the people can see and hear God." As for age, he said, since John Paul II was elected at fifty-eight and Benedict XVI at seventy-eight, he felt the conclave might go for someone between those two extremes.

In his interview, the third Brazilian elector, Dom Raymundo Damasceno Assis, archbishop of Aparecida and current president of the Brazilian bishops' conference, said he believed that the next pope "should, above all else, be a pastor. A person who is reasonably modern, and sufficiently open to the questions of today's world, but at the same time faithful to the questions of the deposit of faith. Because the Church is subject to this deposit and must protect it."

Their comments already suggested the direction they would be moving in at the conclave, and that they would very likely work closely together. They will be worth watching, as they carry weight in the Latin American church.

IN HIS BLOG TODAY, Luigi Accattoli recalled that at various times in the past unrest broke out in the streets of Rome, Viterbo, or Avignon in France in attempts "to condition" the conclave when the election was taking place in one or another of those cities. At other times troops were sent to where the cardinals were gathered in conclave. In later centuries, one of the electors at the conclave was given "the veto" by a ruling power to prevent the election of a cardinal that it did not want elected pope. But Accattoli observed that, starting a century ago, the media has been used to influence the conclave[66] and, he commented, "whether that is better or worse I don't know, but I imagine that the pressure will cease only when the papacy is no longer seen as a power."

FEBRUARY 27 (WEDNESDAY) _____

Cardinal Bergoglio Arrives in Rome

THIS WAS BENEDICT'S PENULTIMATE DAY as pope, and his last public audience. The sun was shining brightly in the blue sky over Rome as an estimated 130,000 Romans, Italians, and pilgrims from all continents, together with scores of cardinals, bishops, priests, women and men religious, and members of the diplomatic corps gathered in Saint Peter's Square and the Via della Conciliazione for his farewell address.

The atmosphere was quite different from that of last Sunday. There was of course sadness, but nothing that even hinted of depression. By now people had accepted his decision and had come here today to express their gratitude and admiration for this humble, courageous scholar-pope who is making history.

I was seated not far from the Arch of the Bells, on the left-hand side of the steps of Saint Peter's as one faces the basilica, a short distance from where he would speak. I had to provide live commentary and analysis for CTV—Canada's independent English-language television.

The crowd gave the eighty-five-year-old pope a tremendous welcome when he appeared on the steps of the basilica, and he rose to the occasion in a way few had anticipated. He delivered a hopeful, unforgettable, much applauded and inspiring speech,[67] most of which I reproduce here.

As he gazed out at the vast crowd, Benedict looked surprisingly relaxed and at peace. He began by thanking people for coming "in such great numbers to this last General Audience" and added, "heartfelt thanks! I am truly moved, and I see the Church alive!"

"At this moment," he said, "my heart expands and embraces the whole Church throughout the world; and I thank God for all that I have 'heard' in these years of the Petrine ministry about the faith in the Lord Jesus Christ and the love which truly circulates in the Body of the Church and makes it live in love, and about the hope which opens and directs us toward the fullness of life, toward our heavenly homeland."

"At this moment," he added, "I feel great confidence, because I know, we all know, that the Gospel word of truth is the Church's strength, it is her life. The Gospel purifies and renews, it bears fruit, wherever the community of believers hears it and receives God's grace in truth and charity. This is my confidence, this is my joy."

Recalling his election in 2005, he revealed that "when on April 19, nearly eight years ago, I accepted the Petrine ministry, I had the firm certainty that has always accompanied me: this certainty of the life of the Church which comes from the word of God. At that moment, as I have often said, the words which echoed in my heart were: Lord, why are you asking this of me, and what is it that you are asking of me? It is a heavy burden which you are laying on my shoulders, but if you ask it of me, at your word I will cast the net, sure that you will lead me even with all my weaknesses."

Then, in a memorable passage, Benedict told the vast crowd and the millions following on live television, that now, "eight years later, I can say that the Lord has truly led me, he has been close to me, I have been able to perceive his presence daily. It has been a portion of the Church's journey which has had its moments of joy and light, but also moments which were not easy; I have felt like Saint Peter with the Apostles in the boat on the Sea of Galilee: the Lord has given us so many days of sun and of light winds, days when the catch was abundant; there were also moments when the waters were rough and the winds against us, as throughout the Church's history, and the Lord seemed to be sleeping. But I have always known that the Lord is in that boat, and I have always known that the barque of the Church is not mine but his. Nor does the Lord let it sink; it is he who guides it, surely also through those whom he has chosen, because he so wished. This has been, and is, a certainty which nothing can shake. For this reason, my heart today overflows with gratitude to God, for he has never let his Church, or me personally, lack his consolation, his light, his love."

Benedict's words produced prolonged, emotional applause. People were deeply touched by what he had said.

As he prepared for his abdication the next day, he told them, "I should like to invite all of us to renew our firm confidence in the Lord, to entrust ourselves like children in God's arms, certain that those arms always hold us, enabling us to press forward each day, even when the going is rough. I want everyone to feel loved by that God who gave his Son for us and who has shown us his infinite love. I want everyone to feel the joy of being a Christian."

In these past days, some in the media, especially in the Italian press, have reported that Benedict felt alone during his eight years, and that this had weighed heavily on him. In this last public discourse, he denied this.

"The Pope is not alone in guiding the barque of Peter, even if it is his first responsibility. I have never felt alone in bearing the joy and the burden of the Petrine ministry; the Lord has set beside me so many people who, with generosity and love for God and the Church, have helped me and been close to me," he stated.

He went on to thank various groups of people who had assisted him in these eight years: his "dear brother cardinals" for their "wisdom," "counsel," and "friendship" which "have been invaluable to me." He thanked his "co-workers," beginning with Cardinal Bertone, "my Secretary of State who has faithfully accompanied me in these years," and followed by "the Secretariat of State and the whole Roman Curia." He thanked "all those who in various sectors offer their service to the Holy See: many, many unseen faces which remain in the background, but precisely through their silent, daily dedication in a spirit of faith and humility they have been a sure and trustworthy support to me."

Then looking out beyond the Vatican City State, the smallest state in the world by both size (110 acres) and population (under a thousand inhabitants), Benedict thanked "most heartily all those people throughout the world who in these recent weeks have sent me moving expressions of concern, friendship, and prayer. Yes, the Pope is never alone; now I once again experience this so overwhelmingly that my heart is touched. The Pope belongs to everyone and so many persons feel very close to him."

He revealed that while "it is true that I receive letters from world leaders—from heads of state, from religious leaders, from representatives of the world of culture, and so on, I also receive many, many letters from ordinary people who write to me simply and from the heart, and who show me their affection, an affection born of our being together with Christ Jesus, in the Church. These people do not write to me in the way one writes, for example, to a prince or some important person whom they do not know. They write to me as brothers and sisters, as sons and daughters, with a sense of a very affectionate family bond."

All this, he said, has enabled him to "sense palpably what the Church is—not an organization, an association for religious or humanitarian ends, but a living body, a communion of brothers and sisters in the Body of Christ, which makes us all one." Indeed, "to experience the Church in this way and to be able as it were to put one's finger on the strength of her truth and her love, is a cause for joy at a time when so many people are speaking of her decline. But we see how the Church is alive today!"

His affirmation that "the Church is alive today" drew prolonged and enthusiastic applause. People felt the ring of truth in his words.

Pope Benedict went onto explain to his worldwide audience, and to the 1.2 billion members of the Catholic Church, the reasons for his decision to resign. "In these last months I have felt my energies declining, and I have asked God insistently in prayer to grant me his light and to help me make the right decision, not for my own good, but for the good of the Church. I have taken this step with full awareness of its gravity and even its novelty, but with profound interior serenity. Loving the Church means also having the courage to make difficult, painful decisions, always looking to the good of the Church and not of oneself."

Referring again to the moment of his election as pope, Benedict said, "the real gravity of the decision [to resign] was also due to the fact that from that moment on I was engaged always and forever by the Lord. Always—anyone who accepts the Petrine ministry no longer has any privacy. He belongs always and completely to everyone, to the whole Church. In a manner of speaking, the private dimension of his life is completely eliminated. I was able to experience, and I experience it even now, that one receives one's life precisely when one gives it away."

He recalled that "many people who love the Lord also love the Successor of Saint Peter and feel great affection for him; that the Pope truly has brothers and sisters, sons and daughters, throughout the world, and that he feels secure in the embrace of your communion; because he no longer belongs to himself, he belongs to all and all belong to him."

Then in a highly significant passage, which read also like a response to those who had asserted that he shouldn't have abandoned the cross of the papal office, Benedict told the hushed crowd, that "the 'always' is also a 'for-ever'—there can no longer be a return to the private sphere. My decision to resign the active exercise of the ministry does not revoke this. I do not return to private life, to a life of travel, meetings, receptions, conferences, and so on. I am not abandoning the cross, but [am] remaining in a new way at the side of the crucified Lord. I no longer bear the power of office for the governance of the Church, but in the service of prayer I remain, so to speak, in the enclosure of Saint Peter. Saint Benedict, whose name I bear as Pope, will be a great example for me in this. He showed us the way for a life which, whether active or passive, is completely given over to the work of God."

Turning to the overwhelming majority of people who had responded positively to his decision to resign, Benedict said, "I also thank each and every one of you for the respect and understanding with which you have accepted this important decision." He assured them, "I will continue to accompany the Church's journey with prayer and reflection, with that devotion to the Lord and his Bride which I have hitherto sought to practice daily and which I would like to practice always."

He called on everyone "to remember me in prayer before God, and above all to pray for the Cardinals, who are called to so weighty a task, and for the new Successor of the Apostle Peter: may the Lord accompany him with the light and strength of his Spirit."

He urged believers everywhere to invoke "the maternal intercession of the Virgin Mary, Mother of God and Mother of the Church, that she may accompany each of us and the whole ecclesial community" and "to commend ourselves with deep confidence" to her.

He concluded his memorable address with this consoling message to the faithful people in Rome and worldwide: "Dear friends! God guides his Church, he sustains it always, especially at times of difficulty. Let us never lose this vision of faith, which is the one true way of looking at the journey of the Church and of the world. In our hearts, in the heart of each of you, may there always abide the joyful certainty that the Lord is at our side: he does not abandon us, he remains."

Again, referring to his resignation, he told them, "The decision I have made, after much prayer, is the fruit of a serene trust in God's will and a deep love of Christ's Church. I will continue to accompany the Church with my prayers, and I ask each of you to pray for me and for the new Pope. In union with Mary and all the saints, let us entrust ourselves in faith and hope to God, who continues to watch over our lives and to guide the journey of the Church and our world along the paths of history. He is close to us and he surrounds us with his love. Thank you!"

When he finished speaking, the overflow crowd in Saint Peter's Square gave him a standing ovation that lasted several minutes, with many chanting "*Bene-detto, Bene-detto, Bene-detto.*" He acknowledged the applause, and extended a final greeting in different languages. "Thank you for these eight years among you," he said, smiling broadly with outstretched hands. He seemed greatly relieved.

WHILE BENEDICT WAS SPEAKING, life was continuing at a hectic back inside the papal apartment, on the third floor of the Apostolic Palace, as his secretaries and the four consecrated laywomen from Memores Domini hastened to pack and get everything ready for the move to Castel Gandolfo. They packed many things, including the teddy bear that his mother had given him as a child for Christmas in 1935, and another teddy bear that he has had since 1939.[68]

IN HIS BLOG TODAY, Luigi Accattoli, recalled that when Celestine V abdicated in front of the cardinals on December 13, 1294, he took off his papal robes, put on his grey habit and took back the name he had had before his election, Pietro da Morrone. When Gregory XII abdicated on July 4, 1415,[69] he put on again his cardinal's robes and took back the title of cardinal. Benedict XVI, on the other hand, will continue to wear white and be called "Holiness" and known as "emeritus pope." The Italian writer attributes this to the great importance the figure of the pope has today compared to that in the Middle Ages.

FOUR HOURS BEFORE BENEDICT BEGAN his final public audience, Cardinal Bergoglio arrived at Rome's Leonardo da Vinci airport aboard an Alitalia plane after a thirteen-hour flight from Buenos Aires. He had traveled in economy class, as he always does. He stepped off the plane wearing, as usual, a simple black clergyman's suit. He was not wearing his pectoral cross and chain as most cardinals and bishops do; indeed there was no visible sign that he was a prelate, except for the ring on his finger. He passed through immigration control and went to the baggage claim area to pick up his case. There he happened to meet the youthful, ever-smiling Cardinal Luis Antonio Tagle, who had just arrived on a plane from Manila after a fifteen-hour flight. The Filipino was wearing jeans and a Barong, the traditional shirt that is considered the national dress, and he too gave no sign of being a cardinal, except for his ring. Tagle had received the red hat less than three months earlier from Benedict XVI, at his last consistory on November 24, 2012. He was in fact in the last batch of cardinals that Benedict created, just as Ratzinger was in the last batch created by Paul VI on June 27, 1977.

At the airport, the Argentinian and Filipino cardinals greeted each other and chatted briefly. When their baggage eventually arrived, Tagle took the car provided for him by the Filipino College where the Filipino cardinals usually stay and where he would reside in the pre-conclave period. Bergoglio took public transportation from the airport to the Domus Paulus VI on Via della Scrofa 70, the international residence that John Paul II had refurbished fifteen years earlier for the use of Holy See diplomats or clergy working in the Vatican as well as for visiting prelates and priests.

The original building dates back to the fourteenth century and was once closely linked to the Jesuits because Saint Ignatius of Loyola, their founder, established the German College here in 1552, and the Jesuits ran the place until the order was suppressed by Clement XIV in 1773. After that, the building had to be partially demolished and then, after being rebuilt, soon served as the Vicariate of Rome.

After becoming archbishop of Buenos Aires on February 28, 1998, Bergoglio always stayed here whenever he came to Rome for meetings in the Vatican. The location is ideal: it is a mere twenty minutes' walk from Saint Peter's Basilica and close to Piazza Navona, the Pantheon, and the Church of St. Louis of the French, which contains great works of art by the famous Baroque painter Caravaggio (1571–1610), including "The Calling of St. Matthew," a story that is at the heart of Bergoglio's spirituality.

LIKE MANY OTHER CARDINALS, Bergoglio did not attend the Wednesday public audience. But one who did was Jean-Pierre Ricard, archbishop of Bordeaux, who was made a cardinal by Benedict in 2006 and is one of the four French electors at this conclave. He had arrived some days earlier, and afterwards spoke to *Il Messaggero*,[70] the Rome daily, about Benedict. "I saw his face tired, with the weight of age, but I was struck that he was a man at peace, a serene man with trust in the Lord who explained the motive for his resignation. He did not make this choice for his own personal good, but for the good of the Church. And he will continue to serve God in prayer."

Looking ahead to the conclave and the kind of pope he is looking for, Ricard said that "after a pontiff who resigned because of fatigue and tiredness linked to age, I would imagine a younger pope. It's not important whether he has sixty, sixty-five or seventy years. But it would be better that he is not over seventy-five." While the nationality of the next pope is not a matter of "fundamental importance," he said, "the determining factor, above everything else, is the personality of the one who will be elected." Asked about the impact Vatileaks and the pedophile scandals might have on the cardinals when they meet for the General Congregations, Ricard said that while he did not expect them to be "unduly affected," he was convinced that all those issues "would strengthen the will of the cardinals to continue in the work of truth started by Benedict, with regard to the pedophile scandal and the other problems." But, he added, "At the same time, our eyes will be turned to the conditions of the world, and the great challenges the church is facing." He excluded himself as a candidate; he considered the role of pope "a gigantic responsibility" that inspired fear in him.

THAT SAME AFTERNOON, I visited Cardinal Thomas Collins, the tenth archbishop of Toronto, a biblical scholar and friend of Ouellet. He was staying at the Domus Romana on Via Traspontina, near the Vatican, where I had interviewed him before. We talked for about an hour and, on the record, he said he didn't have much of an idea about the conclave, since it was his first, nor how long it might last. Right now he was "in the process of gathering information on his fellow cardinals, including those whom the media has listed as *papabile*." He knew the North American cardinals and some others, including Ravasi, who had come to Canada recently to address the bishops' conference, and Bergoglio, who had come to Quebec in 2008 for the Eucharistic Congress, but there were many he didn't know. Collins felt it was too early for him to comment further, as he was still "in a learning process."

ACCORDING TO EL PAÍS,[71] social activists and former members of the Mexican clergy have sent a protest letter to the Vatican objecting to the participation of Cardinal Norberto Rivera Carrera in the conclave. They allege that as bishop of Tehuacan in the 1980s he covered up the sexual abuses of the priest Nicolas Aguilar in Mexico and the United States. Alberto Athié, a former priest of the archdiocese of Mexico, had started the protest by making public their request to the Vatican "that Cardinal Rivera...not vote for the successor of Benedict XVI." Speaking to El País, Mr. Athié emphasized that "all cardinals involved in this tragedy that wrought damage on so many children should not go to the conclave"; he confirmed that he had invited Mexican Catholics to send letters of protest to the Vatican. El País reported that José Barba had joined the protest as well. A former member of the Legionaries of Christ, Barba, who had denounced the cases of pedophilia involving Fr. Marcial Maciel, the founder of the Legionaries, alleged that Rivera was indirectly involved in the Maciel case too because he had ignored the protests of those who denounced him. Furthermore, the Spanish daily reported that "one of the letters" sent to Cardinal Mahony and published by the tribunal of Los Angeles last January in the investigation of cases of pedophilia "indicated that Rivera was aware of the pedophile and homosexual tendencies of Aguilar." But like other cardinals touched by the scandal, the Mexico City cardinal did not cave in under the media pressure; he participated in the conclave.

ELISABETTA AND I did not meet with Cardinal Bergoglio today, as he had already accepted our invitation to come to dinner tomorrow night, but we spoke by phone. This evening, he went for dinner at the home of Gianni Valente,[72] a journalist who had worked for *Trenta Giorni nella Chiesa e nel Mondo* (*Thirty Days*, in English), an Italian monthly magazine linked to the movement Communion and Liberation. Published in six languages between 1983 and 2012, it focused on issues related to the Catholic Church and geopolitics and was read by many cardinals, bishops, priests, and laypeople in 110 countries, as well as by officials in the Roman Curia. From the mid-1990s onwards, the magazine was directed by Senator Giulio Andreotti, a former Italian prime minister and statesman who was close to the Roman Curia and the popes.

Gianni, a friend of Elisabetta and mine, first got to know Bergoglio in Buenos Aires in 2002 when the editor in chief of the magazine sent him there to report on the severe economic and political crisis in Argentina and on how the Catholic Church, led by the cardinal, was responding to the plight of the people in that fraught situation.

On the evening of February 27 Gianni's wife, Stefania Falasca, a journalist who had also worked for *Trenta Giorni* for many years, cooked dinner for Bergoglio and two of Gianni's friends and former colleagues from *Trenta Giorni* who had also been invited: Andrea Tornielli, founder of Vatican Insider and reporter for *La Stampa*, and Lucio Brunelli, an Italian state television reporter who had published the secret diary on the 2005 conclave.

FEBRUARY 28, THURSDAY ———————————————————————
The Era of Benedict XVI Ends

TODAY WILL BE REMEMBERED as the day when the eighth German pope in the history of the Church resigned, the first Roman pontiff to do so in six hundred years.

This morning 144 of the 208 members of the College of Cardinals assembled in the Sala Clementina of the Apostolic Palace, which Clement VII had decorated with frescos and art in the sixteenth century in honor of Clement I, the third pope, after whom it was named. They came to listen to Benedict deliver his farewell address and to greet him individually before he abdicated.

I watched the highly emotional audience, which was transmitted live by Vatican television (CTV). I saw the cardinals arrive and greet each other and then sit on red chairs. I noted that Cardinal Bergoglio was seated in the second row next to Cardinal Zen, chatting.

When Pope Benedict walked into the hall, wearing the red ermine-trimmed *mozzetta* (cape), the cardinals stood and applauded warmly. Once they were seated again, Cardinal Angelo Sodano, the eighty-five-year-old dean of the College of Cardinals and for a short while Benedict's secretary of state, stood up and, greeting him on their behalf, expressed their "heartfelt gratitude for your selfless witness of apostolic service, for the good of the church of Christ and of all humanity." He recalled that "on April 19, 2005, you joined the long line of successors of the Apostle Peter, and today, February 28, 2013, you are about to leave us as we wait for the helm of the barque of Peter to pass into other hands." In this way, he said, "the apostolic succession continues, which the Lord promised to his holy church, until the voice of the Angel of the Apocalypse is heard to proclaim on earth 'there is no longer time, the mystery of God is finished' and so at that moment the history of the Church ends with the history of the world, with the advent of a new heaven and a new earth."

Cardinal Sodano recalled that the cardinals had walked with him over the past eight years, reliving the experience of the disciples as Jesus accompanied them on the road to Emmaus and, like those disciples, "we too felt our hearts burning within us as you spoke to us." Reiterating their immense gratitude for these years, he concluded in German: "Vergelt's Gott!" ("May God reward you!") The cardinals applauded warmly.

When the cardinal dean finished speaking, Benedict XVI stood up, embraced him, and then sat down again. He remained seated as he delivered his memorable farewell speech.[73] The following is the official Vatican translation of that historic discourse:

> Venerable and Dear Brothers,
>
> I welcome you with great joy and I offer each one of you my most cordial greeting. I thank Cardinal Angelo Sodano who, as always, interpreted the sentiments of the entire College: *Cor ad cor loquitur* [heart speaks to heart] I warmly thank you, Your Eminence. And I would like to say—taking up your reference to the disciples of Emmaus—that for me too it has been a joy to walk with you in these years, in the light of the presence of the Risen Lord.
>
> As I said yesterday to the thousands of faithful who filled St Peter's Square, your closeness and your advice have been of great help to me in my ministry. In these eight years we have lived with faith very beautiful moments of radiant light on the Church's journey, as well as moments when several clouds gathered in the sky. We sought to serve Christ and his Church with profound and total love, which is the heart and soul of our ministry. We gave hope, the hope that comes to us from Christ, which alone can give light to us on our journey. Together we may thank the Lord who has enabled us to grow in communion and, together, pray him to help us to grow even more in this profound unity, so that the College of Cardinals may be like an orchestra where

differences—an expression of the universal Church—contribute to a superior and harmonious concord.

I would like to leave you a simple thought, which is deep in my heart: a thought about the Church, about her mystery, that constitutes for us all—we can say—the reason and passion for life.

I will allow a sentence of Romano Guardini to help me. It was written in the very same year that the Fathers of the Second Vatican Council approved the Constitution *Lumen Gentium*. In this, his last book, which also has a personal dedication to me—which makes the words of this book particularly dear to me, Guardini says the Church "is not an institution conceived and built in theory...but a living reality...She lives through the course of time, in becoming, like every living being, in undergoing change...And yet in her nature she remains ever the same and her heart is Christ."

It seems to me that this was our experience yesterday in the Square: seeing that the Church is a living body, enlivened by the Holy Spirit and which is really brought to life by God's power. She is in the world but not of the world: she is of God, of Christ, of the Spirit. We saw this yesterday. That is why Guardini's other famous saying is both true and eloquent: "The Church is reawakened in souls." The Church is alive, she grows and is reawakened in souls who—like the Virgin Mary—welcome the Word of God and conceive it through the action of the Holy Spirit; they offer to God their own flesh. It is precisely in their poverty and humility that they become capable of begetting Christ in the world today. Through the Church, the Mystery of the Incarnation lives on forever. Christ continues to walk through the epochs and in all places.

Let us stay united, dear Brothers, in this Mystery: in prayer, especially in the daily Eucharist, and, in this way, we shall serve the Church and the whole of humanity. This is our joy that no one can take from us.

Before I say goodbye to each one of you personally, I would like to tell you that I shall continue to be close to you with my prayers, especially in these coming days, that you may be completely docile to the action of the Holy Spirit in the election of the new pope. May the Lord show you the one whom he wants. And among you, in the College of Cardinals, there is also the future pope to whom today I promise my unconditional reverence and obedience. For this reason, with affection and gratitude, I cordially impart to you the Apostolic Blessing.

The assembled cardinals applauded with gratitude, admiration, and profound emotion. They gave him a standing ovation. Then one by one, they went to him to say farewell, some with tears in their eyes. There were many profoundly touching moments as the cardinals greeted Benedict for the last time as pope. It was a truly moving scene, but Benedict remained composed and serene throughout. A man at peace.

THIS FAREWELL CEREMONY was followed by the 3,641 journalists and television or radio crews from 989 media outlets, representing twenty-four languages and sixty-one nations, who had already arrived in Rome and obtained accreditation at the Holy See's Press Office to cover Benedict's resignation and the election of the new pope. They broadcast it to the world.

DAVID WILLEY, the BBC's longest serving foreign correspondent reported it this way to his global audience: "In normal times, popes make their final exit from the Vatican in a coffin and—after a period of mourning —are laid to rest in the crypt of Saint Peter's Basilica as the great bells of the first church of Christendom boom out. But not Pope Benedict XVI. His nearly eight-year-long pontificate has ended not in death, but with a remarkable resignation."

THAT AFTERNOON, around five o'clock local time, Vatican TV treated the world to a historic and stunning spectacle worthy of Hollywood, directed by Mgr. Dario Vigano and inspired by Fellini's film, *La Dolce Vita*. It started with Benedict XVI's farewell to the priests, nuns, and lay people working in the Vatican's Secretariat of State. He walked out of the Apostolic Palace for the last time, leaning on a black walking stick, and waved to the usually invisible Vatican employees who are at the heart of the papal civil service and were now gathered in the courtyard of San Damaso. Many were in tears as he waved goodbye before getting into the limousine that took him to the small city-state's heliport, behind St. Peter's basilica. The TV tracked every stage of his journey, enabling people to accompany him on his dramatic departure from the Vatican in a white Italian Air Force helicopter for the town of Castel Gandolfo, overlooking Lake Albano, where the papal summer residence has been ever since 1626 when Clement VIII first went there.

We watched the helicopter take off and twice circle around Saint Peter's Basilica as the mighty bells of Saint Peter's rang out before it soared into the air on this sunny winter afternoon and set course on the fifteen-minute ride to Castel Gandolfo, sixteen miles southeast of Rome. It flew low over the city, passing close to Piazza Navona, the Pantheon, and the Colosseum. The bells of every church in Rome rang out their farewell as Benedict left the eternal city for the last time as pope. People watched from their apartment windows and from the streets and waved as the helicopter flew over.

Our family too watched from our fifth-floor balcony window. Carolina seemed transfixed; Juan Pablo waved. Benedict touched the hearts of the Romans in these days, in a way that he had never succeeded in doing in his almost eight-year pontificate.

By the time his helicopter touched down in the grounds of the papal summer residence in Castel Gandolfo, thousands of people had gathered in the area in front of the palace, where the Swiss Guards were standing on duty. They knew Benedict would come out on the central balcony to give them his last blessing as pope.

He drove the short distance from the heliport to the palace and then went straight to the balcony overlooking the square to greet the crowd for the very last time as pope. His appearance on the central balcony was greeted with prolonged applause. He waved, and then spoke briefly. These were his last words as pope:

Thank you. Thank you all.

Dear Friends,

I am happy to be with you, surrounded by the beauty of Creation and your kindness, which does me so much good. Thank you for your friendship and your affection. You know that this day is different for me from the preceding ones. I am no longer the Supreme Pontiff of the Catholic Church, or I will be until 8:00 this evening and then no longer. I am simply a pilgrim beginning the last leg of his pilgrimage on this earth. But I would still, thank you, I would still—with my heart, with my love, with my prayers, with my reflection, and with all my inner strength—like to work for the common good and the good of the Church and of humanity. I feel greatly supported by your kindness. Let us go forward with the Lord for the good of the Church and the world. Thank you. I now wholeheartedly impart my blessing.

May Almighty God bless us, Father, Son, and Holy Spirit. Good night! Thank you all![74]

The crowd broke into sustained, emotional applause. Many shouted "*Viva il Papa!*" Others just wept. Nobody remained indifferent. Benedict waved and then disappeared back into the palace. It was his last public appearance as pope.

IT HAS BEEN THE DUTY OF POPES to provide for the inter-regnum, or the period of vacancy known as *sede vacante*, between the end of the pontificate of one pope (either by death or resignation) and the election of the new pope.

John Paul II had updated the norms for the period of the vacant see in the apostolic constitution of 1996, *Universi Dominici Gregis*, to ensure that the Church's central administration is not brought to a halt. According to that decree, four cardinals remain in office during the *sede vacante*: the camerlengo (or chamberlain), the major penitentiary (who can absolve the most serious cases of conscience), the vicar of Rome (like the vicar general of a diocese), and the archpriest of Saint Peter's. All other senior office holders in the Roman Curia, including the cardinal secretary of state, the prefects of the congregations, the presidents of the pontifical councils and other offices, cease to have authority. The number-two officials of the various dicasteries remain in office, however, as do the apostolic nuncios and apostolic delegates in countries across the globe.

On April 4, 2007, Benedict XVI appointed Cardinal Tarcisio Bertone, his long-time friend and secretary of state, as camerlengo. He will serve as acting head of state for the Vatican City State and administrator for the Holy See until the election of a new pope. At eight o'clock this evening, when Benedict ceases to be pope, Cardinal Bertone will hold a meeting of the Apostolic Camara and, with the help of his collaborators, put the seals on the papal apartment where the pope had lived in the Vatican, as a visible sign that the pontificate of Benedict XVI has ended. The papal twitter account (@Pontifex) with its three million followers will be closed. The apartment will remain sealed until the new pope enters.

ALL AFTERNOON we had been following on television the unfolding events at the Vatican and Castel Gandolfo. Elisabetta had nonetheless managed to prepare dinner for Cardinal Bergoglio, who was due to arrive by eight o'clock. In fact, he came about ten minutes early, dressed in a black clergyman's suit.

Following the Argentinian tradition, Elisabetta and the children gave him a kiss of welcome. I shook hands. As usual, he brought a gift for Juan Pablo and Carolina: a box of Alfajores, an Argentine delicacy.

When he entered the living room, the television was showing the heavy, wooden doors of the papal residence at Castel Gandolfo, waiting for them to be closed. Bergoglio had arrived just in time to see history being made. He stood there with us watching as the doors closed at eight o'clock exactly, signaling the end of Benedict XVI's papacy. With us he saw the Swiss Guards abandon their positions; there was no longer a pope to guard. We watched in total silence. It was an awesome and truly historic moment. The See of Peter was now vacant. Little did we know that his 265th successor was standing next to us.

After his election, Bergoglio told us that he had absolutely no inkling that evening that God would call him next to step into the shoes of the fisherman. He had set his sights on retirement later that year and had bought his return airline ticket so that, immediately after the Mass for the inauguration of the new pope, he could fly back to Buenos Aires for the Holy Week ceremonies.

At dinner, Elisabetta sat at the head of the table as usual; he always insisted on that. We wanted him to say the grace before meals, but he insisted that I, as father of the family, should do so.

Over dinner, he told us that this happened to be the fifteenth anniversary of his becoming archbishop of Buenos Aires. His predecessor, Cardinal Antonio Quarracino, had died on February 28, 1998, at the age of seventy-five and, as coadjutor-bishop, Bergoglio automatically became archbishop. He took over without any big ceremony to mark the event.

We talked about Benedict's resignation, its significance, the situation in the Church, the upcoming conclave, and much else. He spoke freely, and at one stage during the conversation, Elisabetta told him: "If you say what you think at the General Congregations you will be elected!" He laughed heartily, totally dismissing the possibility.

It was a most enjoyable, relaxed evening. Before leaving, he gave the children his blessing, and then I accompanied him back to the Domus Paulus VI, which is less than five minutes' walk from our home.

PART II

THE SEE OF PETER IS VACANT

(March 1–11, 2013)

Cardinals Begin to Caucus

FR. FEDERICO LOMBARDI began his daily press briefing by anticipating questions about the emeritus pope. He reported the news from Castel Gandolfo: Benedict XVI "slept well" last night and "is serene" after his abdication.

He told reporters that Cardinal Sodano, as dean of the College of Cardinals, had sent a letter to all 209 cardinals worldwide summoning them to attend the important pre-conclave meetings of cardinals, called the "General Congregations," that will begin on Monday, March 4, at 9:30 AM. Sodano informed them that the meetings will be held in the new hall of the Synod of Bishops that is located under the Paul VI audience hall, on the left-hand side of Saint Peter's Basilica, close to the place where Saint Peter, the first pope, was crucified upside down.

Following is the text of Cardinal Sodano's letter, written on letterhead from the Vatican and dated the first of March:[1]

> Lord Cardinal,
>
> Analogously to what is prescribed by the Apostolic Constitution "Universi Dominici Gregis" of February 22, 1996 at no. 19, for the case of death of the Sovereign Pontiff, I perform my duty to communicate officially to Your Eminence the news of the vacancy of the Apostolic See due to the resignation presented by Pope Benedict XVI, and effective since yesterday evening, February 28, at 8:00 p.m. in Rome.
>
> In communicating the foregoing, I fulfill my duty to convoke Your Eminence to the first of the General Congregations of the College of Cardinals, to be held Monday, March 4 at 9:30 a.m. in Paul VI Hall, in the room of the Synod of Bishops.
>
> The General Congregations will then continue regularly until the complete number of Cardinal electors has been reached and the College of Cardinals then decides the date of entry into

the Conclave of those Cardinal electors as prescribed by the recent Motu Proprio of this past 22 February concerning some changes to the rules regarding the election of the Roman Pontiff.

For my part I am pleased to take this opportunity to extend my fraternal greetings.

Cordially in the Lord,
+ Angelo Card. Sodano

Lombardi explained that there would be two plenary assemblies of the cardinals on that first day, one in the morning at 9:30 AM, the other in the afternoon at 5:00 PM. From then on, the cardinals would decide from day to day when the subsequent congregations would be held. He explained that these meetings would continue "until the full number of cardinal electors has been reached" and then the college would decide "the date on which the cardinal electors enter the conclave."

For the many journalists present with little knowledge of the preconclave process, the ever-patient Jesuit explained that while all the cardinals, irrespective of age, can participate in the General Congregations, only those under the age of eighty on the day the See of Peter became vacant can enter the conclave and vote in the election for the next pope. Paul VI had introduced this revolutionary norm on November 20, 1970, in his motu proprio *Ingravescentem Aetatem*,[2] in the face of strong opposition from many cardinals. John Paul II refused to rescind it, despite pressure to do so.

Lombardi confirmed that on March 1, the day the See of Peter became vacant, there were 117 cardinal electors, and another 92 cardinals who have lost the right to vote because they are over eighty. But the number of electors has been reduced to 115, he said, because two electors are not able to participate in the conclave. He was referring to Indonesia's Cardinal Julius Darmaatmadja, SJ, who could not travel to Rome because of ill health, and Scotland's Cardinal Keith O'Brien, who had recused himself, as mentioned earlier.

To everyone's surprise, Lombardi announced that Egypt's Cardinal Antonios Naguib, 77, the Catholic Coptic Patriarch of Alexandria, would participate in the conclave. The leader of the Catholic Coptic Church, which counts for around 10 percent of the population of this majority Muslim country of 84 million people,[3] had suffered a cerebral hemorrhage on December 31, 2012 and had previously announced that he could not travel to Rome. He changed his mind, however, as he explained to Fides,[4] the news agency of the Congregation for the Evangelization of Peoples: "It was something I no longer dreamed of, and so at the beginning I said that it was not possible for me to go to the eternal city for the conclave. But then I reflected on the fact that the primary duty of a cardinal is to participate in choosing the Successor of Peter, and so I changed my initial decision."

This means that 115 cardinals will vote in the conclave to elect the next leader of the 1.2 billion-member Catholic Church, 41.3 percent of whom live in Latin America.

AT THE PRESS CONFERENCE, Fr. Lombardi also provided more mundane information that is sure to be of interest to collectors of stamps (philatelists) and of coins (numismatics) worldwide. The Vatican has been printing stamps since 1852, and he announced that it has already issued postal stamps commemorating the *sede vacante* (with the symbol of the crossed-keys, a sign of papal authority) and, in the coming days, it will mint coins bearing the same message. The stamps and coins are usually in great demand on these occasions because, aside from their being a memento of this historic moment in the life of the Church, they are an investment for collectors and gain in value over the years. The sale of stamps and coins is one of the Vatican's sources of revenue. Since I am a stamp collector, I bought some stamps after the briefing.

THE SEE OF PETER IS VACANT. The search is on for the new pope. The 115 cardinal electors from forty-five countries are expected to have identified the leader of the Catholic world before Saint Patrick's Day, March 17.

After the high emotions and drama of the final days of the pontificate of Benedict XVI, cardinals have begun to engage in serious discussions on the situation of the Church today and possible candidates to be next pope. While many electors already have a favorite candidate, the majority has no one in mind. But all that could change over the coming week.

Unlike the conclave of April 2005, when Cardinal Joseph Ratzinger went in as the front-runner with more than forty cardinals having already identified him as their candidate, at this moment there is no clear favorite, and in that sense this conclave is more open to a surprise result, according to several electors that I have spoken with in recent days.

Right now, most cardinals say they are at the stage of information gathering and sharing. The pre-election process takes many forms, and the cardinals are listening attentively, knowing full well that the Holy Spirit can enlighten them in different ways and through different actors.

A cardinal resident in Rome and working in the Vatican, for example, may invite fellow cardinals from his same language group, nationality, or theological outlook for lunch, or dinner, or a drink at his apartment to discuss the situation of the Church today and the relative strengths and weaknesses of possible candidates, and perhaps to suggest a name.

This time, the lead-in period to the conclave is decidedly shorter than the previous time; there will be no opportunity for the long-term relaxed lobbying that preceded the 2005 conclave. That was ensured by Benedict XVI's shock resignation on February 11; he left the cardinals just one month to identify possible candidates to lead the Catholic Church on the next stage of its pilgrim journey. Many think the conclave could begin as early as March 10.

FROM NOW TO THE OPENING of the conclave, cardinals from the Italian, English, French, German, Spanish, and Portuguese speaking worlds respectively are likely to caucus in small groups behind closed doors in cardinals' apartments, colleges, or religious houses across the city as they seek to identify the candidate who would be best suited for this moment in history.[5]

Early on, for example, Cardinal Walter Kasper invited all the German-speaking cardinals (among them eight electors from Germany, Switzerland, and Austria) to his apartment near the Vatican to review and discuss the present situation in the Roman Curia and the universal Church in advance of the General Congregations. But they did not discuss who the *papabili* might be at that first meeting, a participant told me.

Seven of the eleven electors from the United States—plus at least one other cardinal, Theodore Edgar McCarrick,[6] now over eighty—are staying at the North American College, That makes it easier for this second largest bloc of electors to share ideas.

MORE SIGNIFICANTLY, perhaps, small groups of like-minded cardinals, transcending national and linguistic boundaries, will gather together for the same purpose at locations not visible to the press. If a group concurs on one candidate, they will then test his chances with other cardinals.

It is in these small groups that certain cardinals, known as "kingmakers," can play a highly important role in promoting or gathering support for a candidate. This time round, "kingmakers" could include the following: Italy's Angelo Sodano and Giovanni Battista Re, who held top-ranking positions in the Secretariat of State under John Paul II and the early part of Benedict XVI's pontificate; Poland's Stanislaw Dziwisz, former secretary to John Paul II, who knows most if not all of the cardinals; Nigeria's Francis Arinze, considered among the *papabili* at the 2005 conclave[7] and an esteemed figure in Africa, with good contacts in other parts of the world as well; Honduras's Óscar Rodríguez Maradiaga, who got votes in the last conclave and is well known not only in North and South America but also in Europe; and the English cardinal, Cormac Murphy-O'Connor, who has many friends not only in the Roman Curia but also in Europe, Asia, the Americas, and Africa. Other "kingmakers" could emerge in the coming days.

IN THIS PRE-CONCLAVE PERIOD, the new lay movements or groupings in the Catholic Church, most of which have arisen since the Second Vatican Council (1962–1965) and flourished under the pontificate of John Paul II, do discreet lobbying—though their leaders vigorously deny this. They invite their cardinal friends for dinner, or lunch, or find other ways to talk with them. These conversations can help boost or lower a cardinal's chances in the conclave, or even promote one not yet on the radar screen.

According to various sources, the Focolare movement is said to favor the Brazilian Cardinal João Braz de Aviz, who reminds many people of Pope John XXIII, though they also like the Indian cardinal Telesphore Toppo, the world's first tribal cardinal. The Neo-Catechumenate movement is believed to be firmly backing the former Holy See diplomat, the Italian cardinal Fernando Filoni, head of the Congregation for the Evangelization of Peoples, which oversees the Church's work in missionary lands and the third world. The Communion and Liberation movement is clearly supporting its former leader, the Italian front-runner, Cardinal Angelo Scola, even though he might feel more comfortable—and stand a better chance—without this backing. Opus Dei, though a prelature and not a new lay movement, appears to be gently suggesting two candidates: the archbishop of São Paulo, Brazil, Odilo Pedro Scherer, who once worked in the Vatican's Congregation for Bishops, and the Italian Cardinal Mauro Piacenza, head of the Congregation for the Clergy and spiritual son of the late Cardinal Siri of Genova. The Sant'Egidio Community is said to favor three candidates: Italy's Cardinal Agostino Vallini, the pope's vicar for Rome; Mexico's Cardinal Francisco Robles Ortega; and Argentina's Jorge Mario Bergoglio, though they consider him an outsider.

WITH THE DIGITAL REVOLUTION and the development of various new means of social communication, the media has come to play an increasingly important, sometimes decisive role in society. This is also true of its role in relation to religion, the Church, and the election of the pope.

The first mobile phone came into use in 1973, but was not yet much in evidence when John Paul II was elected in 1978; some reporters had mobile phones, but not many. Most of the means of social communication we have today came into existence after that conclave. Google started in 1998, and blogging around the same time; smartphones began to be more widely used from 2000 onwards. Facebook came on the scene in February 2004 and doesn't appear to have had any impact on the 2005 conclave. Twitter came into existence in March 2006, and Instagram in October 2010. This rapid development in the instruments of social communication has had an enormous impact on news gathering and broadcast, and this was more evident than ever at the papal election in March 2013.

A story about a statement made or an interview given by a cardinal, for example, can be read by another cardinal that same day on Twitter or Facebook and can influence him. It has the potential to boost or deflate, even make or break a *papabile* in the run-up to the papal election, just as it does in politics or any other field in the twenty-first century. How much it is actually doing this in 2013 is a matter for future study.

As mentioned earlier, over the past half-century or more, the Italian media have played a most important, if not unique, role around the election of a pope, particularly through the work of their expert reporters or analysts on the Vatican and the papacy.[8] Indeed, there is no other country in the world where the papacy and the Vatican get as much mainstream media coverage as in Italy.

The historical record shows that for more than half a century, with few exceptions, the Italian media has led the conversation nationally and internationally on both the papacy and the Vatican. The same is true as we move into the 2013 conclave. Every foreign reporter accredited to the Holy See's press office for the conclave—the number is already around four thousand—is monitoring the Italian press and its related websites every day. Many cardinals read Italian because they studied here, and not a few of them monitor the Italian and other media, too, as do people close to them. The embassy staffs of the 180 or more states that have diplomatic relations with the Holy See do likewise.

It should be acknowledged, however, that the relation between cardinals and journalists is often a two-way street: the cardinals not only give interviews, they also talk to journalists whom they trust and from whom they can gather valuable information, including information regarding brother cardinals about whom they may have only minimal knowledge. They often benefit from the media's input and comments. Such input, of course, has the potential to impact a candidate's chances of becoming pope.

AT THIS CRUCIAL MOMENT in the life of the Church, Catholics across the world in dioceses, in parishes, in enclosed orders or religious houses, in movements and in families play an important role by praying to God to enlighten the cardinals in their search for next Successor of Saint Peter. The emeritus pope, Benedict XVI, is praying too for the electors, who have the momentous responsibility before God and the community of believers.

FROM NEXT MONDAY, March 4, all the cardinals—both the electors and those over eighty years of age—will meet in plenary assembly, known as General Congregations, once or twice each day (except Sunday) until the conclave opens.

The meetings will be held in the synod hall. Following Vatican protocol, the cardinals will come dressed in black cassocks with red piping, a red sash, and skull cap, while the patriarchs wear their distinctive dress. They will sit in green chairs in a semi-circle in front of the table of the presidency. Members of the Vatican's Secretariat of State, after taking an oath of secrecy, will translate the various interventions into five main languages: English, French, German, Italian, and Spanish.

It should be emphasized that the General Congregations are of great importance in the pre-election period, because they provide an opportunity for cardinals to get to know each other. Very many cardinals do not know their brother cardinals, and certainly not in any depth; they may have met them perhaps on only one or a few occasions at a synod, a consistory, or another Vatican event. These plenary assemblies allow them to gain a deeper insight into the different personalities and their vision of Church and the world. Since there is no longer a pope, the cardinals feel free to speak boldly and say what is on their minds regarding the last pontificate, consider the main problems of the Church and the world today, and identify the priorities the next pope must address. All this enables the electors to reflect on what type of man might be best to lead the Church in the coming years.

As dean of the College of Cardinals, Cardinal Angelo Sodano will chair these meetings at which each cardinal will be given one or more opportunities to speak. But it is only when the electors cast their first vote in the Sistine Chapel on the opening evening of the conclave that the names of the actual candidates will be revealed.

ON THE EVENING OF MARCH 1, several cardinals let it be known, in private conversations or through the media, that they were anxious to discuss in-depth the major problems that had surfaced during the pontificate of Benedict, starting with Vatileaks, which had interfered with the functioning of the Holy See and risked compromising the central government of the Catholic Church.

An anti-Italian sentiment appeared to have begun to surface among some foreign cardinals as they came to realize that almost all the actors involved in the Vatileaks scandal were Italian; several of the foreign cardinals tended to blame the Italians in the Roman Curia, and particularly some in top positions, such as Cardinal Bertone, for much of the mess at the Vatican bank and the problems in the Roman Curia.

A number of cardinals confided in private, and some stated in public, that the Roman Curia would be a major topic on the agenda of the General Congregations. Thus, for example, upon his arrival in Rome on February 26, Cardinal Christoph Schönborn, a highly esteemed European church leader who is very close to Benedict XVI, told the press: "The Curia must be organized in [such] a way that it services the primacy of the pope and does not substitute for it."

Another cardinal elector, described as "authoritative" but whose identity was not revealed, told *Corriere della Sera*'s Vatican correspondent, Gian Guido Vecchi,[9] "I don't know what the dossier on Vatileaks contains; none of us really knows, but we must know what happened. This is a fundamental presupposition for voting in the conclave." While it's not necessary to read the entire report, he said, "we need a solid summary, we need to know the present situation in the Roman Curia so as to be able to make responsible decisions."

REFORM OF THE ROMAN CURIA, however, is not the only issue being raised. The Italian cardinal Agostino Vallini, former prefect of the Church's Supreme Tribunal[10] and since 2008 vicar general of the diocese of Rome, tells reporters that he believes the Church needs "a pope with younger strength, more vigorous."

Benedict's resignation and the reasons he gave for it have brought the question of age to the fore in the pre-election period. I have heard this mentioned frequently in these days.

The historical record[11] offers an interesting perspective in this regard. It shows that while the age of many popes at the time of their election in the first millennium is given only in generic terms ("old," "young"), we know the exact age of the last 102 popes at the time of their election, starting from 858 with the election of the thirty-eight-year-old Nicholas I.

Of the 109 popes elected since then:

- three were under the age of twenty-five (the youngest was John XX, who was elected in 955 at the age of eighteen)
- seven were between the ages of twenty-five and forty
- eleven between forty-one and fifty
- twenty-four between fifty-one and sixty (John Paul II was fifty-eight when elected in 1978)
- thirty-seven between sixty-one and seventy and (John Paul I was sixty-five when elected in 1978)
- seventeen between seventy-one and eighty (Benedict XVI was seventy-eight when elected in 2005)
- three were over the age of eighty (the last was Gregory XII, who was eighty-one when elected in 1406)

Nationality too can be a factor in the election of the pope, but it should not be a major one, cardinals have said. Indeed, the historical record[12] shows that over the past two thousand years, including the 2005 conclave, popes were elected from thirteen different countries: Africa (*sic*),[13] Dalmatia (one of the four historical regions of Croatia), England, France, Germany, Greece, Holland, Italy, Palestine, Poland, Portugal, Spain, and Syria.

IT IS WELL KNOWN that during the interregnum period cardinals go for lunch or dinner with brother cardinals either in Vatican apartments, restaurants, or other locations.

Cardinals Bergoglio and Murphy-O'Connor, for instance, had dinner together this evening, March 1, at the Pollarolo restaurant, not far from the Campo di Fiori in the historic center of Rome. They have known each other since February 2001, when they were both made cardinals by John Paul II, and they have had meals together on previous occasions. The English cardinal wrote in his autobiography[14] that they had arranged to meet for dinner "to have a chat together" before the General Congregations started. He reveals that "over a meal of risotto and a glass of wine we talked about the sort of person we felt the cardinals should elect," but adds significantly, "If he had any inkling at all that evening that he himself might be in the running, he gave me no indication of that possibility and nor did I raise the issue. There was a lot of talk among the cardinals of the need for someone younger, with the vigor and energy that would be needed to take on the problems and challenges that faced the Church. Bergoglio was seventy-six years old."

When I would have dinner three months later with Cardinal Murphy-O'Connor,[15] he recalled that evening meal and told me, "It was clear to me that night that Bergoglio never considered himself as a candidate to be pope." But he added that after listening to what the Argentinian had to say, and having reflected on it in the following days, he reached the conclusion that "this man could be pope." He told me that subsequently, on occasions when he was with fellow cardinals discussing possible candidates to succeed Benedict, he introduced Bergoglio's name as a possibility, just as other cardinals suggested the names of different cardinals that they thought could fill that role.

MARCH 2 (SATURDAY) _____

"The Sherer Ticket" Revealed

THE FORTHCOMING CONCLAVE is now daily news in the Italian media, which is hardly surprising in a country that has given so many popes to the Church down the centuries and where still today 87 percent of its sixty million people identify themselves as Catholics.

I ALREADY KNEW this was going to be a busy day for me; I had two interviews lined up and much else to do. But I began the day as usual with a review of the Italian press, and some articles caught my attention.

Italy's highest circulation daily, *La Repubblica*, a center-left paper, devoted four full pages to the conclave. On the front page, it carried an article by Professor Hans Küng, the famous Swiss theologian, which had been published as an op-ed in the *New York Times* on February 27, under the title, "A Vatican Spring?"[16]

In it, Professor Küng noted that, apart from Ratzinger, he is the only other living theologian to have participated in the Second Vatican Council (1962–1965). He recalled how the Arab Spring had shaken autocratic regimes in the Middle East to their foundations and wondered if Benedict XVI's resignation could open the door to something similar in the Catholic Church.

Describing the Roman Curia as "a product of the eleventh century," he denounced it as "the chief obstacle to any thorough reform of the Catholic Church, to any honest ecumenical understanding with the other Christian churches and world religions, and to any critical, constructive attitude toward the modern world." While lamenting that under John Paul II and Benedict XVI "there has been a fatal return to the church's old monarchical habits," he asserted that the whole world is asking: "Might the next pope, despite everything, inaugurate a new spring for the Catholic Church?"

The controversial theologian, who crossed swords many times with Cardinal Ratzinger when he was head of the Congregation for the Doctrine of the Faith but had lunch and spent four hours with Benedict XVI at Castel Gandolfo at the latter's invitation on September 24, 2005, wrote in the *New York Times* that he felt that "in this dramatic situation the church needs a pope who's not living intellectually in the Middle Ages, who doesn't champion any kind of medieval theology, liturgy, or church constitution."

According to Professor Küng, the Church "needs a pope who is open to the concerns of the Reformation, to modernity. A pope who stands up for the freedom of the church in the world not just by giving sermons but by fighting with words and deeds for freedom and human rights within the church, for theologians, for women, for all Catholics who want to speak the truth openly. A pope who no longer forces the bishops to toe a reactionary party line, who puts into practice an appropriate democracy in the church, one shaped on the model of primitive Christianity. A pope who doesn't let himself be influenced by a Vatican-based 'shadow pope' like Benedict and his loyal followers."[17]

Strong words, indeed!

I was struck by the fact that while *La Repubblica* published this article on the front page today it also carried a two-page spread inside the paper that was widely interpreted as what one elector described as "campaigning" for Cardinal Scola to be next pope. It is perhaps worth mentioning that *La Repubblica*'s deputy editor in chief is a member of Communion and Liberation (CL), an international Catholic lay movement founded in 1954 by an Italian priest, Luigi Giussani, and present today in ninety countries, and with which Scola has been closely identified.

The article presented the cardinal's life story. It recalled how this son of a socialist truck-driver father and a pious Catholic mother was always first in his class, met Don Luigi Giussani, the founder of CL and became its standard bearer, fell in love with a beautiful woman but left her to enter the priesthood, and was ordained at the age of twenty-nine. It said this scholar-priest went on to become a professor at Freiburg University, Germany, and noted that his mentors were Hans Urs von Balthasar and Karol Wojtyla, while his close friends included men who are today cardinals: Schönborn, Erdo, Ouellet. It argued that Scola has strong credentials to become pope, having been rector of the Pontifical Lateran University (1995–2002) and bishop in three dioceses, including two—Venice and Milan—that have given five popes to the Church in the last century. It highlighted the fact that Benedict, in a surprise and unprecedented move, transferred Scola from Venice to Milan on June 28, 2011, in what was universally interpreted as a clear signal that he considered him the heir-apparent and the most qualified to succeed him.

The article revealed that when a collaborator phoned Scola on February 11 to inform him of Benedict's resignation, Scola reacted incredulously: "Impossible, impossible!" Now, on the eve of the conclave, *La Repubblica* is asserting that this cardinal could be elected pope.

Corriere della Sera, Italy's establishment daily and rival to *La Repubblica*, also devoted two pages to the conclave today. In one article, it predicted that the clash at the conclave would not be between "the progressives" and "the conservatives" but between "the Ratzinger-group" and the "non-" or "anti-" Ratzinger bloc. It quoted a "progressive" cardinal elector, who wished to remain anonymous, as saying: "Before the reform of the Curia or whatever else, it's necessary to begin from what was the fundamental intention of Ratzinger: to go back to the apostolic origins, to start from the Gospel, to frame the renewal of the Church starting from the essence of the faith, that's the starting point."

La Stampa, another Italian national daily, ran a different kind of article under the title "South American temptation for the first extra-European pope." Written by Andrea Tornielli, the article opened by quoting an unnamed prelate and longtime friend of the archbishop of Buenos Aires who asserted, "Four years of Bergoglio would [have been] sufficient to change things." It noted, however, that Bergoglio's name is not being mentioned among the *papabili* because of his age—he is now seventy-six. Nevertheless, it recalled that he was runner-up in the 2005 conclave, and that since then his "prestige" has grown in the Latin American church and in the College of Cardinals, and so those in the conclave who want change might look to him and therefore "it cannot be excluded that he could get votes." In any case, the author predicted that Bergoglio "will certainly be one of the key figures in the General Congregations and in the conclave."

In Tornielli's view, Cardinal Odilo Pedro Scherer, 63, the archbishop of São Paulo, Brazil, is the Latin American front-runner. Tornielli listed in his favor the fact that he worked at the Congregation for Bishops with Cardinal Re (1994–2001) and since then has been on the important commission of six cardinals who oversee the Institute for the Works of Religion (the Vatican bank) as well as being a member of the council of fifteen cardinals studying the organizational and economic problems of the Holy See. Tornielli also mentioned as other possibilities Cardinals Francisco Robles Ortega, 64, archbishop of Guadalajara, Mexico, and the Canadian Marc Ouellet, who worked many years as a priest in Latin America. Significantly, however, he listed only two European *papabili*: Angelo Scola, 71, and Peter Erdo, 60, the archbishop of Budapest.

La Stampa's leading Vatican reporter quoted Cardinal Coccolpamerio as saying, "In my view the moment has come to look outside Italy and Europe and, in particular, to consider Latin America." Tornielli claimed that former nuncios who had worked in Latin America, such as Cardinals Giuseppe Bertello (Italy) and Leonardo Sandri (Argentina) as well as Giovanni Battista Re who held top Vatican positions—including president of the Pontifical Council for Latin America—under John Paul II and Benedict XVI, could be of a similar mind.

When I asked Cardinal Coccopalmerio some years after the conclave[18] why he had spoken to reporters then about the possibility of a Latin American pope, he told me, "We had been talking for a long time about the need to give value to candidates for the papacy from churches in other parts of the world, and in particular from Latin America, and so as the General Congregations were about to begin I asked myself: Why don't we think seriously about this possibility? I hadn't hypothesized, I hadn't prophesied a pope from Latin America, I just felt it would be good to think seriously, to decide for a choice of that nature. And so I directed my thoughts, I oriented my conversations in this direction."

He confirmed that Cardinal Murphy-O'Connor, a friend of his, was one of those who was very sensitive to this same idea but added, "I can assure you my vision was not '*ad excludendum*' but '*ad promovendum*.' To promote (the candidacy of) one does not necessarily mean to exclude the other. That seemed to me to be right."

He recalled that in the pre-conclave period, apart from the General Congregations "which are of a more institutional type, we had other meetings too between cardinals who knew each other and with whom we could express our own thoughts freely and so on." He confirmed what I already knew, that Cardinal Murphy-O'Connor hosted one such meeting at the Venerable English College, Via Monserato 45, near Piazza Farnese and Campo di Fiori. He recalled, "We were less than ten that evening. It's not appropriate to give the names. It's not necessary to give the names because otherwise one would have to give all the names of those who participated. But, later on, this like-minded group expanded further and we were maybe fifteen to twenty persons, I can't remember exactly, but there still wasn't a precise candidate. There were candidates from Latin America who one thought could be suitable ones. That's what I remember of that time. There weren't many meetings, perhaps two or three."

Cardinal Coccopalmerio treasured memories of that pre-conclave period, including "the good friendship, good understanding between persons who wanted the good of the Church." He confirmed that the name of Bergoglio as a candidate to be pope "was not there at the beginning but matured as the days went on. It was not something that we had thought about two years ago!"

HAVING REVIEWED THE PRESS that Saturday morning, I took a taxi to San Isidoro, the house of the Irish Franciscans, just off Via Veneto, which the famous Fr. Luke Wadding, an Irish-born Franciscan and historian, had set up as a house of studies and recollection in the 1600s.

South Africa's Cardinal Wilfrid Napier Fox was staying there in the pre-conclave period, and I had arranged to meet him. A member of the Franciscan Order of Friars Minor and a graduate of Galway University in Ireland, he was ordained to the priesthood in 1970 and consecrated bishop ten years later. This dynamic, outspoken cardinal, who would celebrate his seventy-second birthday on March 8, has been archbishop of Durban since 1992 and participated in the 2005 conclave. He is one of the eleven African electors in this conclave. I have been to South Africa several times and have known him for many years. We talked off the record first, and then I conducted an interview with him, which *La Stampa* later published.[19]

Cardinal Napier feels that Benedict's resignation has changed the nature of the papacy because "the next pope knows the precedent has been set. While the possibility was always there in the Code of Canon Law, the fact that Benedict XVI has taken it I think will open up more possibilities for any future pope if he reached a similar stage."

He recalls that John Paul II, especially, but also Benedict XVI had traveled to many countries to strengthen the faith of their brothers and promote the new evangelization. He believes the new pope should follow suit, but "for this kind of task you need a man who has got some energy," and so "I think we need a younger man for pope—possibly in the sixty- to sixty-seven age group." He notes that there are "quite a number" of cardinals in that age bracket "from parts of the world where the faith is vibrant, alive, being challenged and searching for answers, and if one of those were elected he would bring something of that vitality with him."

Although he comes from a country where Nelson Mandela was elected president at the age of seventy-six, Napier said he'll be looking for "a young pope," under the age of seventy.

Above all else, Cardinal Napier says he'll be looking for "one for whom the relationship with Jesus is primary. That's the first quality I am looking for: the man to be the next pope has to be a deeply spiritual person."

He believes a reform of the Roman Curia is badly needed and says, "If the Church is going to be reformed, the people who are running the Church with the pope would have to be reformed internally, from the inside, through a moral reform, a spiritual reform, a whole faith reformation." He emphasizes that this kind of reform requires "simplicity and humility; the simple following of Jesus Christ, the humble admission that we are sinners and that we need Jesus Christ."

He confesses he was "deeply touched" by Benedict's "final advice" to the cardinals on February 28, when he told them, "Be united in harmony like an orchestra; there's diversity among you but there must be harmony." He interpreted his words this way: "Now you are going to elect a new pope; he is going to be your leader, but he has to have around him people from diverse backgrounds who are going to work together with him like musicians in an orchestra. He is calling for like-mindedness, like-action, and like-intention. I would say that's the basis for the reform of the Roman Curia." He believes the new pope "would have to look very closely at the composition of the leadership at the Curia level. He has that option, that freedom, to select the people that he wants to work with." Moreover, he thinks the new pope should find "a new way" of relating to the bishops, besides the five-yearly *ad limina* visits.

He feels the dynamic in this conclave will be different from that of 2005 when only two cardinals—Ratzinger and Baum—had ever been in a papal election before, "whereas it was a totally new experience for the rest of us. We were like absolute novices. That was part of the awe that the conclave held for us. I remember I felt terrified when I went up there, as you have to do to place your ballot paper on the paten, and you stand before the altar and call on the Lord Jesus, who will be my judge, be my witness that I am voting for the one that I consider to be worthy. That was the most solemn, most frightening moment in the whole of the conclave." This time round, forty-eight electors will have participated in a conclave, and he believes this fact will create a very different dynamic.

Napier expects the 2013 conclave to last longer than the 2005 conclave: "I expect the spread is going to be much wider in the opening ballots. There are lots of younger cardinals in their sixties and so on, which I believe will get somebody's notice. I think those first two ballots are probably going to be like a shotgun with a wide spread. Thereafter, I expect people would be re-adjusting and taking a second look at some candidates who got a certain number of votes in those first ballots. Then maybe some consultations will take place in the informal settings in Santa Marta and so on, until we elect the new Pope."

INTERESTINGLY, Cardinal Francis George of Chicago also highlighted the difference between the 2005 and 2013 conclaves. He told John L. Allen, in an interview for the *National Catholic Reporter* published today, that "the central difference is that the names out there, I've found, are all reasonable candidates. Last time there were a lot of names, and it seemed to me [the press] was searching for names. While there was truly more than one candidate going into the conclave, a lot of the names that had been discussed beforehand in the press were not serious candidates, and we all knew that. This time the names that are before us in the public media are, in fact, serious candidates. That's not to say they'll all stay that way, but for right now there are good reasons their names are out there. I mean a reason in terms of the church, and not just somebody wishing for something he or she would like to see happen."

Expounding on the qualities he's looking for in the candidate to be the next pope, Cardinal George said, "He has to have some sense of how to govern, or else he won't choose people who will make the government work." Besides global understanding, a commitment to the new evangelization, and reform of the Roman Curia, the candidate must have "personal stability, the depth of character founded upon his conversations with Jesus. There's got to be an identification with Jesus as shepherd of his church."

The Chicago-born cardinal said the candidate to be pope "has to know Jesus enough to represent him to his people, so it's governance. Hopefully, he'll be a pious man...he better be! Hopefully, he'll be an intelligent man. He should have a good open personality, which is very important. But all that comes together with the question, can he govern in Christ's name?" George said, "He has to have a heart for the poor around the world. Most Catholics live in poorer countries, and their agenda is very different..."

For Cardinal George, age is a "secondary consideration, provided he has enough physical force to do the job well." Nationality too is secondary "but I think most of us, out of courtesy, would see whether the Italians have someone, because the pope is the bishop of Rome. But the question is, is he able to rise above his culture in order to govern the universal church?"

REVIEWING THE ITALIAN PRESS, I noted a curious article in *La Repubblica*, written by Paolo Rodari, one of its Vatican reporters, that spoke of "the hypothesis of an over-eighty pope" on the basis that "to change the Curia, a veteran is needed." He listed five candidates: Ruini and Sodano—both Italians; Saraiva Martins (Portugal); Tomko (Slovakia); and Herranz (Spain). He explained the task for a short-term pope: to clear up the mess in the Curia and to establish a new working relationship between the pope and the world's bishops. He recalled that on the eve of the 2005 conclave Cardinal Camillo Ruini, then powerful president of the Italian bishops' conference, emphasized the need "to integrate better the two powers: the collegial and the primatial," and observed that "with John Paul II, papal primacy has touched its high point but also its end point."

It's not clear how this hypothesis originated, but one thing is certain, it never gained traction.

IN PAST CENTURIES the ruling powers frequently took great interest in papal elections, even to the point of exercising the veto or "the right of exclusion" of a candidate from being elected. This happened for the last time on August 2, 1903,[20] when Poland's Prince Cardinal Jan Puzyna de Kosielsko stunned the cardinals in conclave and caused turmoil by announcing the veto by Franz Josef, emperor of Austria and king of Hungary, against Cardinal Mariano Rampolla del Tindaro, who was then in the leading position to succeed Leo XIII. The veto effectively doomed his candidacy, and the conclave elected Cardinal Giuseppe Melchiore Sarto, who took the name Pius X. Six months later, on January 20, 1904, Pius X promulgated the apostolic constitution *Comissum Nobis* that abolished "the right of exclusion."

John Paul II also sought to inoculate the cardinals against external pressures of any kind, as did Benedict XVI.

Given this history, it came as a surprise to read in *Corriere della Sera* today[21] that a well-known American politician was promoting a candidate to be pope. Mario Cuomo, former governor of New York, father of its present governor and a Catholic, did just that in an interview with the influential Italian daily when he launched the candidacy of Cardinal Timothy Dolan, the jovial, media friendly president of the US bishops' conference. Describing him as "a pastor," "an educated man with a good sense of humor," he touted him as "the right man for this extraordinary moment in history" who could bring about "The Vatican Spring."

He dismissed the possibility of a pope from Asia or Africa because these are regions "where the faithful are a minority." He expressed optimism that with the new pope the Church "can return to the origins of Christianity" and claimed that to make this happen it would be sufficient "to pick up again the threads of the Second Vatican Council, at which John XXIII proposed extraordinary reforms that then fell into the void. We've lost half a century and it would be sufficient to pick up where the good pope left off." What's important at the conclave, he said, "is to exclude whoever pushes to maintain the status quo."

Cardinals who learned of Cuomo's intervention did not like it one bit. While it is one thing for a cardinal to promote the candidacy of a fellow cardinal to be pope, it is quite another for a politician to do so. It was rumored at that time that Philadelphia's cardinal-archbishop, Justin Rigali, who once worked in the Vatican's Secretariat of State and was on the powerful Congregation for Bishops and very good friends with Cardinal Re, was pushing the New York cardinal's candidacy. It was one of the many difficult-to-verify rumors that mushroomed in Rome during these days.

AVVENIRE, the daily paper of the Italian bishops' conference, today carried an interview with Cardinal Re, 79, who, as the senior cardinal-bishop, will preside over the conclave, since the dean of the College of Cardinals, Angelo Sodano, is over eighty. Re described Benedict XVI as "the pope of a faith that is the friend of reason," whose pontificate "will go down in history" and whose resignation is "a gesture to be admired because of the high sense of responsibility at a time when the attachment to power dominates." He declared that he will enter the Sistine Chapel "with a great sense of responsibility, to help to choose the pope that the Church and the world need at this moment of history."

The same Catholic daily reported that the cardinal vicar of the diocese of Rome, Agostino Vallini, has sent a letter to the faithful and church communities in the city asking them "to pray especially to the Lord, so that the Holy Spirit may enlighten the cardinal electors to whom has been entrusted such an important task." He instructed the priests of the diocese to include a prayer for the election of the pope at all Masses and he granted them the faculty to celebrate a special Mass each day for this same purpose. He appealed especially to the cloistered women and men religious to pray for this intention too. I noted that bishops across the globe are asking their priests and people to do likewise.

Interestingly, *Avvenire* announced the publication of an instant book on the resignation of Benedict: *Il gran rifiuto: Perche' un papa si dimette*.[22] Written by Roberto Rusconi, an Italian church historian who teaches at Roma Tre, a state university, it recalled that while the resignations by earlier popes (Pontiano in 235, Celestine V in 1294, and those in the 1300s and 1400s during the schism and conciliar crisis of the Church in the West) were formally free, they were in fact to a large extent forced by events, often ones external to the Church. On the other hand, Benedict resigned freely and will still be alive when the new pope is elected. His resignation was very different from theirs.

Rusconi stated that there is only one precedent in the history of the Church for the co-existence of two legitimately elected popes: that of Boniface VIII who in 1294 was elected pope eleven days after Celestine V voluntarily resigned, having been pope for a mere five months. But he recalled that Boniface feared that Celestine's supporters could give rise to a schism, and so put him in prison and kept him there until he died some two and a half years later.

ON A LIGHTER NOTE, *Corriere della Sera*, as well as other papers, reported the eating habits of several cardinals. It revealed that many go for lunch or dinner at Al Passetto del Borgo, a restaurant in the Borgo Pio 60 near the Vatican, which offers a menu of Roman and Abruzzo cooking. Open since 1962 and owned by Roberto Fulvimari and his son Antonello, it was a favorite haunt of Cardinal Ratzinger before he became pope. Cardinal Wuerl comes here too and likes a double first course of pasta—lasagna and rigatoni *alla norcina*. Other habitués include Cardinals Coccopalmerio and O'Malley. I should add that it is also a place frequented by journalists.

The Italian press mentioned another restaurant on the same street called "La Venerina," which specializes in fish dishes. Clerics frequent this restaurant. Cardinal Ratzinger used to eat here, as do Cardinals Jean Louis Tauran[23] (who will announce to the world the name of the new pope) and Marc Ouellet, both of whom like fresh fish.

AS MENTIONED EARLIER, for almost a century the Italian press has led the conversation on the election of the pope, but publishing in those decades is nothing compared to what is possible today in the age of Twitter, Facebook, and Instagram, not to mention blogs and myriad websites.

Italy's main news outlets are gearing up in a big way for the conclave, especially in the social media field. *Corriere della Sera*, for example, has established a multi-author blog that includes its Vatican correspondent, Gian Guido Vecchi, together with NCR's John Allen, who gives the view from across the Atlantic, Jean-Marie Guenois from *Le Figaro*, providing a French perspective, and Paul Badde of *Die Welt*, who shares insights from the German-speaking world. The team was further boosted by Massimo Franco, one of the paper's opinion columnists, and Alberto Melloni, a recognized church historian, expert on the Second Vatican Council, and director of the prestigious religious studies center, Fondazione per le Scienze Religiose Giovanni XXIII, based in Bologna.

La Stampa too is moving fast. Around midday, Paolo Mastrolilli, its special coordinator for reporting on the conclave, called all of its Vatican Insider reporters, including me, to come to the newspaper's Rome office this afternoon for a "Scribble-in" training session to enhance the speedy flow of information to its special news outlet for the papal election. *La Stampa* has set up a special channel to cover the conclave that includes an app (for Apple and Android appliances) and a "liveblog" by Vatican Insider reporters, supported up by the newspaper's other reporters.

The Vatican Insider website, for which I have worked since its founding, has a wide international following, which includes cardinals, Vatican officials, and bishops. Boston's Cardinal O'Malley confesses he is one of them. He says he knows "many but not all" of the cardinals and, in preparation for the conclave, visits this and other websites to gather information on his fellow electors. "I read articles to familiarize myself with the themes faced in other conclaves. I read *Le Monde* and *La Stampa* on Kindle," he adds.

At the end of our training session at *La Stampa*'s office, Andrea Tornielli and I had a long chat and in the course of our conversation we discovered that each of us had heard, from different sources, about the "Scherer ticket" plot, as we called it. This was a plan by the Secretariat of State's old guard to promote the candidacy of a Latin American cardinal as pope and so give a "New World face" to the papacy and the hope for change in the Church while, at the same time, accompanying the new pontiff with a secretary of state who would ensure that things did not really change. The Italians call this a "*gattopardesco*" move, meaning "everything needs to change, so everything can stay the same," as Giuseppe de Lampedusa wrote in *Il Gattopardo* (*The Leopard*), one of the most important novels in modern Italian literature.

Andrea and I were both so certain of our information that we took the unprecedented decision to jointly write an article and publish it that same evening on the Vatican Insider website, under our two names.

In the article that appeared first in Italian and later in English under the title "A Ticket to Vote for the First Latin American Pope," we wrote:

> In 2005, some influential cardinals from the Roman Curia worked for the election of Joseph Ratzinger. Today, eight years later, informed sources both within and outside the Vatican confirm that a new group in the Vatican are seeking to bring for the first time in history a Latin American to the See of Peter, accompanied by a Secretary of State who is Italian, or an Argentinian of Italian origins. Among the proponents of this initiative are two leading cardinals: Angelo Sodano, the Secretary of State, and Giovanni Battista Re. Other important Italian curial cardinals could join this initiative.
>
> The candidate to be pope of this group is the archbishop of São Paulo, Brazil, Odilo Pedro Scherer, 63, who worked in the Vatican's Congregation for Bishops from 1994 to 2001. He worked for some time with Cardinal Re, who became head of that Congregation, and later ensured that he became a bishop. Scherer is a well-respected Latin American prelate, of German extraction. A man of measured and less Latin style, he speaks Italian well.
>
> His name has circulated in these days as a possible successor to Benedict XVI. His sponsors aim to bring the first South American to the See of Peter but bringing at the same time with

him—almost as part of a "ticket" a Secretary of State who knows the Roman Curia well. Among the names being mentioned for this second post is that of Cardinal Mauro Piacenza, the Prefect of the Congregation for Clergy. Another name being suggested for the post of Secretary of State is that of Cardinal Leonardo Sandri, the Prefect of the Congregation for the Oriental Churches. Sandri had the post of "Substitute"—that is the third ranking position in the Vatican, in the last phase of the pontificate of John Paul II and the beginning of Benedict XVI's reign.

The idea of a ticket of a Pope with a Secretary of State is not new. It's known that something similar happened in the 1958 conclave when some cardinals of the Roman Curia got assurances that if the Patriarch of Venice, Angelo Roncalli, would be elected that he would not appoint the Archbishop of Milan, Giovanni Battista Montini, as Secretary of State, but would instead choose Monsignor Domenico Tardini for that post. This is in fact what happened on the same evening that John XXIII was elected. Could history repeat itself in the coming days?

Our breaking-news story was quickly picked up and recycled in a variety of news outlets worldwide, and on Twitter and Facebook. No one denied it. Several cardinals told me they read it. Cardinal Seán Patrick O'Malley found it "very interesting." Another elector, who didn't want to be named, said he was "shocked."

The ever-alert John Allen, working also for CNN, spotted it and wrote about it in the *National Catholic Reporter* (March 3) noting that "this news story yesterday got tongues wagging in Rome." His comment: "Although the air is always full of speculation in the run-up to a conclave, the byline on this particular report gives it gravitas: Andrea Tornielli, widely seen as the best-connected of the Italian Vatican writers, and Gerard O'Connell, a respected Vatican-watcher not normally given to spitting in the wind."

HAVING FINALIZED THE TEXT of the "Scherer ticket" article with Andrea, I took a taxi from *La Stampa*'s office to the Universal Bar in Via della Conciliazione where I had arranged to meet the Indian cardinal, Oswald Gracias, 69, archbishop of Mumbai and president of the Federation of Asian Bishops' Conferences (FABC), who had just arrived in town. I have known him for many years and wanted to interview him.

He is one of the five Indian electors at the conclave. Three are from the Latin Rite: Gracias, Ivan Dias, and Telesphore Toppo; the other two are from the Oriental Rites: George Alencherry of the Syro-Malabar church and Baselios Cleemis Thottunkal of the Syro-Malankar church, who is the youngest elector. It is the first time that any country in Asia has had so many cardinal electors in a conclave. The five Indians count for half of all the Asian electors.

Sitting at a table near the window looking out on the Via della Conciliazione, we ordered tea and biscuits. Gracias had just arrived in Rome and was keen to hear about Benedict's resignation and what had happened since. I told him about the "Scherer ticket" article. We talked for most of an hour. He granted me the interview that was subsequently published in Vatican Insider. We agreed to meet again after the conclave.

Gracias felt a special bond with Benedict XVI, who had made him a cardinal in 2007, and confided that he felt "very sad, very surprised and shocked" by his resignation, but said, on reflection, "I see that this is an act of humility, an act of love for the Church, a courageous act." He believed his "courageous step" would "have an impact on the future of the papacy" because now "it's easier for other people to resign."

Looking ahead to the conclave, Cardinal Gracias said, "we would need somebody" as pope "who likes administration, who likes organization, who likes leadership in that sense." Age is a factor, "but not *the* factor." Nationality, he also said, "is not a factor": "The Church needs the best person, the one whom really God wants to be the authentic face of Jesus Christ, to make the Church more, and more what Our Lord wants it to be."

The archbishop of Mumbai had clear ideas about the qualities he's looking for in the candidate to be pope: "I would like a man who is very holy, really a spiritual leader of the Church and of the world. That is very important. I would like to see a man who is also intelligent, has a world vision, and is able to grasp problems; a man who is able to see the needs of the world, and is able respond to them. I would like to see a man who is compassionate, who has got a heart for people in difficulties, with problems, understands them and wants to reach out to them. I would also want a man with courage, who has the wisdom and courage to go ahead in spite of what people say, to give the right leadership that we need."

Living in Asia, a continent where 60 percent of the world's population lives but where Christians are a tiny minority of 3 percent, with Catholics counting for a mere 2 percent, Cardinal Gracias said, "Since we are such a small minority, I would like the new pope to give effective leadership, moral leadership. I would like that he strengthen the Church from within and without...so that the non-Christian world is able to really see in the Church authentic Gospel values, able to see something special in the Church. Because, besides being effective the Church must also have a high level of authenticity, a good image, the image of Jesus Christ. That's so important. This is what we need in Asia. I am sure the Holy Spirit will guide us to choose the man that we need for this moment in history."

Given that in Asia the other major religions are strongly present— Islam, Buddhism, Hinduism, Sikhism, and Traditional Religions—Cardinal Gracias believes it is important that the next pope be "a person who is sensitive to other religions, sensitive to all the people who are searching for truth, searching for God, searching for meaning in life," and is someone for whom "dialogue is important, openness is important." He believes that "a pope who could give spiritual leadership to the Church, and through the Church to the world, would make a very big difference to the whole world, and especially to us in Asia."

As for the reform of the Roman Curia, he believes "a continuous renewal is needed, a spiritual renewal."

He considers it "important, though not essential" that the new pope could travel "so that he meets people in the world and that people in the world meet him. This direct personal contact makes a big impression in today's world." It would be an asset too if he could speak several languages but, he added with a laugh, "you can't get a perfect combination!"

He confirmed he did not have a candidate in mind "because this has taken us all so much by surprise. I am looking and praying, and trying to match the qualities, reflecting on the needs of the Church and the qualities the man should have. I am gathering information, and then praying and reflecting and talking." He didn't rule out an Asian pope, nor did he anticipate "a very long conclave."

THAT SAME EVENING (March 2), Cardinal Ouellet, who had received no less than 120 requests from around the world for an interview after Benedict announced his resignation, accepted the invitation to be interviewed in English by the Canadian Broadcasting Corporation (CBC), Canada's national public television and radio broadcaster.

His fellow Canadian, Fr. Thomas Rosica, chief-executive of Salt and Light Television, the Catholic channel in Canada, who has collaborated with CBC ever since John Paul II went to Canada for World Youth Day in 2002,[24] "arranged and mediated" this exclusive interview,[25] "the only one of its kind" with "the cardinal who is thought to be a strong candidate for the Papacy."

This world exclusive was a very big scoop for CBC. Given the possibility that Ouellet could be elected pope, interest was mounting in Canada and wider afield. Peter Mansbridge, the English-born anchor of CBC's flagship nightly television news and a friend of Rosica, flew from Ottawa to Rome to interview the cardinal at his residence near the Vatican. It was an unusually long (more than one hour) interview and was broadcast in two parts, at prime time on CBC News on March 4 and 5, the first two days of the pre-conclave plenary assembly of cardinals known as General Congregations.

At one stage in the interview,[26] when Cardinal Ouellet said, "[my] faith is defining who I am" and "my identity is to be missionary from the beginning," Peter Mansbridge spotted his opportunity to raise the big question. He began by drawing attention to the fact that the cardinal is being mentioned by all the media as a man who could become the next pope, and then remarked, "Most of us who would see our names included on a list like that would obviously think about it, about that possibility, and quite likely most of us would probably say, I want that. I would like that to happen. Would you like that to happen?"

The grey-haired, bespectacled cardinal seemed taken aback by the question. He smiled, breathed deeply, laughed, hesitated a little, and then said: "So,...I...I...I have to be ready even if I think that probably others could do it better. But we enter there [the conclave] and since with everything that is going on we have to some extent to be prepared. And then you know there is this saying, the one that gets in as pope gets out as cardinal. (Laughs). It's a famous saying here in Rome, we know it. So that's why I think my name is circulating, but I am very careful to go beyond this sort of media expectation which is different."

The last time a leading papal contender gave an interview on the eve of the conclave was in October 1978, when the Italian cardinal Giuseppe Siri did so. He was then widely considered the front-runner to succeed John Paul I; the Italian press were confidently claiming that he had fifty votes before the conclave started. He agreed to give an interview on Friday, October 13, to *Gazetta del Popolo*, one of the two most influential papers in northern Italy. He spoke freely and expressed his very conservative views. He claimed it would take fifty or more years for the Catholic Church to recover from the pontificate of John XXIII and he indicated his intention to roll back many of the new initiatives that had flowed from the Second Vatican Council.

Cardinal Siri allowed the reporter to record the entire interview, but he is reported to have verbally abused him, something that did not play well with the paper's editors. They had agreed in advance that the interview would be published on Sunday, October 15, when the cardinals were already in conclave, but for some unexplained reason the paper ran it in its Saturday morning edition, October 14, just before the cardinals went into the conclave. It quickly made waves. Several cardinals were seen with copies of the paper in their hands before entering the conclave. Cardinal Siri had shot himself in the foot. As expected, he topped the list on the first ballot but only got twenty-three votes, not the fifty predicted by the Italian press. But that was only the beginning of his decline. He fell back to fourth place on the second ballot with eleven votes and scored only five on the third ballot and so was then no longer in the running. This led to a seismic shift within the conclave and, on the eighth ballot, the election of John Paul II—the first non-Italian pope in 455 years.[27]

Did Ouellet damage his chance of becoming pope by giving the interview? It's difficult to say. All I know is that several cardinals told me they considered that he had shown a lack of judgment and prudence by doing so on the eve of the conclave.

MARCH 3 (SUNDAY)_____

Searching for "God's Candidate"

THE LARGER-THAN-LIFE Cardinal Dolan is a newsmaker. He was so in the run-up to the conclave too. He hit the headlines this morning when he celebrated Mass in the Chapel of Our Lady Queen of the Hungarians, in the grottoes of Saint Peter's Basilica, for an invited congregation of about twenty people that included the New York media, among whom was Anne Thompson of NBC news, who read one of the scripture readings. The US Catholic intellectual and biographer of John Paul II, George Weigel, was among the guests.

Reporting on what happened this morning, the *New York Times*[28] said Dolan made clear he wanted to get on with the conclave and return home, and he joked that the chapel where they were at Mass was "just a 9-iron shot from the tomb of Saint Peter."

Referring to the next pope, he explained in his homily that the task of the new pope is not to make changes in the Church but to preserve the Church's traditions. "That's the very nature of the papacy; it is to hand on faithfully what God told us of Jesus, what Jesus told his apostles, and what his apostles hand on to us—tradition, with a capital T." Looking at the media operators present he remarked, "Many of you professional, excellent journalists ask, very often, 'Do you think the new pope will make changes in the church?'" He responded by telling them: "The Church is in the business of change, big time: change of human heart. Jesus through his Church calls us, first-and-foremost, not to change structures, not to change all this stuff out there—we'll get to that if, first of all, we let God change us inside."

AT TEN O'CLOCK this Sunday morning I went to the NH Hotel Giustiniano, on the Via Virgilio not far from the Japanese Embassy to the Holy See and about fifteen minutes' walk from the Vatican. The twenty-four-member CTV crew are staying at this four-star hotel for the conclave's duration. I was asked to participate in the morning's editorial board meeting in preparation for the big day.

We reviewed, among other things, the list of *papabili*, starting of course with Marc Ouellet, who is big news in Canada, and on whom the CTV staff in Toronto were preparing substantial background and news reports. They did not yet know of the CBC interview. As we reviewed the list of *papabili*, I strongly advised them to make sure they have a substantial dossier on Cardinal Bergoglio.

ASKED AT A PRESS BRIEFING at the North American College how a cardinal elector prepares for the conclave, Cardinal George told reporters, "I think all of us have been giving a great deal of thought to this for some time, and even before [Benedict XVI's resignation] we saw people and knew they could be suited to the job. So, I imagine each of us has a list of favorite candidates, as well as a list of other second or third favorites and so on..." He said these names are repeated in the personal and private conversations that go on between cardinals ahead of the big election day. "What do you know about this candidate?—cardinals ask. How do you think he would react in such a situation? What kind of a person is he?

How would he react if...? and so on, and all this information is included in their prayers." The archbishop of Chicago explained that in this way "cardinals test the waters and look around them and it is only normal that the same front-runners start coming up again, and again."

For his part, Boston's Capuchin cardinal Seán Patrick O'Malley said he reads articles and visits websites to gather information and, commenting on the fact that there are some "obvious candidates," he added that it is "a comforting thought" that there is clearly a choice of figures who could make "competent popes." But, he remarked, "I don't think any of us has arrived here saying 'this is who I am voting for.' We are still in the phase of gathering information, praying, getting to know one another; there are definitely some excellent candidates and we all recognize their talents."

THAT AFTERNOON, Cardinal Telesphore Toppo, the world's first tribal cardinal and friend of Saint Mother Teresa of Calcutta, phoned. He had arrived in Rome from India earlier in the day and invited me to come for tea at the convent on the Via della Pisana where he usually stays during his visits to the Vatican.

We have known each other for many years, from the time I was Vatican correspondent for UCAN (the Union of Catholic Asian News), the main Catholic news agency in Asia. As archbishop of Ranchi, the capital of Jharkand State in northeastern India, he has shown great faith and courage in these years, standing up to the state's Hindu fundamentalists who burned his effigy every day for a whole month during the pontificate of Benedict XVI. I was happy to meet him again.

On the record, he told me that, like all the foreign cardinals, he was trying to figure out the true reason for Benedict's resignation. Then, in a comment that I would hear later from other cardinals, Toppo lamented, "We cardinals left Benedict alone during his papacy, and that must not happen again!" He had no idea who the next pope might be; he had no candidate in mind; he was trying to work out who the real *papabile* might be.

A humble, deeply spiritual and astute man, Toppo is serving his second term as president of the Catholic bishops' conference of India, the umbrella conference that includes both the Latin and the two Eastern-rite churches that together have around two hundred bishops and roughly twenty million Catholics. When I noted that this is the first time ever that an Asian church has had so many electors in a conclave, he commented, "This is true, but it is not too much because India has the fourth largest conference of Catholic bishops in the world, after Brazil, the USA, and Italy."

Since news media in Asia, Europe, and the United States have listed the Filipino cardinal Luis Antonio Tagle as *papabile*, I asked Toppo what he thought about the possibility of an Asian pope. "The possibility is definitely there, but how long it will take to make it a reality we do not know," he responded. He then went on to expound his own thesis about the election of a pope: "It is not simply a question of any personal quality of an individual cardinal or anything like that which makes the pope, at least so far. It is the Church that produces the pope."

He elaborated on his personal thesis: "I think it is the local church with a strong Catholic faith that could produce the next pope. We saw that it was the Polish church with its strong Catholic faith that produced John Paul II. His successor too came from a church with a strong Catholic faith because, in spite of Lutheranism and the Protestant Reformation in Germany, the church in Bavaria remained strongly Catholic. So, to my way of thinking, it is that kind of church which produces the pope. The pope should somehow represent the whole Church and he should have his roots in a truly unified local church."

In that sense, he remarked, "The Filipino church is united with a strong Catholic faith and tradition and so it could produce a pope. Certainly, Tagle, the archbishop of Manila, is well qualified to be pope. When I met him at the consistory last November (at which Benedict gave him the red hat) I told him, 'You were the last on the Pope's list, but you are by no means the least! You are Number 1 in Asia!'"

Cardinal Toppo had participated as an elector in the 2005 conclave, and he referred to that experience when answering my next question about what he was looking for in the candidate to be pope. "It is not simply a question of looking," he responded. "For instance, in the 2005 conclave it was clear to me who was the candidate. For those who wanted to see they could already see at the very beginning the way things were moving. They could see Ratzinger was the man. He was dean of the College of Cardinals and then he was moderator of the meetings of cardinals before the conclave. Moreover, he was the main celebrant at the funeral of John Paul II, and prior to that he had written the meditations for the Way of the Cross. Everything somehow seemed to indicate that he was the man. It was just like that."

He disclosed that he is not going into the upcoming conclave with an identikit of the next pope. "No. I think we must listen to what the Spirit is telling the Church. That is my attitude. Of course, 'whisperings' go on. Cardinals speak to one another. Those who are here in Rome do so. I try to listen to the Holy Spirit more than to people, but among the 'whisperings' of course the Holy Spirit is also whispering."

I found his thesis particularly interesting in the light of what was to come.

MARCH 4 (MONDAY)
DAY 1 OF THE GENERAL CONGREGATIONS ⸻
Cardinals Speak from the Heart

THE GENERAL CONGREGATIONS began this morning in the Vatican's new synod hall. The dean of the College of Cardinals, Angelo Sodano, presided over the first session, as he will over all the other ones. He was flanked by the camerlengo (chamberlain), Tarcisio Bertone, and the secretary of the College of Cardinals, Archbishop Lorenzo Baldisseri, a composer of music. All three are Italian.

Since many cardinals do not speak Italian or fully understand it, the Vatican has provided a translation service in Italian, Spanish, English, French, and German, staffed by members of the Secretariat of State.

According to the norms established by John Paul II in *Universi Domenici Gregis*, every three days during the General Congregations, the College of Cardinals must choose by lot three of its members, one from each of the three orders into which the college is divided: bishops (this order has 10 members, but only 4 are electors); priests (this order has 154 members, of whom 83 are electors); and deacons (this order has 45 members including 30 electors). Their task is to assist the camerlengo during the congregations.

The College of Cardinals has a total of 209 members. Today, 142 were present for the first session, including 102 electors, Fr. Lombardi reported at the daily press briefing.

He explained that on arrival in the synod hall, the cardinals took their seats in order of precedence according to the three orders to which they belong. They began with morning prayer and the singing in Latin of the *Veni Creator*—the hymn to the Holy Spirit asking for enlightenment.

Cardinal Sodano greeted all present and underlined the great importance of this event for the Church and the world. He explained how these assemblies will be conducted and then, in accordance with number

12 of the apostolic constitution *Universi Dominici Gregis*, he read in Latin, in an audible voice, the following oath in which they swore, as a body and individually, "to observe exactly and faithfully" all the norms of that apostolic constitution and "to maintain rigorous secrecy" regarding all matters relating to the election of the pope, or those which "by their very nature" during the *sede vacante* call for such secrecy. Once the dean had read the formula, each of the cardinals, in order of precedence, came forward to take an abbreviated form of that same oath.

Fr. Lombardi had to take the oath too. He said the whole process took up most of the morning, after which the cardinals drew lots to choose the three assistants to the camerlengo, as required by the constitution. Those selected were: Cardinals Giovanni Battista Re and Crescenzio Sepe (Italy), and Franc Rodé (Slovenia). Once chosen, they took their seats beside the camerlengo at the head table facing the assembly of cardinals; they will assist him in dealing with minor matters relating to these sessions.

Cardinal Sodano next proposed that the General Congregation send a message of greeting and gratitude to Benedict XVI for his "luminous Petrine ministry" and his "tireless work in the vineyard of the Lord." This was approved unanimously.[29]

THE CARDINALS TOOK a half-hour coffee break during this morning's session. These breaks are precious because they give the cardinals the opportunity to renew old acquaintances, or to get to know another cardinal for the first time, or to exchange information or plan informal meetings outside the institutional setting.

After the mid-morning break, several cardinals spoke. Lombardi reported that some talked about the process, others identified questions to be addressed, taking account of the conclusions of the last synod. While his report was rather generic, the following day's Italian newspapers provided more substantial information thanks to one or more "deep throat(s)" at today's congregations, who found ways of getting around the oath of secrecy that he (or they) had taken.

Fr. Lombardi also reported that five more cardinals had arrived in Rome and participated in the afternoon session after taking the oath of secrecy.[30]

Then, in accordance with the constitution for the papal election,[31] the cardinals listened to the first of two meditations "on the problems facing the church at this time and on the need for careful discernment in choosing the new pope." The constitution has decreed that two churchmen "known for their sound doctrine, wisdom and moral authority" are to be chosen to present these meditations. The two chosen were Fr. Raniero Cantalamessa, OFMCap, and Cardinal Prosper Grech.

Fr. Raniero Cantalamessa, 78, the well-known, bearded, charismatic Franciscan preacher from the Pontifical Household, delivered the first meditation, just as he had done at the beginning of the General Congregations for the 2005 conclave. While the Vatican has not yet disclosed what he said, I learned that, among other things, he raised two important issues that he believed the cardinals should address in these meetings: the question of communion for the divorced and remarried, and the question of the ordination of mature married men to the priesthood.

Cardinals told me the second proposal provoked several reactions in the plenary session that followed. Cardinals Adrianus Johannes Simonis of the Netherlands and Murphy-O'Connor from the UK were among those who spoke in favor of the ordination of mature married men; Cardinal Re was one of those who spoke against.

A total of nine cardinals spoke this afternoon, but we had to wait for the next day's Italian dailies to find out what they said.

THE EMERITUS POPE BENEDICT XVI is now resting at the papal residence in Castel Gandolfo and is praying and following with great interest, by television and the press, all that is happening in Rome, Fr. Lombardi told reporters.[32]

IN AN EFFORT AT TRANSPARENCY, the United States cardinals decided to give daily briefings to the press, the only group of cardinals from any country to do so. Organized by Sr. Mary Ann Walsh, longtime spokesperson for the US bishops' conference, the plan was to have a daily briefing at the North American College each afternoon, starting today with Cardinals Francis George and Donald Wuerl. Reporters from all over the world, hungry for information, flocked to this event.

The cardinals have taken an oath of secrecy, but Cardinal George explained to the more than one hundred journalists present—including TV units from the United States, Canada, Mexico, Brazil, Italy, and several other countries that he and his fellow US cardinals intended to keep lines of communication open with the media and the public even if they might not be able to say that much. He reported that Cardinal Sodano had explained the tightrope act of observing the oath of secrecy over conclave matters and being free to talk to the press. "It seems they've decided perhaps that it's better to talk to the press rather than not talk to the press," George remarked. Then with a conspiratorial smile he added, "They said nothing about a problem in making yourself available, but they did point out that we all just took an oath of confidentiality. So, the problem is content."

He recalled that at today's plenary session, "Someone quoted Saint Thomas of Aquinas, who said you should be slow in deliberation and quick in decision-making. So, decision-making is the conclave, and deliberation is the General Congregations. I think that caught the sense of everyone there, that we need to take the time necessary."

The eighth archbishop of Chicago, who served as president of the US bishops' conference from 2007 to 2010, explained that the rules of confidentiality are designed to keep the cardinals free from "outside pressures and hopefully free from internal pressures, too, because of the profound spiritual mission that brings us there." He asserted that "the conclaves are held in the way they are to ensure that the cardinals are free —free to stand before God—and take that oath that we vote for the one best suited for the office of the papacy."

He claimed to detect a different tone at the General Congregation today compared to those of 2005; he attributed this to a different style of leadership by the dean. Cardinal Sodano acts "more as a canonist," he remarked; his style is "a bit more direct perhaps, but he's very clear in giving instructions, and very clear in presenting the issues." He recalled that in 2005, Cardinal Ratzinger, who was the dean then, "was a genius, not only in his own thinking but in encapsulating the thinking of others so there was a synthesis at the end of the day." He recalled too that Ratzinger instructed the cardinals not to speak to the media, and some, like George, heeded that, but others did not.

Cardinals George and Wuerl responded to questions about some of the leading candidates for the papacy, the date of the conclave, sexual abuse by clergy, and coffee breaks. They asserted that the new pope must uphold the Church's zero tolerance policy for clergy who abuse children. "I think that will be an important issue in the minds and hearts of the cardinals," George stated. "It's certainly in the minds and hearts of many of us because we now have victims of sexual abuse. They're not just victims of sexual abuse by teachers, or politicians, or even fathers or uncles. They've been abused by a Catholic priest and sometimes by a Catholic bishop. And sometimes the abuse was not addressed as it should have been by Catholic bishops. That is a terrible wound on the body of the Church, and it has to be looked at."

Asked about the admission of improper sexual conduct by Scotland's Cardinal Keith O'Brien, the Chicago cardinal remarked, "It's a tragedy for him. But the tragic moment was when he was guilty of misconduct, and then the consequences play themselves out now."

The two American cardinals confirmed that Vatileaks would be a topic on the agenda and that questions would be asked of the three cardinals who carried out the investigation at Benedict XVI's request. They did not reveal much more, but the Italian press compensated for that on the following day.

FROM THE PUBLIC COMMENTS of many cardinals and my conversations with others it is obvious that the reform of the Roman Curia will be a major topic in the General Congregations. Cardinals want to raise questions about structure, the need to rationalize and reduce the number of offices, personnel, and the insistence that people are employed to serve the pope and the Church, not to fashion a career. They are also likely to insist on the need for greater coordination and communication between the different offices of the Curia, and the need to clean up and radically reorganize Vatican finances, including the Institute for the Works of Religion, mistakenly called the "Vatican Bank," which has been plagued by scandals for more than a quarter of a century under John Paul II and Benedict XVI.

The demand for reform of the Roman Curia was strongly felt among foreign cardinals who think the problems of recent years, as revealed by Vatileaks, are the result of Italian mismanagement. In *La Stampa* today, Andrea Tornielli quoted an unnamed foreign cardinal as saying, "I am convinced that what happened in these last years will weigh heavily on the choices of the conclave." He recalled that on March 1, Cardinal Carlo Caffarra[33] of Bologna had spoken about "the clash of light and darkness in the Church and in the world in these times" and said, "Benedict had called the darkness by its names: in the Church, the immorality and ambition of clerics, and in the world, the rejection of God."

Gian Maria Vian, a professor of patristic philology who has been editor in chief of *L'Osservatore Romano*, the Vatican daily, since 2007, told *National Catholic Reporter* that "the government of the Church" would be the key to the conclave.

Alberto Melloni, a distinguished Italian church historian and recognized scholar on the Second Vatican Council, told *La Stampa* he believed "greater collegiality is desirable" and envisaged that, in the future, the pope could be assisted by "a senate of communion" or "a council of state."

Several cardinals with whom I have spoken emphasized that the Church needs a pope who can present the Gospel in a way that is attractive to people in the modern world.

TO ELECT A POPE who will be able to respond to these demands is the challenge facing the 115 electors in the conclave. It is worth mentioning that 48 of these electors participated in the 2005 conclave and understand how a conclave works; the other 67—all created cardinals by Benedict XVI—enter as novices.

MY VATICAN INSIDER COLLEAGUE, Andres Beltramo Alvarez, published an interview in *La Stampa* today with the president of the Brazilian bishops' conference, Cardinal Raymundo Damasceno Assis, 76, archbishop of Aparecida, who said the cardinals want to know "the contents" of the report of the three cardinals tasked by Benedict to investigate Vatileaks, so as to understand the challenges facing the new pope. The Brazilian, who is participating in a conclave for the first time, said they will have to choose "someone who is up to the task," but with "pastoral experience." Moreover, he should "know the Curia from the inside and its structure." Asked if the new pope should be a young man, he replied, "We must look at the person: certainly, it wouldn't be good to elect a pope of advanced age." Nevertheless, he noted, "there are some cardinals who do not yet feel the weight of age and have a vigorous physical disposition," but "obviously, we can't elect an eighty-year-old who feels the weight of old age and has delicate health, because then we run the risk of convening a new conclave within a short time."

THE SPANISH DAILY, *El País*, in an article today by Pablo Ordaz and Juan Arias, highlighted the fact that Brazil is not only an emerging economic and political world power, it is also a heavyweight in the Catholic world because it has the largest Catholic population and five cardinal electors in the conclave, and is already making its presence felt in the General Congregations. It too reported that Cardinal Damasceno affirmed that "all the cardinals" desire to have information about the Vatileaks investigation before electing the successor to Benedict XVI. *El País* reported that another Brazilian cardinal, Geraldo Majella Agnelo, who participated in the 2005 conclave and is well versed in Vatican politics, having worked in the Roman Curia, said he agreed with Damasceno and asked, "Why have they not given us anything from this secret report? I want to know its contents... All the cardinals wish to know."

THERE WAS PALPABLE DISCONTENT at the end of the day when Cardinal Sodano announced that a prayer service would be held in Saint Peter's Basilica next Wednesday evening. Several electors read this as an attempt to reduce the free time they have at their disposal for private discussions.

MARCH 5 (TUESDAY)
DAY 2 OF THE GENERAL CONGREGATIONS ⎯⎯⎯⎯⎯⎯⎯⎯⎯⎯
Leaks to the Press

AS THE CARDINALS ENTERED the synod hall this morning for the third of the General Congregations they learned—to their great surprise and some to their dismay—that much of what had been said in the previous day's meetings had been published in the Italian press. While everyone at the congregation is sworn to secrecy, it was clear that some person or persons had leaked significant information to Andrea Tornielli and, to a lesser extent, to a few other Italian reporters.

"The Vatileaks case explodes: the cardinals want to know more," Tornielli reported in *La Stampa*. He said three leading European cardinals asked to know the secret information about Vatileaks: Walter Kasper, a leading German theologian and former president of the Pontifical Council for the Promotion of Christian Unity, who had just managed to get into the conclave because his eightieth birthday fell on March 5; Christoph Schönborn, OP, archbishop of Vienna and secretary of the editorial team that had drafted the new Catechism of the Catholic Church; and Peter Erdo, archbishop of Esztergom-Budapest, Hungary, and president of the Council of the Bishops Conferences of Europe.

Their request drew a response of a general nature from Spain's cardinal Julián Herranz, 83, former president of the Pontifical Council for the Interpretation of Legislative Texts, a member of Opus Dei and a disciple of its founder—Saint José Maria Escrivà de Balaguer; it satisfied nobody.

Benedict had appointed him head of the commission set up to investigate Vatileaks and the situation in the Roman Curia. The other two members of the commission—Jozef Tomko, 88, from Slovakia, former prefect of the congregation for the evangelization of peoples, and Salvatore De Giorgi, 82, emeritus archbishop of Palermo, Italy—were present as he spoke. Herranz informed the cardinals that Benedict XVI did not want the report to be made public but had given permission to the three cardinal-investigators to provide their brother cardinals with information of a general character.

"Cardinal Herranz was the most criticized man among the cardinals" at the General Congregation, because he told his 148 fellow cardinals that the secret report does not consider the involvement of cardinals, *La Repubblica*'s Marco Ansaldo reported. He said the Spanish cardinal's remark raised the hackles of not a few fellow prelates, including Schönborn, Dolan, O'Malley, and the Germans, who insisted on knowing whether he was taking this stance out of respect for Benedict or because he had been counseled to do so by the "Roman party."

La Repubblica revealed that Cardinal Sodano, who is chairing the meetings, came to Herranz's rescue by suggesting that the cardinals could discuss this matter with the three investigators outside the synod hall. His intervention, however, only increased suspicion among several foreign cardinals, who read it as an attempt to bury the report. The discussion raised strong feelings against the Curia.

However, Vatileaks was not the main topic of the day, Tornielli reported. Peru's cardinal Cipriani Thorne, a member of Opus Dei and archbishop of Lima, raised questions about the functioning of the Roman Curia, while some US cardinals made clear that they considered pedophilia a top priority issue and wanted assurances that Benedict's "zero tolerance" would be continued by his successor.

Given that they will soon be in conclave, most cardinals, not surprisingly, were looking for a candidate to be pope who knows how to speak to the world and proclaim the Gospel in a positive way, Tornielli wrote. He quoted an "influential" cardinal, whom he did not identify, as saying, "We need a pope like Saint Francis, a man who knows how to smile like John Paul I, who can show the merciful face of God [to the world], and who knows how to reform the Curia and make it more credible and transparent."

AT TODAY'S GENERAL CONGREGATION, Cardinal Bertone, who had been secretary of state under Benedict, spoke for fifteen minutes about the work of the Roman Curia in a way that some cardinals read as aligning him more closely to Sodano in what they called "a Romano-centric logic."

Two other Italians spoke: Angelo Bagnasco, archbishop of Genoa and president of the Italian bishops' conference, and Giuseppe Betori, archbishop of Florence and former secretary general of that same conference. They are on the same page. Poland's Cardinal Stanislaw Dziwisz, longtime secretary of John Paul II and now archbishop of Krakow, reportedly caused some eyebrows to be raised when he offered a description of the pope-to-be that looked remarkably like what had gone before.

TODAY'S MEETING OF CARDINALS, the third in the series, lasted just over three hours. Seven newly arrived cardinals took the oath; three were electors.[34]

A total of 148 cardinals attended this morning's session, 110 of them electors. Fr. Lombardi reported that 11 spoke today on a range of topics including the activities of the Holy See and its relations with bishops around the world.

A cardinal told me afterwards that Scherer spoke "but didn't come off well, and went over time," whereas Mahony, the retired archbishop of Los Angeles who has been strongly criticized for his handling of cases of sexual abuse of minors by priests, gave "a very humble intervention."

My source said Godfried Danneels, archbishop of Malines-Bruxelles, considered one of the progressive figures in the Church, told his brother cardinals, "The new pope needs a group of wise men to help him." The idea was not new, however; his predecessor in Belgium, Cardinal Leo J. Suenens, who played a major role at the Second Vatican Council, made a similar suggestion at the 1978 conclave that elected John Paul II, but it gained no traction then.

Another cardinal commented to me on four of today's speakers. He said that Cardinal Ouellet had spoken and emphasized that "we should reflect seriously on the meaning of the resignation of Benedict XVI," but his speech didn't have great impact. The American cardinal Raymond Burke, prefect of the Supreme Tribunal of the Apostolic Signatura since 2008, also spoke on Benedict's resignation, but from a canonical perspective. The Australian cardinal George Pell urged the assembly to move slowly: "Let's not push the process, let's take our time." The Colombian cardinal Darío Castrillón Hoyos, former secretary general and president of CELAM and an opponent of liberation theology, who, as prefect of the Congregation for the Clergy (1996–2006), once told a Vatican press conference that the scandal involving abuse of minors by clergy was a problem only of the Anglophone world, today urged his fellow cardinals, and by implication the new pope: "Let's go out against those who attack the Church."

WHILE THE CARDINALS HELD morning and afternoon sessions on the first day of the General Congregations, they decided to hold morning sessions only on Tuesday and Wednesday (March 5 and 6), as they felt the need to have more free time to meet, discuss, and exchange ideas with each other in informal settings.

SOME OF THE CARDINALS would like the conclave to start soon, but Cardinal Kasper is of the opposite view. He told *La Repubblica*: "This is a time for a long reflection... this conclave must be prepared calmly. As cardinals we almost do not know each other. There's no rush. The '*extra omnes*' (the call for everyone except the cardinals to exit the Sistine Chapel) can wait for now."

Kasper is a renowned theologian, on the progressive wing of the Church. He taught dogmatic theology at the German universities of Münster and Tübingen before becoming bishop of the Rottenburg-Stuttgart diocese in 1989. He was nominated co-chair of the International Commission for the Catholic-Lutheran dialogue in 1994, and five years later John Paul II appointed him to the Pontifical Council for the Promotion of Christian Unity, first as secretary and then in 2001 as president, a post he held with distinction until 2010.

Speaking with *La Repubblica*, he emphasized "the need for a new mode of exercising the government of the Church, a more horizontal mode called collegiality." He asserted that "it is necessary to get out of the straits of Roman centralization by growing in understanding that the center does not mean centralism." He believes "the reform of the Curia is a priority" but recognizes that "it is also a big problem, because today internal dialogue is lacking in the Roman Curia; there's no communication." He said, "the Curia must be revolutionized; it must begin to open itself, and not fear transparency." He recalled that Cardinal Ratzinger, in his Good Friday meditations of 2005, "indicated a new road, which is the line of cleanup in the Church."

As a diocesan bishop in Germany, he and several fellow bishops issued a paper in 1993 proposing an opening on the question of communion for the divorced and remarried, but it was shot down by the then prefect of the Congregation for the Doctrine of the Faith, Cardinal Ratzinger. In today's interview, Kasper returned to the subject and asserted that "the prohibition of communion for the divorced and remarried is a wound" and "there is need for serious reflection on this. It requires humility to address the question."

He concluded by insisting that in the search for the next pope "nobody is to be excluded. We must be open to everyone, of whatever nationality or ecclesial geography."

THIS MORNING, *La Stampa* published my interview with Cardinal Pell, 71, reported earlier. He is the only elector from Oceania, and as a strong defender of orthodoxy in the Church, he is considered to be on the other side of the theological spectrum from Kasper on many issues.

THERE IS MUCH SPECULATION in the Brazilian media that Scherer could become pope. *O Globo*, the main Brazilian newspaper, carried an interview today with a veteran expert on the Vatican, the German journalist Andreas Englisch, under the title "*Brasileiro Odilo Scherer é um nome limpo em Roma.*" Englisch, one of those who had predicted the election of Ratzinger in 2005, said he believed that this time around the conclave would not elect an Italian or a North American but could opt for the Brazilian archbishop of São Paulo. He asserted that "Dom Odilio Scherer is the favorite in the Americas, with good chances. Brazil is the largest Catholic country in the world and is experiencing a great problem, which is the loss of Catholics. A Brazilian pope could regain the faithful of all Latin America and that would be very important. Scherer is new, he speaks several languages and is considered a clean name in Rome."[35]

THIS AFTERNOON, the US cardinals held their second press briefing at the North American College, at which Seán Patrick O'Malley and Daniel DiNardo fielded questions from the press. O'Malley, a Franciscan who prefers to walk around in the brown habit of a Capuchin friar rather than in his cardinal's robes, is much liked by the Romans. Commenting on the General Congregations, he explained that they provide "an opportunity for all of the cardinals to share their ideas concerning the situation of the Church throughout the world, and the possible needs of the Church going forward, particularly as we prepare to elect a new Holy Father." He described the Congregations as "an opportunity for us to hear also from the retired cardinals who have a wealth of experience. They will not be coming into the conclave, but it is an opportunity for them to share their ideas with us."

Asked if Vatileaks and the reform of the Roman Curia had been major topics in their plenary sessions, the Boston cardinal said, "there's certainly a lot of reflection going on throughout the Catholic world about the governance of the Church, about how to improve it and make the Holy Father's ministry more effective and supported by the bureaucracy of the Holy See." He acknowledged that Vatileaks "grabbed the headlines for a long time," but remarked, "I don't know how important those issues are in terms of the work of the conclave." He expressed confidence that "the cardinals will share with each other the information that is really germane and important for us to know as we try to make this important decision."

Cardinal DiNardo, archbishop of Galveston-Houston, Texas, and a chain-smoker, told the press it was "good to hear from the cardinals who are over eighty years of age who will not enter into the conclave. A lot of them have been bishops of dioceses for years, or [have worked] in the Curia, and they have some interesting points of view to bring to our discussions."

Cardinal O'Malley told reporters that "many cardinals" are "concerned" at "the push/rush" to conclude the General Congregations and anticipate the entry to the Sistine chapel, but said he believes that if there is insufficient time to discuss everything at the Congregations then they risk a longer conclave. "For one of the most important decisions of life we must have the necessary time. It's important to have discussions first, so that when we enter the conclave we have rather clear ideas on whom to vote for. Better to discuss beforehand," he stated.

Various media have listed O'Malley as a candidate for pope, but when asked today about this possibility, the archbishop of Boston said: "I have worn the habit for forty years, and I believe I will not change it in the future."

ON A LIGHTER NOTE, one that proves the point that the cardinals do not know each other, *Der Spiegel* reported that an eccentric German, Ralph Napierski, posing as a bishop by the name of Basilius, and wearing "a cassock that was too short and a strange-looking chain with a crucifix and a purple shawl, managed to slip into the Vatican on Monday and mingle with the cardinals." He posed for photos with cardinals but was "eventually identified and kicked out, to the visible amusement of journalists nearby," ANSA (Italy's state news agency) reported. The spokesperson of the German bishops' conference, Matthias Kopp, warned reporters against taking Napierski seriously. He told Germany's mass circulation *Bild* newspaper that "he claims to be a Catholic bishop. We refute that. He is not listed in the Pontifical Yearbook, in which all legitimate Catholic bishops are registered." He politely labeled his behavior as "unacceptable."

THIS EVENING, one cardinal elector told me that at the General Congregations "were talking a lot" about the need for the reform of the Roman Curia, but he remarked, "I personally think that it depends on the pope; he has to bring in people from outside to help him." He recalled that "Benedict XVI had in mind to reform the Curia, but what did he do?"

Speaking about the search for the new pope, he mentioned that "dinners and meetings" were being set up but "we're also talking among ourselves." He confirmed that there is "no clear candidate emerging yet."

Another elector agreed and said he too didn't see any candidate emerging strongly. He reported that "Re and company" are claiming that forty cardinals are supporting Scherer, but he didn't believe them: "It's just not possible!" He said he didn't know when they might go into conclave, maybe early next week.

THE CARDINALS WILL VOTE again tomorrow, Wednesday, March 6, to decide whether to have a full day of interventions (with morning and afternoon sessions) on Thursday and Friday. "This is a very important vote," one of them told me.

BESIDES THEIR PRESS BRIEFINGS, the American cardinals meet every day in the "red room" of the North American College to discuss the day's events. They enter through the red door, move to the right, and sit near the grandfather clock that was a gift of the late Cardinal John Wright, former bishop of Pittsburgh and prefect of the Congregation for the Clergy. With eleven electors, they are the second largest voting bloc in the conclave, after the Italians who have twenty-eight, and so they carry considerable weight in the election if they all vote for the same candidate. Eight of the eleven are residing at the college in the pre-conclave period.

The Survivors Network of those Abused by Priests (SNAP), an organization founded in the United States in 1989 to help victims of such abuse but now with branches in fifty-six countries, today named a "dirty dozen" cardinals whom it alleged had failed, in one way or another, to protect minors or vulnerable people from such abuse and declared that to elect any one of them "would be the worst choice for children."[36]

The Vatican announced today that the Sistine Chapel is now closed to visitors until the end of the conclave, as work has begun in preparation for that big event. Many now think it could start on March 11.

MARCH 6 (WEDNESDAY)
DAY 3 OF THE GENERAL CONGREGATIONS _____
Gag Order on the Cardinals

Much to the chagrin of Cardinal Sodano, who is chairing the meetings, and of Cardinal Bertone, the camerlengo who sits next to him, the Italian press today, and in particular *La Stampa*, again carried reports based on leaks from yesterday's General Congregation. This led to a humorous incident at the beginning of the morning's session, when one cardinal asked in a loud voice, "Is Cardinal Tornielli here today?"

Cardinals later told me that at the start of the morning session a clearly annoyed Sodano was overheard whispering an instruction to Bertone to ask the secretary of the College of Cardinals, Archbishop Lorenzo Baldisseri, to prohibit cardinals from talking to anybody about the conclave and especially what's said at these congregations. Unfortunately for Sodano, the microphone happened to be switched on and his instruction was heard by all the cardinals in the hall. Commenting on that episode, one elector described Sodano as a "*cafone*" (a bad-mannered person) for the way he's running the meetings.

BY THE END OF TODAY'S ASSEMBLY, a climate of tension and nervousness was palpable among the cardinals, as evidenced, for example, by the reaction of a seventy-nine-year-old Italian elector, Cardinal Severino Poletto, emeritus archbishop of Turin, a usually mild and friendly man, who, when approached by journalists for a comment, pleaded in an agitated way, "Please have pity on me!"

THE US CARDINALS, who are the only ones to have brought their communications team to the conclave, were deeply unhappy at the prohibition against talking to the press, but to cover their backs they decided they could no longer continue their daily briefings. Sr. Mary Ann Walsh, their spokesperson, communicated the decision to journalists in a text message at 13:56 PM, canceling the briefing that was scheduled to start thirty-four minutes later. She wrote that the decision was taken because of "concerns expressed at the General Congregation at the leaks of confidential news that were reported in the Italian papers" and "as a precaution, the cardinals have decided not to give interviews."

New York's Cardinal Dolan, who has been getting much media coverage here, was scheduled to appear with Cardinal George today, but it is rumored that Sodano had asked him not to attend, and so the retired archbishop of Washington, Theodore McCarrick, an accomplished polyglot—he speaks seven languages—was to take his place. Sadly, it was not to be.

Lola Galan, writing in *El País*, reported the comment of an unnamed "veteran *Vaticanista*" on the forced cancellation of the US press conference: "It's further proof of Italian hypocrisy. They don't want press conferences, but they're not concerned that Italian cardinals tell whatever they want to those Vaticanisti they trust."

John Thavis, author of *The Vatican Diaries* and former Rome bureau chief for Catholic News Service (1996–2012), expressed surprise and disappointment too. "I thought the balance had swung a little, but more [to] the transparency side—and I guess that isn't true," he remarked. "What inevitably happens is there's an order to not talk to the press, and that just guarantees information will come through leaks. It seems counterproductive. It's pretty sad that the Americans who do things out in the open, on the record, are being punished."

Aware that the gag on cardinals would not be popular with journalists, Fr. Lombardi sought to lower the temperature at today's briefing by offering a rationale for the interdiction. "Reserve is the tradition of the conclave," he stated; the task of the cardinals is to "find the way to move ahead to the election of the Holy Father," and this "reserve" aims "to safeguard their spiritual freedom."

Thomas Rosica, who serves as Lombardi's assistant for the Anglophone media, reminded the press that "we are not dealing with a congress or a synod during which you would try to get as much information as possible about what's taking place. We are dealing with a journey, and part of that journey includes the pre-conclave meetings that are taking place right now and then the conclave itself. So, there's a certain respect that grows among the participants in the conclave as they get deeper into the conversations."

CARDINAL GEORGE HAS A HABIT of speaking frankly, and before the cardinals were muzzled he told reporters (*La Stampa*, March 6): "I can tell you, without violating the oath of secrecy we are bound by in the General Congregations, that the list of candidates for the papacy is getting longer rather than shorter. The names you have seen published in the newspapers make sense, but we are also considering other candidates that no one has discussed before."

George, a member of the Missionary Oblates of Mary Immaculate, was also frank about the progress being made in the discussions: "Everything is going according to plan, in the sense that there is no plan; the discussions are very free. But the Congregations do have some very specific rules, so real contact between cardinals takes place outside these discussions. If a colleague approaches you and asks you what you think about a potential candidate, it means he and the group he leads support that individual. So you reflect on the candidate, aware that he has a certain backing. But proof of this consensus will be given only when we start to vote. The voting process must not be hurried. It is better for long discussions to take place before the votes are cast and keep the conclave brief rather than the opposite."

A TOTAL OF 153 CARDINALS attended the fourth of the General Congregations this morning, Fr. Lombardi reported. Among them were four new arrivals who took the oath.[37] Since three are under the age of eighty, this brings the total number of electors to 113. The assembly is now waiting for the last two to arrive before deciding the date of entry to the conclave.

Cardinal Sodano began the morning's session on a cheerful note by a wishing happy birthday to three electors: Walter Kasper, who turned eighty yesterday; Francesco Coccopalmerio, who is seventy-five today; and Julio Terrazas Sandoval, CSSR, who will be seventy-seven tomorrow. The news was greeted with warm applause.

Eighteen cardinals spoke today, which brings the total number of interventions so far to fifty-one, according to Fr. Lombardi. But since a great many more cardinals want to speak, he said they have decided to hold morning and afternoon sessions tomorrow. Hoping to accelerate the proceedings, Cardinal Sodano again invited the cardinals to limit their interventions to five minutes; he noted that some have exceeded the time limit, thereby depriving others of the opportunity to speak.

FR. LOMBARDI TOLD THE PRESS that the topics raised today included those related to the Church in the world, the needs of the new evangelization, the Holy See, the offices of the Roman Curia and their relations with bishops. He said the prefect of the four-hundred-year-old Congregation for the Evangelization of Peoples, Cardinal Fernando Filoni, gave a presentation on the work of his congregation, which oversees the Church's activities in missionary countries, and Cardinal Mauro Piacenza, prefect of the Congregation for Clergy, spoke about the situation regarding the priesthood and vocations.

LA STAMPA, again drawing on insider information, revealed that Cardinal Camillo Ruini, now over eighty, sketched a profile of the future pope and, like some others, suggested electing a "dynamic" pope who is young enough to adequately deal with the challenges currently faced by the Church.

The Turin-based paper furthermore reported that a foreign cardinal asked for information about two laymen whom he named: one is a Vatican employee, the other is not but has frequent contacts and collaborates at a high level with Holy See institutions. The cardinal sought clarification on their roles in the Vatican which, he claimed, has been a cause for concern in recent times. His request was further evidence of the widespread desire to obtain more information about Vatileaks and the kind of situation the new pope may have to deal with. Cardinals Sodano and Bertone, however, clearly did not like the direction the questioner was taking and, soon after, issued an internal communiqué asking cardinals "not to name individuals" if they are not "certain" of their information; otherwise they risk fomenting a climate of suspicion and resentment.

CARDINAL SODANO looked clearly relieved as he closed the morning's session. He invited everyone to join in the prayer service in Saint Peter's Basilica at five o'clock this evening, at the altar of the chair behind the main altar in Saint Peter's Basilica. He announced that the archpriest of the basilica, the Italian cardinal Angelo Comastri, would lead the service, which would include a recitation of the rosary, vespers, and adoration of the Blessed Sacrament.

I VISITED CARDINAL TONG this afternoon at the Domus Romana Sacerdotalis on the Via Traspontina, very close to the Vatican. John Paul II set this up in 1999 as a residence for clergy working in the Vatican and for visiting cardinals, bishops, priests, and lay faithful. I have known the cardinal for many years and met him in Hong Kong last summer. It was his first conclave. We spoke together for an hour, but all he would say on the record was "I feel like a novice." He is the only Chinese elector at this conclave, but he is not the first Chinese cardinal to vote in a papal election. That honor belongs to Thomas Tien Ken-sin, SVD, the former archbishop of Peking, who was made a cardinal by Pius XII in 1946 but expelled from China in 1951; he voted in the 1958 conclave that elected John XXIII and in the 1963 conclave that elected Paul VI.

WHEN I ASKED ONE ELECTOR what impression some of the *papabili* mentioned in the press and some others now mentioned in the Italian media are making in the General Congregations, he told me: Filoni, who showed courage by staying in the Holy See's nunciature in Baghdad during the US-led war on Iraq, "has little support"; Scherer was not helped by the "Operation Scherer," and moreover he's considered "too cold"; Scola is definitely a candidate, but some are asking whether the Church needs another theologian pope at this time in history; Tagle is much appreciated but "too young"; Bergoglio—"nobody speaks about him"; Ouellet is a candidate, but people are not inspired by him; Dolan's name is being pushed, but people fear the idea of a US pope; O'Malley's name is mentioned too but he's "not sufficiently well known."

Another elector told me Bertone wants to stay on as secretary of state for some time after the conclave "to clean things up." He said Scherer "is feeling down" after having exceeded the time limit when he spoke in the General Congregations. Ouellet came across as the weakest of the front-runners. Scola came across strongly when he spoke, and Cipriani was heard to remark, "He's the man!" O'Malley is being noticed, but an American as pope is a long shot. Robles is not being mentioned as a candidate, nor is Sandri (but some say his sights are set on being secretary of state). Piacenza is not considered *papabile*. Some are even talking of the possibility of an impasse or deadlock in the conclave, he said.

THE CARDINALS HAVE NOT YET DECIDED on the date for the conclave because they are still waiting for two more electors to arrive. One cardinal told me he thinks there's "a secret plan" to have the Mass for the Election of the Roman Pontiff on Sunday and begin the conclave that evening, because the meetings are "getting heated."

A VETERAN FRENCH CORRESPONDENT on Vatican affairs, Jean-Marie Guenois, offered an interesting analysis today in *Le Figaro*, France's oldest and second-largest national daily, which has a center-right editorial line. He described "the tension" and discussion over the date of the conclave as "a symptom of a much deeper tension among the cardinals which is being expressed as never before." It is "not a question of theological quarrels or political sensibilities" nor is it "a debate between conservatives and progressives, as was the case in recent times," he said, because "the crisis of governance in the Roman Curia and the resignation of the pope are truly far beyond that."

Guenois, who knows the Francophone cardinals well, wrote: "Many cardinals think that the hour has come to review the operations of the Curia from top to bottom. They want a reform of the system: a secretary of state with fewer powers; an effective Council of Ministers surrounding the pope; a Vatican designed as a place of service for the continental churches and not as a place of power. But this makes the Italian old guard, which has in fact controlled everything for a long time, fear a crisis at the institutional level that could therefore be very serious."

Expressing a widely shared view in Rome, Guenois stated: "After Paul VI, neither John Paul II nor Benedict XVI really governed the Curia. So now, after more than thirty years of excesses of power (*"dérives de pouvoirs"*) things are imploding." He observed that "in these days, this fundamental calling into question of those who refuse to entrust the keys of the kingdom to anyone who is not of the curial kind is being done not by the progressive left but by the College of Cardinals, in a way that was not seen at the 1978 and 2005 conclaves. The tensions come from here. So, too, does the sacred Italian alliance, but this time it may be in vain."

The French journalist concluded, "It is important to mention that this eagerness to reform the Curia is not without ambiguities. Certainly, some dysfunctions have been apparent in recent years, and one can only hope that the new pope will remedy them, as some cardinals are legitimately demanding. But others would like to see a structural reform to decentralize the Curia and foster again the collegiality promoted by Vatican II. Despite the various declarations on either side during the days of the pre-conclave Congregations, this dangerous ambiguity has not been dispelled—far from it."

Le Figaro, I-Media (the French Catholic news service), and other media today reported comments from the highly respected French cardinal, Jean-Louis Tauran, president of the Pontifical Council for Interreligious Dialogue and former secretary for relations with states (the Vatican's foreign minister from 1991–2003), about what he hopes from the man who becomes the next pope.

"I think, in the first place, it will be necessary to continue what Benedict XVI did, in other words, to teach the content of the faith. In today's world, Christians must be capable of giving a reason for their faith by having an understanding of the content of that faith, because you can't hand on impressions," Cardinal Tauran stated. "It will have to be a pope who is very open to dialogue with other cultures and religions. Of course, I am thinking of interreligious dialogue, but also dialogue with the other Christian Churches," he said.

Moreover, he added, "it will be necessary too for him to be able to carry out a reform of the Curia, in such a way that there is more coordination." But when it was pointed out to him that "before his election, Joseph Ratzinger wanted to carry out that reform...," Tauran responded, "Yes, but the Curia is a huge machine! Maybe it will take a younger pope." In his view, "the ideal age" for the next pope "is more-or-less sixty-five, or even seventy if he is in good shape."

Another curial cardinal, Francesco Coccopalmerio, president of the Pontifical Council for Legislative Texts, in speaking to Italian media today recalled that the Jesuit cardinal-archbishop of Milan, Carlo Maria Martini, to whom he was very close, gave an interview shortly before he died on August 31, 2012 in which he declared: "The Church is two hundred years behind. Why is it not being stirred? Are we afraid? Afraid instead of courageous? Faith is the Church's foundation—faith, confidence, courage."[38]

At this time too, the Italian press, drawing on more leaks, reported that during the General Congregations, Coccopalmerio had proposed that the new pope should consider establishing the role of "moderator" in the Roman Curia. Several years later,[39] I recalled this and asked the cardinal to explain his proposal. He began by saying that all the cardinals had taken an oath of secrecy regarding all matters discussed in those congregations, but since someone had leaked this piece of information to the press he felt free to speak about it. He recalled that, during the General Congregations, cardinals were asked what they desire of the new pope, and so he made several proposals but, because of the oath of secrecy, he would speak only of the one that had been reported in the press. He said he addressed the cardinals as one who has worked in the Roman Curia for many years and proposed "that in the Roman Curia there be a moderator like that which is envisaged by the Code of Canon Law and exists in big dioceses like Milan." He explained that the moderator would have to be "one who works in the Curia and knows the various parts of the Curia." The moderator's role would be "to coordinate internally what is happening in the Curia, to know each part of the Curia, so that each one does not just go its own way," and "to give direction and be like the motor of the Curia." This role could not be carried out by a single person but would require "a small staff that is concerned with and knows what each dicastery does and what's its role is. The moderator would also be responsible for finding the most suitable persons for the different posts and taking care of the ongoing formation of those who work in the Curia, and so on." The cardinal said he received "positive reactions" to his proposal, while the only negative one was that this is the competence of the Secretariat of State but, he added, "I'm totally in agreement with that. I think there's a need for a new organism, a new unit in the Secretariat of State that will deal precisely with this."

THAT WEDNESDAY EVENING, Cardinal Cormac Murphy-O'Connor invited a small number of cardinals whom he knew well to a private meeting at the Venerable English College. He had lived there first as a student, then as rector, and was now staying there for the conclave. He invited, among others, Cardinals Kasper, Coccopalmerio, Barbarin, Brady, Poletto, and Antonelli.

They sat at the round table in the *"salone"* (lounge) on the first floor of this, the oldest English building outside the UK, which was first opened in 1362 as a hospice for English pilgrims but in 1579 was transformed into a seminary to train priests for the English mission. Surrounded by portraits of famous Englishmen, they spoke freely as friends do, discussing the situation in the Church and the Vatican and the upcoming conclave. It emerged that they shared a common feeling of unease about the three front-runners —Scola, Scherer, and Ouellet; they felt that none of these three could offer the kind of inspiring leadership they believed the Church greatly needed at this moment in history. At this stage they did not have any alternative. A few cardinals were mentioned as possibilities, including Bergoglio, but they left that evening without having a common candidate.

MARCH 7 (THURSDAY)
DAY 4 OF THE GENERAL CONGREGATIONS _____
The Last Elector Arrives

"THE AMERICANS HAVE LAUNCHED the challenge to elect their own candidate," *Corriere della Sera*'s chief Vatican correspondent, Gian-Guido Vecchi, reported in an article today. He listed three candidates: Dolan, 63, "the most media-celebrity (mediatic) candidate"; O'Malley, 68, the Capuchin friar famous for his efforts in dealing with the clergy child-abuse scandal in Boston; and Wuerl, 72, who "could be the most reassuring to the European electors" because he has worked in the Curia and speaks Italian. Vecchi noted, however, that some days ago Wuerl seemed to rule out an American pope when he told the press, "a pope from the US superpower would encounter many obstacles in presenting a spiritual message to the rest of the world."

Italy's paper of record went on to assert that the candidacy of Ouellet, 68, is gaining support because he is close to Ratzinger and a polyglot with Latin American experience and no "superpower problems." It mentioned two other candidates as "strong" runners: Brazil's Scherer and Mexico's Robles Ortega, as well as two Italians, Scola and Ravasi.[40] The article concluded by alerting its readers that "the wind from across the ocean is blowing ever more strongly in the College of Cardinals."

THE CHICAGO TRIBUNE reported that Cardinal George, in an exclusive interview, revealed that "there are attempts to vet candidates to avoid surprises." He said, "Ties to anyone guilty of sexual misconduct—whether intended or unintended—could put a man's candidacy in question if it could distract from his spiritual mission." He said, "Given the troubling circumstances surrounding the issue of priest sex abuse, cardinals aren't just asking about leadership and communication style. They are asking about each man's moral character. 'Does he have a past?'"

POPE JOHN XXIII'S GRAND-NEPHEW, Marco Roncalli, writing in *Corriere della Sera* today, provided an interesting insight into the history of "tickets for pope and secretary of state." It seems he did so in the wake of the article that Tornielli and I had written in Vatican Insider on the proposal for a Latin American–Italian ticket at this conclave. He recalled that at the 1958 conclave, before his election, Cardinal Angelo Roncalli gave the cardinals the assurance that he would appoint Domenico Tardini as secretary of state, a decision that gained him the necessary votes for election. Likewise, in the first conclave of 1978, Cardinal Albino Luciani assured fellow cardinals that he would not appoint Cardinal Giovanni Benelli[41] as secretary of state. He recalled that at that same conclave, Belgium's Cardinal Leo-Joseph Suenens, who played a very important role at the Second Vatican Council, had proposed that the next pope should "be able to count on," or establish what he called "a council of the crown," in other words, an advisory group of cardinals, for which there is a precedent in church history.

Roncalli reported that during the General Congregations in this past week, Cardinal Coccopalmerio called for a reform of the Roman Curia, and Cardinal Bertello, president of the Governorate of the Vatican City State, emphasized the need for a reform and reorganization of Vatican finances, including the Institute for the Works of Religion, the Administration of the Patrimony of the Apostolic See, the Governorate, the Prefecture for Economic Affairs, and the Congregation for the Evangelization of Peoples, formerly known as Propaganda Fide. He recalled that these matters were raised too in the October 1978 conclave, but that the Polish cardinal Stefan Wyszynski, archbishop of Warsaw, had rejected the idea saying, "We are not here to concern ourselves with financial matters."

With stories like these, the Italian media continues for the most part to direct the conversation, even internationally, in the lead-up to the conclave.

I was particularly struck, however, by an entry today in the "Blog do Camarotti," by Gerson Camarotti, a respected Brazilian commentator for *O Globo*, the leading quality daily in Rio de Janeiro and the flagship newspaper of the largest media group in Latin America.[42]

O Globo News sent Camarotti to Rome to report on the conclave, and under the headline "*Os riscos da candidature precoce do cardeal Odilo Scherer*" ("The risks of the premature candidacy of Cardinal Odilo Scherer"), he wrote that some members of the Brazilian bishops' conference (CNBB, Conferência Nacional dos Bispos do Brasil) were "concerned" at "the early launch" of Scherer's candidacy by American cardinals. They felt this would ruin his chances, as it would draw attention not only to his positive features but also to his negative ones. On the positive side, Camarotti said, he's a Latin American who has worked in the Roman Curia and now "courageously" leads one of the largest dioceses in the world. Further, he "has not shown timidity" in meetings with university students. On the negative side, Camarotti reported that he had learned that when in recent days Brazilian cardinals were consulted by brother cardinals from other parts of the world about Scherer they said he has "a rather rigid personality" and had been defeated in the election to be president of the Brazilian bishops' conference in 2011 by Cardinal Raymundo Damasceno, who obtained 198 votes (71 percent of the total votes cast) in the second ballot, against Scherer's 75. Camarotti said this revealed that there is resistance to him even within the bishops' conference where he is considered "conservative" and "not very political" in relating to fellow bishops and that, moreover, when he was secretary general of the conference, his fellow bishops found his style "too German," "very direct and objective." Camarotti said a Brazilian bishop told him that he believed the Americans had launched Scherer's candidacy early to "burn" it, to the benefit of Dolan.

Camarotti, however, omitted another significant fact: Scherer suffered an even greater defeat in 2007 when, soon after becoming archbishop of São Paulo, he stood, for the first time, for president of the CNBB, but the archbishop of Mariana, Geraldo Lyrio Rocha, obtained 92 percent of the votes.[43]

It is perhaps worth mentioning here that if a cardinal does not have strong support within his own bishops' conference, this fact is never a good sign for other cardinals when they consider him as a candidate to be pope. Interestingly, this was the case not only with Scherer but also with Scola and Ouellet in relation to their respective bishops' conferences, where neither of them had great support and neither had been elected president. Bergoglio, on the other hand, enjoyed strong support within the Argentine episcopal conference and had been elected president for two terms.

AN AIR OF EXPECTATION seemed to grip the cardinals as they assembled for the fifth of the General Congregations; everyone knew the last of the electors was due to arrive in Rome and would be present today. Fr. Lombardi reported that two newly arrived cardinals, one of them an elector,[44] had been sworn in at the morning's session, This means the total number of electors present now stands at 114, just one short of the full complement.

Following the rulebook, three new cardinals were chosen by lot to assist the camerlengo over the next three days.[45]

After that, Cardinal Sodano introduced an item that was not on the agenda. He read out the draft text of a telegram of condolence to be sent, on behalf of the College of Cardinals, to the government of the Bolivarian Republic of Venezuela on the death of President Hugo Chavez, who had passed away on March 5. It is customary for the pope to send a telegram to the government of a country on the death of its head of state, but Sodano explained that during the *sede vacante* this duty falls to the College of Cardinals. The text was approved.

NEXT, IN ACCORDANCE WITH THE CONSTITUTION, Cardinal Sodano gave the floor to the three cardinal-presidents of the Holy See's economic departments: Giuseppe Versaldi, of the Prefecture for the Economic Affairs of the Holy See; Domenico Calcagno, of the Administration of the Patrimony of the Apostolic See (APSA), who is known in Italy as "Cardinal Rambo," because of his private collection of guns;[46] and Giuseppe Bertello, president of the Governorate of Vatican City State. Each gave a brief report on his area of competence in accordance with the provisions outlined in the apostolic constitution *Pastor Bonus* (The Good Shepherd).[47] By the end of these three reports, the cardinals were more than ready for their half-hour coffee break.

When the session resumed, thirteen other cardinals gave five-minute interventions covering a wide range of topics, including ecumenism, the Church's charitable efforts, and attention to the poor.

The air of expectation gave way to excitement as cardinals and journalists learned that the 115th cardinal elector had arrived in Rome and would be attending the remaining Congregations: Cardinal Jean-Baptiste Pham Minh Mân, metropolitan archbishop of Ho Chi Minh Ville (formerly Saigon), Vietnam, who had completed part of his studies in the United States and whom I had interviewed on several occasions.[48]

Since all the electors would now be present, the cardinals could at last decide on the date for entry into the conclave. Fr. Lombardi urged caution, however, when he briefed the press. He noted that although eighteen cardinals had spoken today, "There is still a long list of cardinals who want to speak." Clearly, they were not yet ready to vote, and so they decided to hold General Congregations tomorrow and the following day—Friday and Saturday.

SOURCES REPORT that some speakers today have named and blamed curial cardinals for the current problems in the Vatican. Some attacked Bertone for trying to impose silence. But, according to *La Stampa*, the Italian cardinal Giovanni Lajolo, former president of the Governorate of the Vatican City State and before that secretary of relations with states, defended the Curia against attacks by cardinals who charged that the Roman Curia was beset by a lack of coordination and difficult relations with bishops' conferences.

So too did Slovenian-born cardinal Franc Rode, who fled with his family from Yugoslavia to Argentina in 1948. There he joined the Vincentians and later served as prefect of the Congregation for Institutes of Consecrated Life and Societies of Apostolic Life from 2004 to 2011. He is the first Slovenian in history to participate in a conclave. His motto in old Slovene, "*Stati inu obstati*," means "Stand and withstand," and today he abided by that motto as he strongly rebutted the criticism of the Curia.

CARDINAL TOPPO was one of those who spoke today, and an elector told me afterwards that he was struck to hear the Indian say: "I have the feeling that we are standing at the crossroads of history in the Church." Like many others, Toppo called for a reform of the Roman Curia, starting with a spiritual reform, and urged his fellow cardinals "to collaborate and cooperate fully with the man God has chosen to lead us."

THE VETERAN VATICAN AFFAIRS REPORTER, Marco Politi, writing in *Il Fatto Quotidiano*, a daily founded in 2009 in which the columnists own 30 percent of the shares, noted that Fr. Lombardi said speakers highlighted the urgent need for "positive proclamation of the Gospel in a joyous, love-filled, merciful way."

La Repubblica reported that since the cardinals have been muzzled, the Americans have adopted a self-imposed silence, the Germans talk to no one—not even to the German press—and almost the only ones willing to comment are the French. Cardinal André Vingt-Trois, archbishop of Paris, told the press on leaving the synod hall, "There's no date yet for the conclave!" His confrère, Philippe Barbarin, the cardinal-archbishop of Bordeaux, who wears a black beret, hinted, "Maybe we vote tomorrow," and then rode off on his bike.

FR. LOMBARDI confirmed that the Sistine Chapel is almost ready for the conclave. According to the Italian press, a jamming device has been installed to block electromagnetic fields and prevent communication by means of electronic equipment. The camerlengo and his team are determined to do everything in their power to prevent the sending of messages from the conclave such as happened in 2005.

ON THE MORE SPIRITUAL SIDE of the preparation, following a long-standing Roman tradition, a triduum of Masses *Pro Eligendo Pontifice* (For the Election of the Pope) has started at the Basilica of Santa Maria Maggiore. It is a sure sign that we are near the opening of the conclave.

FROM CONVERSATIONS with two electors today I gleaned the following information: Scola is in with a good chance and still in the lead, but several electors are now asking the question raised many times before: "Do we need another Italian? Do we need another theologian pope?" Ouellet is also in, but weaker than Scola, though he is said to have backing from some cardinals in Benedict's circle, as well as a few Spanish- and French-speaking electors, and there is talk that the Americans are considering him seriously. Scherer has not been helped by "the ticket" operation; his chances are slim. Tagle is considered too young and inexperienced. Some are pushing Dolan's name, others O'Malley. According to my sources, "a few, but not many" are now talking about Bergoglio as the candidate to be pope.

I LEARNED THAT the ambassadors to the Holy See from Latin American countries held a meeting and invited two outsiders: Anne Leahy from Canada (former ambassador to the Holy See and now serving as acting ambassador during the period of the conclave) and Nigel Baker (British ambassador to the Holy See with Latin American experience), both of whom speak Spanish. The ambassadors were interested in hearing about who their fellow-diplomats considered *papabile*. When Juan Pablo Caffiero, the Argentine ambassador, mentioned Bergoglio, "there was no reaction, because they thought he was too old," Anne Leahy told me much later over a coffee in Hotel Columbus.[49] She said they identified two candidates: Scola (though they thought he would not be able to get enough votes) and Ouellet (whom they felt had a real chance because he not only knew Spanish but had worked in Colombia for seven years and had served in the Roman Curia).

I met Cardinal Bergoglio by chance today. I had come out of the Holy See's press office and was heading across the road to the CTV television studio when our paths happened to cross. He was returning from the General Congregation. I greeted him, and the first thing he asked was, "How is Elisabetta's father?" He knew that her father, Piero, had not been well in recent times and had come from Buenos Aires to spend some days with us. I told him he felt somewhat better now that he was with his daughter and grandchildren.

I was particularly struck by the fact that, notwithstanding all the issues that must have been on his mind after the morning's session at the General Congregation, the Argentinian cardinal could think of Piero. Concern for people has always been a hallmark of "Padre Jorge," the man we have come to know over these years.

In addition to the arrival of the 115th elector, another important thing happened today that was directly linked to the papal election. The previously mentioned British ambassador to the Holy See, Nigel Baker, whom I know well, hosted a dinner in his attic residence at Palazzo Pallavicini, which is a stone's throw from the Quirinal Palace, (the "Qurinaleas" as it is called in Rome).[50]

In consultation with the English cardinal, Murphy-O'Connor, he invited all the cardinals from the Commonwealth, all of whom are English speakers, giving them a precious opportunity to meet and discuss together.

Most of the invitees attended, including Brady (Ireland), Collins (Canada), Gracias and Toppo (India), Onaiyekan (Nigeria), Turkson (Ghana), and Murphy-O'Connor (UK), but three did not: Ouellet (Canada) and Pell (Australia), as they had other engagements, and Cardinal Dias (India), who was not well enough to come. The ambassador and the English cardinal welcomed them all on arrival. They first enjoyed aperitifs, and then sat at table. At the end of dinner, the ambassador, an ever-gracious host, offered digestifs and then, in an extraordinary act of diplomatic sensitivity, retired to let the cardinals talk in private without any outsider present. They discussed the *papabili*. More than one of them brought up Bergoglio's name, but at the end of the evening there was still no clarity among them; they would continue to search, seeking to identify the person many called "God's chosen one."[51]

MARCH 8 (FRIDAY)
DAY 5 OF THE GENERAL CONGREGATIONS _____
Cardinals Decide the Entry Date to the Conclave

THE SEVENTH OF THE GENERAL CONGREGATIONS was held this morning, attended by 153 cardinals, including the 115 electors. Cardinal Sodano, as dean of the College of Cardinals, in accordance with the apostolic constitution,[52] informed the assembly of the reasons given by two cardinal electors to justify their absence: Julius Riyadi Darmaatmadja, SJ, for health reasons, and Keith O'Brien, for personal reasons. He asked if the assembly accepted the reasons presented and, on receiving a positive response, he formally declared that the definitive number of cardinal electors to enter the conclave was thus established at 115.

Then, noting that all the electors were present, he told the assembly that there was no need to wait fifteen days from the beginning of the *sede vacante* for entry to the conclave. He explained that this was justified by the recent motu proprio of Benedict XVI[53] that states: "The College of Cardinals is granted the faculty to move forward the start of the conclave if it is clear that all the cardinal electors are present." Everyone agreed. Surprisingly, however, he did not propose a date for entry to the conclave. They did not vote.

After dealing with these matters, eighteen cardinals spoke, bringing the total number of interventions since the beginning of the week to more than a hundred, Fr. Lombardi told the press briefing. In addition to topics already touched upon, he said cardinals spoke about interreligious dialogue; bioethics; justice in the world; the Gospel as a proclamation of love, joy, and mercy; collegiality; and the role of women in the Church.

He confirmed that the cardinals are expected to vote on the date for the conclave this afternoon, and he expected it to start on one of the first three days of the coming week: March 11, 12, or 13.

SALT AND LIGHt, the Catholic TV channel in Canada, interviewed me this morning on "the papal transition."[54] As we neared the end of our conversation, Sebastian Gomes, the interviewer, asked what I expected the conclave to do. I responded that I thought the cardinals "are likely to cross the Atlantic" for the next pope. The field was still open, I remarked. In my heart, however, though I did not say it, I felt they could choose Bergoglio.

ONE HUNDRED AND FORTY-FIVE CARDINALS attended the eighth of the General Congregations, which was held this afternoon from 5:00 to 7:00 PM. It began with the taking of the oath by two newly arrived cardinals, both non-electors.[55]

Once that was done, the cardinal dean ended the weeklong suspense by proposing that the cardinals vote on the date for entry to the conclave. Given that preparations for this are still under way in the Domus Santa Marta and in the Sistine Chapel, he proposed beginning the conclave on March 12. An overwhelming majority approved. Leaving the synod hall that evening, Cardinal George broke his silence and told reporters, "We're ready!"

After the vote, fifteen cardinals spoke. They included Cardinal Sepe, archbishop of Naples and former prefect of the Congregation for the Evangelization of Peoples, who gave a brief intervention; Cardinal Collins, archbishop of Toronto, who used Paul VI's quote that "modern man listens more willingly to witnesses than to teachers, and if he does listen to teachers, it is because they are witnesses"; and the Portuguese cardinal Saraiva Martins, former prefect of the Congregation for Saints, whom some had considered as a possible compromise candidate at the 2005 conclave if Ratzinger was blocked by Bergoglio and neither one could obtain the necessary votes.[56]

THAT EVENING, one cardinal summarized the situation for me this way: Scola is "very strong, and likely to be elected"; cardinals "are not convinced" that Ouellet can do the job; Scherer "is burnt out, because there's a fear that he would be a puppet, and moreover he's too cold"; no other candidate is gaining much traction.

From conversations with several cardinals, I have come to realize that the odds against Ouellet becoming pope have increased, though he certainly has supporters. I noted with interest that when Salt and Light, the Canadian Catholic channel, interviewed John Allen and asked about Ouellet's candidacy, he listed on the positive side the fact that he has spent several years in Latin America and three or four in the Vatican, "so he knows where the bodies are," but when it comes to the ability to re-form the Roman Curia, "that's the big question mark. Many people would say maybe he's too nice a guy for this job. Does he have steel in his spine to make the tough decisions, changes?" Some weeks earlier, an edi-torial in Toronto's *Globe and Mail* on February 16, had asked: "Can the cardinal who couldn't save his Quebec church save the Vatican?"[57] That said, he still has a chance.

LA REPUBBLICA too seems to have concluded that Ouellet will not become pope. It ran a page-long article in today's edition under the headline: "A game between two at the conclave: Scola with a 'packet of 40' against the candidate of Bertone." The subtitle revealed Bertone's choice: "The curia chooses the Brazilian Scherer, the strong man of the IOR [Institute for the Works of Religion, the Vatican bank)."

The authors, Paolo Rodari and Marco Ansaldo, asserted that Scola would enter the conclave with forty votes and with the support of "many foreign cardinals," including "not a few" from the United States and "several" from Central Europe encouraged by Schönborn. They pre-sented Scola as the candidate of "the reform party" against the one spon-sored by "the Roman party" in which the former adversaries—Sodano and Bertone, together with other Italian curial cardinals—are backing Scherer, to maintain the status quo. They reiterated "the Scherer ticket" story. On the other hand, they alleged that the reform party desires a radical change in the leadership of the Catholic Church and a cleanup of the Roman Curia, something the Roman party resists.

According to *La Repubblica*, the reform party has two fallback candi-dates if Scola fails to get the seventy-seven votes necessary for election: Dolan, whom they liken to Wojtyla in 1978, and O'Malley, whom they consider as a more spiritual choice, much respected for his cleanup of the pedophilia scandal in Boston. According to this Italian daily, the Roman party has two fallback candidates if Scherer fails to get elected, both "for-eigners": the Italo-Argentinian cardinal Leonardo Sandri and the Sri Lankan cardinal Malcolm Ranjith.

Cardinal Sandri has been prefect of the Congregation for the Eastern Churches since 2007, and prior to that he held the third-ranking position in the Roman Curia as *sostituto* (substitute) in the last years of John Paul II's pontificate and the first two years of Benedict XVI's. The authors of the article noted, however, that Cardinal George was opposed to Sandri and his mentor, Angelo Sodano, over their appalling handling of the case of the Mexican priest Marcial Maciel Degollado, the disgraced founder and head of the Legionaries of Christ from 1941 to 2005.

The Roman party's other alternative is Sri Lanka's Cardinal Ranjith, the polyglot archbishop of Colombo, who was very close to Benedict XVI and much liked by the traditionalists. He served as secretary of the Congregation for the Evangelization of Peoples and was then sent as nuncio to Indonesia before Benedict appointed him secretary of the Congregation for Divine Worship. Informed sources said Benedict XVI sent him as archbishop to Colombo in 2009 to help promote peace in this war-torn land at the request of the country's president, Mahinda Rajapaksa, and a year later gave him the red hat.

La Repubblica concluded that if the candidates of the reform and Roman parties cancel each other out, then the most acceptable cardinal to succeed Benedict would be the archbishop of Budapest, Peter Erdo, who was formed in the theological school of the *Communio* review.

SEVERAL CARDINALS from different continents tell me they do not believe that Scola has forty votes already in the bag; they interpreted *La Repubblica*'s article as a campaigning piece. Italian sources confirm that the Italian electors are deeply divided between the pro-Scola group, which includes Caffarra, Bagnasco, Betori, and Romeo, and the anti-Scola Italians, who include Coccopalmerio, Nicora, and Re.

LA STAMPA published my interview with Wuerl today under the title: "A clear chain of command is needed for the future of the church." An accompanying note clarified that the interview was conducted before silence was imposed on the cardinals.

CARDINAL JEAN-PIERRE RICARD, archbishop of Bordeaux, told France's I.Media news agency, in an interview published today, that cardinals are hoping for a pope who will be "capable of truly entering into the dynamic of the new evangelization," but this requires that he be "a man of faith" who "brings the Church forward." He considers it important to have "a theologian" pope after John Paul II and Benedict XVI, but he revealed that many cardinals felt that after "a great teacher" the time has come for a "more pastoral" pope. In any case, he considered it of utmost importance that the new pope be "a man of government," who can review the relations between the local churches and Rome. In the General Congregations, he said, many cardinals were critical of the dysfunction in relations between the Roman Curia offices and dioceses, and some made "suggestions for better operations, for more coordination and openness"; they want "less compartmentalization" among the different curial offices for the sake of "more harmonious collaboration"; they want to "prevent a situation where everyone is doing his own work," and "not coordinated with the others." He said many cardinals desire "more collegiality" in the governance of the Church.

ON A LIGHTER NOTE, the Italian media are taking great interest in the means of transport used by the cardinals to arrive at the General Congregations. Bergoglio always walks to the meetings, as do several others. Barbarin hit the headlines because he rides a bicycle. The Americans arrive by bus. Some take taxis; others use the Vatican's blue service cars or arrive in private cars provided by the colleges or religious houses where they are staying. Some of those living in Rome, like Turkson, drive their own cars. But Senegal's Cardinal Théodore-Adrien Sarr reportedly outclassed them all by arriving in a chauffeur-driven Cadillac.

SR. MARY ANN WALSH, who coordinates media communications for the US cardinals and writes a daily entry on the USCCB blog, noted today that "reports on security measures are beginning to dominate the news. Jamming devices will be installed in the Sistine Chapel to prevent electronic eavesdropping. Staff who serve meals at the Casa Santa Marta, where the cardinals will stay during the Conclave, will be sworn to secrecy. Even who said, 'pass the salt' is a secret. In this electronic age, I worry some cardinals may go into iPad and Twitter withdrawal."

ANOTHER IMPORTANT PRIVATE MEETING over dinner was held in the "red room" of the North American College (NAC) this evening, hosted by

Chicago's Cardinal George. More than sixteen English-speaking cardinals were present, including ten of the eleven American electors (O'Malley was absent). Other electors present included Brady (Ireland), Collins (Canada), Gracias (India), and Pell (Australia), who also has students at the NAC. Some cardinals who are over the age of eighty and no longer electors were present too: Bernard Law, former archbishop of Boston, "who said nothing"; Theodore McCarrick, the emeritus archbishop of Washington; and Cormac Murphy-O'Connor, the emeritus archbishop of Westminster.

"The American cardinals were quite divided. Many were going for Ouellet, though some were for Scola," Cardinal Murphy-O'Connor recalled later.[58] When at one stage he introduced Bergoglio's name, "they said he is a good man but there was no enthusiasm." Cardinal George was concerned about Bergoglio's age, and asked, 'Does he still have the vigor?'"[59]

MARCH 9 (SATURDAY)
DAY 6 OF THE GENERAL CONGREGATIONS _____
A Turning Point

WHILE THE MARCH 8 DECISION to start the conclave on March 12 caused a tsunami of articles in today's Italian press, this penultimate session of the General Congregations will go down in history because Cardinal Bergoglio was to deliver a brief but electrifying talk that would cause many electors to think that maybe he was the right man to be pope.

IN THE ITALIAN PRESS, one of the more interesting articles came from Marco Politi, who in 1997 coauthored with Carl Bernstein *His Holiness: John Paul II and the History of Our Time.*

"Habemus Conclave in the hands of the undecided," Politi headlined his article in *Il Fatto Quotidiano.* While he confidently reported that after more than 110 interventions in the weeklong General Congregations "the contest is now between Scola and Scherer, as we wrote immediately after the resignation of BXVI," he nevertheless injected a note caution because "the greater part of the 'independents' are still un-decided."

He noted that Scola depended on support from the former and current presidents of the Italian bishops' conference, Ruini and Bagnasco; several European cardinals, including Stanislaw Dziwisz, formerly John Paul II's secretary and now archbishop of Krakow; and some extra-Europeans impressed by his dialogue with Islam and his defense of the Church in the public square.

Politi claimed that Scherer, archbishop of São Paulo, former secretary general of the Brazilian bishops' conference and secretary adjunct of CELAM, is being backed by Bertone and "part" of the Curia's old-guard diplomats.

In addition to those two front-runners, he mentioned Ouellet as "something new," but observed that he has a cold temperament and clashed with clergy and laity in Quebec. He listed two other candidates as possible successors to Benedict: the "silent and reserved" Hungarian president of the European bishops' conference, Peter Erdo, who is a canon lawyer but not a communicator, and the jovial Braz de Aviz from Brazil, a John XXIII–like pastor, whom he thinks "could be the surprise of the conclave."

In *La Stampa*, Giacomo Galeazzi raised the possibility of an African pope and recalled that in 2004 Cardinal Ratzinger told a German TV station that "we are ready for a black pope." (He would not be the first, he noted, as three popes in the early centuries of Christianity were from the Roman Africa province.) He listed four possible Africans: Turkson, whose photo has appeared on the streets of Rome on posters, urging cardinals to vote for him; Monsengwo—perhaps the outstanding African candidate; Sarah and Napier, who are rarely mentioned.

IN AN UNUSUAL MOVE, *Corriere della Sera* polled its eight top reporters and commentators on Vatican affairs, including Luigi Accattoli, Gian Guido Vecchi, Massimo Franco, and Alberto Melloni, asking whom they considered the most likely to be elected pope. The poll assigned three votes to each one's first choice, two votes to the second choice, and one vote to the third choice.

It published the results, with photos, on page 5 of today's edition. Ten candidates were identified: Scola, Scherer, Ouellet, O'Malley, Ranjith, Robles Ortega, Sandri, Ravasi, Tagle, and Dolan. The surprising result: first, O'Malley (12 votes); second, Scherer (9 votes); third, Scola (8 votes).

Many cardinals would have read these and other press reports before they entered the ninth General Congregation this morning at 9:30 AM.

CARDINAL SODANO opened today's session by proposing that the cardinal electors take possession of their rooms at the Domus Santa Marta on the morning of March12, the day the conclave begins, starting at 7:00 AM. A majority approved his proposal. The rooms were then assigned by lot, in accordance with the provisions outlined in the apostolic constitution.

Having settled these practical matters, seventeen cardinals took the floor to speak, bringing the total number of interventions delivered so far to at least 133, according to Fr. Lombardi. He reported that subjects addressed today included expectations regarding the new pope, how to improve the service of the Roman Curia, and information regarding wider areas of Church life.

The archbishop of Buenos Aires, Jorge Mario Bergoglio, was one of the seventeen. He delivered[60] an unforgettable three-and-a-half-minute intervention in Spanish that catapulted him onto the radar screen of many electors. That speech is now considered as one of the decisive moments in the lead-in to the conclave, a turning point. He touched hearts, and many more cardinals began to see him as the candidate to succeed Benedict. Cardinal O'Malley, who was sitting behind him in the synod hall, recalled that moment much later. "Everybody had spoken about everything, and again about everything. But Bergoglio said something new and fresh. Cardinals took note."

The individual interventions are normally kept secret, but we know what Bergoglio said because Cardinal Jaime Lucas Ortega y Alamino, the archbishop of Havana, Cuba, asked him for the text that same day. Since Bergoglio didn't have a proper script, just some bullet points in his small handwriting, he could not give it to him immediately, but promised he would do so later. After the election, Ortega obtained Pope Francis's permission to share that text with a wider public. He read it at Mass in Havana Cathedral on March 23, and three days later published it the diocesan newspaper (www.palabranueva.net). As would soon become clear, the speech was the blueprint for his papacy.

The following is the full text of Cardinal Bergoglio's discourse:

> Reference has been made to evangelization. It is the Church's reason for being. "The sweet and comforting joy of evangelizing" (Paul VI). It is Jesus Christ himself who drives us from within.
>
> 1. Evangelizing supposes Apostolic Zeal. Evangelizing presupposes a boldness ("parrhesia") in the Church to go out from herself. The Church is called to go out from herself and to go to the peripheries, not only geographically, but also the existential

peripheries: those of the mystery of sin, those of pain, those of injustice, those of ignorance and religious indifference, those of intellectual currents, and those of all misery.

2. When the Church does not go out from herself to evangelize, she becomes self-referential and then gets sick. (cf. The woman bent over on herself of the Gospel [Luke 13:10–17]). The evils that, over time, happen in ecclesial institutions have their root in self-referentiality. In the book of Revelation, however, Jesus says that he is at the door and knocks [Rev 3:20]. Obviously, the text refers to his knocking from the outside in order to enter... but I think about the times in which Jesus knocks from within so that we let him out. The self-referential Church seeks to keep Jesus Christ within herself and does not let him out.

3. When the Church is self-referential, inadvertently, she believes she has her own light; she ceases to be the *mysterium lunae* ["the mystery of the moon"] and gives way to that very serious evil which is spiritual worldliness (which according to de Lubac, is the worst evil that can befall the Church). Living to give glory to one another.

   Put simply, there are two images of Church: the evangelizing Church which goes out from herself, that of Dei Verbum *religiose audiens et fidente proclamans* [Latin, "which devoutly listens to the Word of God and proclaims it with faith"]; or the worldly Church that lives within herself, of herself, for herself. This should shed light on the possible changes and reforms which must be done for the salvation of souls.

4. Thinking of the next pope: [He must be] a man who, from the contemplation of Jesus Christ and the adoration of Jesus Christ helps the Church to go out to the existential peripheries, who helps her to be the fruitful mother, who lives from "the sweet and comforting joy of evangelizing."[61]

CARDINALS APPLAUDED when Bergoglio finished speaking. In his autobiography, *An English Spring*, Cardinal Murphy-O'Connor reported what happened next: "There was stillness when he sat down. I looked at the faces of the cardinals around me. Many were moved by what he said.

This was the moment, I think, when some of them began to wonder if they might not have heard the voice of the man who would lead the church to recover its vigor and give it a fresh sense of direction."

After the conclave, he told me, "It was one of the two most inspiring talks given during these General Congregations; the other was Tagle's."

Years later, Cardinal Óscar Rodríguez Maradiaga said: "The speech of the archbishop of Buenos Aires impressed us. Cardinal Bergoglio presented himself humbly, almost asking pardon for speaking, raising questions that were in the hearts of many of the cardinals, but which had not been faced up to that point."[62]

Cardinal Schönborn turned to a fellow cardinal who was near him and remarked, "That's what we need."[63] Cardinal Ortega described the speech as "magisterial, illuminating, committed and true."[64]

Significantly too, Cardinal Scola, the front-runner, went to the archbishop of Buenos Aires to shake his hand and compliment him for what he had said.

In an insightful comment, Austen Ivereigh later wrote, "Bergoglio was a once-in-a-generation combination of two qualities seldom found together: he had the political genius of a charismatic leader and the prophetic holiness of a desert saint."[65]

Not everyone, however, was moved by Bergoglio's speech. Cardinal Coccopalmerio told me later, "I don't remember it. That is, I don't remember exactly its content. It's a strange thing that I don't remember, but that's how it is."

Even after that powerful speech, one of Bergoglio's strong backers told me, "Bergoglio spoke well, very movingly, from the heart. But I think he's not really in with a chance; he's too old. Scola is very strong and is most likely to be elected."

THIS SATURDAY was clearly not a good day for the Roman Curia, as Andrea Tornielli reported in *La Stampa*.[66] Based on his deep-throat information, he said that several cardinals expressed strong criticism of the way the Curia is being managed and of the scandals and financial problems that have mushroomed in these years. They criticized too the excessive nomination of Italians to positions in the Curia under Benedict XVI; they pointed to problems related to the functioning of the Roman Curia offices ("dicasteries"), including the Secretariat of State.

According to *La Stampa* and other media, one of the strongest criticisms came from the Brazilian cardinal, João Braz de Aviz, who has been prefect of the Congregation for Institutes of Consecrated Life and Societies of Apostolic Life since January 2011. He pulled no punches when he criticized the way the Institute for the Works of Religion (the Vatican bank) was being managed. He went on to make a more general cutting critique of the Roman Curia, which greatly upset Cardinal Bertone and some other curial cardinals

I learned too from a cardinal elector that, to everyone's surprise, the eighty-four-year-old German Cardinal Karl Josef Becker, a theologian and professor at the Gregorian University who had been a consultor of the Congregation of the Doctrine of the Faith since 1977 and is close to Benedict XVI, "thrashed" or "clobbered" (*bastonato* in Italian) the Roman Curia.

AT THE END OF THE MORNING, the cardinals were informed that the Mass *"Pro eligendo Romano Pontifice"* (For the Election of the Roman Pontiff) will be held in Saint Peter's Basilica at 10:00 AM on Tuesday morning, March 12. It will be presided over by the cardinal dean, and all the cardinals are invited to concelebrate.

They were also informed that the entry to the conclave will begin at 4:30 PM that same afternoon, with a procession of cardinal electors from the Pauline Chapel to the Sistine Chapel. They were briefed too on the general schedule of daily procedures during the conclave.

The cardinal dean concluded today's session by announcing that the tenth and final General Congregation will be held on Monday morning, March 11. He added that many cardinals had already signed up to speak.

AT THE DAILY BRIEFING, Fr. Lombardi told the press that all the auxiliary personnel required for the smooth functioning of the conclave would take the oath of secrecy in the Pauline Chapel on Monday afternoon at 5:30 PM in the presence of the camerlengo.

He informed us that the "ring of the fisherman," which Benedict XVI wore and which exists in two forms—as a ring and as a stamp used to seal documents—have been destroyed, together with two other stamps and the master lead seal that is used for papal documents. He explained that the images on these items were scratched out in the form of a cross with a burin (a chisel-like graving tool).

He announced that the new ring of the fisherman for the next pope would bear the identical image of Peter casting his net but will have the new pontiff's name inscribed above the image.

Fr. Lombardi also revealed that a commission has been set up that will work under the direction of the camerlengo to seal the entrances to the areas of the conclave and conduct other operations necessary for the safeguarding of that event.

He informed reporters that the chimney that will release the *fumata* (smoke) from the conclave was installed by Vatican firemen this morning on the top of the Sistine Chapel. He explained that during the conclave "if the smoke is released after dark, a spotlight will be trained on the chimney so that it can still be seen." (In actual fact, ever-alert TV producers and photographers had already spotted the chimney this morning and had transmitted images across the globe.)

WHILE THE CARDINALS were at the General Congregation this morning, we journalists were given a special viewing of the Sistine Chapel, now almost ready for the conclave. A wooden platform covers the floor to eliminate the steps, and on either side of the chapel are two long rows of tables, one behind the other, a front row and a back row, covered with beige and Bordeaux fabric, and 115 cherry wood chairs, each with an elector's name on it, at which the cardinals will sit and write the name of the man they believe should be the next pope.

I tweeted two pictures: the first showed the two stoves and the flue that leads up to the chimney from where the black or white smoke will billow forth sending a signal to the world of the result of the voting; the second was a photo of the tables and chairs, ready for the cardinals to arrive.

As we left the Sistine Chapel, Irene Hernandez Velasquez, correspondent for *El Mundo*, surveyed fifteen Vaticanisti, including me, regarding the next pope.

She asked three questions:

1. What characteristics or qualities should the pope have?
2. Who do you think will be the next pope?
3. Who would you like to be the next pope?

She published answers from four of us in her paper as follows.[67]

– John Allen (*National Catholic Reporter*) said the new pope should have "a global vision and be a pastor"; he should "know how to govern and be capable of taking the reins of the situation and reforming the Curia." He predicted the conclave would choose Scola, or Ouellet, or Dolan. He did not have a preference.

- Andres Beltramo (Notimex) asserted that the new pope "should have been in charge of a large diocese and know the Curia well." He would "need physical and spiritual vigor" and "should be between sixty-five and seventy-five." He expected Scherer to be elected, "because he is Latin American," but he would like to see the conclave choose Ouellet "because he has all the requisites."

- Marco Politi (*Il Fatto Quotidiano*) thought the new pope "should open a debate in the Church and transform the synod of bishops into an organ of effective collaboration with the pope." He found it "very difficult" to predict who would be elected "because with votes any pre-fabricated candidate can be blocked." He had no preference.

- Gerard O'Connell (Vatican Insider) said the new pope "should be a spiritual figure, a saint," someone "who has an important pastoral track record," "the qualities of an administrator" and be able to "excite" people. He noted "much indecision" regarding the election, and while Scola, Scherer, and Ouellet are mentioned he said, "I believe that there could be a surprise." He would like to see Argentina's cardinal, Jorge Bergoglio, elected pope.

CARDINAL BERGOGLIO had lunch today with Cardinal Javier Lozano Barragán in the latter's apartment. "We have been friends for thirty years, and he brought me a pair of slippers as a gift," the Mexican cardinal later told Televisa in an interview with his friend, longtime Vatican correspondent Valentina Alazraki. There were a few other Mexican cardinals at the lunch, together with Rodríguez Maradiaga (Honduras), and Amigo Vallejo, OFM (Spain). All were electors except Barragán who turned eighty on January 26. As Bergoglio was leaving, Sr. Maria Stella, one of the nuns who cares for Barragán, must have had a sudden premonition. "Eminence," she said, "if you become pope you must invite us to a celebration in the Vatican!" Bergoglio laughed, not taking it seriously, but he promised he would do so if that unlikely event should come to pass.[68]

A NON-EUROPEAN ELECTOR, who tells me he is "still undecided," says he is looking through the biographies of each of the electors, which, he says, are much better than those prepared for the 2005 conclave. He believes the ones who are now the front-runners may not pull through, and says Scola and Scherer are paralyzing themselves. He doesn't think any Asian or African will emerge. He thinks the conclave could take some time.

Another non-European elector tells me they are looking for "a man of God," and adds, "one can find managers anywhere, but men of God are less easy to find." He too doesn't believe Scola has forty votes, as *La Repubblica* is stating; "maybe he's got twenty to thirty," he muses. He reveals that more cardinals are now beginning to mention Bergoglio's name. He too thinks the conclave could take some time.

AS THE DAY CLOSES, John Raphael Quinn, the emeritus archbishop of San Francisco and author of the groundbreaking book *The Reform of the Papacy*, speaking at Stanford University, says this week's conclave has the potential to be one of the most critical moments in the history of the Church since the Reformation. The cardinals "need to see themselves and the whole Catholic Church poised at a moment of far-reaching consequences."[69]

MARCH 10 (SUNDAY) _____

Front-runners in the Spotlight

FOLLOWING A LONG-STANDING ROMAN TRADITION, on the Sunday before they enter the conclave the cardinal electors celebrate Mass in their titular churches across the city. These are the churches that the pope assigned to them at the consistory after he gave them the red hat and cardinal's ring. (On becoming cardinals they automatically become pastors of the Rome diocese too.)

These Masses have always attracted much media attention, particularly those celebrated by front-runners or other *papabili*, and this is even more the case in the new age of social communications. Hordes of photographers and reporters with TV cameras descended on the churches where the cardinals celebrated to get a sense of the *papabili* and to hear what they might have to say about the conclave. The faithful of those parish churches, and fellow nationals of the cardinals, came in great numbers to pray for—and perhaps greet—the man who could be the next pope.

There was a media scramble as Cardinal Scola arrived to celebrate mass at 9:00 AM in the Basilica of the Santi Apostoli (the basilica of the twelve apostles), close to Piazza Venezia. Pope Julius I had a church built here in the fourth century. Then in the sixth century Pelagius I built another on the ruins of the first one. This second church was destroyed by an earthquake in 1348 but later restored by Martin V in 1417. Now under the care of the Conventual Franciscans, the basilica is close to the Jesuit-run Gregorian University and Biblical Institute where many future church leaders from all continents —including many of the cardinals in this conclave—have been educated,

Preaching on the Gospel of the day—the story of the prodigal son (otherwise known as the story of the merciful father)—the tall, heavily built, bespectacled cardinal-archbishop of Milan told his large Italian congregation that "the mission of the Church is to announce always the mercy of God, even to the sophisticated and lost people of the new millennium." He referred to "the limits" and "the sins" of members of the Church and said that only in Jesus, who "took on himself our evil," can it find the strength to announce God's mercy. He concluded by asking the faithful to pray to God for the cardinals in conclave, because the Church needs "a holy pastor" who knows how "to build the Church with the witness of his life," one who can follow "in the footsteps of the great popes of the last 150 years." The timeframe was significant; it was a reference to the period from the end of the Church's temporal power in Italy in 1870 to the present day.

Corriere della Sera, which is published in Milan, naturally gave wide coverage to Scola on its website and in the next day's edition, but it also gave visibility to Scherer. Like other Italian media, it was convinced that the choice in the conclave lay between Scola and Scherer, or to use a football image—between Italy and Brazil. Nevertheless, it seemed confident that the cardinal of Milan would bring the papacy back to Italy after a lapse of thirty-five years.

Since Elisabetta reports for *La Nación*, the Argentine daily, and Bergoglio had decided not to offer Mass in his titular church, she attended Cardinal Scherer's Mass at 10:30 AM at the church of Sant' Andrea al Quirinale. Located next to the Quirinal Palace, the residence of the president of Italy and former summer residence of the popes, the church was designed by Bernini and completed by 1661. It is an important example of Roman Baroque architecture.

The archbishop of São Paulo has been getting considerable media coverage throughout Latin America, and especially in Brazil, as Elisabetta knew from her friend Alberto Armendáriz, the correspondent for *La Nación* in Rio de Janeiro. Not surprisingly then, when Scherer arrived for Mass at the church, Brazilians and Italians alike shouted out, "He's the new pope!" He smiled and pretended not to hear. Originally built for the Jesuit seminary in this area, this church is still run by the Jesuits; Fr. Giovanni La Manna, the Jesuit director of the city's Centre Astalli that assists refugees, concelebrated with Scherer. La Manna began the Mass by welcoming the cardinal: "The Church needs a pope who is close to God and to people, a spiritual man, capable of leading the Church with true charity." He greeted Cardinal Scherer as "a true witness" in this sense.

Having spent many years in Rome, the Brazilian cardinal speaks Italian fluently. In his homily on the gospel story of the prodigal son he told the congregation, "We all have to ask forgiveness. Jesus did not come for the just but for the sinners." God wants "conversion of heart" and, for the future too, "reconciliation is needed." These last words were interpreted as an allusion to the current divisions in the Church. Referring to the upcoming conclave, he said, "We're all preparing for the conclave because we need to make the right decision to decide who is going to be the new pope." He told them, "We need to trust the Church. This is a beautiful moment in the life of the Church. People from all around the world are following what we are doing with joy and hope."

Later, as he distributed communion in front of the TV cameras and photographers, a host fell from his hand to the ground, but he picked it up and carried on unperturbed. At the end of Mass, he blessed an elderly couple who were celebrating seventy years of married life together.

Later that Sunday, Scherer drove to Assisi "to pray at the tomb of Saint Francis to ask God to inspire the election of the pope" and, in an interview after the conclave[70] he disclosed that in the lead-up to the conclave he had tried to avoid any kind of outside influence and so "I did not read the newspapers, nor did I take notice of messages."

CARDINAL OUELLET DECIDED to celebrate Mass at 6:30 PM in his titular church of Santa Maria in Transpontina, on the Via della Conciliazione that leads to Saint Peter's. Pope Sixtus V designated it as a titular church on April 13, 1587, and tonight it was under the spotlight of the international media.

The cardinal's decision fitted in nicely with the agenda of CTV, because it had scheduled an editorial board meeting that Sunday morning in preparation for the conclave. We reviewed our plans then and I again strongly advised the editors in Toronto to have a bio ready not just for the three front-runners—Scola, Scherer, and Ouellet—but also for Cardinal Bergoglio, whom I believed had a real chance.

Torrential rain was pouring down that evening as Cardinal Ouellet arrived for Mass. This was big news in Canada, and so of course I was there with the CTV crew. But we were only one of about fifty other media units also present. The Carmelite fathers who are in charge of the church struggled hard to make way for the cardinal through the crowd of cameramen, photographers, and reporters. It is not a big church by Roman standards, but it was packed to capacity this evening. Among those in the crowd was Anne Leahy, Canada's former distinguished ambassador to the Holy See, who is now serving as acting ambassador for the conclave until the government in Ottawa appoints a new ambassador.

Like all the cardinals, Ouellet preached on the parable of the prodigal son and reminded those present that "no one is ever abandoned by the mercy of God." He called for unity in the Church and told those present that "the Lord never ceases to come to meet us and to walk the road that separates us from him: every man can enter into communion with God." He concluded with this invitation to the faithful: "Let us pray that the Holy Spirit will indicate to the College of Cardinals the one whom God has already chosen." As he left the altar at the end of Mass, he waved somewhat timidly to the reporters.

ANOTHER *PAPABILE*, much-liked by the Romans, is Boston's Seán Patrick O'Malley. He too attracted much media attention when he came to celebrate Mass in the church of Our Lady of Victories (Santa Maria della Vittoria) on the Via XX Settembre. Built in 1605, the church was originally dedicated to Saint Paul for the Discalced Carmelites, but after the Catholic victory at the battle of White Mountain in 1620, which reversed the Reformation in Bohemia, it was rededicated to the Virgin Mary.

O'Malley likes this church, not because of the Turkish standards that were captured at the 1883 siege of Vienna and now hang on its walls as part of the theme of victory, but because it contains the Ecstasy of Saint Teresa, one of the masterpieces of the famous Italian sculptor and architect, Gian Lorenzo Bernini, who also designed Saint Peter's Square.

The Capuchin cardinal and former missionary bishop in the Virgin Islands is well known in Rome for preferring the Franciscan habit to the cardinal's robes. His presence this morning attracted a large congregation and a battery of TV cameras, photographers, and reporters. Interest had been heightened because this morning *Il Messaggero*, Rome's daily newspaper, ran an article in which it wondered whether O'Malley, who has been touted as *papabile*, could emerge from the conclave as Pope Francis I! He must surely have read this on his iPad before coming here, because he went out of his way to assure the congregation that after the conclave he would return to the small room in the diocesan seminary in Boston where he lives, ever since he sold the archbishop's residence to compensate victims of sexual abuse by priests.

In his homily on the gospel story of the prodigal son, he reminded everyone that for Jesus, the Good Shepherd, "every sheep is precious."

NEW YORK'S CARDINAL DOLAN too sparked lots of excitement when he arrived at the church of Our Lady of Guadalupe in the Monte Mario district of the city. When he first took possession of this church on October 12, 2012, he described Our Lady of Guadalupe as "the Empress of America" and said "her image is the most popular shrine at Saint Patrick's Cathedral in New York City! She will keep us together."

One thousand faithful managed to squeeze into the church for his Mass this morning, but the television camera operators, photographers, and reporters from all over the world were forced to wait outside, much to their annoyance. There was no room for them inside! Commenting on the parable of the prodigal son, Dolan told the congregation that because of God's mercy "we should all be particularly content." Ever ready to crack a joke or provoke a laugh, he confided that after Saint Patrick's Cathedral, New York, "this is the church I prefer, but don't tell that to the people of New York." He explained his preference: "Here I am what I want to be: a parish priest, a Roman parish priest, and as a parish priest of this city I will enter the conclave to choose a new bishop of Rome." His allusion to the conclave reminded those present of an incident some days earlier when a journalist informed him that the Italian media were saying he could be the next pope, Dolan quipped: "Have you been smoking marijuana?"

THE AUSTRIAN CARDINAL, Christoph Schönborn, also attracted the media and a packed church when he celebrated Mass in the church of the

Divin Lavoratore (the Divine Worker), that was built in 1955 in a work-ing-class area of the city. The cardinal, who is a member of the Domini-can order, is descended from a princely house. He was very close to Joseph Ratzinger long before he became pope; they worked together in the *Communio* review of theology and on the new Catechism of the Catholic Church. It came as no surprise, therefore, that in his homily he spoke about Benedict XVI's resignation. Describing it as "a gesture of humility" that had moved him to tears, he told his congregation that "the renewal" of the Church has started with this resignation. Then, looking ahead to the conclave, he reminded the faithful that "in a few days we will have the new pope. And I can say that in this week of meetings of the cardinals before the conclave I have experienced a spirit of fraternity rarely lived." He concluded by asking them to pray for the conclave, and added, "Get the children also to pray for the conclave; their voice will be listened to especially by God!"

THE GHANAIAN CARDINAL, Peter Turkson, was given a rapturous wel-come when he came to celebrate Mass at the church of San Liberio at Ponte Mammolo, on the periphery of Rome, which John Paul II blessed in 1998. In his homily, this humble, jovial cardinal, who is president of the Pontifical Council for Justice and Peace, emphasized that "the church exists to accompany humanity."

HUNDREDS OF SRI LANKAN MIGRANTS working in Rome, many of them victims of the twenty-six-year-long internal conflict in their homeland (1983–2009), flocked to the Mass celebrated by Cardinal Malcolm Ran-jith, the archbishop of Colombo, in the Basilica of San Lorenzo in Lu-cina. This enormous church traces its origins to the fourth century and is dedicated to Saint Lawrence the martyr and deacon. Damasus I, son of a man who later became priest of this church, was elected pope here in 366 and is also buried here.

In his homily, the polyglot, dark-skinned cardinal, who is very close to Benedict, reminded his fellow countrymen and women that "there is not just a God of justice, there is a God of forgiveness and mercy," and one should respond to the logic of an eye for an eye and a tooth for a tooth by turning the other cheek. He concluded by referring to the con-clave and said, "We are gathered to listen to the word of the Holy Spirit: he will inspire the choice of pope who is called to guide a church that has to give the world the great message of the love of God and his infinite mercy." There was loud applause at the end of his Mass.

NIGERIA'S FEARLESS, DYNAMIC CARDINAL, John Onaiyekan, archbishop of Abuja—the federal capital of this country of 171 million inhabitants— reminded his congregation that "we must bring joy to this world that is full of things, also ugly ones, but it is our world. The angels without sin are in paradise, we must bring peace among sinners."

SOME CARDINAL ELECTORS decided not to celebrate Mass in their titular churches today, including Tagle, Ravasi, and, as previously mentioned, Bergoglio.

True to character, the archbishop of Buenos Aires wanted to avoid the media circus and so celebrated Mass in private, for a small group of friends, at the Domus Paulus VI where he is staying.

Later that day, he went for lunch with the ninety-year-old sister of the late Archbishop Ubaldo Calabresi, the former nuncio in Argentina (1981–2000) who had played such an important role in his life and in his nomination as bishop.[71]

WITH THE CARDINALS SET to enter the conclave in two days, it is hardly surprising that speculation in the media has rocketed about who stands the best chance of being elected pope.

In *Le Figaro* today, Jean Marie-Guenois, analyzing the situation, concluded that the conclave "is more open than ever"; there is no clear favorite.

The Globe and Mail (Toronto) today reports that the US Jesuit, Fr. Thomas Reese, analyst with the *National Catholic Reporter*, has suggested a few reasons why there is no clear front-runner in the conclave: "One is that 24 of the 115 elector cardinals were appointed last year and the new-bies are still matching faces to bios—they probably don't know yet whom they are going to back. Another is that the 28 Italian elector cardinals, who could make or break the election if they were to vote as a bloc, are divided."

Associated Press (AP), the American news agency headquartered in New York, agreed with that assessment of uncertainty, and said, "The preliminaries over, Catholic cardinals are ready to get down to the real business of choosing a pope" and while there is no clear front-runner "there are indications they will go into the conclave Tuesday with a good idea of their top picks."

AP, which provides news to more than seventeen hundred newspapers and five thousand television and radio broadcasters across the globe, has been busy trying to identify the likely successor to Benedict, but it had to admit that "in the secretive world of the Vatican, there is no way to know who is in the running, and history has yielded plenty of surprises. Yet several names have come up repeatedly as strong contenders." Seeking to cover all eventualities, it listed a wide spread of fifteen names: Scola, Scherer, Ouellet, Erdo, Ravasi, Turkson, Dolan, Bergoglio, Sandri, Tagle, Schönborn, Ranjith, Maradiaga, Bagnasco, and O'Malley.

Like most other media, it said Scola "is seen as Italy's best chance at reclaiming the papacy" and "is one of the top names among all of the papal contenders," while Scherer is "Brazil's best hope" and, with Vatican experience, "is increasingly being touted as one of the top overall contenders." It presented Ouellet as "a favorite to become the first pontiff from the Americas" because of his Latin American and Vatican experience.

It said Erdo "is increasingly seen as a compromise candidate" if cardinals can't agree on one of the front-runners, while Ravasi is "one of the favorites among Catholics who long to see a return to the tradition of Italian popes." It noted that Turkson "is viewed by many" as "the top African contender" and "the social conscience of the church."

AP put Dolan on its list but said that "scholars question whether his charisma and experience are enough for a real shot at succeeding Benedict."

Profiling Bergoglio, AP noted that "he has long specialized in the kind of pastoral work that some say is an essential skill for the next pope" and "has shown a keen political sensibility as well as the kind of self-effacing humility that fellow cardinals value highly."

It described Sandri as "a Vatican insider who has run the day-to-day operations of the global church's vast bureaucracy and roamed the world as a papal diplomat."

It highlighted Tagle as "Asia's most prominent Roman Catholic leader [who] knows how to reach the masses," but rated his chances as "remote" because "many believe that Latin America or Africa—with their faster-growing Catholic flocks—would be more logical choices if the papal electors decided to look beyond Europe."

It portrayed Schönborn as "a soft-spoken conservative who is ready to listen to those espousing reform" and who "could appeal to fellow cardinals looking to elect a pontiff with the widest possible appeal," but said "electors may be reluctant to choose another German speaker as a successor to Benedict."

AP claimed that "there are many strikes against a Ranjith candidacy —Sri Lanka, for example, has just 1.3 million Catholics, less than half the population of Rome," but "the rising influence of the developing world, along with the 65-year-old's strong conservative credentials, helps keep his name in the mix of papal contenders."

It asserted that Maradiaga, on the other hand, "embodies the activist wing of the Roman Catholic Church as an outspoken campaigner of human rights, a watchdog on climate change and advocate of international debt relief for poor nations." But despite charges of supporting a coup and accusations of anti-Semitism, AP ranked him "among a handful of Latin American prelates considered to have a credible shot at the papacy."

In AP's view, Bagnasco, the archbishop of Genoa and head of the Italian bishops' conference, could have "outsize influence in the conclave, where Italians represent the biggest national bloc," but concluded that "his lack of international experience and exposure could be a major liability."

The fact that O'Malley is mentioned as a potential papal candidate, it reported, "is testament to his efforts to bring together an archdiocese at the forefront of the abuse disclosures," but they felt his papal prospects suffer because "many papal electors oppose the risk of having US global policies spill over, even indirectly, onto the Vatican's image."

THE UNCERTAINTY about who could be elected was also reflected in *La Stampa*, which identified eleven "strong candidates" in an article by Andrea Tornielli. He listed them in order of likelihood: Scola, Scherer, Dolan, Ouellet, Erdo, O'Malley, Robles Ortega, Bergoglio, Ranjith, Erdo, and Ravasi. Tornielli recognized there is no authoritative candidate, as Ratzinger was in 2005, and, based on the information he had gathered in recent days, he claimed the cardinals were looking for "a man of government who is able to dialogue and communicate and is spiritually deep."

Like everyone else, he acknowledged that "the true test" will come at around 6:00 PM (Rome time) in the Sistine Chapel on March 12 when the electors cast their vote in secret for the first time; the results then will reveal the true challengers to Scola. Meanwhile, according to his information, Scola's candidacy "was being consolidated," and Scherer would be the most likely challenger. Erdo, he noted, was among the strong candidates, but not in the first round. He advised readers to keep an eye on two other Latin American outsiders who could emerge if the conclave went on for a long time: Robles Ortega and Bergoglio.

His conclusion: if the conclave ends in the first two days, then one of the stronger candidates has won, whereas a longer election could bring surprises, and the outsiders could have a chance.

I SPOKE TO SEVERAL ELECTORS this afternoon and evening and got the distinct impression that neither Scola, nor Scherer, nor Ouellet will be elected. As one told me, "Scola is a scholar, too much of a scholar!" while Scherer "is too German for Latin America," and Ouellet "is too ordinary." Another said he detected "an air of anxiety" and believed that Scola, Scherer, and Ouellet could cancel each other out. He saw "no enthusiasm" for any other European, but confided that electors are beginning to look carefully at Bergoglio. A third elector told me, "Bergoglio's name is cropping up everywhere, including at coffee breaks"; cardinals from the different continents, not just Latin America but also Asia and Africa, now have him on their radar.

CARDINAL BERGOGLIO went for dinner this evening at Gianni Valente's. Gianni's wife Stefania Falasca cooked. They had both met Bergoglio in Argentina when they were with Communion and Liberation and interviewed him for the movement's journal, *Trenta Giorni*. "Since then, he has been a friend of the family, and he would come to visit us every time he was in Rome," Stefania told *La Repubblica* after the conclave. "We saw him for the last time not long before he entered the conclave; he came to dinner. We never imagined that he would become the new pope." Lucio Brunelli and Andrea Tornielli were also present that evening.[72] I learned later that the four journalists were all sad, because they were convinced that Scola would be elected.

That evening too, Fr. Tom Rosica and Sebastian Gomes from Salt and Light had just eaten a pizza together and were on their way back to the Jesuit Curia where they were staying when they happened to meet Bergoglio walking through Piazza Navona. Rosica later reported that when he asked the cardinal if he was nervous, the Argentinian replied, "a little" and then quickly, before moving on, asked them to "pray for me!"

IN ITS POST-CONCLAVE ANALYSIS, the *Wall Street Journal* got it right when it said that "by March 10 a new narrative was taking hold among the cardinals. Jorge Mario Bergoglio was now a contender." Few had noticed that an underground shift was taking place inside the College of Cardinals, bringing Bergoglio to the fore. The Italian media never picked up on it.

MARCH 11 (MONDAY)
THE SIXTH AND FINAL DAY
OF THE GENERAL CONGREGATIONS _____
Cardinals Have Their Final Say

AS THEY PREPARED to go into the synod hall this morning for the final session of the General Congregations, many cardinals would have read or received press reports not only on what the front-runners had said at Mass yesterday but also the latest speculation in the Italian and international media regarding the candidates considered most likely to succeed Benedict XVI—speculation that was for the most part based on conversations with cardinals or those close to them.

La Stampa carried photos of four cardinals on its front page—Scola, Scherer, Dolan, and Ouellet—under the headline: "Scola in the lead, but with half the quorum." In an accompanying article, under the subtitle, "Ouellet shoots up among the rivals of Scola," Andrea Tornielli reported "what seems an already consolidated fact" that Scola would get "a good number of votes, some say thirty-five, others forty" on the first ballot. He predicted that Scherer would get some twenty-five votes, and Ouellet around twelve (from the United States and Latin America backers). He expected Dolan, O'Malley, and Ranjith to get "some votes" and said, "It is not to be excluded" that Bergoglio and Tagle could also get some votes.

He highlighted the uncertainty surrounding this conclave by quoting Cardinal Barbarin, who said that while at the 2005 conclave Ratzinger "stood out as three or four times superior to all the other cardinals, this is not the case now. Therefore, the choice has to be made on one, two, three, four…[even] twelve candidates. Right now, we know nothing, we have to wait at least until the results of the first ballot." The cardinal-archbishop of Paris, André Armand Vingt-Trois, appeared to share this view; speaking to another reporter, he referred to "half a dozen candidates."

Corriere della Sera's expert on Vatican affairs, Gian Guido Vecchi, reported that at most the leading candidates could have around thirty votes, and contended that many electors "keep two or three options." He expected three or four options to emerge in the first ballot, including Scola ("supported more by the Europeans than the Italians"), Ouellet and Scherer ("supported by the Curia"), and one of the three United States cardinals: Dolan, Wuerl, or O'Malley. He anticipated that, given their close ties, the Europeans and Americans could agree to "converge" their votes on one of their candidates. In the case of a stalemate, he thought that Robles Ortega, Erdo, Schönborn, or even an African or Asian candidate could emerge.

CORRIERE DELLA SERA today highlighted an astounding fact, that the northern Italian region of Lombardy has six electors in this conclave: Coccopalmerio, Nicora, Ravasi, Re, Scola, and Tettamanzi. This means that Lombardy has more electors than any of the forty-eight countries from five continents represented at the conclave, with the exceptions of Germany, which also has six, Italy with twenty-eight (including the six from Lombardy), and the United States with eleven.

IN HIS CLOSELY WATCHED NCR COLUMN, John Allen also analyzed the situation on March 11 and wrote: "At the moment the consensus seems to be that three candidates could have significant support when the cardinals cast their first ballot on Tuesday evening: Scola, backed by a number of Europeans and some Americans, who profiles as the best insider/outsider combination to turn over a new leaf in the Vatican; Ouellet, an intellectual disciple of Benedict XVI with deep ties to the Americas, both North and South; and Scherer of Brazil, who would bring on board many Latin Americans as well as Vatican veterans who remember him from his stint at the Congregation for Bishops."

Allen added that many Vatican-watchers believe a couple of US cardinals could be in the running too: Timothy Dolan and Seán Patrick O'Malley, but early voting could eliminate one of them, or they could continue to split the vote for an "American pope." He envisaged that if none of the above seemed capable of obtaining the two-thirds majority, then several other options could come into focus with Schönborn, Ranjith, Bergoglio, Tagle, Erdo, and Ravasi as possibilities.

His conclusion: "If we have a pope by Wednesday night, the best places to watch for celebrations will be Milan, Quebec City, and São Paulo."

JOHN THAVIS, former Catholic News Service (CNS) bureau chief in Rome, had also picked up rumors that Bergoglio could be a contender, but not even he understood that the Argentinian had become a front-runner. He wrote in his blog on March 11: "In the last few days, some serious voices have mentioned Cardinal Bergoglio as a contender in the coming conclave. Not simply because he came in second the last time around, but because he impressed cardinals when he took the floor in the pre-conclave meetings that began last week. His words left the impression that even at age 76, Bergoglio had the energy and the inclination to do some house-cleaning in the Roman Curia." His conclusion: "This conclave has multiple contenders but no real front-runner, and it's quite possible that if early voting produces a stall, the College of Cardinals could once again turn to Cardinal Bergoglio as someone who would bring key changes but without an extra-long reign." Few gave credence to his report.

ALL THIS, AND MUCH MORE was in the public domain as 152 cardinals entered the synod hall this Monday morning for the tenth and final General Congregation. Again, in accordance with the norms, three were chosen by lot to assist the camerlengo for the next three days in the lesser affairs of the proceedings.[73]

The cardinals spent little time in preliminaries today as many wanted to take their last opportunity to speak. Twenty-eight cardinals took the microphone, bringing the total number of interventions to 160. Cardinal Sodano proposed an afternoon session if others wanted to speak, but the majority voted to conclude by lunch time.

AT HIS DAILY BRIEFING, Fr. Lombardi reported that Cardinal Bertone, in his role as president of the Commission of Cardinals for oversight of the Institute for the Works of Religion (IOR, the Vatican bank), gave "a concise" report about the nature of the institute, its service to the Holy See and the Church, and the process now under way to ensure its insertion into the international system of controls (that is, Moneyval, a monitoring body of the Council of Europe) that work against money-laundering and the financing of terrorism.

Under questioning from journalists, Lombardi admitted that many cardinals had asked for clarity about recent events at the Vatican bank. He emphasized, however, that these money issues are not the key criteria for choosing the next pope; the cardinals, including many foreign ones who want change in the Curia and the IOR, are looking for a spiritual leader, not an expert in countering money-laundering!

Summarizing the seven days of the General Congregations, the ever-patient Lombardi, whom many consider "a saint," told reporters it had become "unequivocally clear that the main task of the new pope is to be first and foremost one of evangelization: to fulfill the command of Jesus to bring the Good News to all peoples and to baptize them." But to achieve this, he said, the cardinals felt "it is necessary" that the new pope should "promote great collegiality in the Church, bring about a radical reform of the Roman Curia and of Vatican finances, and examine whether the Vatican really needs a bank."

It was an interesting wrap-up. But as we learned from the leaks to the Italian media, and as I did from other sources, there has been some forthright talk during the General Congregations, and there have even been heated interventions regarding the Roman Curia, the Vatican bank, and Vatican finances in general, along with numerous calls for a reform of the Roman Curia. This remained true in the case of this very last session, which made it clear, as the 115 electors prepared to enter the conclave, that the winds of change were blowing strongly.

IN THESE PAST DAYS, according to various sources, Cardinal Bertone, whose role as secretary of state ended on February 28 with Benedict's resignation, felt hurt by the implicit and sometimes explicit criticism of how the Roman Curia and the IOR were managed, especially in the last two turbulent years, under the former pope's administration in which he had the lead role.

While Cardinal Becker's razor-sharp criticism last Saturday did not reach the press, Cardinal Braz de Aviz's hard intervention did, and Bertone was furious. Not always known as one to turn the other cheek, Benedict's right-hand man gave vent to his feelings this morning by harshly criticizing Braz de Aviz's intervention and even insinuating that the Brazilian himself may have leaked the story to the press!

That was just too much for Cardinal Braz de Aviz, who has carried fragments of bullets in his body since 1983, when he was caught in the crossfire between police and bandits in the diocese of Apuccarana. Feeling he could not let this accusation pass, he demanded the right to reply and Cardinal Sodano granted it. The Brazilian flatly denied Bertone's allegation that he had leaked the information and suggested instead that perhaps "the organization"—by which he meant the old guard in the Curia—had passed the news to the press. Many cardinals applauded. It was the strongest signal yet that they had had more than enough of the way things had been run in the Vatican under Bertone and his team; they now demanded real change; they wanted a cleanup and transparency in all Vatican finances as well as a reform of the Curia. "It was so obvious that something had to change," Cardinal Kasper commented much later.[74]

The fireworks had not ended, however. Without considering the personal consequences, Cardinal Scherer spoke out strongly in defense of the Roman Curia. He did so by drawing on his personal experience as a member of the commission of five cardinals tasked with overseeing the IOR and as a member of the council of fifteen cardinals that oversees the management of Vatican finances and the organization of the Roman Curia. His intervention revealed beyond the shadow of a doubt that he was not the candidate for change. With that speech, he destroyed whatever chances he had of being elected—and they were already few, as several cardinals told me later.

Cardinal Re, who had spent most of his life in positions of power in the Roman Curia and was a backer of Scherer, surprised not a few cardinals by stating clearly that he too firmly believed the Curia must change. This was a highly significant remark from a man who has spent so many years of his life in the Roman Curia and who would soon preside over the conclave. It was another signal that Scherer's candidacy was doomed. Most cardinals wanted change.

CARDINAL MURPHY-O'CONNOR, who had already spoken twice at the General Congregations and had, in his first speech, emphasized the need for the new pope "to build bridges," now asked to address his fellow cardinals one last time; over eighty years old, he would not be present inside the conclave. Cardinal Sodano, with whom he has been on friendly terms for many years, granted his wish. Then, in what one cardinal later described to me as "a final pitch," the English cardinal told the electors: "You are going to elect a pope. I will not be there with you, but I will pray for you." Describing the kind of pope that in his view the Church needs today, he said, "We need a pope who goes out to the world, and not just one who is looking in on the situation in the Church." He concluded with an appeal from the heart: "If you don't see a candidate here in Europe, don't be afraid to go to another continent, to cross the Atlantic to the Americas where there's [been] a Catholic tradition for many centuries, and don't let age be a barrier to your choice." Many understood he was referring to Bergoglio.

THIS WAS THE FINAL MEETING of all the cardinals, both electors and non-electors, before the conclave, and there seemed to be agreement that the General Congregations had proved fruitful and enlightening. And, overall, a generally fraternal spirit had prevailed, even if, as one elector told me, "it was in many ways like a synod, but many good things came out."

O GLOBO TV, BRAZIL, in its news report today from Rome, highlighted that the Brazilian Scherer, a moderate conservative, was "among the favorites," along with Scola and O'Malley.[75]

In a post-conclave comment on the spirit that prevailed in the week-long General Congregations, Cardinal Scherer told *Il Giornale*,[76] "I got to know many persons "on the ball" (*in gamba*), and it gave me immense joy to see that there are cardinals of great stature in the local churches." He recalled that in the plenary sessions "we spoke with openness and frankness about all the questions about the life of the Church which the new pope has to take account of. It was an experience of truth, responsibility, serenity, and brotherhood, knowing well that the Church is not only on the shoulders of the pope but of everyone."

LOOKING BACK at these General Congregations, Cardinal Maradiaga, who played an important role in getting cardinals to opt for Bergoglio, later said, "In those days we spoke about the need to make the Vatican and the Church still more collegial and universal, and how to face the wound of the persecution of Christians in the world, about [the need for] interventions in the IOR, reform of the Roman Curia, and many other things, including freemasonry, lobbies, and Vatileaks."[77] These assemblies, he noted, "were lived by us cardinals called to elect the next pope, with that spirit, a spirit of service to the universal Church to find a worthy successor of Benedict XVI who could heal the wounds of the Church hit by various scandals."[78]

ONE OF THE MAIN PURPOSES of the General Congregations was to get a clear, in-depth picture of the situation in the Church and in the world today, and identify the principal challenges and tasks facing the future pope. The other, equally important one was to identify the kind of candidate who could best respond to these challenges and lead the world's 1.2 billion Catholics in the rapidly changing world of the twenty-first century. By Monday, March 11, the cardinals seemed satisfied that they had gone a long way to achieving both objectives. Now it was up to the electors to choose the 266th successor of Saint Peter.

FROM THE INFORMATION at my disposal I understood that many cardinals were still uncertain about whom to cast their vote for in the first ballot.

While thirty-four of the forty-seven countries represented in the conclave had only one elector each, eleven—Argentina, Brazil, Canada, India, Italy, France, Germany, Mexico, Nigeria, Spain, the United States, Poland, and Portugal—had more than one.

The Italians with twenty-eight electors were the biggest voting bloc, but everyone knew they were deeply divided about Scola. Several had opted for Bergoglio, while a small number backed Ouellet or Scherer.

The eleven American electors appeared to be mostly in favor of Ouellet, at least at the start. Like their fellow electors, they too had fallback choices.

The six German electors were divided too, and it was no secret that Kasper, Lehmann, and Marx were not on the same page as Cordes and Meisner. Woelki was in between. My friend Ludwig Ring Eifel, head of the German Catholic News Agency (CIC) told me several years later[79] that when he met Cardinal Lehmann before the conclave and asked him, "Have you a name in mind?" Lehmann answered: "I have four." Ludwig asked: Scola? "No!" Ouellet? "Not really." Scherer? "No!" O'Malley? "No!" He didn't ask if Bergoglio was one of the four, but he knew that a lay group in Germany had suggested his name to Lehmann, saying, "Bergoglio would be a good choice." Later he learned that Bergoglio had not appeared on Lehmann's radar in the 2013 conclave until after the second ballot.

The five Spanish electors were not of the same mind either.

India's five cardinal electors, like Brazil's five, seemed largely united and impressed by Bergoglio, particularly after his speech. The other Asians could take their lead from them.

France's four electors were divided, while Poland's four electors were thought to be united behind Scola. Mexico and Canada had three electors each, but it was still unclear where they were moving. Argentina, Nigeria, and Portugal each had two.

Although the eleven African electors had not met as a group before the conclave, from their discernment in these days many were convinced that Bergoglio was best qualified to be next pope.

AFTER THE GENERAL CONGREGATION this morning, Cardinals Bergoglio, Abril y Castelló, and Cañizares went to pray in Saint Peter's Basilica, and there they happened to meet Cardinal Amigo. Cañizares, known as "the little Ratzinger," invited them to lunch in his apartment in Piazza della Citta Leonina. Abril y Castelló and Bergoglio have known each other since the Spaniard was nuncio in Argentina (2000–2003). The lunch was a frugal one, since it was a Friday in Lent: a simple broth soup, fish, and fruit. As I learned from Paloma Garcia Ovejero,[80] the Spanish correspondent for Radio COPE, while the cardinals did not discuss names over lunch, they all agreed that the next pope should be a "Saint Francis of Assisi type" person, with love for the poor; he should possess a sense of humor and have a "religious" outlook that rejects the "them vs. us" mentality.

DURING THE PRE-CONCLAVE PERIOD, the Americans used to meet every day to discuss the General Congregations and to share information. Cardinals George and Dolan took the leading roles, with Wuerl adopting a more reserved stance.

After the conclave, the *Wall Street Journal* quoted George as saying, "We came into this process thinking the next pope had to be vigorous and probably younger and there you have a man who isn't young, he's seventy-six years old. The question is: does he have vigor?"

CARDINAL TOPPO PHONED at lunch time to ask if I could assist him that afternoon with a video interview that he had agreed to do with a young couple who are running an "adopt a cardinal" campaign, inviting people to adopt and pray for a cardinal in advance of the conclave. The campaign has been running for weeks and tens of thousands of people have been assigned a cardinal. The Indian cardinal felt a little uneasy, so he asked me to be present as his press advisor. I went to the convent where he was staying and was present throughout the interview, which went very well indeed.

Afterwards, we chatted over tea about the upcoming conclave and I came to understand that the situation was "still not clear."

THE *BOSTON GLOBE* today reported that a new app called "Conclave" has been created by Logos Bible Software, a major vendor of digital products for religious folk, "to let us track the proceedings from start to finish." It has an interface "that links users to the latest news about the papal selection conclave," as well as links to videos from Rome, and it points to the best Catholic news sites. It provides a Twitter feed "that singles out tweets relating to the selection process—even tweets that make fun of the whole thing," and offers "a section with mini-biographies of the cardinals and a numerical 'buzz' ranking that attempts to estimate the popularity and influence of each man."

THE COUNTDOWN TO THE CONCLAVE has started. This afternoon, some ninety people—"auxiliary personnel involved in the care of the coming conclave"—took the oath of secrecy in the Pauline Chapel, a ceremony presided over by the camerlengo. These included the secretary of the College of Cardinals, Archbishop Lorenzo Baldisseri; the master of the Liturgical Celebrations of the Supreme Pontiff, Msgr. Guido Marini and other masters of pontifical ceremonies; the religious who supervise the pontifical sacristy; the religious priests charged with hearing confessions in the various languages; doctors and nurses; the personnel for preparing meals and cleaning; the staff of florists and technical service personnel; drivers responsible for transporting the cardinal electors from the Domus Santa Marta to the Apostolic Palace.

AS I WAS RETURNING HOME that evening after taking part in an eve-of-the-conclave program on CTV from the platform on top of the Augustinian house overlooking Saint Peter's Square, I happened to meet Matilde

Burgos, a Chilean journalist whom I have known since the 2005 conclave and who is working for CNN Chile. She was standing at the intersection between Via Paolo VI and Via Borgo Santo Spirito, across the street from Bernini's colonnades and Saint Peter's Square. She had placed her computer on the low wall at the corner of the intersection and was preparing her text for transmission. We started chatting.

She is close to Cardinal Francisco Javier Errázuriz Ossa, who has been a major figure in the Latin American church in these years. Elected president of the Chilean bishops' conference (1998–2004), he was made a cardinal by John Paul II in 2001. He was elected president of CELAM— the Latin American Episcopal Council, in 2003, a post he held until 2007.

Matilde, who has been close to his family, surprised me by asking if I thought Bergoglio had a chance of being pope. She revealed that when she had asked the Chilean cardinal about the likely candidates to be pope, he had mentioned the Argentinian's name. And when she remarked, "Isn't he too old?" Cardinal Errázuriz responded, "Four years of Bergoglio would be enough to change things!"

Since she was aware that Elisabetta and I both know Bergoglio, she wanted my opinion on whether he stood a chance of being pope. I responded: "Yes, this is a possibility, but there's still a lot of uncertainty, and so it's difficult to predict what will happen in the conclave."

THE BRAZILIAN JOURNALIST Gerson Camarotti wrote on that same evening, March 11, that it was becoming clear that the Latin American cardinals were not going to vote for Scherer on the first ballot. Camarotti discovered "strong resistance" to him from cardinals in Mexico, Argentina, and other countries on the continent. From conversations with "influential prelates" in the Vatican, he had come to understand that at the eleventh-hour Bergoglio's candidacy was being launched. Late that evening, a source in the Holy See assured him that "age" was not an impediment to his becoming pope and added, "Cardinal Bergoglio is one of the few that could capitalize on this sentiment for change."[81]

ELISABETTA SPOKE WITH BERGOGLIO that afternoon and said she hoped to meet him again for her birthday on March 15. We decided to write him a short letter of good wishes before he entered the conclave. We handed it in at the reception desk of the Domus Sacerdotalis Paulus VI at around 9:30 PM. I didn't want to disturb him by phoning.

In my heart, I wanted to tell him: "If God calls you, do not say no!" but I didn't write that. I didn't want to make him nervous. Instead, we assured him of our prayers and good wishes, and said we looked forward to meeting him again after the conclave.

NINE MONTHS AFTER THE CONCLAVE, on December 26, 2013, Elisabetta and I learned from Clare (whom the Italians called Chiara), a consecrated lay woman from the island of Tonga, Polynesia, that on that last Monday night before entering the conclave Cardinal Bergoglio ate dinner alone at the Domus Paulus VI. Maybe his thoughts went back to 1958 when, on this same day, he first entered the Society of Jesus to become a Jesuit.

Chiara was a member of the Third Order of Carmelites, and one of the managers at the Domus. She had known Bergoglio since before the 2005 conclave. He used to call her "Madre Badessa" ("Mother Abbess"). She got to know him well over the years and assured us, "He is a saint." She revealed that he never wanted people to serve him, unlike the many other prelates who have stayed there over the years. Moreover, she disclosed that one of the cleaning ladies at the Domus told her that "he is the only priest who makes his own bed."

Chiara recalled that on the eve of the conclave when he came into the dining hall, the first two tables were full, so he went to the third table on the left and sat there all alone. "He looked worried," she recalled. "He didn't have the tranquil look that he always used to have." She got the feeling—"it was a sensation"—that he would be elected pope. So, she told him, "You will not come back here!" But he responded, "I'll return on Thursday." And so he did—as pope—to thank all the staff individually, to pay his bill, and to pick up his few belongings from his room.

THAT SAME MONDAY EVENING, as Bergoglio was eating alone in the Domus, the Italian and Roman Curia cardinal, Attilio Nicora,[82] was hosting a crucial meeting of cardinals in his Vatican apartment.[83] A priest of the archdiocese of Milan, Nicora worked in the Vatican from 1992 to 2011 as chief financial officer administering Vatican properties. In 2011, Benedict XVI appointed him president of the Vatican's Financial Information Authority.

At the gathering in Nicora's apartment there were around fifteen or more from many countries and different continents, including Roman

Curia cardinals and Italians. All, it turned out, were supporting Bergoglio's candidacy. At least five were from Italy: Nicora, Antonelli, Bertello, Coccopalmerio, and Poletto. There were other Europeans too, including Brady, Kasper, Tauran, and Murphy-O'Connor (the only non-elector). Most significantly of all, perhaps, there were three key figures from Latin America, Africa and Asia: Maradiaga, Turkson, and Gracias. It was noteworthy, however, that there was no American cardinal among them.

During the meeting, each one confirmed or revealed that he had decided to support Bergoglio on the first ballot, and also mentioned other cardinals that he believed were thinking along the same lines and could vote for him then.

When they had all given their input, Coccopalmerio, who was keeping a tally of what was being declared, added up the numbers. The result showed that Bergoglio had at least twenty-five votes. They concluded the evening knowing that Bergoglio would enter the conclave with between twenty and thirty votes. "It was crucial that he had that support in the first ballot," the English cardinal told me later; he understood this after his experience at the 2005 conclave.

Indeed, no fewer than three participants confirmed to me that "this was the decisive meeting."

Nevertheless, as one of the electors told me, there was still uncertainty even after that evening meeting; nobody knew for certain what would happen on the first ballot.

When, more than three years later, I asked Cardinal Kasper about that meeting,[84] he confirmed that "two days before the conclave, there was a small group from different countries, not just Italians, but also some from the Vatican, and they said we should go for Bergoglio. Then it was clear for me. Beforehand it was very unsure, but his intervention in the pre-conclave meetings had been very important; his speech made a great impact."

The following year,[85] when I told Coccopalmerio that I knew about that meeting and asked if they were all convinced that last night that Bergoglio was the candidate to be pope, he responded, "That's difficult to say. It was a good hypothesis, but it was difficult for me to understand if they were all on board. Yes, that night we knew there was a bloc of persons supporting him. It's necessary to enter the conclave with an orientation because otherwise you lose time, so there were conversations, meetings, comparisons ahead of time before supporting a candidate, and I think all this is right. But it was not certain, though we knew he had a good chance. I was not certain as I entered the conclave. I couldn't be sure of a solution, but, knowing how the others thought, I knew he had a chance."

When I asked how he himself had reached the conclusion that Bergoglio was the best candidate to be pope, he replied: "I can't easily say. Sometimes it's a sensation, an 'instinct,' I don't know. The Lord gives us voices which we do not immediately recognize at that moment; maybe we think 'that's just my idea,' but it was he who said it to you."

He first met Bergoglio in Buenos Aires in 1999 when he was sent by the Holy See to visit the Company of Saint Paul (La Compagnia di San Paolo), a secular institute founded in Milan by Cardinal Andrea Ferrari in 1921. He went to Buenos Aires to visit some families of that institute and had to meet the archbishop—Cardinal Bergoglio—to discuss the case of a young man who wanted to join the institute but whose family was very dubious and had protested to the archbishop that he was being brainwashed.

Cardinal Coccopalmerio told me that when he happened to meet Bergoglio before the conclave and said, "Eminence, we met some years ago in Buenos Aires," the Argentinian replied, "Yes, I remember, and I also remember the Company of Saint Paul." The Italian cardinal said he was very impressed that Bergoglio remembered all that and added, "I immediately saw that he was a person who considered you important. When he looked at you, he made you feel that you were important for him." He added, "Maybe it's that, this pastoral approach that 'you're important to me' that made me support Bergoglio. It's difficult to say exactly, but maybe it is that relationship of trust, of being important to him, that I am dedicated to you at this moment, and what you are saying to me."

Sources told me that before the conclave Cardinal Bergoglio knew nothing about this meeting at Cardinal Nicora's apartment, or the earlier meetings at the English and American Colleges and the British Embassy mentioned in this book. He learned about them only years later.

Indeed, Cardinal Maradiaga, who actively supported his candidacy, revealed that "before entering the conclave, I remember that the then Cardinal Bergoglio confided to me that he was happy that he had prepared his letter of resignation as archbishop of Buenos Aires (as every bishop must do at the end of his mandate), to hand to the future pope, which evidently he did not think would be him. In fact, he had brought to Rome only a few personal belongings, and so, after his election—which took him by surprise—he found himself lacking various things."[86]

REFLECTING BACK ON THE PAPAL ELECTION many months later, Cardinal Murphy-O'Connor told me: "The key was getting the Asians and Africans to support Bergoglio." Indeed, he said, "when the history of the conclave is written it will be shown that over the week of the General Congregations, a small minority helped lead the cardinals to understand that the front-runners (Scola, Scherer, and Ouellet) were not the men to lead the Church at this time in history, and that the only candidate was Bergoglio."

PART III

THE CONCLAVE

(March 12–13, 2013)

The Cardinal Electors Enter the Sistine Chapel

THE SKY WAS DARK this morning and torrential rain poured down as the cardinals set out from the places where they had been staying to travel to Santa Marta and take possession of their rooms before participating in the Mass *Pro Eligendo Pontifice* (For Electing the Roman Pontiff) in Saint Peter's Basilica, scheduled to start at 10:00 AM. They had drawn lots for the rooms at last Saturday's General Congregation. They knew when they had to enter the conclave. What they didn't know was when they would come out.

Early in the morning, at the Domus Paulus VI, Fr. Fabián Pedacchio, a young priest from the archdiocese of Buenos Aires who works in the Congregation for Bishops, informed Cardinal Bergoglio that the priest-friend whom he had asked to drive them to the Vatican could not come because of problems with his car; they would have to go by taxi. Bergoglio wanted to walk to the nearby taxi rank in Piazza delle Cinque Lune, but Don Fabián, insisting that the cardinal should not get drenched, took his umbrella and went to fetch a taxi.

Some minutes later, he returned in a taxi, having told the driver that he had to take someone important to the Vatican. The cardinal got into the taxi. Don Fabián accompanied his archbishop to Santa Marta and instructed the driver not to stop at the entrance, even if journalists wanted him to do so.

They traveled without mishap through the entrance on the right-hand side of what was long known as the Holy Office, today the office of the Congregation for the Doctrine of the Faith, next to Bernini's colonnades. At the cardinal's request, the taxi stopped just before they reached the entrance to Santa Marta. As they got out of the car they could see some cardinals, already dressed in their scarlet robes, queuing up to enter because everyone first had to go through the security scanning system that had been specially installed for the conclave. Bergoglio, wearing his black overcoat and carrying a black briefcase, joined the queue. Don Fabián stood beside him holding the cardinal's small suitcase.

When his turn came, Cardinal Bergoglio went through the metal detector and took his briefcase with him. Don Fabián then placed the cardinal's small case on the track for the scanner and shouted "Bergoglio" so the security controllers would know whose case it was. It so happened that the Chilean cardinal Errázuriz Ossa was also checking in his bag at the same time, and when he heard the name "Bergoglio" he came to Don Fabián and asked if he was from Argentina or spoke Spanish. When the priest confirmed both and said he was with Bergoglio, the Chilean commented, "I hope that if, this time, the Holy Spirit calls him, he will say 'Yes!'"

Don Fabián didn't tell Bergoglio this until after the conclave.

When the names were drawn last Saturday at the General Congregation to decide which room each cardinal would have at Santa Marta, Bergoglio was assigned Room 207. After going through the security controls that morning, he went to his room to deposit his case and settle in.

The Sicilian cardinal Paolo Romeo, a former Holy See diplomat who had worked in the Vatican Secretariat of State monitoring the Church in Latin America (1976–1983) and was now archbishop of Palermo, had been assigned a room across the corridor from Bergoglio.

So too had Cardinal Kasper, and since his book *Barmherzigkeit* (Mercy) had been translated into Spanish and published recently, he gave a copy to Bergoglio, who commented, "This is the name of our God."

SR. MARY ANN WALSH reported in the USCCB blog that she was up early this morning "to see" the eight US cardinals who were staying at the North American College set off for the conclave: Cardinals DiNardo, Dolan, George, Mahony, O'Brien, O'Malley, Rigali, and Wuerl. Paul Haring, Catholic News Service photographer, took their photo for the historical record before they boarded the bus for Santa Marta.

IL MESSAGGERO'S CORRESPONDENT, Franca Giansoldati, reported that if one were to judge by the size of the bags the cardinals were taking into Santa Marta, it was clear that some thought they were in for a long haul. Cardinal Raymond Burke arrived in his car with four cases, she wrote. Cardinal Kasper, on the other hand, came by foot pulling a trolley case, while an Italian cardinal (not named) came with a medium-sized Samsonite case.

AT TEN O'CLOCK THIS MORNING, more than 150 cardinals, both electors and those over the age of eighty, walked in procession into Saint Peter's Basilica to concelebrate the solemn, sung Latin Mass. Around seven thousand faithful—bishops, priests, women and men religious, and thousands of lay people—were present in the basilica for this important moment. The ambassadors from most of the more than 180 states that have diplomatic relations with the Holy See were also present, together with television crews, photographers, and other media personnel from many countries.

Thunder sounded several times during Mass as the storm raged outside bringing heavy rain. The emeritus pope, Benedict XVI, followed the celebration from the papal residence at Castel Gandolfo, as he would do later in the day for the procession of cardinals into the Sistine Chapel for the conclave. As dean of the College of Cardinals in 2005, he had been then the main celebrant at the hour-and-forty-minute liturgy. Cardinal Sodano had that role today, presiding at the solemn, sung Latin celebration with its songs, prayers, and readings in different languages.

In his homily,[1] Sodano began by thanking God for his constant assistance to the Church and for giving it "a brilliant pontificate" under Benedict XVI, and asked that he might "soon grant another Good Shepherd to his Holy Church." The mention of Benedict drew warm, spontaneous applause from the congregation.

Addressing his brother cardinals, Sodano told them, "It's necessary to build the unity of the Church and cooperate with the successor of Peter."

Then, drawing on the scripture readings of the day, he spoke about what he saw as some of the tasks facing the next pope. First, he must bring "a message of love" to the world (Isaiah 61). "Jesus came into the world to make present the love of the Father for all people," he said, and "this is a love that is especially felt in contact with suffering, injustice, poverty, and all human frailty, both physical and moral." He recalled that this "mission of mercy" has been entrusted by Christ to the pastors of his Church and, in a special way, "to the Bishop of Rome, Shepherd of the universal Church." The mission involves bringing "the Good News of the Gospel" to all people.

Second, he said, the new pope's task is to bring "a message of unity." In the second reading, Saint Paul writing to the Ephesians from his prison in Rome urged them to "make every effort to keep the unity of the Spirit through the bond of peace." Sodano recalled that Jesus "established his apostles and among them Peter, who takes the lead as the visible foundation of the unity of the Church," and he told his fellow cardinals, "each of us is therefore called to cooperate with the Successor of Peter, the visible foundation of such an ecclesial unity."

He next referred to a third aspect of "the mission of the pope." The Gospel of the day (John 15) recalled that Jesus told the first apostles, "This is my commandment: that you love one another as I have loved you." Cardinal Sodano said, "The basic attitude of every Shepherd is therefore to lay down one's life for his sheep" and "this also applies to the Successor of Peter, Pastor of the Universal Church. As high and universal as the pastoral office is, so much greater must be the charity of the Shepherd." He reminded them that the words Jesus addressed to Peter have resounded in the heart of every Successor of Peter: "Do you love me more than these? Feed my lambs . . . feed my sheep!"

Sodano, formerly the Vatican's top diplomat, recalled that in this service of love toward the Church and all humanity, "the last popes have been builders of so many good initiatives for people and for the international community, tirelessly promoting justice and peace." He urged his brother cardinals to "pray that the future pope may continue this unceasing work on the world level." It is, he said, "a mission of charity that is proper to the Church, and in a particular way is proper to the Church of Rome," which, as Saint Ignatius of Antioch said, is "the Church that presides in charity." He invited all the faithful present and the millions watching on television to pray "that the Lord will grant us a pontiff who will embrace this noble mission with a generous heart."

WHEN THE MASS ENDED, the cardinals again walked out in procession down the central aisle of the basilica amid the flashes of cameras and smartphones, as the faithful wondered which of them would be the next pope.

While the cardinals were greeting and chatting with one another after removing their vestments, Archbishop Vincenzo Paglia, president of the Pontifical Council for the Family and ecclesiastical advisor to the Sant' Egidio Community, ran up to Bergoglio and said, "You could be the next pope!"

IN HIS MEMOIR,[2] Cardinal Murphy-O'Connor recalled, "As I left Saint Peter's after the Mass ended, I found myself walking beside Cardinal Bergoglio. It was the first time we had spoken since we shared a risotto together nine days earlier. He was on his way back to the Casa Santa

Marta for lunch and a rest before the beginning of the conclave that evening. We chatted for a minute or two and as we parted my final words to him were, '*Stai attento!*' (Watch out!). He nodded, '*Capisco!*' (I understand!). He was calm. Did I know Bergoglio was going to be elected pope? No! Neither of us knew what was about to happen. Any of the men entering the conclave might emerge as the next pope."

When I asked the English cardinal about this much later, he confided that he got the impression then that Bergoglio "had accepted in his heart that he could be pope." Indeed, he felt the Argentinian knew he could be elected. He revealed, moreover, that at one stage during the General Congregations, he went up to Bergoglio and said, "I think we need this and this kind of pope." When Bergoglio responded, "I agree," Murphy-O'Connor told him, "You are the man!"

Although before the conclave a number of people had alerted him to the possibility that he could become pope, Bergoglio didn't take them seriously because, as he told close friends the summer after the election, "I never thought it would happen. Going into the conclave, I never thought I would be elected."

CARDINAL SCHÖNBORN OF VIENNA, addressing an audience of five thousand people in the Royal Albert Hall in London on May 14, revealed[3] that after the Mass in Saint Peter's he happened to meet a Latin American couple, friends of his. "I met them outside the basilica," he said, "and I asked: 'You have the Holy Spirit, can you give me advice for the conclave that will start in a few hours?' And the woman whispered in my ear 'Bergoglio,' and it hit me really: if these people say Bergoglio, that's an indication of the Holy Spirit." He added, "And I'm sure many of us have received similar signs during the Conclave; it wouldn't have been possible [otherwise] to have this election so soon and so rapidly."

The Latin American couple that Schönborn referred to were Dr. Guzmán Carriquiry Lecour, the Uruguayan-born secretary of the Pontifical Commission for Latin America, and Lídice María Gómez Mango, his wife. Carriquiry, now vice president of the Commission for Latin America and the highest ranking layperson in the Roman Curia, confirmed this episode in a conversation with me long after the election.[4] He revealed that when John Paul II died on April 2, 2005, he was convinced that Ratzinger would be elected pope, "because after the giant John Paul II it was necessary to change gears and find another giant with a different way of thinking." He recalled that his mentor, friend, and fellow Uruguayan, Alberto René Methol Ferré, was of the same view and wrote, in a much-publicized article in *La Nación* on the eve of that conclave, that "the time has not yet come for a Latin American pope."

Carriquiry said that after Benedict announced his resignation he felt sure that Bergoglio would succeed him in the See of Peter. He recalled that he and his wife "told many friends in the Curia that the next pope would be Bergoglio, we were totally convinced, but nobody believed us." And when Cardinal Schönborn asked them for their advice, he said she whispered in his ear "Bergoglio, Bergoglio, Bergoglio!" They had never spoken about this to anyone until the cardinal disclosed it in public more than once, though without naming them. Carriquiry revealed that even Pope Francis came to know of this and one day joked with him saying, "I hear you were campaigning for my election." Carriquiry felt somewhat embarrassed about this and told me that they had never suggested Bergoglio's name to any cardinal prior to the conclave but when Schönborn, whom they knew well, asked them explicitly for their input as lay people, they gave it, thinking it would remain confidential.

Carriquiry told me also that he too came from that Mass in Saint Peter's convinced that Bergoglio could be pope.

WRITING IN HER USCCB BLOG after the 2013 election, Sr. Mary Ann Walsh recalled that as they were leaving Saint Peter's Basilica after Mass they saw a Roman junior seminarian standing outside "with a glossy sheet of pictures of the electors from the *L'Osservatore Romano* newspaper." He cornered cardinals to sign their photo she said, and added, "odds are that he got a papal signature for his work." She saw cardinals George, Dolan, and Tagle kindly giving him autographs.

AS THE 115 CARDINAL ELECTORS went for lunch that Tuesday, photographers spotted an elderly man with a beard, dressed like Saint Francis of Assisi, and holding a pilgrim staff in his hand, kneeling in prayer in the middle of Saint Peter's Square. His message was clear: we need a pope like Saint Francis.

The photographers also captured another sight of a very different kind in the square that same day: two young Ukrainian women from the Femmen activist group bared their breasts in a protest against the Church and the papacy. Italian police quickly removed them from the square, followed by at least a dozen TV cameras. The next day's papers carried this story too.

AT A PRESS BRIEFING on the eve of the conclave, Fr. Lombardi advised the more than six thousand journalists gathered here for this global event not to expect a result on the first day. "It's difficult that the first ballot would have a positive result; one should not expect white smoke." His words were reported everywhere as "there will be black smoke today."

Cardinals and observers alike agreed that the first round of balloting this evening, which is expected to take place around 6:00 PM, would be like a primary; it will reveal who the real runners-up are and what support each one has. Most commentators expect a result by Thursday at the latest. If the conclave were to continue into Friday, it would be a sign of deep division among the cardinals.

Under the rules for the conclave promulgated by John Paul II, but significantly modified by Benedict XVI, if the conclave went to the thirty-fourth ballot, then the cardinals would have to vote for the two candidates that who obtained the most votes at that stage. But, it would still require a two-thirds majority to be elected pope.

RESPONDING TO QUESTIONS from reporters, some cardinals had earlier speculated on the length of the conclave.

South Africa's Wilfrid Fox Napier, who was also an elector in the 2005 conclave told *Corriere della Sera*,[5] "It will be longer than the last [conclave] when there was a very strong candidate—Ratzinger, who got elected on the fourth ballot. This time one looks a little farther ahead, perhaps to the second vote tomorrow evening, or the first two votes on Thursday." The *New York Times*[6] quoted him as saying: "I expect the first vote is going to be quite scattered around" given "the wider field of candidates with the potential [to become pope]."

Cardinal Dolan told the press, "I foresee the election of the pope by Thursday evening [March 14], and the inaugural Mass on March 19, the feast of Saint Joseph."

Cardinal Collins of Toronto, when asked for his prediction on the length of the conclave while having a meal at La Venerina restaurant in the Borgo Pio, said with a smile, "I am having a carbonara [spaghetti with eggs and bacon sauce], because if we do not elect the pope by the third day [March 14], they will put us on [a diet] of bread and water."

THE HISTORICAL RECORD offers some perspective on the length of the conclave. It shows that eight conclaves were held over the past hundred years, and most were short. The longest was for the election of Pius XI in 1922, which took fourteen votes. The most rapid came on the eve of World War II in 1939, when Pius XII was elected in three ballots. Since then, John XXIII was elected in 1958 after eleven ballots, Paul VI in 1963 after five ballots, John Paul I after four and John Paul II after eight—both in 1978—and Benedict XVI in 2005 after four. This would suggest that the 2013 conclave could also be short, but cardinals seemed unsure about this as they began.

THE FRENCH CARDINAL Paul Poupard, former rector of the Institut Catholique de Paris (1972–1980) and president of the Pontifical Council for Culture (1988–2007) but now over eighty and no longer an elector, emphasized the difference between this conclave and that of 2005 in which he was an elector. He told *La Repubblica*, "Then we went into the Sistine Chapel more prepared, with rather clear ideas; each one of us had much time to prepare himself." But this time, "the cardinals, and not just the electors, had to face the shock of the announcement of Benedict XVI. That is why the week of the General Congregations was most useful. I spoke several times. I listened with great attention to the contributions of the others. Now all is in the hands of Divine Providence. And as a Portuguese proverb says, God is able to write straight even with crooked lines."

According to *La Stampa*'s Andrea Tornielli, "The situation seems not to have changed much with respect to the past days." He predicted that Scola would receive the most votes on the first round, about thirty, with two other candidates having "weight" from the beginning: Ouellet, with support from North and South American cardinals, and Scherer, with support from curial cardinals. He envisaged that Bergoglio, "whose speech in the hall had impacted positively on some cardinals," could gain votes, as could Ranjith and Tagle. He expected that the second, third, and fourth round of balloting would be decisive in seeing which of those who emerged strongly on the first ballot had gained strength. As for the three Americans—Dolan, O'Malley ("who devoted his whole talk in the General Congregation to the fight against pedophilia"), and Wuerl—he noted that according to John Allen only Wuerl had all the qualities to be pope.

The Guardian, a British daily, also ruled out Dolan as a possibility. It quoted an unidentified "senior church source" who said: "Dolan is just too brash to be acceptable to the Europeans." The BBC did not think so, and it included him in its final list of "Runners and Riders" at the conclave: Scola, Ouellet, Ravasi, Schönborn, Scherer, Sandri, Turkson, Tagle, Braz de Aviz, Dolan.

Le Monde, in an article by Stephanie Le Bars based on conversations in Rome in these days, presented "portraits" of ten cardinals who could be pope, but did not include Bergoglio. Le Bars sought to capture a key feature of each one and ranked them in order of likelihood: Ravasi, 70, the communicator; Scola, 71, the politician: Schönborn, 68, the reformer; Ouellet, 68, the theologian; Scherer, 64, the emerging one; Sarah, 67, the discreet one; Tagle, 55, the young shoot (*pousse*); Ranjith, 65, the conservative: O'Malley, 68, the American outsider; and Erdo, 60, the European. Significantly, however, she concluded, "the game remains open and, at this stage, dangerous."

Corriere della Sera's Gian Guido Vecchi also listed ten *papabili*, but not Bergoglio.[7] He reported "strong support" for Scola, with his backers claiming he has forty-five to fifty votes, but said he could pay dearly for his links with the Communion and Liberation movement, as an elector had hinted recently. Vecchi reported backing for an "American candidate"—either Ouellet or Scherer or one from the United States (Dolan, O'Malley, Wuerl), but noted that Scherer suffers from being supported by diplomats in the Roman Curia and because of his speech in defense of the IOR at the last General Congregation. Given this scenario, he thinks Mexico's cardinal Robles Ortega, who is a devotee of Padre Pio and has made a good impression in the General Conferences, could emerge as the Latin American candidate.

The same Italian daily asserted that the eleven US electors "will have a central role in the election, even if they cannot make one of their own the pope." It suggested that "there is a solid possibility that Ouellet, the disciple of Hans Urs von Balthasar and very close to Ratzinger, could gain a 'transversal' consensus."

CARDINAL NORBERTO CARRERA, archbishop of Mexico City, speaking to *La Stampa*'s Andrés Beltramo Álvarez, reported that the three Mexican electors who represent 10 percent of the world's Catholics want "to elect a pope who is close to the whole Church." Nationality is not an important factor. He revealed that some were looking for "a more academic type who can establish a dialogue with culture," others seek "someone who is close to the people," but many want "someone with greater authority to put order into some internal church questions." Up to now, he said, "there's not a majority [view], and we thank God for this diversity." Carrera believes the new pope "must be different from those who have preceded him and must have his own characteristics. He can't be a repetition, a copy of another pontificate." He predicted: "We'll reach an accord very quickly."

La Stampa's Giacomo Galeazzi reported that Venezuela's cardinal Jorge Urosa Savino, archbishop of Caracas, had told journalists that "this is the moment" for a South American pope, but noted that there is division among the Latin Americans regarding whom to support. Cardinal Claudio Hummes, for example, opposes the candidacy of Scherer, his successor in São Paulo. In this context, Galeazzi claimed Santos Abril y Castelló, one of the three Spanish electors, "could serve as mediator to get agreement on a Latin American candidate" because he knows many of the Latin American electors, having served as nuncio in Bolivia and Argentina for twenty years. He listed four Latin American *papabili*: Maradiaga, Braz de Aviz, Bergoglio, and Robles Ortega. Urosa noted that O'Malley is much liked by the Latin Americans for his work with Hispanics in the United States. Significantly, he asserted that Sodano, Bertone, and Re are all seeking an alternative to Scola.

Le Figaro's correspondent, Jean-Marie Guenois, presented his list of *papabili* based on conversations with electors in these weeks.[8] He predicted the top three on the first vote will be Scola, Scherer (who's chances have decreased), and Ouellet.

IN MY VIEW, one of the more interesting analyses came from Luigi Accattoli, in an article on the front page of *Corriere della Sera*. He recalled that just over fifty years ago John XXIII called the Second Vatican Council, and Paul VI brought it to completion and guided its implementation. John Paul I, John Paul II, and Benedict XVI continued that effort at implementation, having absorbed "the reforming gene." But this time, he observed, the next pope will not belong to that conciliar generation.

He speculated that the crisis of the Church in Europe, and the fact that the majority of Catholics are no longer European, "could push the conclave to take the papacy outside the old continent," and if this were to happen "it would be an epochal choice comparable to that made by the second conclave in 1978, which reached beyond Italy and elected a Polish cardinal."

Accattoli suggested that "a leap toward the Americas would constitute an almost painless passage to a new constellation, given the cultural continuity between the old and new worlds." He rated the election of an African or Asian pope as "more difficult to imagine" at this time in history, but "the choice of a Latin American—a hypothesis that is mature today, but which was tasted and discarded by the 2005 conclave—would indicate a passage from the North to the South of the world, one of extraordinary interest in a phase in history that sees the global reshuffling of cultures and economies." He claimed some European cardinals are ready for such a move.

Accattoli concluded that "the decision that will mature in the coming hours before the 'Last Judgment' of Michelangelo is important not only for Christians but also for the secular world, which has more than one motive of interest that the Church of Rome should accept the challenge of new times with the hard-fought but proven trust in the Gospel, and in the history that has made it an expert in humanity."

Notwithstanding his insightful analysis, Accattoli did not include Bergoglio on his list of "the most named" cardinals to be pope. He named Dolan, Erdo, O'Malley, Ouellet, Ravasi, Robles Ortega, Scherer, Scola, Tagle and Turkson.[9]

GERMANY'S *DER SPIEGEL* offered its own analysis as the cardinals entered the conclave. It claimed that the cardinals "are seeking a leader who will stand out, one who can lead the crisis-plagued church into a better future." It noted that the leaks from the pre-conclave assemblies "revealed that cardinals from around the world are sharply critical of the papal administrative machinery. Everything was discussed, including Vatileaks, the Vatican bank affair, and the sexual abuse scandals. Cardinals from Africa and Asia sharply criticized the Vatican's patronizing attitude toward local churches. An American cardinal admonished the central administration, saying that its focus must be on serving the church rather than on serving itself."

Der Spiegel claimed that "even most of the ultraconservatives no longer want the kind of church that the two chairmen of the College of Cardinals represent. Angelo Sodano and Tarcisio Bertone stand for the past."

It alleged that "candidate-bashing is standard Roman practice in the pre-conclave phase, as is canvassing for one's own favorite candidate." By way of example, it revealed that the German cardinal, Walter Brandmüller, "one of the staunch conservatives, has been meeting with other cardinals every day in his apartment directly above the vestry at Saint Peter's Basilica, and is campaigning for Albert Malcolm Ranjith, the archbishop of Colombo in Sri Lanka."

Reading the conclave from an entirely political perspective, *Der Spiegel* commented that "there are few elections or political party conventions in which the high arts of tactics, diplomacy and intrigue are as important as they are in the conclave." It claimed that "so far, none of the camps has been strong enough to push through its candidate of choice. Coalitions must painstakingly be formed." Concluding its analysis, it stated: "The current mood can be quickly summed up: We now need a new pope surrounded by new people who will turn their attention to repairing the system."

FOLLOWING THE SOLEMN MASS in Saint Peter's this morning, the cardinal electors said goodbye to those over eighty and returned to their rooms in Santa Marta, where the windows were locked and the blinds closed to prevent contact with the outside world. The cardinals, as well as all others directly linked to the conclave, now reside in Santa Marta and the Vatican, incommunicado, without any access to the outside world. A strict cordon of security protects the whole building and the entire area from there to the Sistine Chapel.

The electors entered the dining hall for lunch at one o'clock in the afternoon and sat in groups at various tables. Not everyone likes the food here, as Cardinal Dolan, attending his first conclave, remarked some days ago: "At the conclave one eats badly." Since it was Lent, the organizers decided there would be no dessert, just a first and second course, followed by fruit.

After lunch, some cardinals, like Bergoglio, went to their rooms to rest, while others, like Portugal's chain-smoking cardinal, José da Cruz Policarpo, went outside for a smoke. Some chatted, others prayed or read in their rooms as they prepared to cast their first vote.

THIS CONCLAVE WILL TAKE PLACE in the Sistine Chapel but, as the historical record shows, it was not always so. Down through the centuries, popes were elected in different places and different ways. While some, like Gregory III in 731, were chosen "by acclamation," and others, such as Sixtus V in 1585, by "quasi inspiration," the rest were elected by secret ballot. The first papal election in a conclave was held at Arezzo, 135 miles north of Rome, in 1276 and, with one exception, all subsequent papal elections have been held in conclave since 1294. This is the seventy-fifth conclave.

Almost all papal elections have been held in Italy,[10] and most took place in Rome. Fifty-one papal elections in conclave were held in the Vatican, and since 1513 twenty-four of these were held in the Sistine Chapel. Another ten took place in the Pauline Chapel between 1550 and 1700. This is the fifty-second conclave to be held in the Vatican and the twenty-fifth in the Sistine Chapel.

THIS AFTERNOON the 115 cardinal electors were profoundly conscious of their enormous responsibility. It was not surprising, therefore, that some nervousness and tension could be felt as they waited to be taken by coach to the Apostolic Palace. They came from forty-eight countries and five continents: Europe sixty (twenty-eight are Italian), Latin America nineteen, North America fourteen (eleven from the United States, three from Canada), Africa eleven, Asia ten, and Oceania one (Australia).

Eighteen were members of institutes of consecrated life or societies of apostolic life. Among them were one Jesuit, three Franciscan Friars Minor, one Franciscan Capuchin, four Salesians, two Dominicans, one Redemptorist, one Lazzarist, one Sulpician, one Oblate of Mary Immaculate, one Scalabrinian, one from the Institute of Schonstatt priests, and one from the Mariamite Maronite order.

BY 3:30 THAT AFTERNOON I was with the CTV special panel for the papal election and the rest of the twenty-five-member television crew on a platform overlooking Saint Peter's Square, waiting for the opening of the conclave. The panel, led by Lisa LaFlamme (the news anchor), included Fr. Michael Bechard, chaplain at Kings University College, Ontario; Solange Lefebvre, professor in the faculty of theology and the science of religions at Montreal University; and myself as Vatican affairs analyst.

Back in Canada, the news editors told us there was mounting interest and excitement at the possibility that a native son might become pope. CTV broadcast a report from La Motte, Quebec, the home-town of Cardinal Ouellet, in northwestern Quebec. It said the little town, "was besieged Tuesday by dozens of journalists—creating a sudden jump in the local population of almost 10 per cent." Ouellet's family told reporters that the Canadian front-runner liked ice-skating and family moose-steak dinners and has been known to eat dessert off a sibling's plate and gun his uncle's tractor until it broke. They fear, however, that if he becomes pope such intimate moments will be lost forever. "We know that it would be over," his younger brother, Roch, said in an interview; "we would prefer to have a brother [than a pope]."

In Rome our panel was ready, and waiting for the ceremony to start.

BY 3:45 PM THE CARDINAL ELECTORS were already dressed in their scarlet robes and waiting to be transported by coaches from Santa Marta to the Pauline Chapel. The chapel is named after Paul III, the Farnese pope, who had it built between 1537 and 1540; it is located at the top of the Scala Regia, the Royal Staircase designed by Bernini (1663–1666) to connect the Vatican Palace to Saint Peter's Basilica.

On arrival there, the cardinals assembled in the chapel, and as they waited for the ceremony to begin many gazed at the two magnificent paintings by Michelangelo on the walls: "The Conversion of Saint Paul" (1542–1546) and "The Crucifixion of Saint Peter" (1550). He painted these at the request of Paul III after having completing the "Last Judgment" in the Sistine Chapel.

By now almost everyone had decided on the name of the man to whom they would give their first vote. A significant number would have a second and perhaps a third name at the back of their minds in case their original choice failed to gain much support. It is likely, however, as has happened in past conclaves, that those who are still unsure will cast their first vote for someone they esteem, respect, or wish to encourage.

Their thoughts were suddenly interrupted by the loud announcement that it was time for the ceremony to start, a ceremony rich in history, ritual, and pageantry.

It opened in great solemnity at 4:30 PM with a prayer in the Pauline Chapel, in accordance with the *Ordo Rituum Conclavis*[11] (the *Book of Rites of the Conclave*). Cardinal Re presided and delivered a brief exhortation. Then the cardinals began to walk slowly in procession to the Sistine Chapel. The cross was carried at the head of the procession, followed by the Sistine choir, two masters of ceremonies, two sacristans, and an ecclesiastical assistant to the cardinal dean. They were followed by the secretary of the College of Cardinals, Archbishop Baldisseri; Cardinal Grech, who would give the meditation to the electors; and then the cardinal electors, walking in the reverse order of their hierarchical precedence and seniority by age: first the cardinal-deacons, then the cardinal-priests, and in last place the cardinal-bishops.

Next came a deacon, carrying the book of the Gospels.

CARDINAL KARL LEHMANN, a big, sturdy man who had for many years been president of the German bishops' conference and a leader in the Church's more progressive wing, walked slowly with crutches. Cardinal Dias, an accomplished Vatican diplomat, emeritus archbishop of Bombay and prefect of the Congregation for the Evangelization of Peoples, now in failing health, walked with the aid of a stick. Cardinal Okogie of Nigeria moved slowly.

Cardinal Giovanni Battista Re, who is presiding at the conclave, came last in the procession, accompanied by the master of ceremonies, Msgr. Guido Marini, a tall, thin, friendly man with glasses who somehow always managed to keep his composure and look serene.

While some cardinals smiled and waved to people they knew, most had pensive or serious looks on their faces as they made their way to the Sistine Chapel amid the flashes of the photographers and under the glare of the Vatican's television cameras broadcasting the whole ceremony to a global audience that was difficult to quantify.

As they moved slowly forward, the renowned Sistine Choir led the cardinals in singing in Latin, first, the Litany of the Saints, invoking the intercession of all the saints, and then the *Veni Creator Spiritus*—the ninth-century hymn invoking the guidance of the Holy Spirit, as they prepared for their momentous decision that is destined to impact the life of the universal Church and the world.

They entered the Sistine Chapel two by two, walked to the center, bowed before the cross, and then went to their pre-assigned seats on either side of the central aisle.

Many looked around with awe and admiration, some for the very first time, at the magnificent frescoes on the walls of the chapel that were commissioned by Sixtus IV and made by a team of Renaissance artists that included Botticelli, Perugino, Pinturicchio, Ghirlandaio, and Rosselli. The frescoes depict the life of Moses and the life of Christ. They were completed in 1482, and Sixtus IV celebrated the first Mass in the Sistine Chapel (which is named after him) on August 15, 1483. The first conclave to be held here was in 1513.

As they waited for everyone to reach their seats, the cardinals cast their eyes on the magnificent achievements of Michelangelo, one of the most famous artists of the Italian Renaissance. They could see the ceiling with its scenes from the Book of Genesis, the best known of which is that of the creation of Adam, which depicts God stretching out his hand to create Adam, which Michelangelo painted between 1508 and 1512 under the patronage of Julius II. Above the altar, they could see the imposing, awe-inspiring scene of the Last Judgment, which Michelangelo painted for Clement VII and Paul III between 1535 and 1541.

Cardinal Bergoglio took his place in the second seat at the top end of the back row on the left-hand side of the chapel. As he looked at the scene of the Last Judgment, he could see that he was sitting on the side of the just. His great friend from Brazil, Cardinal Hummes, sat on his left, while the Italian cardinal, Severino Poletto, was on his right, and next to him was the patriarch of Portugal, Cardinal José da Cruz Policarpo. Farther down that same back row sat the front-runner, Cardinal Angelo Scola.

India's Cardinal Gracias, who was seated on the right hand side of the Sistine Chapel, in the back row, across from Bergoglio, described his feelings on entering the chapel in an interview with me[12] shortly after the pope's election: "When I entered the conclave we were all apprehensive, uncertain. I was personally nervous to be taking part in a decision that is so important for the Church, so important for the world. How could we do that? Yet there was a good preparation in the Congregations, we knew each other—but also much, much more important at the higher level there was the spiritual preparation, we prayed a lot."

"It was an emotional experience, the Mass for the election of the pope before the conclave began and, then, when we entered the conclave, there were prayers too," he recalled. "It was exciting to see all the cardinals there, deep in prayer, all of us conscious that we had to participate in a decision that was so important. I felt very, very strongly, that the presence of the Holy Spirit was guiding us, and I felt too the effect of prayers. People all over the world were supporting us with their prayers."

"Being in the conclave has been almost like being in a retreat, alone with God," he stated. "We cardinals met and were speaking to each other, of course, but it was not a social gathering. It was not a business gathering either, nor was it an executive committee meeting trying to plan something. Rather, it was trying to open oneself to God, to see what God wants."

On the tables in the Sistine chapel, in front of each cardinal there were three texts: The apostolic constitution *Universi Dominici Gregis*, which governs the election process; the *Ordo Rituum Conclavis*; and a prayer book of the Liturgy of the Hours. There was also a sheet with the names of all the cardinal electors present.

Once they had all been seated, Cardinal Re, who was presiding over the conclave, recited the common formula of the solemn oath[13] that bound the cardinals to observe faithfully and scrupulously all the norms and prescriptions of the apostolic constitution regarding the papal election, and to maintain strict secrecy at all times regarding all that happens at the conclave. The oath bound them to secrecy on everything they saw or heard during the conclave pertaining to the new pope's election unless explicitly granted special faculty by the new pope or his successors. It also bound them to refrain from using any audio or visual equipment to record anything pertaining to the papal election during the conclave. Finally, it required that they not support or allow any interference or intervention by any secular authorities, groups of people, or individuals in the election of the pope. The penalty for breaking the oath is automatic excommunication.

When the cardinal dean of the conclave finished reading the oath, each of the electors, in order of precedence, went to the lectern at the center of the Sistine Chapel on which there was an open copy of the Gospels. There, with his hand on that book, he repeated a short, personal form of the oath. Vatican television transmitted all this live to the outside world.

After the electors had taken the oath, master of ceremonies Msgr. Marini, gave the order, in a loud voice, for everyone to leave the chapel: "*Extra omnes!*" (All out!). Millions around the world watched this riveting scene. Everyone who was not an elector, except for Msgr. Marini and Cardinal Prosper Stanley Grech, immediately left, and Marini then slowly closed the two wooden doors of the Sistine Chapel. Two Swiss guards, wearing the blue, yellow, and red uniforms and holding halberds, stood on guard outside to prevent anyone from entering.

The eyes of the electors then turned to the eighty-seven-year-old Cardinal Grech, a member of the Augustinian order and renowned scholar of the early fathers of the Church. Benedict XVI had named him a cardinal on February 18, 2012, making him the first Augustinian cardinal in 111 years and the first Maltese cardinal in 168 years. He spoke frankly, from the heart and from long pastoral experience. The Vatican published the full text some months later.[14]

He began by reminding the cardinal electors that "the act which you are about to fulfill here in the Sistine Chapel is a *kairos*, a powerful moment of grace in the history of salvation that continues to unfold in the Church until the end of time." It "requires the utmost responsibility from all of you," he said. "It does not matter whether the pope you elect is of one nationality or another, of one race or another. It only matters that when the Lord asks him, 'Peter, do you love me?' he be able to reply in all sincerity: 'Lord, you know everything, you know that I love you' (cf. Jn 21:17–19). Then the sheep entrusted to him by Jesus shall abide secure, and Peter will follow Christ, the chief Shepherd, wherever he goes."

Speaking in Italian—even though not everyone was fluent in it and there were no translators—the Maltese cardinal assured the electors that he did not intend to offer a profile of the new pope, much less suggest a plan of action for him, as "this most delicate task belongs to the Holy Spirit." He reminded them that their task is to proclaim the Gospel "without diluting the word of God," because "when one compromises one empties it of its power, as though one had removed the explosive from a hand grenade." One compromises by presenting Christ as "one savior" among others, he stated.

For their part, he said, they must preach "the scandal of the cross." He recalled that in the first centuries of Christianity "it was the precisely the preaching of the folly of the cross that in less than three hundred years reduced the religions of the Roman Empire to a minimum and opened the minds of men to a new vision of hope and resurrection." He told them: "Today's world thirsts for the same hope, as it suffers from an existential depression."

He reminded them that "Christ crucified is intimately bound to the Church crucified, the Church of the martyrs," of yesterday and today and that "we must embrace the cross, but we must also remember that persecution is not always physical." There is also "the persecution of falsehood," he said, as they had "recently experienced this through various media outlets that do not love the Church." His words appeared to allude to the pressure put on some cardinals through the media not to participate in the conclave for allegedly having mishandled of cases of sexual abuse of minors by clergy.

Cardinal Grech counseled the cardinal electors, and among them the next pope, that "when false accusations are made one must not pay attention to them, even if they are a cause of immense sorrow." But, he said, "it is quite another thing when the truth is spoken against us, as has happened in many of the accusations of pedophilia. Then one needs to humble oneself before God and men and seek to eradicate evil at any cost, as Pope Benedict XVI did with great anguish and sorrow. Only thus does one regain credibility before the world and offer an example of sincerity."

The electors listened as the Maltese cardinal underlined the need to proclaim "the kerygma," the nucleus of the Christian faith, in a language and a way that people can understand. He drew their attention to the fact that "today many people do not arrive at believing in Christ because his face is obscured or hidden behind an institution that lacks transparency." He seemed to be urging the next pope to promote transparency in the Vatican and in the Church worldwide.

He spoke of "the mystery of evil" that strives constantly to infiltrate the Church, and because of this, he said, one of the hardest tasks for the next pope will be to preserve unity in the Church. His task will not be easy because of "ultra-traditionalist extremists and ultra-progressive extremists, between priests who rebel against obedience and those who do not recognize the signs of the times" and added that "there will always be the danger of minor schisms that not only damage the Church but also go against the will of God: unity at all costs." But, he noted, "Peter will make his task easier to the extent that he shares it with the other apostles." His words reflected the need for greater collegiality in the Church, something that had been mentioned many times in the General Congregations and goes back to the teaching of the Second Vatican Council.

Then, referring to the crisis of faith in Europe, the scholarly cardinal emphasized the need for a new evangelization that involves reaching out to non-believers. At the same time, he assured the electors, "the Lord is never defeated by human negligence and, it seems that, while they are closing the doors to him in Europe, he is opening them elsewhere, especially in Asia. And even in the West God will not fail to keep for himself a remnant," also through the new movements. He reminded the electors that "God cannot be defeated by our indifference. The Church is his, the gates of hell can wound its heel but can never suffocate it."

He urged the cardinals and future pope to pay attention to the simple faith of the ordinary people, saying, "The embers of devout faith are kept alive by millions of simple faithful who are far from being called theologians, but who in the intimacy of their prayer, reflections, and devotions can give deeply meaningful advice to their pastors." The Word of God, he said, "shines forth in simple hearts that form the marrow from which the backbone of the Church is nourished."

In his challenging exhortation, Cardinal Grech told the electors that "while professing that the Holy Spirit is the soul of the Church, we do not always take him into consideration in our designs for the Church. He transcends any sociological analysis and historical forecast. He exceeds the scandals, internal politics, the social climbing and social problems that obscure the face of Christ, which must also shine through the dense clouds."

He concluded his profound, incisive meditation by reminding the electors that as they stand and vote under Michelangelo's fresco of the

Last Judgment, they do so "beneath the figure of Christ with his hand raised, not to crush but to illuminate your voting, so that it may be according to the Spirit, not according to the flesh." He assured them that if they act in this way then "the one who is elected will not only be yours but will essentially be His."

Once he finished speaking, Msgr. Marini accompanied the elderly cardinal out of the Sistine Chapel and then, in accordance with the rules of the conclave, the junior cardinal-deacon, James Harvey from the United States who had worked in the Vatican for almost thirty years, firmly closed the doors, leaving the 115 electors all alone. The Swiss Guards stood outside the doors to prevent anyone coming near or entering while the cardinals voted. Vatican television captured this solemn moment too, letting the world see what was happening.

What took place next inside the Sistine Chapel was hidden from the outside world. Cardinal Re first explained the voting process and then asked the cardinals if they were ready to vote. They were! Everyone was anxious to do so, as this would reveal where the Holy Spirit was leading them. The first phase of the process began with the distribution of ballot sheets to the electors. Before the voting started, and in accordance with the constitution, the most junior cardinal elector then extracted at random the names of three "scrutineers" and three "revisers" to supervise the first voting session.

The second phase was the secret ballot. Each cardinal had before him a ballot form, rectangular in shape, on which were printed in Latin the words *Eligo in Summum Pontificem* (I elect as Supreme Pontiff...), and underneath there was a space for the name of the person to whom he wished to give his vote. The electors were expected to write in such a way that they could not be easily recognized by their handwriting. Once the cardinal completed his ballot form, he had to fold it lengthwise, in such a way that the name of the person he voted for could not be seen.

Once all the electors had written the name of their chosen candidate and folded the ballot sheets, then each cardinal, in order of precedence, took his ballot sheet between the thumb and index finger and, holding the ballot aloft so that it could be seen, carried it to the altar at which the scrutineers stood and where there was an urn, made of silver and gilded bronze by the Italian sculptor Cecco Bonanotte, with an image of the Good Shepherd on it. The urn was covered by a similarly gilded plate to receive the ballot sheets.

On arrival at the altar, the cardinal elector stood under the awesome painting of Michelangelo's Last Judgment and pronounced the following oath in a clear and audible voice: "*I call as my witness Christ the Lord, who will be my judge, that my vote is given to the one whom, before God, I think should be elected.*" He then placed his ballot sheet on the plate and tilted the plate in such a way that the sheet fell into the urn. Finally, he bowed in reverence to the cross and returned to his seat, and the next elector then walked to the altar.

After all 115 electors had cast their votes, the three scrutineers came forward to count them. It was a moment of high tension. Everybody watched the ritual with rapt attention. The first scrutineer shook up the ballot sheets in the urn, which was first used at the last conclave, to mix them. Then another scrutineer began to count them, taking each ballot form separately from the first urn and transferring it to a second urn, exactly like the first, that was empty. The constitution decrees that if that the number of ballot sheets cast does not correspond exactly to the number of electors present then that ballot is declared null and void.[15]

When the number of ballot sheets corresponds exactly to the number of electors, the process continues with the opening of the ballots. The three scrutineers sit at the table in front of the altar. The first opens the ballot sheet, reads the name silently, makes a note of it, and passes it to the second scrutineer. The second does likewise, and then passes it to the third, who reads the name written on the sheet and then, in a loud voice, announces it to the whole assembly, and next records it on a paper prepared for this purpose.

The windows of the Sistine Chapel had been blacked out. But that was considered totally inadequate given the advanced state of modern communications technology and the risk of electronic interception and so, as in 2005, the conclave organizers took high-security measures to prevent the possibility of transmission by smartphone from inside and electronic interception by outside agencies or individuals. They installed state-of-the-art jamming systems, including a Faraday cage.[16]

This time, however, the organizers went even further than at the last conclave to prevent the possibility of interception; they took the extraordinary decision not to use the sound-amplification system inside the Sistine Chapel. The reason for this, it seems, goes back to the 2005 conclave, when the Swiss Guard standing on duty outside the doors of the chapel could sometimes hear what was being said inside, especially when the vote counts were announced over the PA system.[17]

Consequently, before the first vote, Cardinal Re asked Cardinal Juan Sandoval Íñiguez, the seventy-nine-year old emeritus archbishop of Guadalajara, who was known to have a powerful voice, to stand in the middle of the chapel and proclaim in a loud voice the names read out by the third scrutineer.[18]

As the third scrutineer read out a name on a ballot sheet, Cardinal Sandoval repeated it so that all could hear. There was an air of high suspense inside the Sistine Chapel as the results were being announced. For the first time the electors were revealing their choices; they were putting their cards on the table.

After reading out the name on each individual ballot, the third scrutineer pierced the sheet through the word "*Eligo*" with a needle and thread; this was done to combine and preserve the ballots. When the names on all the ballots had been read out, a knot was fastened at each end of the thread and the joined ballots were set aside.

This was followed by the third and last phase of the voting process, which began with adding up the votes each individual had received. The results held several big surprises.

Before the conclave, several cardinals had predicted that there would be a wide spread on the first ballot, but few had imagined how wide: twenty-three cardinals received at least one vote each on the first ballot; this meant that one out of every five in the College of Cardinals got a vote, with four of them getting ten or more votes, and another getting four.

Scola 30
Bergoglio 26
Ouellet 22
O'Malley 10
Scherer 4

Scola came first with thirty votes, but he did not receive as many votes as had been predicted by some cardinals and the Italian media.

The big surprise was Bergoglio, who came in at second place, close behind Scola, with twenty-six votes. His total, in fact, would have been twenty-seven if an elector had not misspelled his name, writing "Broglio"[19] instead of Bergoglio on the ballot sheet. It was a most promising start for the archbishop of Buenos Aires.

Ouellet scored well too, better than expected, and arrived in third place, having obtained twenty-two votes. He seemed a strong candidate.

O'Malley was a surprise also; with ten votes, he became the first American in history to score so highly in any papal election.

On the other hand, Scherer, the much-touted Brazilian, had a surprisingly low score; he got a mere four votes.

Besides these front-runners, five cardinals received two votes each in that first ballot: Schönborn, Turkson, Pell, Monsengwo Pasinya, and Dolan.

Another thirteen cardinals got one vote each: Bačkis, Maradiaga, Antonelli, Caffarra, Vingt-Trois, Gracias, Collins, Tagle, Sandri, Sarah, Piacenza, Ravasi, and Broglio (which, as mentioned earlier, seemed an obvious misspelling of Bergoglio).

The voting process ended with the burning of the ballots. After a final check of the report sheets on which the scrutineers had recorded the votes, the ballot sheets and the reports were taken to one of the two specially installed stoves at the back left-hand side of the Sistine Chapel as one faces the altar.

The two stoves join together in one flue that is connected to the chimney erected outside the chapel, a chimney that is now the center of attention for the world's media. The origin of the stove goes back to the eighteenth century, when the master of ceremonies came up with the brilliant idea of communicating to the world whether or not a new pope has been elected by dispelling white or black smoke from the chapel chimney as the ballot sheets and records are burned.[20]

Following the norms for the election process, the ballots from the first vote at this conclave were burned in the older stove that has been used at every conclave since 1939. This was done by one of the scrutineers, with the assistance of the secretary of the conclave, Archbishop Baldisseri, who had been re-admitted after the votes had been counted. As they began the burning, they activated an electronic smoke-producing device in the newer stove, first used at the 2005 conclave, which contained a cartridge containing five types of chemical mixtures that can produce black or white smoke as required. As per the rulebook, the burning and smoke signal operation had to be completed before the cardinals left the Sistine Chapel.

Given that no candidate had gained the two-thirds majority on the first vote, the ballot sheets were burned, the electronic smoke producing device was activated, and at 7:41 PM (Rome time), black smoke streamed forth from the slender rust-colored chimney of the Sistine Chapel, announcing to the world that the pope had not been elected.

The sight of the black smoke provoked an audible NOOOOOH from the thousands of faithful and tourists huddled in the cold under multi-colored umbrellas in Saint Peter's Square and wearing raincoats, plastic ponchos, or other waterproof gear to protect themselves from the incessant rain. They stood there, constantly shifting their gaze from the small chimney lit by a spotlight to the maxi-screens in Saint Peter's Square that showed the live scene as television units and radio networks from many countries that were located outside the square broke the news to a global audience.

AT THE MOMENT THE FIRST SMOKE APPEARED, I was with the CTV panel led by Lisa LaFlamme, its talented chief anchor and news anchor, on a platform in a spectacular position on top of the Augustinian House overlooking Saint Peter's Square, with a magnificent view of the chimney on the Sistine Chapel and the central balcony of Saint Peter's.

We were on air when the black smoke began pouring out of the small chimney. Lisa announced the breaking news: Black smoke! No pope! Led by Lisa, our panel engaged in a round of comment and speculation as to what this meant and what tomorrow might bring.

BACK IN THE SISTINE CHAPEL, since the constitution did not envisage a second round of voting this evening, the 115 cardinals sang vespers, the Church's evening prayer, and were then transported back by bus to Santa Marta as the rain continued. On arriving there, they went to their rooms, changed from their ceremonial garb into cassocks or suits, and then came down for dinner in the rather impersonal dining hall.

The nuns who cook for the 115 cardinals during the papal conclave at the Casa Santa Marta residence had prepared "meals of soup, spaghetti, small meatballs, and boiled vegetables," as *Corriere della Sera* had reported that morning.

Over the frugal evening meal, the cardinals talked together and exchanged reactions as they reflected on the result of the first ballot.

When Cardinal Bergoglio entered the hall just after 8:00 PM he spotted his fellow Argentinian, Cardinal Sandri, and said to him "Come here, sit next to me, let's have dinner together." Sandri revealed this to Elisabetta Piqué in an interview after the conclave.[21] They sat side by side at the table, at which there were also other electors.

Bergoglio and Sandri have known each other for almost half a century, since Bergoglio was nineteen and Sandri thirteen or fourteen. Bergoglio was Sandri's prefect at the Villa Devoto diocesan seminary in Buenos Aires before he decided to join the Jesuits. Since then, their paths had moved in vastly different directions.

Leonardo Sandri entered the Holy See's diplomatic corps and served in numerous posts, from Madagascar and Mauritius to the Vatican's Secretariat of State and Holy See's nunciature (embassy) in the United States, where he served as a counselor. In 2000 the pope recalled him to the Vatican as "substitute" (*sostituto* in Italian) in the Secretariat of State "for the general affairs of the Church"—the third-ranking position in the Vatican. In 2007, Benedict XVI gave him the cardinal's red hat and appointed him prefect to the Congregation for Oriental Churches, a post he had held until the pope resigned.

Though their relationship went way back, it was well known in Argentina and Rome that they had experienced their share of tensions, especially in recent years, when Angelo Sodano was secretary of state and Sandri was *sostituto* in the Secretariat of State.[22] The tensions related to, among other things, undue interference in the nomination of bishops, objections arising from different pastoral visions, and aspects of Bergoglio's pastoral ministry. But tonight in Santa Marta, on the first day of the conclave, all that was history and they shared dinner together like old friends.

Sandri was not feeling well; he had pharyngitis and his eyes were watering. Bergoglio, who has a background in chemistry, looked at the antibiotic that Sandri was taking and told him how many milligrams of another substance he should take to get better. Their conversation, like that of the others at the table, inevitably moved to the conclave and the evening's vote. Sandri advised him, "Get ready, my friend!"[23]

Asked by Elisabetta after the conclave if he had foreseen then that Bergoglio would be pope, Sandri responded, "Well, these are things that you see coming. One could see it coming because we were there, and we saw the results (of the first vote)." He knew that a sizable group of Latin Americans, Asians, Africans, and some Europeans, including Italians, were supporting his candidacy.

"I was not surprised at the election of Bergoglio," he added. He revealed that before he went to the conclave his sister and niece accompanied him to the lift and told him, "When you elect Bergoglio we will invite him to the house to eat a *puchero* (an Argentinian stew)."[24]

During dinner that evening at Santa Marta, the cardinals discussed the surprising results of the first ballot and how to move ahead the next morning. Bergoglio for his part went to his room to pray and, as he told friends later, he "slept well" that night.

To an outsider, that scattered first vote might have given the impression of great uncertainty, but the electors saw it in a very different light. Cardinal Gracias, for example, who had been assigned Room 102, told me he read it this way: "The Holy Spirit was indicating already, the Holy Spirit was leading us in a particular direction. God was there right through." Several other cardinals told me they had interpreted the first vote in a way that was similar to that of Gracias.

The vote revealed several things. It showed that Scola was the only strong European candidate in line to succeed Benedict, and while this pastor and eminent theologian had support, it was at the lower end of what had been expected on the eve of the conclave, when cardinals and much of the Italian press had anticipated that he would be out in front with around forty votes. Naturally, this came as a disappointment to his supporters.

More important, the vote confirmed what many already knew or suspected: the twenty-eight Italian electors were deeply divided about Scola. Indeed, as the history of the last two conclaves (October 1978 and April 2005) showed, when the Italians are divided an Italian pope will not be elected. Was history about to repeat itself? That first ballot seemed to indicate to many electors that the next pope would not be European; he would come from the Americas. It also left little doubt that Scherer was out of the race; he was seen as the candidate of the status quo in a conclave that was looking for radical change. Apart from Scola, the result left three other candidates standing: Bergoglio, Ouellet, and O'Malley, in that order.

The archbishop of Boston had much in his favor: he is a pastor, well-liked, with a simple lifestyle; he speaks Spanish fluently and has a sterling track record on handling cases of sexual abuse of minors by clergy. Nevertheless, while before the conclave many cardinals affirmed publicly that nationality was not an issue, the truth was few wanted a pope from the world's main superpower. To elect an American, even if he happened to be a Franciscan friar, would not have gone down well in the southern hemisphere, or in the churches of the developing world. O'Malley, a friend and admirer of Bergoglio, shared that view.

Cardinal Ouellet had scored much better than expected in the first vote, and he was in a strong position. As the cardinals discussed his candidacy in small groups and one-to-one conversations that Tuesday night, March 12, they recognized several positive factors in favor of this polyglot Canadian. He had pastoral experience as a priest in Colombia and as archbishop in Quebec. Important too was the fact that he knew the Vatican from the inside, having worked first in the Pontifical Council for the Promotion of Christian Unity and since 2010 in the powerful Congregation for Bishops. Notwithstanding this very positive side, several cardinals said they found him "uninspiring," "ordinary," and felt that his track record in the Roman Curia gave rise to serious questions about his ability to govern under pressure. These questions, now transformed into serious reservations, surfaced in conversations that first night in Santa Marta and led many undecided electors to conclude that if he could not govern well in the Roman Curia, he might not be able to govern the Catholic Church.

At the same time, however, Ouellet had some highly influential supporters besides the Americans. Among them was Cardinal Joachim

Meisner, archbishop of Cologne, Germany, since 1989, and for nine years before that archbishop of Berlin. Widely considered the leading conservative in the German church, he was known to be very close to John Paul II and a life-long friend of Joseph Ratzinger. He wanted to ensure that the next pope would faithfully follow the line and vision of his two predecessors. And so, that Tuesday night in Santa Marta, he was seen standing outside the door of his room urging fellow electors, "Vote for Ouellet! Bergoglio is too old!"[25]

As for Bergoglio, the first vote revealed that he was indeed a strong candidate, stronger than many had realized. If one counted the misspelled name—"Broglio"—as a vote for him, he would have had twenty-seven votes, just three votes behind Scola. There were many factors in Bergoglio's favor. He was known to be a very holy man, a humble, intelligent, inspiring pastor, devoid of ambition, who avoided the limelight, lived a simple life, and had a passionate love for the poor. He had never lived or studied in Rome and did not have a Roman outlook. He had governed the Buenos Aires archdiocese for fifteen years in a truly pastoral way, with decisiveness, prudence, and creativity; he had a talent for government. Ever since the 2001 synod his stature had grown internationally, and at the CELAM meeting in Aparecida, Brazil, in May 2007, he had emerged as the undisputed leader of the Church in this region where almost 50 percent of the world's Catholics live. Above all, he was a man of courage, with a vision, a missionary vision, able to open new horizons for the Church, a man committed to dialogue—with the Jews, with Muslims, with other Christians, and with those who professed no faith. He was above all a pastor. His brief intervention in the General Congregation as well as his interaction with many cardinals during these days had revealed this clearly.

As the undecided electors considered for whom to cast their vote the following morning, three factors leaned heavily in Bergoglio's favor: first, the great majority of Latin American cardinals were supporting him, with not one of them was speaking badly about him; second, he had revealed his ability to communicate and inspire when he had given his brief but refreshing intervention in the General Congregation; and third, he had support from Asians and Africans as well as Europeans. In addition, sixty-eight electors who had participated in the 2005 conclave knew him as runner-up then, and several—like Maradiaga, Monsengwo, Kasper, Tauran, Turkson, Gracias, and others too—did not disguise their backing for him.

The undecided had this night to make up their minds; tomorrow morning, they would have to cast their votes again.

IT WAS THAT TUESDAY EVENING, after finishing my analysis of the papal election for CTV, that I happened to meet a source who shared a crucial piece of information with me on condition that I not publish it until long after the papal election. He confided the story I have previously described, that on the previous evening, March 11, the eve of the conclave, Cardinal Attilio Nicora had hosted a meeting in his Vatican apartment attended by more than a dozen cardinals from different countries and four continents, all of whom had declared their intention to support Bergoglio, and had mentioned the names of others they knew who were thinking along the same lines.

Having learned that Bergoglio would go into the conclave with between twenty and thirty electors voting for him, and would almost certainly get twenty-five votes, I felt sure he would be elected. My conviction was based not on wishful thinking or intuition but on information I had been gathering over the previous four weeks on the likely voting tendency of the cardinals. I had obtained this information in conversations with cardinals, Vatican officials, and informed fellow journalists who had close relations with cardinals.

Already, before the General Congregations started on March 3, I had made a chart of all the electors. I had identified who would most likely vote for Scola, and who would never do so, and from this calculation I concluded that, because of the strong opposition he faced, including opposition from many Italian electors, he was unlikely to get a lot more than forty votes—far short of the seventy-seven he would need for election as pope.

I felt certain too, for a variety of reasons, that the conclave would not elect a cardinal from the United States, Africa, or Asia this time around.

As for Cardinal Ouellet, I didn't expect him to be elected either. I expressed this view to Canada's acting ambassador to the Holy See, Anne Leahy, on the evening of March 11, when she invited me to the embassy for a chat. I had learned that Ouellet's star had fallen in recent days, for the reasons mentioned earlier. It remained true that many North American electors (mostly in the United States) supported him, along with some French, German, and Spanish cardinals linked to Ratzinger, as well as a few central and eastern European cardinals, who could eventually support him. But, according to my calculations, he was unlikely to get much more than twenty votes.

With all this information in my head, I concluded that if Bergoglio entered the conclave with a package of around twenty-five votes and received this on the first ballot, that would be enough to launch him on the path to the papacy. I knew he had support from most of the Latin Americans and most, if not all the Asian electors, several Africans, several Europeans, and several Italians, including some working in the Roman Curia. In other words, he had trans-continental support. I understood that while Scola could not obtain many more than forty votes, Bergoglio had no such limit. Therefore, I reckoned that if he got twenty-five or more votes on the first ballot, as now seemed highly likely, and could add to that in the second and third ballots, then a dynamic would develop that would make his path to the papacy unstoppable. These calculations left me feeling elated.

It was raining, so I took a taxi from the Vatican to Pollarolo restaurant, near the Campo di Fiori, to join Cardinal Cormac Murphy-O'Connor, who had invited me and around ten other guests to dinner. They included Alexander de Forges and Maggie Dougherty, director and deputy director of communications for the Catholic bishops' conferences of England and Wales respectively; Msgr. Philip Whitmore, rector of the Venerable English College where the cardinal was staying; and Msgr. Roderick Strange, rector of the Beda College, who had been hired by the BBC as its advisor for the papal election.

Not surprisingly, the conclave was the main topic of conversation. Most thought Scola would be the next pope. Having listened for some time, I predicted that Bergoglio would be elected pope tomorrow on the fourth or fifth ballot, but I did not explain the rationale behind my assertion. They were taken aback by my forecast; not even the cardinal found it credible. "Maybe on Thursday," he said, expressing his hope against hope. He did not envisage such a quick result and believed that if Bergoglio were elected it would be on March 14. Msgr. Strange, however, thought I might just be onto something, and some hours later alerted the BBC to this possibility, as he told me later.

As we left the restaurant, I decided to accompany the cardinal to the door of the English College in Via Monserrato, off the Piazza Farnese. As we walked, he recalled that he had had dinner at this same restaurant with Cardinal Bergoglio in early March. He said he prayed and hoped the Argentinian would become pope, but unlike me, he did not feel sure about this. After bidding him goodnight, I set off briskly for home. It was cold and windy, though no longer raining.

MANY THOUGHTS RACED through my mind as I walked through Campo dei Fiori and an unusually deserted Piazza Navona and arrived home around 10:30 PM. Elisabetta had just put Juan Pablo and Carolina to bed and was saying goodnight to her father, Piero, who was spending some days with us. I stopped her in her tracks when I told her: "Bergoglio could be pope this time tomorrow!" Her look of utter disbelief gave way to bewilderment, as she realized I was deadly serious.

After listening to my explanation, Elisabetta phoned Gail Scriven, the foreign editor of *La Nación*, the Argentine daily, for which she works. Gail, like the other persons in top positions at the paper with whom she shared the news, was skeptical, incredulous. They thought it was wishful thinking on Elisabetta's part because she knew Bergoglio and was close to him. But somehow, finally, she managed to convince them that this was at least a real possibility. They agreed to publish a brief story, but only on page 2! It was not until the following afternoon that they realized she had given them a world scoop. She tells the story in her biography of Francis, which was published in Buenos Aires the following November[26] and subsequently inspired the making of a film.[27]

Sometime after midnight, after Elisabetta had filed her story, I decided to share the information with my good friend Andrea Tornielli. I sent him an email in which I wrote: "I believe the pope could be elected on the first or second vote tomorrow evening, and it could be Bergoglio." He later described receiving this tip in his book *Francis: Pope of a New World*,[28] one of the first on the market after the election.

MARCH 13 (WEDNESDAY) _____

Bergoglio Elected Pope

"THE BLACK SMOKE" from the conclave was the top news story in the Italian media this morning. They reported that Benedict XVI was following everything by television from Castel Gandolfo and was praying that the Holy Spirit would enlighten the electors. But the 115 cardinals in conclave knew nothing about all this; they had no access to newspapers, radio, or television, nor could they use their iPads or smartphones; they were totally cut off from all communication with the outside world.

Even though nobody in the press corps knew what was happening inside the Sistine Chapel, this did not stop a spate of stories that claimed to present the latest news, some of it based on information gathered as the cardinals entered the conclave, more the result of creative thinking.

IL MESSAGGERO'S FRANCA GIANSOLDATI, for example, writing under the headline "A brake on Scola, the risk of a stalemate," reported that in the hours preceding the opening of the conclave she had picked up "signs that were unfavorable to Scola, as if the consensus for him was decreasing." She claimed that "traps on the road" to Scola's election are coming from "personal enmities toward him" on the part of several of the other twenty-seven Italian electors, enmities "that would be difficult to overcome."

At the same time, citing unnamed sources, she asserted that the chances of three candidates from the Americas were on the rise: Ouellet ("though the pedophile problem of his brother does not help"), Scherer ("though criticized for his overseer role in the IOR"), and O'Malley ("a third-world figure made in the USA"). She predicted that if the front-runners cancelled each other out, the path to the papacy could open up to outsiders like Robles Ortega, Braz de Aviz, Tagle, or Sarah.

La Repubblica offered a different reading of what it imagined might be happening inside the Sistine Chapel. Under the headline, "A brake on Scherer's race, Scola stable, and out of the pack Erdo surfaces at the conclave." Its correspondent, Paolo Rodari, reported that while Scola entered with thirty-five to forty votes, it was not certain he would be elected, partly because his connections with Communion and Liberation and with Roberto Formigoni, the governor of Lombardy who is now under investigation on charges of corruption, have eroded his Italian support. Rodari reported that support for Scherer had diminished after his final defense of the governance of the Roman Curia, and affirmed that Ouellet and Dolan were the beneficiaries of all this.

Marco Ansaldo, writing in *La Repubblica*, claimed that Scherer understands that he has lost, and asserted that electors of "the Bertone front" are among those opposed to Scola, including cardinals Calcagno and Versaldi, who have responsibility for Vatican finances and are seated next to each other in the Sistine Chapel.

LA STAMPA published today my interview with Cardinal Onaiyekan, a former president of the Nigerian bishops' conference and a leading figure in the African church. I have known him for many years, having met him in Rome and Abuja, the federal capital of Nigeria, where he is archbishop.[29]

Knowing that Bergoglio was now on the radar of many cardinals, but that there was concern about his age, I had asked Onaiyekan if he thought the conclave could elect a man who is over seventy-five as pope. Onaiyekan answered without hesitation: "If a man of seventy-five, from whatever nationality, comes up as the best person, why not? If a seventy-five-year-old becomes pope, he can generally have ten years, which is the average term of a pope's reign, or maybe less." He said he was going into the conclave "to discover God's will for his Church. I do not have any candidate in mind. The Holy Spirit will guide us."

However, given that he comes from a country of more than 170 million people where the relation between Christianity and Islam is a major issue, Onaiyekan told me, "I don't think anybody can be a pope and ignore Islam." The new pope, he said, "will have to relate to other religions too. The pope is the pope for all. Therefore, the concerns of the Catholic Church and of the world in every corner of the globe are his concerns too."

LA STAMPA also carried an interview with Cardinal Schönborn, conducted by my Vatican Insider colleague, Alessandro Speciale. The Austrian cardinal explained that "choosing a pope is an act that is different from a political election. One is not dealing with choosing the director-general of a multinational [corporation] but [with choosing] the spiritual head of a community of faith."

For this reason, he said, "there is a need first of all of a person who has religious qualities: a man of faith and of the Gospel, a credible man." While "managerial qualities are needed, that is not the first quality. Everything depends on his capacity to be a man of faith." Schönborn concluded: "Personally, I believe the decisive characteristic is to be a man of the Gospel. As for the other qualities, the more there are the better it is, but they will all be useless without this high spiritual stature."

THE CANADIAN MEDIA was giving oceans of attention to Ouellet. *The Star* of Toronto, for example, noted that as archbishop he was "a traditionalist in a secular Quebec," but it also quoted Jasmin Lemieux-Lefebvre, who became director of communications for the archdiocese about a year before Ouellet left Quebec City for the Vatican, who described him as "a deeply spiritual man who sometimes allowed the professorial side of his personality to take over when speaking to non-parishioners in the public arena, although he has softened his image over time." He asserted that Ouellet "was a great pastor on the ground. People loved him, he was warm, but when it had to do with the public space I think he was speaking more as at teacher." He recalled that at a June 10 press conference before returning to Rome, Ouellet said, "I tried to give a certain example. I was not perfect, but I hope others will follow."

THE BOOKMAKERS are having a field day with the conclave and hope to make big money. *La Repubblica* published the latest odds they were offering for the different candidates, with comments:

Scola, the favorite, but feared by the Curia: 3.25/1.

- Scherer, a Brazilian much loved in the Curia, but pays a price for defending it: 4.5/1
- Ouellet, the Canadian outsider, could be compromise candidate: 9/1
- Erdo, young, in continuity with Ratzinger, but would be a real surprise: 15/1
- Dolan, a blogger, spirited, energetic, could be the first pope from the USA: 26/1
- Bergoglio, the Jesuit who is attentive to the poor, runner-up in 2005: 41/1

Edwin, my eldest son, a student of political science at Bath University, phoned last evening and asked who I thought would be elected, as he and his friends were following the election and also thinking of placing a bet. But as I did not like the idea of betting on the result of the conclave, I did not say. A Vatican official, a good friend of mine, later told me that a friend of his bet on Bergoglio and made out well.

THAT WEDNESDAY MORNING as the cardinals were preparing to travel from Santa Marta to the Sistine Chapel, I arrived at the CTV studio located on top of the Augustinian House, overlooking Saint Peter's Square. I brought with me a copy of *El Jesuita*, the book by Francesca Ambrogetti and Sergio Rubín based on wide-ranging interviews they had conducted with Bergoglio in Buenos Aires.[30] It had gained little coverage internationally. The front cover carries a photo of the cardinal in a simple clergyman's black suit.

I startled everyone at the beginning of our editorial meeting when I pulled the book out of my bag and, holding it up, predicted: "Bergoglio will be pope this evening!"

One of my fellow CTV conclave panelists was Solange Lefebvre, a spirited and thoughtful young professor at the University of Montreal. She approached me later and said, "Gerry you must be joking, this guy is so conservative and traditional! They can't elect him." She had contacted friends of hers who knew about him and this is what they had told her. "Are these friends of yours Jesuits?" I asked. She admitted it was so. I raised that question because I knew that "a black legend" about Bergoglio had gained credence among Jesuits in many parts of Latin and North America as well as in Rome regarding Bergoglio's period as provincial in Argentina. Not only had they misread his actions to a large degree,[31] but also, and more importantly, they had completely failed to understand or take account of the man he is today.

AS WE PLANNED our day's work, the cardinals in conclave had already had breakfast between 6:30 and 7:30 AM in the Domus Santa Marta and had been taken by bus to the Pauline Chapel, where they concelebrated Mass. Cardinal Re presided and gave the homily. After Mass they spent time in silent prayer before walking to the Sistine Chapel, where they took their assigned seats and recited the morning prayer of the Church.

Once the prayers ended, the process for the second vote began, following the same procedure as yesterday. They drew by lot the names of three new scrutineers and three new "revisers" for the morning's voting sessions, and then the ballot sheets were given to each cardinal.

The 115 cardinals wrote the name of the person they had chosen on the secret ballot sheets, folded them in the prescribed way, carried them to the altar, and then cast their votes in order of precedence. The scrutineers mixed the ballot sheets and then counted them to verify that the number of votes cast matched the number of electors present. Next, they read the names, and then proclaimed aloud one by one the names of those who had obtained votes. As he had last evening, Cardinal Sandoval stood at the center of the chapel and repeated the names in his booming voice for all to hear. The result was as follows:

Bergoglio 45
Scola 38
Ouellet 24
O'Malley 3

Five other cardinals—Turkson, Pell, Gracias, Scherer, and Tagle—got one vote each in this second ballot.

The second ballot revealed a dramatic shift from the previous evening. The undecided cardinals had cast their votes for one of the four cardinals who had come out on top of the previous evening's ballot. Scola gained eight votes, Ouellet gained two, and O'Malley lost seven. Bergoglio was the main beneficiary; he obtained nineteen more votes and was now seven ahead of Scola, which seemed to suggest that many cardinals were ready to take a historic step, similar to what happened in October 1978 with the election of John Paul II, the first non-Italian pope in 455 years.

Since no cardinal had obtained the requisite two-thirds majority of 77 votes needed for election as pope, the electors proceeded immediately to a third vote, following the standard procedure. After checking that there were exactly 115 ballot sheets, the scrutineers opened each one, noted the name on the ballot sheet, and then read out the name of the person who had obtained that vote. Cardinal Sandoval, at the center of the chapel, repeated the names. The electors listened with rapt attention, sensing that this could be the watershed vote, a turning point. The results confirmed this, and were as follows:

Bergoglio 56
Scola 41
Ouellet 14

Four other cardinals got one vote each in the third ballot: Pell, O'Malley, Gracias, and Scherer.

Though the outside world did not know it, the second and third ballots indicated where the conclave was now heading. There was little doubt that the dynamic was clearly in Bergoglio's favor. Many cardinals, as some told me later, interpreted it as a sign from the Holy Spirit that this was the man God was calling to be the successor to Saint Peter.

After the results were announced, the silence was broken inside the Sistine Chapel as cardinals chatted with each other, commenting on the outcome. It seemed the Americans, and perhaps a few others, had switched their votes from Ouellet to Bergoglio in the third ballot, and as a result the Canadian lost ten votes between the second and third ballot. Scola gained only three extra votes; his candidacy seemed to have run out of steam. Bergoglio, on the other hand, gained eleven. Unless something totally unexpected happened over lunch at Santa Marta, the cardinals were poised to turn their sights across the Atlantic later that day to elect the first pope from the New World.

Since no cardinal had obtained the requisite majority on either the second or the third round, the ballot sheets from these two rounds of voting were burned in the stove at the back of the Sistine Chapel, and at the same time the appropriate chemicals were activated in the second stove. At 11:39 AM black smoke poured forth for a second time from the chimney of the Sistine Chapel, to the dismay of the thousands of people from many countries who had gathered in Saint Peter's Square since ten o'clock that morning. It had stopped raining, but that was little consolation. They wanted a pope, not sunshine!

The cardinals began leaving the Sistine Chapel immediately after the burning of the ballot sheets to return to Santa Marta. But not all of them. Cardinal Scola remained behind with a group of Italian cardinals who were supporting him, including Bagnasco, Caffarra, and Betori. The archbishop of Milan saw the writing on the wall and looked as if he didn't want to go on, but his Italian backers sought to convince him otherwise.[32] He urged them to vote for Bergoglio, but they were not listening; they didn't want him to throw in the towel just yet.

BY LUNCHTIME a sense of high expectation had begun to arise among the ever-growing crowd in Saint Peter's Square, but it was escalating even more inside Santa Marta. In both places there was the distinct sensation that the pope would be elected this evening.

I strongly sensed this too when the BBC interviewed me from its platform at the back of Saint Peter's Square where many of the world's TV units were located. As I stepped off the platform, I was struck at seeing two middle-aged women carrying a large photo of Bergoglio; they were praying he would be pope.

INSIDE SANTA MARTA, there was excitement in the air and a sense of suspense and tension, combined with the growing conviction that the cardinals would elect the new pope this evening. It was already clear where the Holy Spirit was leading them. Bergoglio had the wind in his sails.

As the archbishop of Buenos Aires left the Sistine Chapel that Wednesday morning, he understood there was a risk that he could be elected pope, but he still didn't think it would happen, as he would later confide to close friends over the weeks that followed. His reason: he knew from the history of conclaves that electors can quickly change their votes from one ballot to another, and he felt that could still happen.

DURING LUNCHTIME AT SANTA MARTA that day, however, several things happened that led Cardinal Bergoglio to understand that he would most likely be elected pope in the afternoon.

First of all, before the cardinals entered the dining hall, the Cuban cardinal Ortega y Alamino came up to him and reiterated his request for the text of the talk he had given at the General Congregation. When he had first asked for it at that session, the Argentinian confessed he did not have a written text, just bullet points, but he promised he would write up what he had said and give it to him. Thus, when the archbishop of Havana again asked him for it before lunch, Bergoglio went to his room on the second floor, came downstairs with a handwritten page and handed it to him. The Cuban was delighted, thanked him warmly, and then remarked in an audible voice that others heard, "Now I have a text from the new pope!"

A few minutes later, the Chilean cardinal Errázuriz Ossa happened to meet Bergoglio in the hallway as he was on his way to the dining hall and said to him,[33] "You'd better prepare what you are going to say!"

Then, when Bergoglio entered the dining hall, Cardinal Maradiaga invited him to join him for lunch along with a group of mostly European cardinals, including Erdo, many of whom he did not really know. But there was also Cardinal O'Malley, who sat beside him and noted that "he was pensive."[34] The cardinals asked many questions about Latin America and other things, and Bergoglio responded candidly. Weeks later, recalling that lunch, Francis, never a big eater, told close friends, "I didn't feel like eating much then!"

I'VE LEARNED FROM SEVERAL SOURCES that the allegation that Bergoglio has only one lung was spread during the lunch break by supporters of another candidate in a last-ditch effort to block his election. Cardinal Maradiaga, who was one of those openly supporting Bergoglio's candidacy but was suffering from a broken leg during the conclave,[35] confirmed this five years later in his introduction to the book *Tutti Gli Uomini di Francesco*.[36]

He wrote, "I certainly cannot say what happened inside the Sistine during the conclave, but I can recount this: when the figure of the archbishop of Buenos Aires began to emerge as the possible new pope, they began to move to stop the plan of God that was about to be realized. Someone who was supporting another *papabile* cardinal in fact spread the word in Santa Marta that Bergoglio was ill, that he was without one lung.

It was at that point that I took courage. I spoke with other cardinals and I said, 'OK, I will go to ask the archbishop of Buenos Aires if these things are really true.' When I went to find him, I asked pardon for the question I was about to ask. Cardinal Bergoglio was very surprised at the question I put to him, but confirmed that apart from a little sciatica and a small intervention to his left lung for the removal of a cyst when he was young, he had no serious health problems. It was a true relief: the Holy Spirit, in spite of the obstacles of the cliques (*le cordate*), was breathing on the right person."

According to another elector, Cardinal Abril y Castelló also approached Bergoglio and asked him the same question at the end of lunch: "Is it true that you have only one lung?" The archbishop of Buenos Aires again denied it and went on to explain that in 1957, when he was around twenty-one years of age, he underwent surgery that removed the upper lobe of his right lung where he had three cysts, but since then his lung has functioned without a problem.

AN ELECTOR ALSO APPROACHED Cardinal Lehmann and tried to undermine his support for Bergoglio by asserting that he had problems because he had colluded with the military dictatorship in Argentina (1976–1983).

It was an old allegation and had been used at the 2005 conclave, when articles written by Horacio Verbitsky, an Argentine investigative journalist and former member of a left-wing armed group, the Montoneros, but now director of a human rights organization and close to President Nestor Kirchner and his wife Cristina Fernández, were sent to many cardinals. The ruse failed in 2005 thanks to good media work by Fr. Guillermo Marcó, the cardinal's communications officer, and it did not succeed this time either, because Lehmann went straight to Cardinal Hummes to ask if it was true. The Brazilian responded, "I can assure you this is all false!"[37]

Commenting on these efforts to derail Bergoglio's path to the papacy, another elector told me weeks after the election: "The devil is active too in the conclave." He cited his own personal experience. Over lunch that Wednesday a fellow elector had sought to dissuade him too from voting for the Jesuit cardinal on the grounds that he had allegedly "handled badly a case of abuse." My source said he became quite concerned at this allegation and went immediately to a Latin American cardinal whom he knew well and trusted and asked if this was true. The response was a categorical denial: it was not true.

These last desperate efforts failed to block the momentum of Bergoglio's trajectory to the papacy. While real, these attempts should not be overrated. In contrast to the 2005 conclave, when there was strong resistance to the election of Ratzinger, in this case, as several electors confirmed to me after the conclave, there was in fact little opposition to Bergoglio's election. An elector who participated in both conclaves put it this way: "Last time a hard core never accepted Ratzinger and fought against him. This time around it was not like that."

Indeed, as they talked over lunch on March 13, most cardinals felt sure that Bergoglio would be elected pope that same day. Cardinal Tong was one of them. In a post-conclave interview, he told me that at lunch he became so convinced that the Argentinian would be elected pope in the afternoon that before returning to the Sistine Chapel he went to his room to get the small statue of Our Lady of Sheshan that he had brought from Hong Kong to give to the new pope.

The statue, a copy of the one that stands atop the church at the Marian shrine of Sheshan not far from Shanghai, shows Our Lady holding the child Jesus above her head, presenting him to the world. The statue is venerated by Catholics from all over China, as I had seen when I had visited there the previous August. Cardinal Tong said he had taken the statue out of its box and put it in the pocket of his cassock so that he could give it to the new pope after his election.

During lunch that Wednesday, Cardinal Bergoglio too came to realize that he would be elected pope. After the conclave, he told close friends that "during lunch I realized that I was in danger, but I felt great peace and calm." He has enjoyed that peace ever since, as he confirmed on January 16, 2018, in a conversation with the Jesuits of Chile in the capital city, Santiago. He told them, "As soon as I realized during the conclave what was about to happen—a complete surprise for me—I felt great peace. And up to today that peace has never left me. It is a gift of the Lord and I am grateful for it. And I really hope he won't take it away from me. It is a peace that I feel as a pure gift, a pure gift."[38]

That Bergoglio was at peace is evidenced by the fact that he took his siesta after lunch that Wednesday, as he confirmed to close friends later.

BY 4:30 PM I HAD JOINED THE CTV PANEL on the platform overlooking Saint Peter's Square. It was cold, wet, and windy that Wednesday afternoon. We were wearing overcoats and protected by a plastic tent-like covering. We knew the cardinals were returning to the Sistine Chapel at this time, and we had to be ready for whatever happened next.

THE 115 CARDINALS went again to the Pauline chapel and from there returned to the Sistine Chapel at 4:45 PM, aware that they were on the threshold of making a historic decision. Bergoglio walked with Ravasi from the Pauline to the Sistine Chapel, talking on the way.

Once inside, they followed the procedure laid down by the Apostolic Constitution: they chose three new scrutineers and three "revisers" by lot, and then the ballot papers were distributed, more than two to each elector. Next, the cardinals wrote the name of their chosen candidate on the ballot sheets and cast their secret vote as on previous occasions. After the scrutineers had verified that there were exactly 115 ballot sheets, they began the counting and, as before, one of them announced the names of those who had received votes and Cardinal Sandoval repeated what he had said. The results of this fourth vote were as follows:

Bergoglio 67
Scola 32
Ouellet 13
Vallini 2
O'Malley 1

There was little doubt. The Holy Spirit was clearly guiding the papal electors across the Atlantic for the first time in history. Bergoglio had gained eleven votes, Scola had lost nine, Ouellet had lost one. The only surprising element in this fourth ballot was the introduction of a new name—the seventy-two-year-old Italian cardinal Agostino Vallini, who got two votes. Did this mean that someone wanted to derail Bergoglio's trajectory to the papacy at the very last minute by presenting the conclave with a different candidate? Whatever the rationale, it was a futile move.

As mentioned earlier, the Argentine cardinal Leonardo Sandri shared his memories of the conclave in an interview after the election with Elisabetta. He spoke about what had happened as the cardinals voted: "Bergoglio was in front of me, right in front of me. The cardinal-deacons were on the lower level, and I was the fifth and I had in front of me him and Hummes, right in front, and Cardinal Lehmann. And in some moments, I did this (making a sign with his hand) meaning it's your turn, and he responded this way (moving his head, resigned)."[39]

Since no candidate had obtained the two-thirds majority required on the fourth vote, the cardinals proceeded with eagerness to cast their fifth vote. But something totally unexpected happened next that would delay the final result: the scrutineers counted the number of ballot sheets cast and discovered to their surprise that there were 116, one more than the number of electors present. This happened because the cardinals were given more than two ballot sheets each and one cardinal cast his vote without noticing that two of his ballot sheets were stuck together.[40] The fifth vote was therefore declared null and void and, without any of the names on the ballot sheets being read, a second vote was taken immediately. This was in full compliance with number 28 of the apostolic constitution *Universi Dominici Gregis*, promulgated by John Paul II, which states: "If the number of ballots does not correspond to the number of electors, the ballots must all be burned, and a second vote taken at once."[41]

The cardinals lost no time and cast their sixth vote in the normal way. Since the number of ballots cast corresponded to the number of electors, the opening of the ballot sheets and reading of the names began in an atmosphere of great expectation. The names were read out, and Bergoglio's re-echoed repeatedly through Sistine Chapel as he moved ever closer to the seventy-seven votes that would seal his election.

Cardinal Gracias, in a post-conclave interview with me,[42] described the dramatic scene inside the Sistine Chapel as the final votes were being counted. "Cardinal Bergoglio was sitting practically opposite to where I was seated. I was on the right-hand side as you face Michelangelo's Last Judgment and he was on the left. Cardinal Hummes was next to him and next to me was Cardinal Bagnasco, who is a good friend, and Cardinal Sarr. So, I would see Bergoglio every time I looked up. I would see him across from me. I would see him so often. We were in two rows on either side, as you know, he was on the back row on the left side, and I was on the back row on the right side, so we were face-to-face. Bagnasco and I were sharing notes. On the other side of me was a Mexican cardinal and Scherer. So, Scherer and I were chatting about things, and Bagnasco and I too. And there directly opposite me was the man who is now our Holy Father."

Another elector told me that Bergoglio was reciting the rosary with his beads all the while the votes were being counted.

Gracias described the look on his face: "It was like he was accepting God's will. He's a man of God. I could see he was accepting God's will and obeying what the Lord wanted. It was very clear to me that he was the man the Lord wanted. He felt, and we all felt that the Lord wanted him, and he was not going to refuse the cross. That was his attitude: I'll carry the cross, I'll be Simon of Cyrene to Jesus. That was the thought that came to my mind. There was no doubt in our minds. In everybody's mind it was the same thing: here is God's choice. I felt all the time that he was the man chosen by God. He was the chosen one from the beginning. And when Bergoglio reached seventy-seven votes, the number required for the election of the pope, there was tremendous joy, enthusi-asm. You're overtaken by events."

Another Indian cardinal, Telesphore Toppo, who was sitting between cardinals Pell and Turkson in the conclave, recalled in a post-conclave interview[43] the moment when Bergoglio reached the two-thirds majority: "A big clap went up when Bergoglio reached seventy-seven votes. I felt exhausted, also during the pre-conclave meetings. I felt a sense of relief after the election."

Cardinal Coccopalmerio too spoke to me about the moment of election. "Without breaking the rules of the conclave, I can say we were all very happy."

Once the counting was finished, there was no doubt: Cardinal Bergoglio had been elected pope! The first pope from Latin America, the first Jesuit pope.

The results of the sixth vote were as follows:

Bergoglio 85
Scola 20
Ouellet 8
Vallini 2

There was more applause after the final results were announced. Then, immediately after the applause ended, Cardinal Bergoglio got up and went to Cardinal Scola, who was some seats down from him on the same row, and embraced him.

THE APOSTOLIC CONSTITUTION outlines clearly[44] the next steps to be taken once the conclave has reached this stage, and these were followed scrupulously.

First, the junior cardinal-deacon, James Harvey, summoned into the chapel the secretary of the College of Cardinals—Archbishop Lorenzo Baldisseri—and the master of Papal Liturgical Celebrations—Msgr. Guido Marini, and two other masters of ceremonies: Monsignors Francesco Camaldo (Italy) and Konrad Krajewski (Poland).

Then came the moment to ask Bergoglio if he accepted his election. In the apostolic constitution, Saint John Paul II had this to say to the one elected: "I ask the one who is elected not to refuse, for fear of its weight, the office to which he has been called, but to submit humbly to the design of the divine will. God who imposes the burden will sustain him with his hand, so that he will be able to bear it. In conferring the heavy task upon him, God will also help him to accomplish it and, in giving him the dignity, he will grant him the strength not to be overwhelmed by the weight of his office."[45]

Cardinal Re, who was presiding over the conclave, went to Bergoglio and, standing in front of him, asked in the name of the whole college of electors: "*Do you accept your canonical election as Supreme Pontiff?*"

Cardinal Bergoglio responded in Latin, with words that translated into English mean: "I am a great sinner, trusting in the mercy and patience of God, in suffering, I accept."[46]

The apostolic constitution states that "after his acceptance, the person elected, if he has already received episcopal ordination, is immediately Bishop of the Church of Rome, true Pope and Head of the College of Bishops. He thus acquires and can exercise full and supreme power over the universal Church."[47] It declares, furthermore, that "the conclave ends immediately after the new Supreme Pontiff assents to his election, unless he should determine otherwise."[48]

As soon as Cardinal Bergoglio gave his consent, Cardinal Re asked him a second question: *By what name do you wish to be called?* The new pope responded: Francesco (Francis).

Three days later, on March 16, Pope Francis described how he lived that historic moment and how he chose the name Francis. He did so when he greeted the six thousand journalists and media operators who had covered the conclave. He told them:

> During the election, I was seated next to the Archbishop Emeritus of São Paulo and Prefect Emeritus of the Congregation for the Clergy, Cardinal Claudio Hummes: a good friend, a good friend! When things were looking dangerous, he encouraged me. And when the votes reached two thirds, there was the usual applause, because the Pope had been elected. And he gave me a hug and a kiss and said: "Don't forget the poor!" And those words came to me: the poor, the poor. Then, right away, thinking of the poor, I thought of Francis of Assisi. Then I thought of all the wars, as the votes were still being counted, till the end. Francis is also the man of peace. That is how the name came into my heart: Francis of Assisi. For me, he is the man of poverty, the man of peace, the man who loves and protects creation; these days we do not have a very good relationship with creation, do we? He is the man who gives us this spirit of peace, the poor man... How I would like a Church which is poor and for the poor![49]

CARDINAL GRACIAS, in his post-conclave interview,[50] recalled that "after his election and acceptance, one of the things we were looking for was what name is he going to take? I remember we were craning our heads to listen to this, and he said, "I take the name Francis (in memory or in honor of St Francis of Assisi)." We all asked each other which name has he taken? I remember Levada was in front of me and he turned around and asked 'What name has he taken?' I told him. We were happy. For me the name was a message."

Cardinal O'Malley, in his blog on the conclave, said, "That was a very emotional and moving moment, when he accepted and announced that his name would be Francis in honor of Saint Francis of Assisi. He said very explicitly that he was taking it in honor of Saint Francis of Assisi. As a Jesuit, he could have said he was taking the name in honor of Saint Francis Xavier, who is one of the greatest missionaries in the history of the Church. In talking about evangelization, for example, it would have been very understandable, but he specified that he was taking the name of Saint Francis of Assisi."

Cardinal Coccopalmerio said he was "very happy" too, because he is also called Francis, after the saint of Assisi.

But not everyone was happy. Cardinal Rodé, for example, later on turned to Cardinal Levada, who was near him, and commented, "This is going to be a disaster!"[51]

After the acceptance and choice of name, the master of ceremonies, Msgr. Marini, followed the procedure in the constitution and, "acting as notary and having as witnesses two Masters of Ceremonies," drew up "a document certifying acceptance by the new Pope and the name taken by him." The two witnesses were Msgrs. Camaldo and Krajewski.

In the apostolic constitution, John Paul II also decreed: "At the end of the election the Cardinal Camerlengo of Holy Roman Church shall draw up a document, to be approved also by the three Cardinal Assistants, declaring the result of the voting at each session. This document is to be given to the Pope and will thereafter be kept in a designated archive, enclosed in a sealed envelope, which may be opened by no one unless the Supreme Pontiff gives explicit permission."[52]

After accepting the election and declaring his new name, Pope Francis left the Sistine Chapel and went to the so-called Room of Tears, a small robing room adjacent to the Sistine Chapel where the new pope goes to take off his cardinal's robes and put on the white cassock of the pope;[53] it is called the "Room of Tears" because of the strong emotions felt by the newly elected pope, which can sometimes result in tears. Francis entered with Msgr. Marini and "they locked the door," Cardinal Sandri recalled.

Gammarelli, the tailor shop that was established in 1798 and has been the papal outfitter since the time of Pius IX (1846–1878), had prepared three sets of clothes for the new pope: a white wool cassock, a short red ermine cape called a *mozzetta*, and some accessories: a gold string for the cross and a belt with golden tassels which would later bear the coat of arms of the new pope. Each set came in three different sizes: small, medium, and large.

Francis chose the medium size cassock but, breaking with tradition, he declined to wear the gold string and cross that was offered to him; he opted instead to retain his old silver one. Likewise, he insisted on wearing the old black shoes with which he had walked the streets and shanty towns of Buenos Aires, not the red ones that had been specially made for the new pope. He also declined to wear the *mozzetta* over his shoulders as his predecessors had done. When he had finished changing, he came out dressed in white as the pope.

"It was about 7:10 when he came out; I remember looking at my watch," Cardinal Gracias told me. "We watched him come out dressed as the pope but wearing his normal [pectoral] cross and ring," Cardinal Sandri recalled.[54]

WHILE FRANCIS WAS EXCHANGING his scarlet cardinal's cassock for the white papal one, the scrutineers gathered the ballot sheets from the three rounds of voting, took them to be burned in the stove at the back of the chapel, and inserted the appropriate chemical in the second stove to ensure that the smoke would be white.

Outside in Saint Peter's Square, meanwhile, oblivious of the fact that history had been made inside the Sistine Chapel, tens of thousands of people from five continents and many countries had gathered in the cold and rain, huddled under a sea of multicolored umbrellas, while others just wore ponchos or raincoats. It had rained heavily before, but was raining less now. Although it was dark, the square was lit up by television cameras, and people's eyes moved from the long thin chimney on the Sistine chapel, now lit up by a spotlight, to the two maxi-screens in the square that were providing a live video-feed of the chimney.

A feeling of great expectation swept through the crowd as the hands of the clock moved closer to seven. Everyone knew that in a matter of minutes smoke would pour out of the chimney, and all were hoping it would be white. Some prayed the rosary, others held religious objects, hoping for a new pope to bless them, many were talking to those next to them or taking photos with their smartphones, while others just watched and waited in silence. Across the globe millions of Catholics were waiting for news too.

More than half an hour ago, a white seagull had perched on the chimney of the Sistine Chapel, and quickly captured the limelight. Some in the square took this as a portent of things to come, the idea being #habemusbird = #habemuspapa. The television cameras zoomed in on the seagull, photographers took snapshots, and on Twitter the hashtag #habemusbird took off. The bird became an instant star, and soon had its own Twitter account, @SistineSeagull, with several thousand followers.

Expectations had skyrocketed in the square as the clock struck seven. The atmosphere was electric as people waited impatiently for smoke from the chimney of the Sistine Chapel. Then suddenly, at 7:06 PM, the seagull flew away and smoke billowed out of the chimney; an uncertain color at first but then unequivocally WHITE.

A mighty roar went up from the crowd. People cheered, applauded, waved flags and umbrellas, and hugged each other. TV networks, news agencies, and radios struggled to compete with Twitter to flash the breaking news across the globe. At CTV we interrupted programs being broadcast across Canada to give the breaking news.

Then, to remove any remaining doubt, after the white smoke, the mighty bell of Saint Peter's Basilica, known as the "Campanone" rang out. This 1,973-pound bell dates back to 1795. Now, along with its six smaller bells, it pealed out with joy the good news, confirming to the world: "We have a pope!" Twitter was on fire. On CTV, like everywhere else, people were asking: Who has been elected?

Soon after the white smoke and the ringing of the bells of Saint Peter's, to everyone's surprise the news began to circulate that the bells of Milan's cathedral had started ringing too, giving the impression that Scola had been elected. Was this true? Had someone sent a signal? The suspense became almost unbearable. But it took more than an hour before we learned the name of the man the cardinals had chosen.

At the 2005 conclave, forty-five minutes elapsed between the white smoke and the announcement to the world by the cardinal proto-deacon (the senior member of the order of cardinal-deacons) that Cardinal Ratzinger had been elected. At the 2013 conclave, however, it took much longer: sixty-six minutes.

To understand this time lag, it is necessary to return to the Sistine Chapel where things were happening amidst an atmosphere of great joy.

Pope Francis returned to the Sistine Chapel dressed in white. A white chair had been placed in front of the altar for him. There, following tradition, he was to receive the homage and obedience of the cardinals. But instead of going to the chair, he walked straight down the chapel, to the amazement of the cardinal electors who wondered where he was going and whether he was actually leaving the Sistine Chapel. Instead, almost tripping in his new cassock, the new pope went and embraced the Indian cardinal, Ivan Dias, who was in a wheelchair.

Cardinal Coccopalmerio recalled that touching moment. At the end of the conclave, he said, it has been the tradition that the first homage that the new pope receives is from the cardinals in the Sistine Chapel, so he goes to a pedestal, in front of the altar and sits on a footstool or chair for this. "But before that happened he left and went to the central part of the Sistine Chapel, and everyone asked: What's happening? What's he doing? He went to greet Cardinal Dias who was ill and was in a wheelchair. This gesture struck everyone, because normally the pope is the one to whom everyone goes; instead, he was the one who went to greet Dias, and that gave us all a lot of joy."

This act of tenderness greatly impressed the cardinals, several told me afterwards. Cardinal Tong commented, "The new Holy Father really cares for everybody, particularly the weak."

After that embrace, Francis returned to the chair in front of the altar. At this point, following protocol, Cardinal Re led a prayer of thanksgiving to God for the election of the new pope. This was followed by the reading of the passage from chapter 16 (verses 13–19) of the Gospel according to Saint Matthew, which recounts that after Peter had confessed his faith in Jesus, the Lord told him: "You are Peter, and upon this rock I will build my church, and the gates of the netherworld shall not prevail against it. I will give you the keys of the kingdom of heaven. Whatever you bind on earth shall be bound in heaven; and whatever you loose on earth shall be loosed in heaven."

The scripture reading was followed by a prayer for the new pope, and then the cardinals, in order of precedence, went up to greet him in an act of homage and obedience. According to a long tradition, the pope remains seated for this, but Francis, again breaking with tradition, remained standing to greet each one individual on the same level.

Some of the cardinals fell on their knees before him, but he managed to stop many from doing so. When the Vietnamese cardinal, Jean-Baptiste Pham Minh Man, 79, bowed to kiss his ring, Francis blocked him and instead kissed his hands, in an act of homage to the courageous

Vietnamese church that had suffered much in the second half of the twentieth century.

He did likewise when Cardinal Tong, the only Chinese elector, came to express his homage and obedience. The cardinal narrated exactly what happened in a homily at a Mass of thanksgiving for the election of the new pope soon after he returned to Hong Kong. "One by one, we extended our personal greetings and embraces of love to him," he said, "and when it came to my turn, I gave him a small bronze Chinese statue of Our Lady of Sheshan, and told him, 'the Catholics in China love you and will pray for you. Also, we ask for your care for all Chinese Catholics, and please pray for us!' Francis responded, 'Chinese Catholics have given many testimonies to the Universal Church,' and then he kissed my right hand to show his love and devotion for the Church in China. This gesture moved me deeply." Tong recalled that two days later he happened to be in the same elevator with the new pope and Francis told him that the statue, now standing in his own room, reminded him of the Jesuit Saint Francis Xavier who arrived in China more than 460 years ago. "He told me he never forgets to pray for Chinese Catholics."

Cardinal Gracias told me that when his turn came to express his obedience, he told the new pope: "We love you. India loves you. Bless India." Then he added, "Most Holy Father, your name has impressed me so much. The whole program is there in the name." Francis responded, "Greetings to India. Warm greetings to India!" And as he was leaving the pope added, "Please pray for me!" Reflecting on this request, the cardinal commented: "He meant it. He is an ardent believer in prayer. He is a person of deep prayer and deep holiness, and that is what we wanted. That is what the Church wanted."

Cardinal Sandri, in his interview with Elisabetta Piqué for *La Nación*, revealed that he was quite emotional when his turn came to promise obedience to his fellow Argentinian. "I went on my knees and said to him, 'Don't make me cry!'"

Once all the cardinals had greeted the new pope, Cardinal Re concluded the celebration in the Sistine Chapel by leading everyone in a powerful rendition of the *Te Deum*, a hymn of jubilation and thanksgiving to God that dates back to the fifth century.

IMMEDIATELY AFTERWARDS, the senior cardinal-deacon, Jean-Louis Tauran, left the Sistine Chapel and headed for the central balcony of Saint Peter's Basilica to announce to the world the election and name of the new pope.

It had been the tradition that the cardinal dean who presided at the conclave and the master of ceremonies would accompany the new pope from the Sistine to the Pauline Chapel before greeting the world. Francis, however, invited his friend, Cardinal Hummes, and his vicar for the Rome diocese, Cardinal Vallini, to accompany him.

Pope Francis walked out of the Sistine Chapel looking down at the ground, and he went to the Pauline Chapel to pray in silence before making his first appearance as pope on the central balcony of Saint Peter's. He knelt and prayed intensely for some minutes, flanked by the two cardinals. When he finished he stood up, and when he turned around he seemed a different person, Msgr. Dario Vigano recalled. "He was another man, smiling, as if he had entrusted his burden to God."[55]

As all this was happening, tens of thousands of people from across Rome were heading as fast as they could to Saint Peter's Square to be present when Cardinal Tauran revealed the name of the new pope.

Fr. Fabián Pedacchio, the Argentinian priest who had accompanied Bergoglio to the Domus Santa Marta on March 12, after some hesitation and encouraged by a priest friend decided to go to the square too, and arrived in good time to hear the announcement.

The English cardinal, Murphy-O'Connor, as he recounts in his memoir,[56] had just finished celebrating the six o'clock Mass at his beautiful titular church, Santa Maria Sopra Minerva, next to the Pantheon, during which he had asked the congregation to pray for the cardinals in conclave. Suddenly someone rushed up to him and said, "White smoke! White smoke!"

He quickly removed his vestments and set out to walk to Saint Peter's. It was raining when he came out of church but fortunately Msgr. Nicholas Hudson, the rector of the English College where he was staying, had brought a car and so he got in and they headed for the Vatican. But they soon had to abandon the car and walk, because news that a new pope had been elected had spread like wildfire across the city and half of Rome seemed to be moving in the same direction, on foot.

"How well I remember walking down the Via della Conciliazione towards Saint Peter's, with people on either side of me carrying umbrellas, wondering and praying about the man who would soon be coming out on the balcony and giving us his blessing. I had my own hopes in my heart, but I remember saying to myself, a sort of act of faith, 'Whoever comes out on that balcony, he will be pope and he will always have my total loyalty and support,'" the cardinal wrote.

"When we arrived in the square," he recalled, "it was full of people. The rain and the lamps coming on created a curious sensation." Archbishop Arthur Roche, his former auxiliary and now secretary of the Congregation for Divine Worship, invited him to come up to his office where there was a window looking out on the square, and from there they watched and waited for the historic announcement.

Back home, Elisabetta became increasingly nervous, as I would later learn. Deep in her heart, she felt ever more certain that our friend Cardinal Bergoglio would be the new pope—he is an Argentinian, and she, a correspondent for Argentina's paper of record, which he reads. She foresaw that this would be an earthquake for our family and would change her life, indeed all our lives, for many years to come.

She watched the television ever more anxiously and waited impatiently with her father, Piero, and the children to hear the name of the new pope. Juan Pablo had already reached his own conclusion: It will be "Padre Jorge," as we called him.

AT THE CTV PLATFORM we, like everyone else, were watching and waiting for the announcement of the name of the new pope. Then at 8:10 PM, the lights suddenly came on in the Hall of Benedictions and the loggia behind the central balcony of Saint Peter's Basilica. Vatican ushers opened the great windows and drew back the heavy red velvet curtains.

Two minutes later, at 8:12 PM, Cardinal Jean-Louis Tauran, the eminent, seventy-year-old French cardinal, now suffering from Parkinson's disease, appeared on the balcony accompanied by a master of ceremonies who held the microphone for him to make the announcement. The suspense was unbearable.

Cardinal Tauran began reading from a prepared Latin text and told the now silent crowd huddled under umbrellas in the square, and the hundreds of millions worldwide watching the scene on live television or by social media: "*Annuntio vobis gaudium magnum, habemus papam!*"("I announce a great joy to you: We have a pope!") A thunderous roar rose up from the tens of thousands of Romans, pilgrims and tourists in the square, followed by prolonged applause.

CTV was transmitting the dramatic scene live across the different time zones in Canada. Lisa LaFlamme, the CTV anchor, charged me with the task of recognizing and announcing the name of the new pope to the millions in Canada who were following us at this hour. As the crowd cheered, my heart raced with excitement, expectation, and hope.

When the crowd felt silent again, Cardinal Tauran announced the name: "*Eminentissimum ac reverendissimum Dominum, Dominum Georgium Marium Sanctae Romanae Ecclesiae Cardinalem Bergoglio, qui sibi nomen imposuit Franciscum*"—"The most eminent and most reverend Lord, Lord Jorge Mario Bergoglio, cardinal of the Holy Roman church, who has taken the name Francis."

On hearing the name, my heart exploded with emotion and I shouted, "It's the Argentinian! Bergoglio is the new pope!" Lisa LaFlamme remarked, "Gerry, you got it right again!"

Elisabetta too, as she recalled in her biography, was overcome with emotion when she heard Cardinal Tauran's announcement that Bergoglio was pope.[57] "I freeze. My fingers aren't working properly. I start tweeting in capital letters, to make my enormous excitement totally clear: 'THE NEW POPE IS JORGE BERGOGLIO.' I'm so beside myself that he's the new pope that I miss his choice of name: Francis, a revolution, no less."

Fr. Fabián Pedacchio, standing in the square, was overwhelmed with emotion when he heard that his archbishop, whom he had accompanied to Santa Marta for the conclave, was the new pope. "I was knocked out!" he told me.

Cardinal Cormac too recalled[58] the moment Tauran revealed the name: "There was a brief hush. Nobody had heard of this prelate from Argentina. In spite of the feverish speculation by professional Vatican watchers, Bergoglio's name had hardly been mentioned."

BENEDICT XVI REVEALED that he too was totally surprised by the election of Cardinal Bergoglio as pope. In the book based on interviews by Peter Seewald, Benedict says: "No one had expected him. I knew him, of course, but I did not consider him—so it was a great surprise to me."[59]

Asked if he had been expecting someone else, Benedict replied, "Certainly, yes, not anyone in particular, but another, yes." Asked if Bergoglio was one of them, he responded, "No. I did not think he was among the more likely candidates." Even though he was one of the favorites at the last conclave, "I thought that was past." And he added, "When I heard the name I was uncertain at first. But when I saw how he spoke with God on the one hand and with the people on the other, I was truly glad. And happy."

THE ITALIAN BISHOPS' CONFERENCE was caught completely off-guard; they had confidently expected Cardinal Scola to be elected; they were so sure of this that their secretariat made the incredible blunder of issuing a press communique expressing "joy and thanks to God," and welcoming "the news of the election of Cardinal Angelo Scola as successor of Peter"! They managed to correct the statement some forty minutes later.

Avvenire, the daily newspaper of the Italian bishops' conference, was shell-shocked: it had prepared a sixteen-page supplement on the archbishop of Milan that was ready to roll on the printing press. It had to scrap all that.

The mainline Italian media, except for *La Stampa*, were dumbfounded; they had not seen this coming, and even those who had mentioned Bergoglio's name as an outsider certainly never imagined him being elected so soon. And since the Italian media had up to this point led the conversation for the international media on all things relating to the papacy and the conclave, the latter too were badly misled, and not one of them (except *La Nación* in Argentina), predicted the election of the first pope from the southern hemisphere.

Even the Vatican daily *L'Osservatore Romano* was so taken by surprise that it got Bergoglio's age wrong in the first edition printed immediately after the election; it gave it as seventy-seven instead of seventy-six.[60]

AT 8:22 PM, ONE HOUR AFTER THE ANNOUNCEMENT, Pope Francis, dressed in white, appeared on the central balcony of Saint Peter's. The quarter of a million people in the square were ecstatic. They cheered and waved flags—surprisingly many of Argentina, but also of the United States, Canada, Italy, Brazil, Spain, and Mexico. They hugged each other, applauded, jumped up and down with joy.

Francis just stood there in silence, immobile. He seemed stunned by the sea of humanity that stretched out in the darkness before him across the square, right down the Via della Conciliazione reaching toward Castel San Angelo. He just gazed at the crowd as the flashes from thousands of iPads, smartphones, and cameras lit up the square and captured this historic, joy-filled moment.

As he looked down, he could see in the main area under the loggia, in front of the basilica, the Swiss Guards, the Vatican Gendarmerie, and different elements of the armed forces from Italy's army, navy, and air force, all standing at attention.

Finally, Francis spoke. In Italian. But in a way nobody expected, least of all the cardinals who had just elected him and who were now clustered at the windows on either side of him on the loggia, looking out on Saint Peter's Square:

"*Fratelli e sorelle, buona sera!*" ("Brothers and sisters, good evening!")

With that first "*Buona sera!*" the new pope reached the hearts of the Romans, as well as millions of people across the globe now following on live television. Lisa LaFlamme, the CTV anchor standing beside me gasped in awe. "Oh my God!" The crowd in the square went wild and responded with thunderous applause. They loved it! There was new energy in the air.

Then, with a smile on his face, Francis, the first non-European pope in almost thirteen hundred years, continued in a humorous vein:

"You know that it was the duty of the conclave to give Rome a bishop. It seems that my brother cardinals have gone to the ends of the earth to get one... but here we are..."

Again, thunderous applause. The cardinals immediately noted that he had referred to himself as "bishop" not "pope" or "Roman pontiff." The leaders of the other Christian churches and communities also took note of this.

"I thank you for your welcome. The diocesan community of Rome now has its bishop. Thank you!" he said.

He touched their hearts even more, and drew sustained applause, by next referring to his predecessor: "First of all, I would like to offer a prayer for our bishop emeritus, Benedict XVI. Let us pray together for him, that the Lord may bless him and that Our Lady may keep him."

He went on to lead them in praying the Our Father... Hail Mary ... Glory Be... Prayers that everyone, even the children on the street, knew.

It was truly moving to watch the people recite these simple prayers with the new pope. I saw so many with tears in their eyes as they prayed fervently with him. It was a profoundly religious experience.

We learned later that Francis had tried to reach Benedict XVI by phone before coming out on the balcony, but without success. The emeritus pope and those with him at the residence in Castel Gandolfo had been watching it all on television and didn't hear the phone ring!

After praying for his predecessor, Francis turned to his own role as their new bishop and told the Romans:

"And now, we take up this journey: bishop and people. This journey of the church of Rome which presides in charity over all the churches. A journey of fraternity, of love, of trust among us. Let us always pray for one another. Let us pray for the whole world, that there may be a great spirit of fraternity. It is my hope for you that this journey of the church, which we start today, and in which my cardinal vicar, here present, will assist me, will be fruitful for the evangelization of this most beautiful city."

According to an ancient tradition, the new pope gives his first blessing, "*Urbi et Orbi*," to the city of Rome ("*urbi*") and to the world ("*orbi*"). Francis intended to follow suit, but with a striking difference. He put on the ceremonial stole just for the blessing—and not for the entire encounter with the people in Saint Peter's Square as had been the custom, and then told them:

"And now I would like to give the blessing, but first—first, I ask a favor of you: before the bishop blesses his people, I ask you to pray to the Lord that he will bless me: the prayer of the people asking the blessing for their bishop. Let us make, in silence, this prayer: your prayer over me."

Then, to the astonishment not only of the cardinals on either side of him, looking out at the crowd from the loggia, but also of his global audience, the first Latin American pope bowed down in front of the crowd. It was something never before seen in the history of the papacy.

An absolute silence descended on the crowd in the square. It was an awesome moment. An unforgettable one. Total silence!

After about a minute he broke the silence and said, "Now I will give the blessing to you and to the whole world, to all men and women of good will." Then, raising his right hand, he imparted the blessing in Latin.

The bands played the Vatican national anthem. The crowd roared their joy. Francis stood transfixed and watched for some minutes. He concluded this incredible evening with simple words:

"Brothers and sisters, I leave you now. Thank you for your welcome. Pray for me until we meet again. We will see each other soon. Tomorrow I wish to go and pray to Our Lady, that she may watch over all of Rome. Good night and sleep well!"

AFTER BIDDING FAREWELL to the crowd, Francis went back inside the loggia and this time managed to speak with Benedict by phone.

Benedict XVI, in his interview book with Peter Seewald, revealed his own reaction when Francis came out onto the balcony for the first time as pope, dressed in white, and later when they spoke by phone.

"We were all dressed in white. He did not want the mozzetta; that did not matter to me at all. I was very touched, however, that even before he stepped out onto the loggia he wanted to call me by telephone, although unfortunately he did not reach me, as we were watching the television. Also, by how he prayed for me, that moment of reflection, and then the cordiality with which he greeted the people. That made the spark catch immediately, you might say. I knew him of course, but I did not consider him—so it was a great surprise to me. But that convinced me immediately, the way he prayed on the one hand, and, on the other, how he spoke to the hearts of the people."[61]

Msgr. Xuereb, the second of Benedict's two private secretaries, speaking at a conference in northern Italy in October 2017, revealed what had happened in Castel Gandolfo that evening after Francis appeared on the balcony: "We were struck with admiration at the words and gestures of the new pontiff." Then, during dinner, the phone rang. It was Francis wanting to greet his predecessor. Earlier the sound of the phone had been switched off in the TV room as they watched the election, he said. Msgr. Xuereb was present when the phone rang this time: "It was very moving to be present. I heard Benedict say, 'I thank you Holy Father that you have thought immediately of me!'"

AFTER GREETING HIS PREDECESSOR, Francis set out to return to Santa Marta. A limousine driven by a chauffeur was waiting, ready to take him there but, to the amazement and delight of the cardinals, he opted instead to travel back on the coach with them, just as he had come. Fr. Lombardi later told reporters that at the dinner in Santa Marta, the cardinal electors toasted and applauded the new pope. When his turn came to speak, he thanked them, and then raising his own glass, he remarked with a smile, "May God forgive you for what you have done!"

That night he made several phone calls. One was to his sister in Buenos Aires, who was stunned.

Surprisingly, he also found time to send a message to the chief rabbi of Rome, Riccardo Di Segni. During his years as archbishop of Buenos Aires he had developed extraordinarily close relations with the Jewish community, and had participated in a television program with Rabbi Abraham Skorka, which later became the basis for a book that was translated into many languages.[62] He made clear tonight, in his message to the chief rabbi, that as pope he intended to continue his relationship with the Jewish people.

He wrote, "On the day of my election as bishop of Rome and pastor of the universal Catholic church, I send you my cordial greeting, and announce that the solemn inauguration of my pontificate will take place on March 19." Then he added, "Trusting in the protection of the Almighty, I strongly hope to be able to contribute to the progress that the relations between Jews and Catholics have known since the Second Vatican Council, in a spirit of renewed collaboration and service to the world that may always be ever more in harmony with the will of the Creator."[63]

Pope Francis slept peacefully that night after an exhausting day. The next morning he woke up very early, as usual, to pray.

Part IV

EARLY SIGNS OF
A NEW STYLE OF PAPACY

(March 14–19, 2013)

Surprises on Francis's First Day as Pope

THE SURPRISE ELECTION of the first Latin American pope, the first Jesuit, and the first to take the name Francis, made headline news around the world. There was consensus that it marked a seismic shift in the leadership of the Catholic Church, and that his first appearance on the central balcony of Saint Peter's Basilica heralded the dawn of a new style of papacy.

What happened in the days following his election and leading up to the inauguration ceremony on March 19 revealed even more clearly that Pope Francis intended to exercise the papal ministry in a distinctly new and refreshing way that traced its roots back to the origins of the Church, to the apostle Peter, the first pope.

I WOKE EARLY this Thursday morning and scanned the national and international media before heading for the CTV television studio to comment on Bergoglio's election for the Canadian audience. I saw that the front pages of most Italian newspapers carried a photo of a smiling Pope Francis on the central balcony of Saint Peter's after his election. All described his election as a great surprise, on a par with that of John Paul II in 1978.

This morning, however, I was more interested in the headlines of the Latin American press. *La Nación*, the Argentine daily, carried the photo with his name "Francisco" and the subtitle "*El Papa que llegó desde el fin del mundo*" ("The pope who came from the end of the world"). Its rival daily, *Clarín*, also ran the photo with the caption, "*Papa Argentino*." The country's other paper, *Pagina 12*, which had often attacked Cardinal Bergoglio when he was archbishop of Buenos Aires, screamed "*¡Dios Mío!*" ("My God!").

Each paper carried a biography and long commentary on his election, but I had little time to read them, as Francis was already on the move and we had to track him.

AS IS WELL KNOWN, after his first greeting to the world from the balcony of Saint Peter's the previous evening, Francis had opted to ride back with the cardinals on the coach to Santa Marta, having declined the papal limousine that was ready to take him there.

This morning too, continuing his rejection of status symbols, he gave instructions that he wanted to drive in a small economy car, not the papal limousine, to the Basilica of Saint Mary Major where he wished to pray in front of the venerated Byzantine image of the Virgin Mary with the child Jesus, known as *Salus populi Romani* (the Salvation or Protectress of the Roman people), that had arrived in Rome in 590 AD. He was driven in an economy car, a dark-colored Ford Focus.

In the past, whenever the pope drove through the city of Rome, he almost always moved with an escort of outriders, while police stopped traffic and cleared the route as they do for heads of state or government so that his motorcade could pass quickly. This morning, however, Francis insisted that the escort be reduced to an absolute minimum and asked that the police not block the streets for him; he wanted to move as an ordinary citizen. He traveled in the car with his window lowered, so that he could wave to people. It was a refreshing sight, greatly appreciated by the Romans.

He arrived just before 8:00 AM at the basilica that stands on the Esquiline, one of the seven hills of Rome, and is one of the first churches built to the Virgin Mary after the Council of Ephesus (431 AD) proclaimed Mary as the Mother of God.

There he was joyfully welcomed by his friend, Cardinal Santos Abril y Castelló, archpriest of this major basilica. Francis entered by a side door carrying a small bouquet of flowers and went straight to the Pauline Chapel, where he placed them in front of the famous icon. He prayed in silence for around ten minutes, entrusting his pontificate to the Blessed Virgin. It was the first of his many visits as pope to this basilica to pray before the revered image.

Having finished his prayer, he greeted the canons and the confessors of the basilica and told the latter "Be merciful with souls!" It was a significant remark, as mercy has always been a central theme of his ministry as bishop and is in the motto of his papal coat of arms, "*Miserando atque eligendo.*"

He then walked to the nearby Sistine Chapel, where Saint Ignatius of Loyola, the founder of the Jesuits, celebrated his first Mass on Christmas day in 1538, and prayed there too. He also stopped at the tomb in that chapel of one of his predecessors, Saint Pius V, who was pope from 1556 to 1572.

Students from a nearby high school, the Liceo "Albertelli," had spotted him entering the basilica and cheered when he came out. He responded joyfully and waved to them.

On leaving the basilica, instead of returning to the Vatican, he made a detour to visit the Domus Paulus VI, where he had resided before the conclave. On arrival, he greeted the staff, most of whom he knew, collected his meager belongings, and, before leaving, insisted on paying for his sojourn from February 27 to March 12. "In that way, he wanted to set a good example!" Fr. Lombardi commented to reporters.

He had not been pope for even twenty-four hours, but he was already sending a clear message to the world: he didn't want special privileges. This new way of being pope, which Elisabetta in her biography called "the scandal of normality," was warmly welcomed by a great many ordinary people in Rome but it upset not a few traditionalists who then, and in subsequent months and years, would charge him with desacralizing and downgrading the papacy.

FROM THE MOMENT OF HIS ELECTION, Francis wanted, as far as possible, to continue living a normal life. We experienced this in our own relationship with him over the days that followed. Soon after returning to the Vatican that Thursday morning, he called Elisabetta on her mobile phone. She recounted the story in her biography.[1] He made clear then that he wanted to remain in contact with us. He said that he had also tried to contact me, but without success. (My phone was switched off because I was on air with CTV television, or giving interviews to other news outlets.)

Back in Argentina, Francis was accustomed to using the phone a lot, and he didn't change his ways on becoming pope. On the night of his election, in addition to calling his sister and several friends back in Buenos Aires, he also called some friends in Rome, including Gianni Valente's family. Gianni was not at home but his wife Stefania Falasca was, and Francis spoke with her. He would continue making private calls in the days and years ahead.

FRANCIS PHONED FR. FABIÁN PEDACCHIO that Thursday morning and asked him to come to Santa Marta in the afternoon. Don Fabián, as he is called in Rome, was born in Buenos Aires and studied economics before going on for the priesthood. He is an expert in canon law and, with Cardinal Bergoglio's backing, had gone to work at the Congregation for Bishops in 2007. Benedict XVI made him a monsignor in 2012.

Upon meeting his former archbishop at Santa Marta, he learned that Francis wanted him to be his private secretary. He made it clear, however, that the role was to be low profile; he was to work behind the scenes, not in the limelight. This too was a significant break with the recent past, particularly in light of the highly visible and operational roles—including that of gatekeeper—played by the private secretaries of John XXIII, Paul VI, John Paul II, and Benedict XVI.[2]

FRANCIS WAS THE FIRST JESUIT to become pope since the Society of Jesus was approved as a religious order by Paul III in 1540, and so today the order's Spanish-born superior general, Fr. Adolfo Nicolás, issued a statement on this historic fact. The election not only took the world by surprise but stunned the whole order. Fr. Nicolás wrote:

> In the name of the Society of Jesus, I give thanks to God for the election of our new Pope, Cardinal Jorge Mario Bergoglio, S.J., which opens for the Church a path full of hope.
>
> All of us Jesuits accompany with our prayers our brother and we thank him for his generosity in accepting the responsibility of guiding the Church at this crucial time. The name of "Francis" by which we shall now know him evokes for us the Holy Father's evangelical spirit of *closeness to the poor*, his identification with simple people, and his commitment to the renewal of the Church. From the very first moment in which he appeared before the people of God, he gave visible witness to his simplicity, his humility, his pastoral experience, and his spiritual depth.
>
> "The distinguishing mark of our Society is that it is...a companionship...bound to the Roman Pontiff by a special bond of love and service" (Complementary Norms, No. 2, §2). Thus, we share the joy of the whole Church, and at the same time, wish to express our renewed availability to be sent into the vineyard of the Lord, according to the spirit of our special vow of obedience, that so distinctively unites us with the Holy Father (General Congregation 35, Decree 1, No. 17).
>
> P. Adolfo Nicolás S.J.
> Superior General
> Rome, 14 March 2013

ON THAT FIRST EVENING after his election, Francis followed the Roman tradition by celebrating the *Missa pro Ecclesia* (Mass for the Church) in the Sistine Chapel with the cardinals who had participated in the conclave. It was his first Mass as pope, and it was in Latin. The Sistine Choir led the singing. He celebrated with great simplicity, as if he were a parish priest. Whereas in the past the master of ceremonies would remove the pope's miter at various parts of the celebration, Francis removed it himself. And when it came to the time for the homily, he went to the lectern as any parish priest would do instead of remaining seated as had hitherto been the custom for popes.

Following custom, Vatican officials had prepared a homily for the new pope for his first Mass, assuming he would not have time to prepare one. Francis however put it aside and spoke off the cuff, in fluent Italian, for seven and a half minutes, looking into the eyes of the cardinals seated in front of him. In Buenos Aires he had been accustomed to comment on the scripture readings at Mass and was renowned for his ability to highlight their relevance to the lives of those present.

In this case,[3] he linked the three scripture readings to the lives of the cardinals concelebrating with him. The first reading was from the prophet Isaiah, chapter 2; the second was from the first letter of Peter; and the third was from the Gospel according to Saint Matthew, chapter 16, where Jesus tells Peter, "You are Peter and on this rock I will build my church."

He told the cardinals, "In these three readings, I see a common element: that of movement. In the first reading, it is the movement of a journey; in the second reading, the movement of building the Church; in the third, in the Gospel, the movement involved in professing the faith. Journeying, building, professing." He went on to comment on each of those three movements:

"Journeying," he recalled, "is the first thing that God said to Abraham: 'Walk in my presence and live blamelessly.'" He reminded the cardinals, that "our life is a journey, and when we stop moving, things go wrong. Always journeying, in the presence of the Lord, in the light of the Lord, seeking to live with the blamelessness that God asked of Abraham in his promise."

"Building the Church," Francis said, is done with "living stones, stones anointed by the Holy Spirit," and involves building "on the cornerstone that is the Lord himself."

The third movement, he said, involves "professing the faith." Then, with razor-sharp words, he told the cardinals who had elected him, "We can walk as much as we want, we can build many things, but if we do not profess Jesus Christ, things go wrong. We may become a charitable NGO, but not the Church, the Bride of the Lord."

Francis reinforced his message by reminding them, "When we are not walking, we stop moving. When we are not building on the stones, what happens? The same thing that happens to children on the beach when they build sandcastles: everything is swept away, there is no solidity. When we do not profess Jesus Christ, the saying of Léon Bloy comes to mind: 'Anyone who does not pray to the Lord prays to the devil.' When we do not profess Jesus Christ, we profess the worldliness of the devil, a demonic worldliness."

Speaking from his twenty-one years of pastoral experience as a bishop, he acknowledged, however, that "things are not so straightforward, because in journeying, building, professing, there can sometimes be jolts, movements that are not properly part of the journey, movements that pull us back."

He recalled that the Gospel highlighted one such situation when it recounted that "the same Peter who professed Jesus Christ, now says to him: You are the Christ, the Son of the living God. I will follow you; but let us not speak of the Cross. That has nothing to do with it. I will follow you on other terms, but without the Cross."

Then, speaking from the heart with forceful words, Francis told the cardinals: "When we journey without the Cross, when we build without the Cross, when we profess Christ without the Cross, we are not disciples of the Lord, we are worldly: we may be bishops, priests, cardinals, popes, but not disciples of the Lord."

He concluded with these words: "My wish is that all of us, after these days of grace, will have the courage, yes, the courage, to walk in the presence of the Lord, with the Lord's Cross; to build the Church on the Lord's blood which was poured out on the Cross; and to profess the one glory: Christ crucified. And in this way, the Church will go forward."

He prayed that "the Holy Spirit, through the intercession of the Blessed Virgin Mary, our Mother, will grant us this grace: to walk, to build, to profess Jesus Christ crucified. Amen."

After delivering this striking homily, Francis returned to his seat. There was silence. It was but the first of his many powerful homilies that would attract attention, and not only in the Vatican. Francis has the gift of making the Gospel come alive in a new and fresh way. Though no one realized it then, he would reach the hearts of pastors and people alike across the world in the months and years ahead through his homilies at daily Mass, in ways that brought the Gospel and the papacy close to the lives of people.

AFTER MASS, Cardinal Bertone, the camerlengo, and Archbishop Georg Ganswein, the prefect of the Papal Household, as well as other officials, accompanied Francis to the papal apartments in the Vatican's Apostolic Palace, which had been locked and sealed ever since Benedict XVI moved out on February 28.[4]

All the popes of the twentieth century had lived in this apartment on the third floor of the palace, ever since Pius X first took up residence here in 1903. Indeed, for more than six centuries the popes have lived in this palace, or in other places nearby in the Vatican.

On reaching the apartment, Francis, following the norms laid down by the apostolic constitution, broke the seals on the doors and entered "to take possession of" the apartment that had been restructured and refurbished in 2005, before Benedict came to live here. He walked through its ten rooms, including bedrooms, decorated drawing rooms with sixteenth-century marble floors, a chapel, a medical unit, and a study. At one point, looking somewhat perplexed, he exclaimed, "but three hundred people could stay here!"[5] Quite unaware of his inner feelings, they informed him somewhat apologetically that he would have to wait some days before the apartment would be ready for him, as there was still some refurbishment to be done.

Little did they realize that he had no intention of living there. Neither did other senior Vatican officials who were confidently predicting that he would soon transfer from Santa Marta to "the apartment." Since his election, Francis had already moved from Room 207, a single bedroom, to Room 201, which was a suite reserved for special guests, such as the ecumenical patriarch of Constantinople. His new abode was composed of a medium-sized living room, an even smaller study, a bedroom, and bathroom.

It soon became clear that Vatican officials, with few exceptions, were unaware that as bishop in Buenos Aires he had lived an austere life, which he had no intention of changing. They did not know that when he became archbishop of the Argentine metropolis fifteen years ago he had refused to live in the archbishop's residence in the city's upmarket Olivos district, next to the residence of the state president, opting instead for a small apartment in the curial offices off the Plaza de Mayo, a square made famous worldwide by the weekly protests of the Madres de la Plaza de Mayo, the mothers of those who disappeared in the dirty war under military rule.

As pope, Francis wanted to live among people, not to be locked up in "a golden cage"—his own words—where access to him would be extremely difficult. Two weeks later, on March 26,[6] he announced at the end of morning Mass in Santa Marta that he had decided to make his residence there.

While his decision was welcomed by ordinary people, it provoked considerable resistance among many in the Vatican, not only for breaking with tradition and allegedly downgrading his status as pope, but also for reasons having to do with his personal privacy and security.

LATER THIS SAME DAY (March 14), Cardinal Raymundo Damasceno Assis, president of the Brazilian bishops' conference, radiated happiness as he revealed that in a private conversation the previous day Francis had confirmed that he would attend World Youth Day in Rio de Janeiro in July, an event that is expected to attract millions of young people.

MARCH 15 (FRIDAY) _____
"He Hasn't Changed a Bit"

NEWS LEAKS FROM SANTA MARTA revealed that Francis had rejected the idea of having a separate table for meals. He didn't want any special treatment; he preferred to take his meals with the cardinals who had elected him. At breakfast this morning, he sat at table with Cardinal Scola. At lunch he went to a table where there was a free place with other cardinals.

Moreover, he retained his sense of humor, as shown next morning when he came down to breakfast and Cardinal Toppo greeted him *"Buon giorno Santo Padre!"* ("Good morning Holy Father"). Francis responded with a smile, *"Buon giorno Santo Figlio"* ("Good morning, Holy Son!").

THIS MORNING, "Padre Jorge" phoned Elisabetta again, this time to wish her a happy birthday. He never forgets, and as she remarks in her book, "he hasn't changed a bit."[7] I spoke with him too. It was a great joy.

POPE FRANCIS WENT to the Sala Clementina this morning to greet the entire College of Cardinals, not only those who had elected him but also the over-eighties. The last time the college had gathered here was for

Benedict XVI's farewell address, exactly fifteen days ago. Today's meeting was also a farewell, but of a different kind, as Francis bade goodbye to the many cardinals who had come to Rome for the conclave, and who would return home after the inauguration ceremony on March 19 to preside at the Holy Week ceremonies in their respective dioceses.

They stood and applauded warmly when he entered the hall. Cardinal Angelo Sodano opened this joyful encounter by greeting him on behalf of the College of Cardinals. He thanked Francis for having accepted "the Lord's invitation with a big and generous heart." The papal office is "certainly a demanding job," he remarked, "but I am certain that the Good Shepherd will be always close to you and the Holy Spirit will enlighten you from on high, that same Spirit who always rejuvenates the church and continues its renewal." After assuring him that all the cardinals "will seek to provide our humble contribution to the Petrine ministry," he concluded by wishing Francis "*ad multos annos*," the good wish in Latin that means "May you live many years!"

Immediately after Sodano finished speaking, Pope Francis arose and moved to embrace the cardinal dean, unfortunately forgetting that there was a step to navigate. He missed it, and almost fell!

According to a long-standing protocol, Francis should have addressed them as "Lord Cardinals" (*Signori Cardinali*), but with that great inner freedom that he would reveal in his exercise of the papal ministry, Francis ignored the protocol and began his talk[8] by greeting them as "dear brother cardinals."

He recalled that "the period of the conclave has been a momentous time not only for the College of Cardinals, but also for all the faithful." Reflecting on that experience he said, "In these days we have felt almost tangibly the affection and the solidarity of the universal Church, as well as the concern of so many people who, even if they do not share our faith, look to the Church and the Holy See with respect and admiration."

He noted that "from every corner of the earth fervent prayers have been offered up by the Christian people for the new Pope." He revealed that his own "first encounter with the thronging crowd in Saint Peter's Square was deeply moving" and said "that evocative image of the people gathered in joyful prayer is still impressed on my memory."

Francis expressed his "sincere thanks" to the bishops, priests, consecrated persons, young people, families, and the elderly "for their spiritual closeness, so touching and so deeply felt."

He extended his "sincere and profound gratitude" to the cardinals, as a group and individually, for their "ready cooperation in the task of leading the Church during the period of the '*Sede Vacante*.'" He thanked, in particular, the dean, Cardinal Sodano, the camerlengo, Cardinal Bertone, and "our dear friend" Cardinal Re, "who led us during the conclave."

He conveyed special words of "affection" to those cardinals "who, on account of age or ill health, made their contribution and expressed their love for the Church by offering up their sufferings and their prayers." And he revealed that on March 13, his Argentinian friend, Cardinal Mejia, had suffered a heart attack and had been taken to the Pio XI Hospital, but said that his condition was now "stable" and "he has sent us his greetings."

Seeking to be all-inclusive, Francis thanked "all those who carried out various tasks in the preparation and the conduct of the conclave, providing the cardinals with security and peace of mind in this period of such importance for the life of the Church."

He drew spontaneous and warm applause when he told the cardinals, "my thoughts turn with great affection and profound gratitude to my venerable predecessor Benedict XVI, who enriched and invigorated the Church during the years of his Pontificate by his teaching, his goodness, his leadership, his faith, his humility and his meekness." He declared that all this "remains as a spiritual patrimony for us all" and remarked that "the Petrine ministry, lived with total dedication, found in him a wise and humble exponent, his gaze always firmly on Christ, the risen Christ, present and alive in the Eucharist."

He drew more applause when he assured his predecessor that "we will always accompany him with fervent prayers, with constant remembrance, with undying and affectionate gratitude." And, he added, "we feel that Benedict XVI has kindled a flame deep within our hearts: a flame that will continue to burn because it will be fed by his prayers, which continue to sustain the Church on her spiritual and missionary path."

He told the cardinals that his meeting with them today was "intended to be," as it were, "a prolongation of the intense ecclesial communion" that they had "experienced together" in this period. He recalled that, "inspired by a profound sense of responsibility and supported by a great love for Christ and for the Church, we have prayed together, fraternally sharing our feelings, our experiences and reflections." In that "atmosphere of great warmth," he said, "we have come to know one another better in a climate of mutual openness," marked by a sense of "community," "friendship," "closeness," and "mutual openness," that "helped us to be docile to the action of the Holy Spirit." That same Spirit, he remarked, "creates all the differences among the Churches, almost as if he were an Apostle of Babel" but also "creates unity from these differences, not in 'equality,'" but in 'harmony.'"

Then, referring to his new ministry as pope, he expressed his "desire to serve the Gospel with renewed love, helping the Church to become increasingly, in Christ and with Christ, the fruitful vine of the Lord." He called on everyone, "pastors and members of the faithful alike," to strive "together" in this Year of Faith "to respond faithfully to the Church's perennial mission: to bring Jesus Christ to mankind and to lead mankind to an encounter with Jesus Christ, the Way, the Truth and the Life, truly present in the Church and also in every person."

Benedict XVI, he said, "reminded us so many times in his teachings, and at the end by his courageous and humble gesture, [that] it is Christ who leads the Church through his Spirit. The Holy Spirit is the soul of the Church through his life-giving and unifying force: out of many, he makes one single body, the Mystical Body of Christ."

Then, in words reminiscent of John XXIII at the opening of the Second Vatican Council, Francis made a heartfelt appeal to the cardinals: "Let us never yield to pessimism, to that bitterness that the devil offers us every day; let us not yield to pessimism or discouragement: let us be quite certain that the Holy Spirit bestows upon the Church, with his powerful breath, the courage to persevere and also to seek new methods of evangelization, so as to bring the Gospel to the uttermost ends of the earth (cf. Acts 1:8)."

He reminded the cardinals that "Christian truth is attractive and persuasive because it responds to the profound need of human life, proclaiming convincingly that Christ is the one Savior of the whole man and of all men," and he declared, "this proclamation remains as valid today as it was at the origin of Christianity, when the first great missionary expansion of the Gospel took place."

Knowing that most of them would soon return to their home dioceses, others to Vatican offices or their places of retirement, Francis told them, "dear brother Cardinals, take courage! Half of us are advanced in age. Old age is—as I like to say—the seat of life's wisdom. The old have acquired the wisdom that comes from having journeyed through life, like the old man Simeon, the old prophetess Anna in the Temple. And that wisdom enabled them to recognize Jesus. Let us pass on this wisdom to the young: like good wine that improves with age, let us give life's wisdom to the young."

Francis, who spent some time in Germany after his period as Jesuit provincial and also speaks the language, recalled that a German poet once described old age as "a time of tranquility and prayer" (*Es ist ruhig, das Alter, und fromm)* and, the pope added, it is also a time "to pass on this wisdom to the young."

As they prepared to return home "to continue" their ministry, Francis reminded them that this ministry has been "enriched by the experience of these days, so full of faith and ecclesial communion" and, he added, "this unique and incomparable experience has enabled us to grasp deeply all the beauty of the Church, which is a glimpse of the radiance of the risen Christ: one day we will gaze upon that beautiful face of the risen Christ!"

He concluded by entrusting his ministry and theirs to "the powerful intercession of Mary, our Mother, Mother of the Church," and gave them his blessing.

HAVING FINISHED HIS TALK, Francis stood up and greeted each of the cardinals, one by one, with a smile, with words of encouragement or a pat on the shoulder or on the hand, an embrace. There were many touching moments. He bent down to greet Cardinal Dias in his wheelchair. He gave a clenched fist sign and said "*forza*" to Cardinal Caffarra. He spoke for some moments with Cardinal O'Malley, shared a hearty laugh with Cardinals Dolan and Tagle, and as Cardinal Scherer left him, he made a sign with his hand meaning "write to me." He accepted a yellow plastic bracelet from Cardinal Napier that had been made by a priest in South Africa for the young people for the Year of Faith; he looked at it, and then without hesitation put it on his wrist.

CARDINAL MURPHY-O'CONNOR revealed that when his turn came, "We embraced, and I assured him of my prayers. He then said: '*Dov'é la squadra?*' (Where is the team?)." The cardinal explained, "He was, of course, referring to the five cardinals who had sat in a group together at the previous conclave. He asked me to gather them together for a photo, which I did when all the greetings were completed. The last thing he said to me was: 'Don't forget: give the Queen my warmest greetings.'"9

THAT AFTERNOON, Francis again left the Vatican in an economy car, with minimal escort, and made a surprise visit to his friend, the ninety-year-old Argentinian cardinal Mejia, who was hospitalized at the Pio XI clinic in the Via Aurelia. He not only spent time with the cardinal but also met other patients and the medical staff, much to their delight; he encouraged the latter in their work, thanked them for their care of the sick, and then asked everyone, "Pray for me."

Pope Francis is a strategist. He showed this today, at the very begin-ning of his pontificate, when he took the initiative to re-open a dialogue with the authorities in Beijing. He did so by sending his personal greet-ings and good wishes to the new Chinese leader, Xi Jinping, who would take over as president of the People's Republic of China on March 17. In the months and years ahead, Francis would continue with determina-tion his effort to normalize relations with China, first of all by seeking to reach the crucial agreement on the appointment of bishops in the mainland.

MARCH 16 (SATURDAY) _____

Muslim Woman Reporter: "I Just Love Your Pope"

POPE FRANCIS WALKED from Santa Marta to the Paul VI audience hall this morning at eleven o'clock to greet the more than six thousand repre-sentatives from the world's leading secular and Catholic media outlets that had covered the conclave and his election.

He has not given many interviews in his years as archbishop. By and large, he has never wanted to draw attention to himself or to have his words distorted.[10] Yet today he showed a truly extraordinary ability to communicate and to reach the hearts of even skeptical reporters.

Speaking off the cuff,[11] he greeted them as "dear friends" and told them that as he began his ministry as pope, "I am pleased to meet all of you who have worked here in Rome throughout this intense period which began with the unexpected announcement made by my venerable predecessor Benedict XVI on 11 February last."

He noted that the mass media's role "has expanded immensely in these years," and acknowledged that today they "are an essential means of informing the world about the events of contemporary history." He thanked all present "for the professional coverage" they had provided during these days "when the eyes of the whole world, and not just those of Catholics" were turned to Rome and the Vatican, "which has as its heart the tomb of Saint Peter." They laughed and applauded when he joked, "You worked hard, didn't you?"

He recognized that over the past few weeks they had "to provide in-formation" for their news outlets and audiences about "the Holy See and the Church, her rituals and traditions, her faith and above all the role of the Pope and his ministry," and he thanked especially "those who viewed and presented these events of the Church's history in a way which was sensitive to the right context in which they need to be read, namely that of faith."

At this point, Francis emphasized the importance of the accurate interpretation of events, and in particular of matters related to the Church and the faith. Over his fifteen years as archbishop of Buenos Aires he had become well aware of the way the media can present or misrepresent such matters.

He reminded journalists that "historical events almost always demand a nuanced interpretation which at times can also take into account the dimension of faith." He told them that "ecclesial events are certainly no more intricate than political or economic events!" but, "they do have one particular underlying feature: they follow a pattern which does not readily correspond to the 'worldly' categories which we are accustomed to use, and so it is not easy to interpret and communicate them to a wider and more varied public."

While acknowledging that "the Church is certainly a human and historical institution with all that that entails," he reminded reporters that "her nature is not essentially political but spiritual: the Church is the People of God, the Holy People of God making its way to encounter Jesus Christ," and he emphasized that "only from this perspective can a satisfactory account be given of the Church's life and activity."

He then went on to speak about the papacy and sought to put in a proper perspective the role to which he had just been elected. He reminded them that "Christ is the Church's Pastor, but his presence in history passes through the freedom of human beings; from their midst one is chosen to serve as his Vicar, the Successor of the Apostle Peter." He repeated with emphasis: "Christ remains the center, not the Successor of Peter: Christ is the center. Christ is the fundamental point of reference, the heart of the Church. Without him, Peter and the Church would not exist or have reason to exist."

Recalling that Benedict XVI had "frequently reminded us" that "Christ is present in the Church and guides her," Francis told the media that "in everything that has occurred" in these past weeks, "the principal agent has been, in the final analysis, the Holy Spirit. He prompted the decision of Benedict XVI for the good of the Church; he guided the Cardinals in prayer and in the election."

Looking at the representatives of the world's media in the audience hall, Francis remarked, "It is important, dear friends, to take into due account this way of looking at things, this hermeneutic, in order to bring into proper focus what really happened in these days."

Thanking them again for their work, he asked them "to try to understand more fully the true nature of the Church, as well as her journey in this world, with her virtues and her sins, and to know the spiritual concerns which guide her and are the most genuine way to understand her."

Francis assured the world's media that "the Church highly esteems your important work." He emphasized its fundamental importance by reminding them that they have at their disposal "the means to hear and to give voice to people's expectations and demands, and to provide for an analysis and interpretation of current events."

Their work, he said, "calls for careful preparation, sensitivity and experience" and, "like so many other professions, it also demands a particular concern for what is true, good and beautiful." He declared that this is something that the Church and the media "have in common, since the Church exists to communicate precisely this: Truth, Goodness and Beauty in person."

Noting that reporters sometimes tend to present themselves as the news, Francis reminded them that "all of us are called to communicate not ourselves, but this existential triad made up of truth, beauty and goodness."

Having made these crucially important points, Francis surprised and delighted journalists by revealing some of the secrets of the conclave, and giving them the news story of the day.

He recalled that "some people wanted to know why" he had chosen the name Francis, and said some thought it was because of Francis Xavier, Francis de Sales, and also Francis of Assisi. He set the record straight by telling them that, when it had become clear that he would be elected, his good friend who was sitting next to him in the conclave, Cardinal Claudio Hummes, turned to him, embraced him, and told him not to forget the poor. As he sat waiting for the counting of the ballots to be ended, "the name came to my heart," he said. He explained that, for him, Francis of Assisi is the man of poverty, the man of peace." The pope drew loud, sustained applause from the journalists he was addressing when he remarked, "How I would like a Church which is poor and for the poor!"

He went on to reveal that after the election people joked with him saying, "But you should call yourself Hadrian, because Hadrian VI was the reformer, we need a reform..." And someone else said to me: "No, no: your name should be Clement." "But why?" "Clement XV: thus you pay back Clement XIV who suppressed the Society of Jesus!"

After recounting the jokes, Francis concluded by telling the media, "I love all of you very much, I thank you for everything you have done. I pray that your work will always be serene and fruitful, and that you will come to know ever better the Gospel of Jesus Christ and the rich reality of the Church's life." He then commended them to the Blessed Virgin Mary, extended "cordial good wishes" to them and to "each of your families," and said he would impart his blessing.

At that point, however, he broke yet again with tradition, and out of respect for the many reporters present who were not Christians, he did not impart his blessing as his predecessors had done. Instead, speaking in Spanish, he explained why: "I told you I was cordially imparting my blessing. But since many of you are not members of the Catholic Church, and others are not believers, I cordially give this blessing silently, to each of you, respecting the conscience of each, but in the knowledge that each of you is a child of God. May God bless you!"

That meeting with the media was the beginning of what would become an extraordinary relationship with journalists, which would continue during his pontificate with interviews, press conferences on the plane returning from countries that he had visited, interview books, video conferences, and pre-recorded video messages. No pope in history has related to the media to this extent.

A WOMAN REPORTER for Al Jazeera television, a Muslim wearing a headscarf, had asked to interview me after the audience to comment on the new pope's talk. Before we began, she told me: "I just love your new pope! He respects us." She said she was really taken by his concern for the poor and how he had not imposed his blessing on non-Christians.

AFTER FRANCIS FINISHED SPEAKING, the time came for him to meet some fifty representatives of the world's media, starting with Vatican personnel involved in media work. When Fr. Lombardi went to greet him, the six thousand media personnel present broke into loud and sustained applause in appreciation for the great work he had done and the help he had given them over the past month.

Among those who went up to greet Francis was Archbishop Claudio Maria Celli, president of the Pontifical Council for Social Communications. He has known the future pope for many years, ever since he served in the nunciature in Buenos Aires in the late 1970s. Today Francis greeted him warmly. Speaking afterwards to *Avvenire*,[12] the archbishop described the new pope as one "who gives attention to people. He is without preconstituted schemes or attitudes, because he is authentically involved with the person who is in front of him" and expresses himself "in simple gestures that are easily understood" and "in a language that people perfectly understand." He underlined that his "deep spirituality" is joined to a humanity that is marked by "simplicity and spontaneity." He revealed that Francis has already approved the use of his Twitter account—@pontifex—and said his first message would likely appear the next day, Sunday, March 17.

When Alessandro Forlani, a blind journalist from Rai, the Italian state media, went to greet the new pope accompanied by his Saint Bernard guide dog, Francis greeted him, and then caressed the dog, drawing more applause.

ELISABETTA WAS ONE of the fifty reporters chosen to greet Francis. He had asked for her to be included. When she went to greet him, following the Argentine tradition, she kissed him on the cheek, much to the surprise of many onlookers, and then, as she recounts in her biography, "I seize his arms and tell him to go on being as he is, that he's doing fine, that he mustn't change, he must stay the way he is, that I'm with him, that he's not alone."[13]

COMMENTING ON FRANCIS'S BIG IMPACT on the world's media, Msgr. Dario Vigano, head of Vatican television who had directed the live coverage of the conclave with twelve television cameras, two radio cameras, and a staff of thirty-five, and who was now receiving requests for TV images from even the most faraway countries, told *Avvenire*,[14] "Pope Francis is so naturally telegenic, he teaches much with his gestures" and comes across "with a solemn sobriety" that makes him so authoritative.

THE VATICAN PRESS OFFICE announced that Pope Francis has asked the prefects, presidents, secretaries, and members of all the Vatican dicasteries (congregations, councils, and tribunals) as well as the president of the pontifical commission for the Vatican City State and the secretary of state, to continue for the time being in their respective posts of responsibility. A press communiqué explained that he wished "to take some time for reflection, prayer and dialogue before making any definitive nomination, or confirmation (of those in office)." Benedict XVI did likewise after his election.

Importantly, the Vatican also announced that Francis would visit Benedict XVI at Castel Gandolfo on March 23.

THAT AFTERNOON, Francis made yet another phone call, this time to Daniele, the proprietor of the newsstand in the Plaza de Mayo, Buenos Aires, who used to deliver the newspaper *La Nación* every day to Padre Jorge. Francis thanked him for his service all these years, and asked him to cancel his order. Daniele was incredulous at first, but when he realized it was for real he broke into tears.

Padre Jorge phoned our home that day too, after lunch, to invite Elisabetta and me to participate in his Mass the next morning at the parish church of Sant'Anna, just inside the Porta Sant'Anna, one of the main entrances to the Vatican. He also spoke to Juan Pablo and Carolina, and made them so happy.

MARCH 17 (SUNDAY)_____

The World's Parish Priest

THERE WAS AN AIR OF EXCITEMENT and joy in the small parish church of Saint Anna when Pope Francis arrived just before ten o'clock to celebrate Sunday morning Mass for the usual congregation and the invited guests. Some two hundred persons crowded into the small church; there was standing room only.

It was unprecedented for a pope to celebrate his first public Mass in this place and in this way. As he walked down the aisle, he shook the outstretched hands of people on either side and blessed many of the children.

The celebration was transmitted on live television and watched by millions around the world. Fr. Bruno Silvestri, the local parish priest, captured the sense of the pope's presence when he recalled Saint Augustine's famous phrase, "For you I am a bishop, with you I am a Christian."

After the scripture readings, Francis went to the lectern to comment on the gospel story about how Jesus showed mercy to the woman caught in adultery, when her accusers wished to stone her to death.

"This is a beautiful story," Francis said as he began his homily,[15] speaking without a text. "First, we have Jesus alone on the mountain, praying. He was praying alone (cf. Jn 8:1). Then he went back to the Temple, and all the people went to him (cf. v. 2). Jesus in the midst of the people. And then, at the end, they left him alone with the woman (cf. v. 9). That solitude of Jesus! But it is a fruitful solitude: the solitude of prayer with the Father, and the beautiful solitude that is the Church's message for today: the solitude of his mercy towards this woman."

Commenting on the many people who had come to Jesus, he noted "a variety of attitudes": some "wanted to hear the words of Jesus"; they came with "open hearts, hungry for the word of God." There were others "who did not hear anything, who could not hear anything." And then there was a group "who brought along this woman" who was caught in adultery and they told him, "Listen, Master, this woman has done such and such . . . we must do what Moses commanded us to do with women like this," in other words, stone her.

Francis told the congregation, "I think we too are the people who, on the one hand, want to listen to Jesus, but on the other hand, at times, like to find a stick to beat others with, to condemn others." But, Francis said, "Jesus has this message for us: mercy. I think—and I say it with humility—that this is the Lord's most powerful message: mercy."

He recalled that Jesus had said, "I did not come for the righteous. I came for sinners" (Mk 2:17). He reminded them that when Jesus called Matthew, there was gossip and people said 'he associates with sinners!' (cf. Mk 2:16)."

Pope Francis told those present and his global audience that "Jesus comes for us when we recognize that we are sinners. But if we are like the Pharisee, before the altar, who said: 'I thank you Lord, that I am not like other men, and especially not like the one at the door, like that publican' (cf. Lk 18:11–12), then we do not know the Lord's heart, and we will never have the joy of experiencing this mercy!"

He admitted that "it is not easy to entrust oneself to God's mercy, because it is an abyss beyond our comprehension. But we must!" "Oh, Father, if you knew my life, you would not say that to me!" "Why, what have you done?" "Oh, I am a great sinner!" "All the better! Go to Jesus: he likes you to tell him these things! He forgets, he has a very special capacity for forgetting. He forgets, he kisses you, he embraces you and he simply says to you: 'Neither do I condemn you; go, and sin no more' (Jn 8:11). That is the only advice he gives you. After a month, if we are in the same situation...Let us go back to the Lord."

Then in memorable words that he would repeat frequently during his pontificate, Francis declared: "The Lord never tires of forgiving: never! It is we who tire of asking his forgiveness. Let us ask for the grace not to tire of asking forgiveness, because he never tires of forgiving. Let us ask for this grace."

AT THE END OF MASS, Francis spoke again and noted that some of those present were not parishioners, and a few were from Argentina, including his auxiliary bishop. He then introduced Gonzalo, a priest from Uruguay who was also at the Mass, and said, "He works with children and with drug addicts on the street. He opened a school for them; he has done many things to make Jesus known, and to take all those boys and girls off the street. They today work thanks to the studies they have completed; they have the ability to work, they believe and they love Jesus." He invited Gonzalo to greet the people, and asked them to "pray for him." Francis concluded on a humorous note, "I do not know how he came here, but I will find out! Thanks. Pray for him."

THEN, AFTER MASS, like any parish priest, Francis went outside the door of the church, still wearing his green vestments, and greeted individually everyone who had attended the eucharistic celebration, including Elisabetta and me. He asked each one: "Pray for me!"

After greeting the congregation, Francis unnerved Vatican security, the Swiss Guards, and Italian police by suddenly walking outside the Porta Sant'Anna to greet the ecstatic crowds that had gathered in the street and were chanting, "*Fran-ce-sco! Fran-ce-sco! Fran-ce-sco!*" They went wild with excitement, cheered, photographed him with smartphones, and struggled to touch him. Francis looked extremely happy as he moved among them for twenty minutes, shaking hands with men and women, enthusiastic nuns, and overjoyed young people, blessing and caressing children and elderly people. While this was unprecedented at the beginning of a pontificate, it revealed the true character of the new pope, who sees himself first and foremost as a pastor.

Having greeted the faithful, Francis removed his vestments and was driven by car to the Apostolic Palace to greet for the first time, from the papal study window, the more than one hundred and fifty thousand Romans, pilgrims, and tourists who had gathered in Saint Peter's Square and nearby streets to pray the Angelus with him, listen to what he had to say, and receive his blessing.

"Crowds like this have not been seen since the death of John Paul II," *Corriere della Sera* reported the next day. A record audience of some seven million Italians followed the event live on television.

When he appeared at the study window of the papal apartment, the crowd broke into thunderous applause, people cheered wildly, waved flags and scarves, and jumped up and down with joy. One could feel a new energy in the air. Francis, by his humility and simplicity, was reaching the hearts of people. I heard many saying, "he is one of us."

Francis again spoke without script, about "mercy." He talked in a way that was comprehensible to everyone; one did not need an interpreter or high school education to grasp his message. He revealed yet again his great sense of humor, and his visible joy at meeting people.[16]

He began in the most ordinary way: "Brothers and sisters, good morning!" The crowd responded enthusiastically with loud applause—the first of the many rounds of applause that would interrupt his talk.

He told them that after first greeting them on the night of his election, he was "glad" to do so again on this, the Lord's Day! "This is beautiful and important for us Christians: to meet on Sundays, to greet each other, to speak to each other as we are doing now, in the square. A square which, thanks to the media, has global dimensions."

He recalled that today's Gospel "presents the episode of the adulterous woman whom Jesus saves from being condemned to death." He drew their attention to "Jesus' attitude," which, he said, "is striking: we do not hear words of scorn, we do not hear words of condemnation, but only words of love, of mercy, which are an invitation to conversion. 'Neither do I condemn you; go, and do not sin again.'"

Looking at the vast crowd in the square, Francis said, "Ah! brothers and sisters, God's face is the face of a merciful father who is always patient. Have you thought about God's patience, the patience he has with each one of us? That is his mercy. He always has patience, patience with us, he understands us, he waits for us, he does not tire of forgiving us if we are able to return to him with a contrite heart. 'Great is God's mercy,' says the Psalm."

He revealed that in the past few days he had been reading a book on mercy written by Cardinal Kasper, "a clever theologian, a good theologian," which "did me a lot of good, so much good," and then in a humorous comment that drew more applause, he remarked, "but do not think I am promoting my cardinals' books! Not at all!"

Recalling that Cardinal Kasper wrote that "feeling mercy" changes everything, Francis declared, "It is the best thing we can feel: it changes the world. A little mercy makes the world less cold and more just."

He told the attentive crowd, "We need to understand properly this mercy of God, this merciful Father who is so patient...Let us remember the Prophet Isaiah who says that even if our sins were scarlet, God's love would make them white as snow. This mercy is beautiful!"

When Francis gives homilies or talks, he often draws on incidents from his twenty-one years' experience as a bishop. He did likewise today, and recalled that soon after he first became a bishop in 1992, the statue of Our Lady of Fatima arrived in Buenos Aires and a big Mass was celebrated for the sick. "I went to hear confessions at that Mass," he said, "and almost at the end of the Mass I stood up, because I had to go and administer Confirmation. But then, an elderly woman approached me, humble, very humble, and over eighty years old. I looked at her, and I said, 'Grandmother'—because in our country that is how we address the elderly—'do you want to make your confession?' 'Yes,' she said to me. 'But if you have not sinned...' And she said to me: 'We all have sins...' 'But perhaps the Lord does not forgive them.' 'The Lord forgives all things,' she said to me with conviction. 'But how do you know, Madam?' 'If the Lord did not forgive everything, the world would not exist.'"

Francis then remarked, "I felt an urge to ask her: 'Tell me, Madam, did you study at the Gregorian [University]?' because that is the wisdom which the Holy Spirit gives: inner wisdom focused on God's mercy."

Repeating what he had said at Mass this morning, Francis told his worldwide audience, "Let us not forget this word: God never ever tires of forgiving us! 'Well, Father what is the problem?' Well, the problem is that we ourselves tire, we do not want to ask, we grow weary of asking for forgiveness. He never tires of forgiving, but at times we get tired of asking for forgiveness."

Francis encouraged the people, "Let us never tire, let us never tire! He is the loving Father who always pardons, who has that heart of mercy for us all. And let us too learn to be merciful to everyone. Let us invoke the intercession of Our Lady who held in her arms the Mercy of God made man."

When he finished speaking, he recited the Angelus with the crowd, gave them his blessing, and thanked them for their welcome. He asked them, and all those following by radio, television, or the social media, "Pray for me!"

Before bidding farewell, he addressed a special word to the Italians. He told them, "I have chosen the name of the Patron of Italy, Saint Francis of Assisi, and this strengthens my spiritual ties with this country where, as you know, my family comes from." But, he said, "Jesus has called us to belong to a new family: his Church, to this family of God, walking together on the path of the Gospel." He prayed that Jesus would bless them and Our Lady protect him, and told them yet again, "Do not forget this: the Lord never tires of forgiving! It is we who tire of asking forgiveness."

He concluded with words that would soon become like a signature tune at his Sunday audiences: "Have a good Sunday and a good lunch!"

The Romans just loved all this, and especially his familiarity, his humility, his simple touch, his closeness, his humor. He had connected with them when he first appeared on the balcony of Saint Peter's after his election, and today he clearly consolidated that relationship.

A taxi driver confirmed this that afternoon when he told me, "I was born in Rome forty-seven years ago, but this was the first time ever that I went to Saint Peter's Square to listen to a pope speak. I watched him on television on the night of his election and I just felt he was so different, so close to ordinary people. He touched my heart then, and so I came to the square today to listen to him. I think he will be a great pope."

OBSERVING FRANCIS'S SPONTANEOUS WORDS and actions since his election, and the fact that he has requested minimal input from Vatican officials, the veteran Italian journalist Luigi Accattoli remarked: "He's a 'do-it-yourself' pope!" Moreover, he commented, "Francis does not seem concerned about where to put his foot, or what to say. With his disarming security, he seems to have always been pope."[17]

FRANCIS'S EMPHASIS on the theme of "mercy" at Mass and again at the Angelus, together with the fact that mercy is also a key element in his motto, sent a strong signal that mercy would be a central theme of his pontificate.

Two years later, on the second anniversary of his election (March 13, 2015), he announced that a Jubilee Year of Mercy would be held from December 8, 2015, to November 20, 2016. He issued a papal decree, or Bull of Indiction, to that effect on April 11, 2015,[18] and then, breaking with a seven-hundred-year-old tradition, he opened the Jubilee Year not in Rome but in Bangui, the capital of the war-torn Central African Republic, on November 29.[19]

AFTER THE ANGELUS on his first Sunday as pope, Francis sent his first tweet on @pontifex. It said: "Dear friends, I thank you from my heart and I ask you to continue to pray for me." It reached three 3,400,000 followers, in nine languages including Latin. By the end of 2017 he would have more than 40 million followers on Twitter.

ON HIS RETURN TO SANTA MARTA, he joined Cardinal Maradiaga, whom he had invited to lunch. As they ate together, he informed the cardinal that following up on a proposal made in the General Congregations before the conclave, he had decided to create a Council of Cardinals to serve as his advisors in the governance of the universal Church and the reform of the Roman Curia. He said he had chosen eight cardinals in all, including at least one from each continent. He named the eight[20] and then asked the Honduran cardinal if he would serve as the group's coordinator. Óscar Maradiaga accepted. He also asked the Italian bishop, Marcello Semeraro of Albano diocese, whom he has known since the 2001 synod of bishops, to serve as secretary of the council, and he too accepted.

Subsequently, he communicated his decision and the list of names to the Secretariat of State, asking that it be made public but, for some reason, that did not happen until April 13.[21]

It was Francis's first major decision, one of the utmost importance. The council is to serve as an advisory body to the new pope, and this will give him a freedom from the Roman Curia that for centuries his predecessors did not have. Needless to say, not everyone in the Vatican rejoiced.

AT 5:30 PM, THAT SUNDAY EVENING, the father general of the Jesuits, Adolfo Nicolás, went to visit him in Santa Marta, at the pope's personal invitation.[22] They have known each other for more than two decades.

Afterwards, Fr. Nicolás wrote a brief report to the Jesuits on that visit, and said:

> He was at the entrance and received me with the usual Jesuit embrace. We had a few pictures taken, at his request, and at my apologies for not keeping protocol he insisted that I treat him like any other Jesuit, at the *Tu*[23] level, so I did not have to worry about treatments, "Holiness" or "Holy Father."
>
> I offered him all our Jesuit resources, because in his new position he is going to need counsel, thinking, persons, etc. He

showed gratitude for this and at the invitation to visit us for lunch at the Curia he said he would oblige.

Significantly, Fr. Nicolás reported that "there was full commonality of feeling on several issues that we discussed and I remained with the conviction that we will work very well together for the service of the Church in the name of the Gospel."

Then, in reference to the not always easy relationship between Francis and some in the Jesuit order over the past forty years, Fr. Nicolás noted, "There was calm, humor, and mutual understanding about past, present, and future."

He concluded, "I left the place with the conviction that it will be worth cooperating fully with him in the Vineyard of the Lord. At the end he helped me with my coat and accompanied me to the door. That added a couple of salutes to me from the Swiss Guards there. A Jesuit embrace, again, is a good way to meet and send off a friend."

MARCH 18 (MONDAY) ——————————————————————
Preparing for the Inauguration Ceremony

Fr. Lombardi gave a briefing to the world's media regarding tomorrow's inauguration ceremony. He said 132 delegations, including heads of state and of government from many countries and all continents will attend, together with delegations from various religious communities.

Following a tradition dating back to the late Middle Ages, every pope has a coat of arms and a motto. Today, the Vatican released an image of the coat of arms and motto chosen by Pope Francis that shows that both will remain essentially the same as the ones he chose when he first became auxiliary bishop of Buenos Aires in 1992. This is quite unusual.

The Vatican provided an explanation of each.[24] It said the motto—*"miserando atque eligendo"* ("having mercy he chose him") is taken from the Venerable Bede's commentary on the gospel story of Jesus' calling of Saint Matthew,[25] which is an homage to the mercy of God. It is directly linked to Francis's own calling, because it was on the feast of Saint

Matthew, September 21, 1953, that Jorge Mario Bergoglio, then seventeen years old, walking past the Basilica of San José de Flores in Buenos Aires, was moved to enter and go to confession,[26] when he experienced in a most personal and extraordinary—some would say mystical—way the loving and merciful presence of God in his life. That experience led to his decision to take up the vocation to the priesthood and to the centrality of the theme of mercy in his life and ministry ever since.

The coat of arms consists of a blue shield, at the top of which is the emblem of the Society of Jesus: a radiant sun in which there is the red-colored monogram of Christ—IHS (Jesus, Son [of God], Savior), with a red-colored cross over the letter H and three black nails under it. At the bottom of the shield are two images: a yellow star, symbolizing the Virgin Mary, the mother of Christ and of the Church; and a spikenard, symbolizing Saint Joseph, the patron of the universal Church. By putting these two images in his coat of arms, Francis was highlighting his personal devotion to Mary and Joseph. Significantly, the inauguration of his Petrine ministry took place on the feast of Saint Joseph. Above the coat of arms are the insignia of papal dignity: the gold and silver keys and an episcopal miter, bound by red cord.

MARCH 19 (TUESDAY)

In the Shoes of the Fisherman

THERE WERE 132 official state delegations present in Saint Peter's Square this morning for the inauguration ceremony, including 31 heads of state, 11 heads of governments, and members of the royal families from six countries. There were also high-level representatives of thirty-three Christian churches and communities, and official delegations from the Jewish and Islamic communities.

Fifty years ago, when Paul VI began his ministry as pope in 1963, the ceremony was officially called "the rite of coronation" but that reforming pope subsequently changed this, and much else, in keeping with the vision of the Second Vatican Council. Subsequently, the ceremony for John Paul I was called "The Mass for the Beginning of the Ministry of the Supreme Pontiff"; that for John Paul II was titled "The Beginning of the Pontificate," and that for Benedict XVI was similar. Significantly, however, Francis decided that today's ceremony would be officially known as "The Start of the Petrine Ministry of the Bishop of Rome."

WHILE MANY ARGENTINIANS living in Italy and neighboring countries came for the ceremony, very few actually came from Argentina, because immediately after his election Francis asked those who were planning to travel to Rome for the inauguration, including Maria Elena, his beloved sister and only surviving sibling, not to do so but instead to donate to the poor the money they would have spent on the trip. They did his bidding.

At the same time, Francis wanted to let the world know in other ways too that care for the poor will be a top priority for his pontificate.[27] To underline this, he took the extraordinary step of inviting Sergio Sánchez, the leader of the ten thousand "*cartoneros*" (garbage pickers) from Buenos Aires to attend, and assigned him a front-place seat at the Mass. Dressed in his blue and green overalls, with the words "*Movimento de trabajadores excluidos*" (Movement of Excluded Workers) emblazoned on his shirt, Sánchez sat alongside representatives of governments from many lands, including the president of Argentina, Cristina Fernández de Kirchner, with whom Francis had had a long conversation and lunch the previous day.

There were many other presidents at the ceremony, including those from Italy, Brazil, Chile, Costa Rica, Paraguay, Mexico, Ecuador, Honduras, Panama, Taiwan, Ireland, Portugal, Poland, Slovakia, Serbia, and Romania, but the most controversial one of all was Robert Mugabe from Zimbabwe, a country he has ruled since 1987, who had been accused of human rights violations.

Members of the royal families of Belgium, Luxembourg, Monaco, Spain, and the United Kingdom were also present, together with the German chancellor, the prime ministers of Italy, France, and Spain, and the presidents of the European Commission and of the Russian parliament.

Vice President Joe Biden, a Catholic, represented the United States, together with the governor of New Mexico, Susana Martinez; the Democratic leader in Congress, Nancy Pelosi; Rep. Loretta Sanchez of California; and John J. DeGioia, president of the prestigious Jesuit-run Georgetown University.

For the first time since the Great Western Schism of 1054, Bartholomew I, the ecumenical patriarch of Constantinople, the first among equals of the leaders of the Orthodox Churches, attended the inauguration.

So too did the representative of the patriarch of Moscow and All Russia, Metropolitan Hilarion of Volokolamsk. For the first time also the chief rabbi of Rome, Riccardo Di Segni, attended the inauguration ceremony for a new pope. He was accompanied by, among others, the director general of the Grand Rabbinate of Israel, Oded Wiener. The secretary general of the Islamic Organization of Latin America, Mohamed Youssef Hajar, was present too.

AT 8:30 AM, a great roar went up from the crowd as Francis arrived in the square for the first time in an open jeep. He was driven among the cheering crowds for half an hour; he wished to be as close to them as possible on this day. Later he would meet the official delegations.

As his jeep moved slowly through the square, he blessed and kissed children and he waved to the Argentinians who had come with the flags of his homeland, giving them the thumbs-up sign. And then, suddenly, came the first of those iconic moments that have become a hallmark of his pontificate: as he drove among the crowd, Francis spotted a fifty-year-old man named Cesare, lying on a stretcher, totally paralyzed except for one hand. He asked the driver to stop, and then after dismounting from the jeep, he went to the man and kissed him on the forehand, caressed his face, and spent some time talking to him. The man later told the press that the pope had asked him and the friends who had brought him here: "Please pray for me."[28] Millions watching the scene on television were profoundly moved by his gesture, but it was only the beginning of a pontificate that would be expressed as much in gestures as in words.

After driving among the crowd for over half an hour, Francis went inside Saint Peter's Basilica for the start of the solemn, colorful inauguration ceremony that was rich in symbolism and tradition.

MEANWHILE, BACK IN ARGENTINA, millions prayed in churches for the new pope and watched the ceremony on television. In Buenos Aires, an immense crowd, including thousands from the shantytowns around this metropolis, the second largest in South America, had gathered in the famous Plaza de Mayo early on this rainy morning, after a night vigil, to follow the ceremony in Rome on maxi television screens. They sang, they cheered as in a stadium, they danced, they waved the triband blue and white Argentine flags with the sun in the center, they prayed, they wept, they embraced, proud that their former archbishop was now pope.

They watched the ceremony begin as "Padre Jorge" descended to the crypt under the high altar and prayed before the tomb of Saint Peter, together with the patriarchs and major archbishops of the Eastern-rite Catholic churches. They saw him come back up and then walk in procession down the center aisle of the basilica and through its main doors onto the steps of Saint Peter's basilica to celebrate the open-air Mass in the square, not far from the place where Peter, the apostle chosen by Christ to lead his church, was martyred by being crucified upside down.

SOME 180 PRELATES concelebrated with Francis at the Mass for his inauguration. These included not only the cardinals present in Rome together with the patriarchs and major archbishops of the Oriental Catholic churches but also, at Francis's specific invitation, two representatives of the religious orders: the minister general of the Franciscan order of Friars Minor, Fr. Rodríguez Carballo; and the superior general of the Jesuits, Fr. Adolfo Nicolás, then president and vice president respectively of the Union of Superiors Generals.

TWO SYMBOLS OF PAPAL AUTHORITY—the pallium (that is, a circular white stole made from lamb's wool with five red crosses woven into it, representing the five wounds of Jesus) and the fisherman's ring—had been placed on the tomb of Saint Peter in the crypt of the basilica the previous evening. They were brought up from there this morning and carried in the procession of the pope and patriarchs from the basilica to the square, together with the book of Gospels.

Before the start of the Mass, Cardinal Tauran, the proto-deacon who had announced Francis's election to the world, placed the pallium, a symbol of the authority of the chief shepherd, on the shoulders of the new pope. It was the same one that had been worn by Benedict XVI.

Next, the dean of the College of Cardinals, Angelo Sodano, placed the fisherman's ring[29] on the ring finger of the new pope's right hand. Francis had chosen the gold-plated silver ring made for Paul VI (though the Italian pope never wore it[30]) for this occasion, but he intended to use it only for formal ceremonies.

After the new pope had been given these symbols of authority, and following a long tradition, six cardinals, representing the entire college, went and made their act of obedience to him.

FRANCIS THEN BEGAN the solemn pontifical Latin Mass in the presence of an estimated quarter of a million people in the square and on nearby streets and countless millions worldwide who were following the event by radio, television, or social media. It was a truly festive occasion, enriched by the magnificent singing of the Sistine and other choirs, and accompanied by the prayers and singing of the enormous crowd of priests, women and men religious, together with lay men and women from Rome, Italy and other countries, and all continents.

While much of the celebration was in Latin, the Gospel was sung in Greek. The classical Latin and Greek reflected the Western and Eastern traditions of the universal Catholic Church. But there were also scripture reading and prayers in Spanish, English, Italian, Chinese, Russian, French, Arabic, and Swahili.

After the gospel reading, Francis went to the lectern to deliver the homily[31] that he himself had written. But as he read it, he was frequently interrupted by the spontaneous applause of the vast crowd of Romans, Italians, pilgrims, and tourists filling the square.

He began with the simple greeting, "Dear Brothers and Sisters," and went on to "thank the Lord" that he could celebrate this Mass "for the inauguration of my Petrine ministry" on the feast day of Saint Joseph, the spouse of the Virgin Mary and patron of the universal Church. Francis, who has a particular devotion to the saint and has on his desk a statue of Saint Joseph sleeping, described it as "a significant coincidence."

He drew a great round of applause when, next, he recalled that it was also the name day of his predecessor, Benedict XVI, who was called Joseph before he became pope. "We are close to him with our prayers, full of affection and gratitude," he said.

Francis extended his greetings to the cardinals, bishops, priests, deacons, men and women religious, and lay faithful present, and thanked the other Christian churches and communities represented at the ceremony, as well as the Jewish and other religious communities that had sent representatives. In the following days, when he met the delegations from the Christian churches and the other religions, he insisted on sitting on a chair at the same level as these delegates; as pope, he didn't want to be above anybody.

Today also, he expressed "cordial greetings" to the heads of state and government and other official delegations from many countries, as well as the diplomatic corps. He would greet them individually after Mass.

Having dealt with the formalities, Francis went on to comment on the gospel story that recounts that "Joseph did as the angel of the Lord commanded him and took Mary as his wife" (Mt 1:24).

Francis explained that "these words already point to the mission which God entrusts to Joseph: he is to be the *custos*, the protector. The protector of whom? Of Mary and Jesus; but this protection is then extended to the Church."

He noted that Joseph exercised his role as protector "discreetly, humbly and silently, but with an unfailing presence and utter fidelity, even when he [found] it hard to understand."

He recalled that "from the time of his betrothal to Mary until the finding of the twelve-year-old Jesus in the Temple of Jerusalem, he is there at every moment with loving care. As the spouse of Mary, he is at her side in good times and bad, on the journey to Bethlehem for the census and in the anxious and joyful hours when she gave birth; amid the drama of the flight into Egypt and during the frantic search for their child in the Temple; and later in the day-to-day life of the home of Nazareth, in the workshop where he taught his trade to Jesus."

Francis explained that Joseph responded to his calling to be the protector of Mary, Jesus, and the Church "by being constantly attentive to God, open to the signs of God's presence and receptive to God's plans, and not simply to his own."

Joseph is a "protector," he said, "because he is able to hear God's voice and be guided by his will; and for this reason he is all the more sensitive to the persons entrusted to his safekeeping. He can look at things realistically, he is in touch with his surroundings, he can make truly wise decisions." This approach of "looking at things realistically" would soon be recognized as one of the hallmarks of Francis's own ministry, as he adopted the inductive rather than deductive approach to major questions and problems of everyday life, and in the life of the Church.[32]

In the next, and most important part of his homily, Francis focused on what would become another of the hallmarks of his entire pontificate: protection of people and protection of the created world, our environment, our common home. While he would articulate all this more fully two years later in his encyclical *Laudato Si'*,[33] the key ideas were nonetheless present in his homily today, and directly linked to Saint Joseph.

Addressing Christians worldwide as "dear friends," Francis told them that in Saint Joseph "we learn how to respond to God's call, readily and willingly, but we also see the core of the Christian vocation, which is Christ!" He urged them, "Let us protect Christ in our lives, so that we can protect others, so that we can protect creation!"

He went on to tell people worldwide that "the vocation of being a 'protector,' however, is not just something involving us Christians alone; it also has a prior dimension which is simply human, involving everyone."

Declaring that "everyone" on planet Earth is called to be a "protector," Pope Francis explained what this involves in everyday life. He said:

"It means protecting all creation, the beauty of the created world, as the Book of Genesis tells us and as Saint Francis of Assisi showed us.

"It means respecting each of God's creatures and respecting the environment in which we live.

"It means protecting people, showing loving concern for each and every person, especially children, the elderly, those in need, who are often the last we think about.

"It means caring for one another in our families: husbands and wives first protect one another, and then, as parents, they care for their children, and children themselves, in time, protect their parents.

"It means building sincere friendships in which we protect one another in trust, respect, and goodness. In the end, everything has been entrusted to our protection, and all of us are responsible for it."

Francis was well aware of the dramatic reality in today's world, and in his homily he sought to alert people everywhere to this by reminding them that "whenever human beings fail to live up to this responsibility, whenever we fail to care for creation and for our brothers and sisters, the way is opened to destruction and hearts are hardened. Tragically, in every period of history there are 'Herods' who plot death, wreak havoc, and mar the countenance of men and women."

In this context, Francis made his first passionate appeal as pope to "all those who have positions of responsibility in economic, political and social life, and all men and women of goodwill." He pleaded with them: "Let us be 'protectors' of creation, protectors of God's plan inscribed in nature, protectors of one another and of the environment. Let us not allow omens of destruction and death to accompany the advance of this world!"

In order to be "protectors," he said, "we also have to keep watch over ourselves! Let us not forget that hatred, envy and pride defile our lives! Being protectors, then, also means keeping watch over our emotions, over our hearts, because they are the seat of good and evil intentions: intentions that build up and tear down! We must not be afraid of goodness or even tenderness!"

He reminded everyone that "caring, protecting, demands goodness, it calls for a certain tenderness." He recalled that in the Gospels, "Saint Joseph appears as a strong and courageous man, a working man, yet in his heart we see great tenderness, which is not the virtue of the weak but rather a sign of strength of spirit and a capacity for concern, for compassion, for genuine openness to others, for love." He told his global audience, "We must not be afraid of goodness, of tenderness!"

They were gathered here today, he said, to celebrate "the beginning of the ministry of the new Bishop of Rome, the Successor of Peter, which also involves a certain power." He recalled that when Jesus conferred this power upon Peter, he commanded him to "feed my lambs, feed my sheep."

Commenting on this power and how he envisaged exercising it, Francis told his global audience: "Let us never forget that authentic power is service, and that the Pope too, when exercising power, must enter ever more fully into that service which has its radiant culmination on the Cross. He must be inspired by the lowly, concrete and faithful service which marked Saint Joseph and, like him, he must open his arms to protect all of God's people and embrace with tender affection the whole of humanity, especially the poorest, the weakest, the least important, those whom Matthew lists in the final judgment on love: the hungry, the thirsty, the stranger, the naked, the sick and those in prison (cf. Mt 25:31–46). Only those who serve with love are able to protect!"

In the final part of his homily, Francis emphasized the need for Christians, and for himself as pope, to bring hope to people in today's world. "Today, amid so much darkness, we need to see the light of hope and to be men and women who bring hope to others," he said. He explained that "to protect creation, to protect every man and every woman, to look upon them with tenderness and love, is to open up a horizon of hope; it is to let a shaft of light break through the heavy clouds; it is to bring the warmth of hope!"

He explained that "for believers, for us Christians, like Abraham, like Saint Joseph, the hope that we bring is set against the horizon of God, which has opened up before us in Christ. It is a hope built on the rock which is God."

He told his global audience that as bishop of Rome he is called to carry out a service which is "to protect Jesus with Mary, to protect the whole of creation, to protect each person, especially the poorest, to protect ourselves."

He reminded Christians everywhere that "all of us are called" to this service, "so that the star of hope will shine brightly." He invited everyone, "Let us protect with love all that God has given us!"

He concluded his homily, which contained many of the seminal ideas of his pontificate, by imploring the Virgin Mary, Saint Joseph, Saints Peter and Paul, and Saint Francis, and everyone following the ceremony to "pray for me."

THE CROWD BROKE INTO GREAT APPLAUSE when he finished speaking. But then a total silence descended as Francis returned to his seat, and sat down, and people reflected on what he had said.

The silence was broken by the Sistine Choir when it led the congregation in a powerful rendering of the Credo. This was followed by the prayers of the faithful in many languages.

At the end of Mass, the choir again led everyone in the singing of the *Te Deum*, in thanksgiving to God for having given the Church a new chief shepherd. Then the great bells of Saint Peter's rang loudly, conveying to the world the joy of the Christian people.

At the conclusion of the ceremony, Pope Francis re-entered the basilica to greet the official delegations from states and international organizations. He spent more than one hour doing so, standing all the time. Observing all this, Gianni Cardinale, one of the most informed Italian journalists on Vatican affairs who writes for *Avvenire*, commented: "Pope Francis appeared perfectly at ease in the new mission that has been entrusted to him" and "never seemed to tire.[34]

THAT AFTERNOON, Francis phoned Benedict XVI to greet him on his name day. Four days later, on March 23, Francis traveled by helicopter to Castel Gandolfo for their first face-to-face meeting since his election as pope. It was a historic moment. They embraced, prayed together, and then had a long private conversation that marked the beginning of a truly remarkable relationship, one that is without precedent in the two-thousand-year history of the Church, a relationship in which Francis subsequently related to Benedict as the "wise grandfather" in the family.

IT IS WORTH MENTIONING HERE, particularly in the light of what Francis would do three months later, that he received a letter today from the parish priest of the island of Lampedusa, Don Stefano Natasi, that described the dramatic plight of the tens of thousands of migrants and refugees who, fleeing war and poverty, had traveled across the Mediterranean Sea from the Middle East and North Africa and found refuge on this island off the coast of Sicily. He spoke too about the tears of the many who had lost relatives or friends on that perilous sea-journey. He appealed to Francis, himself the son of immigrants, to accompany these suffering people with his prayers, and to come and visit them.[35] Francis went there four months later, on his first journey outside the Vatican, showing that one of the priorities of his pontificate would be care for migrants and refugees, an issue that has become the biggest humanitarian crisis since World War II.[36]

AS THE DAY OF HIS INAUGURATION drew to a close, it had already become clear that a new style of papacy was quickly taking shape in the Vatican. Francis, the first pope from the southern hemisphere, was exercising the Petrine ministry in a new way, different in many ways from that of his predecessors. He was doing so with humility and simplicity, but also with great inner peace and freedom, and he had already revealed many of the issues that would be among the top priorities of his pontificate.

He spelled all this out more fully, as well as much more, in his first apostolic exhortation, *Evangelii Gaudium* (The Joy of the Gospel), in which he set out "to encourage the Christian faithful to embark upon a new chapter of evangelization marked by this joy, while pointing out new paths for the Church's journey in years to come." It was the programmatic document for his pontificate; it opened new horizons and clearly signaled the road ahead. He signed it on November 24, 2013.[37]

Since then, many others have written about the new style of papacy that has taken shape under Francis, one marked by collegiality and synodality, so there is no need for me to add more here, except to say that the reshaping of the papacy is still a work in progress.

CONCLUSION

IT HAS BEEN A MOST EXTRAORDINARY EXPERIENCE to cover the conclave of 2013 and to track the path to the papacy of the man my family and I know so well, and love.

I have written this book to offer the reader a narrative from a historical perspective about what happened at that conclave. I hope I have succeeded.

I am eternally grateful to the many sources both living and dead, who over the past five years shared with me the information published here. There is, of course, much more that I know but cannot put into the public domain, out of respect for them. All that will have to remain in my heart.

NOTES

PREFACE

1. An anonymous cardinal elector at the 2005 conclave kept a secret diary and later shared it with Lucio Brunelli, an Italian journalist, who published it in the geopolitical review, *Limes*, in November 2005. Brunelli, then an Italian state television journalist, is now editor in chief of the Italian Catholic Bishops' Conference's television and radio channels.

INTRODUCTION

1. "Conclave" comes from the Latin word *"cum-clave,"* meaning "with" (*cum*) "a key" (*clave*), or, one might say, "under lock and key."
2. Gregory III, a Syrian, was the last non-European pope. He died in 741.
3. Msgr. Scicluna's official title was promoter of justice at the Congregation for the Doctrine of the Faith. He held that post from 2002 to 2012, when he was appointed first auxiliary bishop and then archbishop in Malta. In 2014, Pope Francis sent him to Scotland to investigate abuse of seminarians and priests by Cardinal Keith O'Brien. In 2018, he sent the Maltese archbishop to Chile to gather testimony regarding the abuse scandal in that country.
4. Fr. Maciel died on January 30, 2008.
5. The original Italian title: *Sua Santità. Le carte segrete di Benedetto XVI.*
6. In Latin, *"promoveatur ut amoveatur."*
7. My article in Vatican Insider, May 24, 2012.
8. Concita De Gregorio, "Sesso e carriera, I ricatti in Vaticano dietro la rinuncia di Benedetto XVI," *La Repubblica* (February 21, 2013).
9. The Focolare movement, the Neocathecumenal Way, the Communion and Liberation movement, the Sant' Egidio Community, and many others. The Opus Dei prelature, while not a movement, was nonetheless one of the new forces that had arisen in the old continent during the twentieth century.
10. Gerard O'Connell, "Saving Brazil," *Our Sunday Visitor* (May 6, 2007); Gerson Camarotti, *Segredos do Conclave* (São Paulo: Geração Editorial, 2013), 128–29.
11. Text of the Aparecida Final Document can be found at: www.celam.org/aparecida/Ingles.pdf.

12. Pope John Paul II sent Cardinal Roger Etchegerary to Saddam Hussein, and Cardinal Pio Laghi to George W. Bush.

13. Cardinal Laghi, in a statement issued in Washington, DC, on March 5, 2003, emphasized that "there is great unity on this grave matter on the part of the Holy See, the bishops in the United States, and the Church throughout the world."

14. Cardinal Giovanni Lajolo.

15. Private conversations with representatives of church and diplomatic sources in these countries.

16. Text of Pope Benedict's letter can be found at: https://w2.vatican.va/content/benedict-xvi/en/letters/2007/documents/hf_ben-xvi_let_20070527_china-note.html.

17. http://w2.vatican.va/content/benedict-xvi/en/speeches/2013/january/ documents/ hf_ben-xvi_spe_20130107_corpo-diplomatico.html.

18. Pew Research figures for 2015. http://www.pewresearch.org/fact-tank/ 2017/04/05/christians-remain-worlds-largest-religious-group-but-they-are-declining-in-europe/.

19. http://w2.vatican.va/content/john-paul-ii/en/encyclicals/documents/hf_jp-ii_ enc_25051995_ut-unum-sint.html.

20. *Ut Unum Sint* 95.

21. One of the few who did respond was Archbishop John R. Quinn, the emeritus archbishop of San Francisco and former president of the United States bishops' conference (1977–1980), with his book, *The Reform of the Papacy: The Costly Call to Christian Unity* (New York: Herder and Herder, 1999). He gave John Paul II a copy of the book. Interestingly, both Cardinal Ratzinger and Cardinal Bergoglio read the book before becoming popes.

22. Apostolic letter *Ordinatio Sacerdotalis* (Priestly Ordination) http://w2. vatican.va/content/john-paul-ii/en/apost_letters/1994/documents/hf_jp-ii_ apl_19940522_ordinatio-sacerdotalis.html.

23. He stated then: "Wherefore, in order that all doubt may be removed regarding a matter of great importance, a matter which pertains to the Church's divine constitution itself, in virtue of my ministry of confirming the brethren (cf. Lk 22:32) I declare that the Church has no authority whatsoever to confer priestly ordination on women and that this judgment is to be definitively held by all the Church's faithful."

PART ONE

1. http://w2.vatican.va/content/benedict-xvi/en/speeches/2013/february/ documents/hf_ben-xvi_spe_20130211_declaratio.html.

2. Benedict XVI, *Last Testament: In His Own Words*, with Peter Seewald, paperback edition (London: Bloomsbury, 2017), 16. He speaks at length about his resignation in chapter 2.

3. Cardinal Murphy-O'Connor died on September 1, 2017.

4. Conversation with Giovanna Chirri. She tells the story too in her book, *L'ultima parola: Gesti e parole di Benedetto XVI che hannon segnato la storia* (Milan: San Paolo, 2013).

5. Elisabetta Piqué, my wife, is correspondent for *La Nación* in Italy and the Vatican.

6. *New York Times*, February 11, 2013.

7. Benedict XVI: *Light of the World: The Pope, the Church and the Signs of the Times*, in conversation with Peter Seewald (San Francisco: Ignatius Press, 2010).

8. Ibid., 9.

9. Benedict XVI, *Last Testament*, 36.

10. Ibid., 16–17.

11. Tarcisio Bertone, *I Miei papi* (Turin: Elledici, 2018), 37.

12. Benedict XVI, *Last Testament*, 18.

13. Vatican Insider, February 23, 2013: "Cardinal Arinze praises the Pope's courageous decision to resign."

14. Talk in northern Italy, October 17, 2017.

15. Interview with Cardinal Coccopalmerio, October 19, 2017.

16. Notes from conversation with Paloma García Ovejero, now deputy director of the Holy See's press office.

17. In a reform of the utmost significance, Paul VI, in the motu proprio *Ingravescentem Aetatem*, November 21, 1970, decreed that a cardinal loses the right to vote in a conclave to elect the pope on reaching the age of eighty. Benedict used the words "*ingravescentem aetatem*" in his speech announcing his resignation.

18. http://w2.vatican.va/content/benedict-xvi/en/speeches/2006/september/documents/hf_ben-xvi_spe_20060912_university-regensburg.html.

19. Benedict XVI, apostolic letter, *Summorum Pontificium*, July 7, 2007. Several people had advised Benedict XVI against doing this, including Cardinal Francis Arinze, then prefect of the Congregation for Divine Worship and the Discipline of the Sacraments.

20. Apostolic letter of Benedict XVI: *Anglicorum Coetibus*, November 4, 2009. http://w2.vatican.va/content/benedict-xvi/en/apost_constitutions/documents/hf_ben-xvi_apc_20091104_anglicanorum-coetibus.html.

21. Gerson Camarotti, *Segredos do Conclave* (São Paulo: Geração Editorial, 2013), 145.

22. The secretariat of the Council of the European Bishops' Conferences is based in Sankt Gallen, Switzerland, and the group usually met there.

23. Lucio Brunelli presented "The Secret Diary of the Conclave" under the title "*Cosi elegemmo Papa Ratzinger*" ("How we elected Pope Ratzinger"), *Limes* 4 (2005): 291–300. Like several other Italian journalists mentioned in this book, Brunelli had started his journalistic career with the magazine *Trenta Giorni* (*Thirty Days*), then went on to work for Italian state television and radio, and since 2014 he has been news editor in chief of the Italian bishops' conference television and radio channels, TG2000 and Radio Blu.

24. Brunelli, "The Secret Diary of the Conclave," 299.

25. Austen Ivereigh, *The Great Reformer* (New York: Henry Holt and Company, 2014), 354.

26. Conversation with Cardinal Murphy-O'Connor immediately after the publication of Ivereigh's book, *The Great Reformer*.

27. The translation of Lombardi's statement from Italian to English was made by the author.

28. The interview with Cardinal Scola was published in the magazine *Inside the Vatican*, founded and edited by Robert Moynihan, and later in Vatican Insider, as well as in the UK Catholic weekly, *The Universe*, and *La Nación*.

29. http://w2.vatican.va/content/benedictxvi/en/audiences/2013/documents/hf_ben-xvi_aud_20130213.html.

30. http://w2.vatican.va/content/benedictxvi/en/homilies/2013/documents/hf_ben-xvi_hom_20130213_ceneri.html.

31. *La Stampa*, March 13, p. 10.

32. Ibid., 10.

33. Ibid., March 13, p. 10.

34. http://w2.vatican.va/content/benedictxvi/en/speeches/2013/february/documents/hf_ben-xvi_spe_20130214_clero-roma.html.

35. *God's Invisible Hand: The Life and Work of Cardinal Francis Arinze*, as interviewed by Gerard O'Connell, was first published in 2003 by the Paulines Publications Africa in Kenya, and later by St. Stephen Publishing Press in Nigeria. It was published in the United States in 2006 by Ignatius Press.

36. John L. Allen, for example, states this in his book *Conclave: The Politics, Personalities, and Processes of the Next Papal Election*" (New York: Doubleday, 2002, 2004), 180–81. Though he does not name him in "the top ten" to succeed John Paul II, a list that included Bergoglio but not Ratzinger, he puts Ouellet among the next "fifteen to watch."

37. Nello Scavo's excellent book, *Bergoglio's List: How a Young Francis Defied a Dictatorship and Saved Dozens of Lives*, reveals and documents much of this. First published in Italian in 2013, months after his election, under the title *La Lista di Bergoglio* (Bologna: EMI, 2013), it appeared in an English translation by Bret Thoman (Charlotte, NC: Saint Benedict Press) in 2014.

38. Elisabetta Piqué, *Francis: Life and Revolution* (Chicago: Loyola Press, 2015), 84–90.

39. https://zenit.org/articles/cardinal-cipriani-i-hope-we-will-be-men-who-listen-to-god-or-we-are-of-no-use-at-all/.

40. Benedict XVI, *Last Testament*, 25–26.

41. Piqué, *Francis: Life and Revolution*.

42. *L'Espresso* 49 (November 28–December 5, 2002).

43. He had received a green light from the Vatican to ask for this permission.

44. My skepticism was confirmed almost three years later when Benedict XVI strongly denied this story in *Last Testament*, pp. 23–24. He said, "No, that is not right, not at all. On the contrary the Vatileaks matter was completely resolved. I said while it was still happening that one is not permitted to step back when things are going wrong, but only when things are at peace. I could resign because calm had returned to this situation. It was not a case of retreating under pressure or feeling that things couldn't be coped with."

45. Text in English can be found at http://w2.vatican.va/content/john-paul-ii/en/apost_constitutions/documents/hf_jp-ii_apc_22021996_universi-dominici-gregis.htm.

46. The motto is taken from the opening words of the Second Vatican Council's Constitution on the Church in the Modern World, a document that opened new horizons and had a great impact on the Catholic world.

47. *Corriere della Sera*, February 21, 2013.

48. On March 5, SNAP published a list of twelve cardinals—its "dirty dozen" —whose election, it was alleged, "would not be good news for children."

49. *Francis: Life and Revolution*, 206.

50. http://w2.vatican.va/content/benedict-xvi/fr/motu_proprio/documents/ hf_ben-xvi_motu-proprio_20070611_de-electione.html (text not in English). Under the rules that prevailed at the 2005 conclave. it was possible to get elected by a simple majority after more than thirty ballots. Benedict changed this, and reinstated the traditional norm.

51. This decree on "certain modifications" (*Normas Nonnullas*) can be found at http://w2.vatican.va/content/benedict-xvi/en/motu_proprio/documents/hf_ben- xvi_motu-proprio_20130222_normas-nonnullas.html.

52. *Normas Nonnullas* 35.

53. *Normas Nonnullas* 37.

54. *Normas Nonnullas* 43.

55. August 1978, October 1978, April 2005.

56. He listed the clerics in *Normas Nonnullas* 46, namely: the secretary of the College of Cardinals, who acts as secretary of the electoral assembly; the master of Papal Liturgical Celebrations together with eight masters of ceremonies; two religious attached to the Papal Sacristy; and an ecclesiastic chosen by the cardinal dean or by the cardinal taking his place, to assist him in his duties.

57. *Normas Nonnullas* 46.

58. The Chilean cardinal was the first non-Italian to do so.

59. *Normas Nonnullas* 47.

60. *Universi Dominici Gregis* 64–70.

61. *Normas Nonnullas* 75.

62. *Normas Nonnullas* 87.

63. http://g1.globo.com/platb/blog-do-camarotti/2013/02/26/cardeais-brasileiros -apontam-o-perfil-do-futuro-papa/.

64. Camarotti, *Segredos do Conclave*, 57–58.

65. It is of course a fact that many cardinals in this conclave (and bishops too), have found their personal faith sustained and spiritually nourished through contact or association with movements such as Focolare, Communion and Liberation, Sant'Egidio, Schoenstatt, and also—though it is not a movement, Opus Dei. Dom Geraldo seems not to be challenging that; his point is another.

66. This whole issue merits a fuller analysis than is possible in this book.

67. http://w2.vatican.va/content/benedict-xvi/en/audiences/2013/documents/ hf_ben-xvi_aud_20130227.html.

68. These background details were revealed by Msgr. Alfred Xuereb, the pope's second private secretary, in a talk he gave at Pordenone, in northern Italy, on October 17, 2017.

69. Gregory XII was forced to resign on July 4, 1415, to end the Great Western Schism.

70. *Il Messaggero*, February 29.

71. Also in Vatican Insider today.

72. Gianni Valente interviewed Cardinal Bergoglio four times for *Trenta Giorni* between 2002 and 2009. Those articles reveal much about Bergoglio's

vision and priorities, which are now known to the whole world. The interviews were published after Francis's election as *Francesco: Un papa dalla fine del Mondo* (Bologna: EMI, 2013). The book appeared in English under the title *Interviews with a Future Pope* (London: Catholic Truth Society, 2013) and was also published in other languages.

73. http://w2.vatican.va/content/benedict-xvi/en/speeches/2013/february/documents/hf_ben-xvi_spe_20130228_congedo-cardinali.html.

74. http://w2.vatican.va/content/benedict-xvi/en/speeches/2013/february/documents/hf_ben-xvi_spe_20130228_fedeli-albano.html.

PART TWO

1. The English translation of his letter was provided by the Vatican.

2. http://w2.vatican.va/content/paul-vi/it/motu_proprio/documents/hf_p-vi_motu-proprio_19701120_ingravescentem.html (text in Italian or Latin).

3. https://www.aljazeera.com/indepth/features/2013/04/2013418135910 379874.html.

4. www.fides.org/.../33312-AFRICA_EGYPT_Coptic_Catholic_Cardinal_Naguib_will_a.

5. It should be noted that many cardinals have studied in Rome and so speak Italian, which can serve as a common language too.

6. Pope Francis accepted Cardinal McCarrick's resignation from the College of Cardinals on July 27, 2018, following allegations of sexual abuse of a minor that rocked the church in the United States, and ordered him to observe "a life of prayer and penance in seclusion." He had earlier removed him from public ministry. McCarrick was the first cardinal ever to resign from the College of Cardinals because of the abuse scandal, and the first to resign since 1927, when the French cardinal Louis Billot did so because of his support of Action Française, a right-wing political movement condemned by Pius XI.

7. During a pre-conclave gathering of ten or more electors at Cardinal Lopez Trujillo's apartment in April 2005, a participant told me that the then still very influential cardinal, Bernard Law, the former archbishop of Boston who had to resign following the abuse scandal there, told the group that if Ratzinger failed to get elected, or did not accept the election, then Cardinal Arinze would be the alternative candidate to succeed John Paul II.

8. Called "*Vaticanisti*" in Italian.

9. *Corriere della Sera*, February 27, p. 35.

10. The Apostolic Segnatura.

11. Ambrogio M. Piazzoni, *Storia delle Elezioni Pontificie* (Milan: Edizioni Piemme, 2005), appendix, 309–13.

12. Ibid.

13. According to the sixth-century *Liber Pontificalis*, the earliest known record of the popes, Victor I (ca. 189–198 AD), the fourteenth pope was from North Africa. Two other popes, Miltiades (311–314 AD) the thirty-second pope, and Gelasius I (492–496 AD) the forty-ninth pope, were born in Rome to families of African origin.

14. Cormac Murphy-O'Connor, *An English Spring* (New York: Bloomsbury Continuum, 2015), 213–14.

15. June 12, 2013.

16. http://www.nytimes.com/2013/02/28/opinion/a-vatican-spring.html.

17. Quotes here are taken from the original op-ed in the *New York Times*, February 27, 2013.

18. October 2017.

19. *La Stampa*, March 9, 2013.

20. Francis A. Burkle-Young, *Passing the Keys: Modern Cardinals, Conclaves, and the Election of the Next Pope* (Lanham, MD: Madison Books, 1999), 5–10.

21. *Corriere della Sera*, March 2.

22. Roberto Rusconi, *Il gran rifiuto: Perche un papa si dimette* (*The Great Refusal: Why a Pope Resigns*) (Brescia: Morcelliana, 2013), 152. The term "the great refusal" is found in Dante's *Inferno*, Canto III, which critics say refers to Pierro Morrone, who was taken from his hermitage when he was eighty years of age and made pope in 1294. He took the name Celestine V but resigned five months later and was succeeded by Boniface VIII. Dante visiting Hell saw him among the damned and wrote: "I saw and knew the shade of him who from cowardice made the great refusal."

23. Pope Francis, who held him in the highest esteem, appointed him camerlengo on December 20, 2015. He died on July 5, 2018 in Hartford, Connecticut, where he had been hospitalized for treatment of Parkinson's, from which he had suffered since 2003. Unusually, Pope Francis attended the requiem Mass, whereas protocol requires him only to give the final commendation.

24. The Canadian Conference of Catholic Bishops appointed Fr. Rosica as the national director and chief executive officer of the Seventeenth World Youth Day (WYD) in Toronto in 2002, a role that brought him into direct contact with John Paul II and top Vatican officials. Shortly after WYD he was asked by the founder of St. Joseph Communications, Gaetano Gagliano, to run a religious television network, and he chose the name "Salt and Light" from the WYD motto. It began broadcasting in 2003.

25. This was posted on the Salt and Light website on the eve of the broadcast: saltandlighttv.org/blogfeed/getpost.php?id=45228.

26. www.cbc.ca/player/play/2340061432.

27. Burkle-Young, *Passing the Keys*, 276. This well-researched book provides a substantial account of what happened in that conclave, including the votes obtained by cardinals in each of the eight ballots that concluded with the election of John Paul II (276–90).

28. https://www.nytimes.com/2013/.../at-vatican-cardinal-dolan-urges-catholics-to-look-bey.

29. The text appeared in *L'Osservatore Romano*, the Vatican daily, March 6.

30. They were: Cardinals Béchara Boutros Rai, OMM, patriarch of Antioch of the Maronites, from Lebanon, the first Maronite to participate in a conclave; Joachim Meisner, archbishop of Cologne, Germany; Rainer Maria Woekli, archbishop of Berlin, Germany; Théodore-Adrien Sarr, archbishop of Dakar, Senegal; and Dominik Jaroslav Duka, OP, archbishop of Prague, Czech Republic.

31. *Universi Dominici Gregis* 13.

32. The information came from Archbishop Georg Ganswein, the emeritus pope's secretary.

33. Cardinal Caffarra died on September 6, 2017. He was one of the four cardinals who sent a letter to Pope Francis on September 19, 2016, asking for clarification of his teaching in *Amoris Laetitia* on the admission of the divorced and remarried to communion. The other three signatories of the letter were Cardinals Joachim Meisner (Germany; died July 5, 2017), Walter Brandmuller (Germany), and Raymond Burke (USA). The text of their letter can be found at https://www.catholicnewsagency.com/news/full-text-of-dubia-cardinals-letter-asking-pope-for-an-audience-15105.

34. The three electors were: Antonio María Rouco Varela, archbishop of Madrid, who has been the dominating force in the Spanish church for many years; Zenon Grocholewski, the Polish prefect emeritus of the Congregation for Catholic Education since 1999; and Anthony Olubunmi Okogie, archbishop emeritus of Lagos, Nigeria. The four cadinals over the age of eighty were: Michael Michai Kitbunchu, archbishop emeritus of Bangkok, Thailand, and one of four members of the College of Cardinals with Chinese ancestry, whom I have interviewed; Emmanuel Wamala, archbishop emeritus of Kampala, Uganda, who, in an interview with a Ugandan paper, described his participation in the 2005 conclave in these striking words: "During the elections I was armed with the power of the Holy Spirit even as I walked to drop my ballot paper in the box. I kept looking straight at the image of the crucified Lord. I was then seized by a second feeling that I was participating in crucifying someone" (April 8, 2018, interview in Uganda's *Daily Monitor*); Eusébio Oscar Scheid, SCI, archbishop emeritus of São Sebastião do Rio de Janeiro, Brazil; and Christian Wiyghan Tumi, archbishop emeritus of Douala, Cameroon, a courageous leader whom I have known for many years.

35. https://oglobo.globo.com/mundo/brasileiro-odilo-scherer-um-nome-limpo-em-roma-7739828#ixzz5Dyl1LhwR.

36. The twelve listed include Rivera Carrera (Mexico), Rodriguez Maradiaga (Honduras), Dolan (USA), Scola (Italy), Pell (Australia), Duka (Czech Republic), Bertone (Italy), Wuerl (USA), Ouellet (Canada), O'Malley (USA), Sandri (Argentina), Turkson (Ghana). http://www.snapnetwork.org/snap_s_dirty_dozen_list_the_papabile_who_would_be_the_worst_choice_for_children.

37. Antonios Naguib, patriarch emeritus of Alexandria, Egypt; Karl Lehmann, bishop of Mainz, who was for twenty-one years chairman of the German bishops' conference (1987–2008); John Tong Hon, bishop of Hong Kong—the only Chinese elector; and Friedrich Wetter, archbishop emeritus of Munich, Germany.

38. Cardinal Martini's memorable last interview in English can be found at: https://datinggod.org/2012/09/04/the-full-english-translation-of-cardinal-martinis-last-interview/.

39. October 2017.

40. It named others too as *papabile*: Tagle, Turkson, Sarah, Schönborn, and Erdo.

41. Cardinal Benelli was the grand elector of John Paul I, as Burkle-Young reports in considerable detail in *Passing the Keys*, 240–60.

42. http://g1.globo.com/platb/blog-do-camarotti/2013/03/07/os-riscos-da-candidatura-precoce-do-cardeal-odilo-scherer.

43. https://noticias.uol.com.br/internacional/ultimas-noticias/2013/03/12/arcebispo-que-bateu-dom-odilo-em-eleicao-diz-que-papa-brasileiro-seria-honra-imensa.htm?cmpid=copiaecola.

44. Cardinal Kazimierz Nycz, archbishop of Warsaw, Poland, an elector, and Cardinal Giovanni Coppa, emeritus apostolic nuncio to the Czech Republic, who is over the age of eighty.

45. From the order of bishops, Cardinal Béchara Boutros Raï, OMM, patriarch of Antioch of the Maronites, Lebanon; from the order of priests, Cardinal Laurent Monsengwo Pasinya, archbishop of Kinshasa, Democratic Republic of Congo; and from the order of deacons, Cardinal Velasio De Paolis, CS, president emeritus of the Prefecture for the Economic Affairs of the Holy See.

46. Cardinal Calcagno owns at least thirteen guns, the Italian media reported, including a Smith & Wesson 357 Magnum and a Turkish Hatsan shotgun, according to *The Daily Mail*, April 14, 2012.

47. *Pastor Bonus* 171, n. 2.

48. The Vietnamese prelate and Cardinal Adam Joseph Maida, the archbishop emeritus of Detroit, Michigan, and now over the age of eighty, attended this afternoon's congregation and took the oath.

49. April 5, 2017.

50. The Quirinale was once the papal summer residence; Pius IX was the last pope to live here. Four conclaves were held in this palace, which is now the residence of the president of Italy.

51. Catherine Pepinster mentions this too in her book, *The Keys and the Kingdom: The British and the Papacy from John Paul II to Francis* (London: Bloomsbury T&T Clark, 2017), 69.

52. *Universi Dominici Gregis* 38.

53. Benedict's motu proprio, as mentioned earlier, amended no. 37 of the apostolic constitution *Universi Dominici Gregis*.

54. Salt and Light, YouTube, March 8, 2013: Papal Transition Special with Vatican affairs analyst Gerard O'Connell.

55. Miguel Obando y Bravo, SD, archbishop emeritus of Managua, Nicaragua, famous for his clash with the Sandinista government; and Gaudencio Borbon Rosales, the humble, wise, and prudent archbishop emeritus of Manila, the Philippines, whom I have known for many years

56. Lucio Brunelli, "*Cosi elegemmo Papa Ratzinger,*" ("How we elected Pope Ratzinger") *Limes* 4 (2005): 299.

57. https://www.theglobeandmail.com/news/can-the-cardinal-who.../article8767944/.

58. In conversation with me. Others too have this story, including Austen Ivereigh, see following note.

59. Austen Ivereigh, in *The Great Reformer* (New York: Henry Holt and Company, 2014), 356, n.9, also mentions that the *Wall Street Journal*'s staff provided an account of this dinner in *Pope Francis: From the End of the Earth to Rome* (New York: HarperCollins, 2013), chapter 8.

60. Some have reported that Cardinal Bergoglio gave his intervention on Friday, March 8, but that does not accord with the information I have.

61. My translation from the Spanish, but also drawing on Matthew Sherry's fine effort in Sandro Magister's blog, Chiesa.

62. Fabio Marchese Ragona, *Tutti Gli Uomini di Francesco* (whose English title would be *All the Men of Francis*) (Milan: Edizioni San Paolo, 2018), 8.

63. Ivereigh, *The Great Reformer,* 359.

64. Ibid.

65. Ibid.

66. *La Stampa*, March 10 and 12, 2013.

67. *El Mundo*, March 12, 2013.

68. It did—and he did!

69. *National Catholic Reporter*, March 10, 2013.

70. *Il Giornale*, March 16, 2013. In the post-conclave interview he said, "God gave us a Jesuit with a Franciscan heart!"

71. Elisabetta Piqué, *Francis: Life and Revolution* (Chicago: Loyola Press, 2015), 97. Long after the conclave, Calabresi's niece, Ms. Milvia Arcese, revealed that her uncle, the nuncio who died in 2004, had predicted that Bergoglio could become pope.

72. *La Repubblica*, March 15, p. 10.

73. From the order of bishops, Antonios Naguib; from the order of priests, Marc Ouellet; and from the order of deacons, Francesco Monterisi.

74. Conversation, November 8, 2017.

75. https://globoplay.globo.com/v/2454013/.

76. *Il Giornale*, March 15.

77. Ragona, *Tutti Gli Uomini di Francesco*, 9.

78. Ibid., 8.

79. March 22, 2017.

80. Pope Francis appointed her deputy-director of the Holy See's press office in August 2016. She is the first woman to hold that post.

81. Gerson Camarotti, *Segredos do Conclave* (São Paulo: Geração Editorial, 2013), 22.

82. Cardinal Nicora died in Rome on April 22, 2017.

83. I learned of this meeting the following day. The list of names provided here is substantially accurate, but not complete.

84. October 22, 2016.

85. October 2017.

86. Francesco Antonioli, ed., *Francesco e Noi*, (Segrate, Italy: Edizione Piemme, 2017), 237.

PART THREE

1. www.vatican.va/sede_vacante/2013/homily-pro-eligendo-pontifice_2013_en.html.

2. Cormac Murphy-O'Connor, *An English Spring* (New York: Bloomsbury Continuum, 2015), 217.

3. John Bingham, "Pope Francis Elected after Supernatural 'Signs' in the Conclave, says Cardinal," *Daily Telegraph*, May 14, 2013, www.telegraph.co.uk.

4. December 19, 2017.

5. *Corriere della Sera*, March 11.

6. The *New York Times*, March 11.

7. *Corriere della Sera*'s ten *papabili*, on March 13: Dolan, Erdo, O'Malley, Ouellet, Ravasi, Robles Ortega, Scherer, Scola, Tagle, and Turkson.

8. *Le Figaro*'s twelve *papabili*: Scola (Italy), Scherer (Brazil), Ouellet (Canada), Schönborn (Austria), Tagle (the Philippines), O'Malley (USA), Bergoglio (Argentina), Robles Ortega (Mexico), Erdo (Hungary), Ranjith (Sri Lanka), Dolan (USA), Toppo (India).

9. After the conclave Accattoli admitted that he had never been right in his papal predictions, but he rejoiced greatly at the election of Bergoglio.

10. Exceptions include papal elections that took place in Avignon, France, between 1316 and 1370.

11. The *Ordo Rituum Conclavis*, prepared by the Office of Liturgical Celebrations of the Supreme Pontiff, outlines in detail, in Latin and Italian, the entire ceremony related to the election of the pope.

12. March 20.

13. The text of the oath is found at no. 53 of the apostolic constitution *Universi Dominici Gregis*, promulgated by John Paul II in February 22, 1996 and amended by Benedict XVI on June 12, 2010 and February 25, 2013. http://w2.vatican.va/content/john-paul-ii/en/apost_constitutions/documents/hf_jp-ii_apc_22021996_universi-dominici-gregis.html.

14. http://www.news.va/en/news/cardinal-prosper-grechs-meditation-to-the-115-card.

15. *Universi Dominici Gregis* 68.

16 . A Faraday cage is an enclosure made of conducting material that shields what it encloses against the entry or escape of electromagnetic fields.

17. John Thavis mentions this in *The Vatican Diaries* (New York: Penguin Books, 2013), 19–20.

18. I have interviewed him on a number of occasions.

19. There was only one bishop named "Broglio" listed in the Vatican Year Book (*Annuario Pontificio*) for 2013: Archbishop Timothy Broglio, the military ordinary for the United States of America. He was not on anybody's list to be pope.

20. *The Election of a Pope* (London: Catholic Truth Society, 1997), 45. This excellent booklet was written by the Scottish monsignor Charles Burns, who served as Vatican archivist for thirty-five years and is one of the most knowledgeable persons in Rome on the history of the Church and the popes. In recent years he has served as ecclesiastical advisor to the British Embassy in the Holy See.

21. Elisabetta Piqué, *Francis: Life and Revolution* (Chicago: Loyola Press, 2015), 23.

22. Ibid., 23. Sodano and Sandri were very close to each other.

23. Piqué, *Francis: Life and Revolution*, 23.

24. Interview with Elisabetta Piqué, March 24.

25. A cardinal elector who witnessed the scene told me this.

26. Piqué, *Francis: Life and Revolution*, 13–14.

27. *Francisco: El Padre Jorge*, September 2015.

28. Andrea Tornielli, *Francesco Insieme* (Milan: Piemme, 2013), 8. English edition: *Francis: Pope of a New World* (San Francisco: Ignatius Press, 2013).

29. I interviewed Cardinal Onaiyekan three days before the conclave.

30. Francesca Ambrogetti and Sergio Rubin, *El Jesuita*: Conversaciones con el cardenal /Jorge Bergoglio, SJ (Buenos Aires: Vergara Grupo Zeta, 2010). In English: *Pope Francis: Conversations with Jorge Bergoglio: His Life in His Own Words* (New York: Berkley Books, 2014).

31. As pope, Francis admitted that he had made mistakes in those early years as provincial.

32. An elector told me this long after the conclave. Some Italian media also reported it.

33. An elector who witnessed this told me.

34. O'Malley told this to reporters.

35. Cardinal Maradiaga confirmed the story about the broken leg in a brief conversation with me on March 7, 2018.

36. Fabio Marchese Ragona, *Tutti Gli Uomini di Francesco* (Milan: Edizioni San Paolo, 2018), 9.

37. A German source close to Lehmann told me this a week after the conclave, March 22, 2013. It was later revealed in Argentina that Horacio Verbitsky, the main accuser of Bergoglio, worked for Argentina's military during the dirty war. I wrote an article on this for *America* magazine, May 18, 2015. https://www.americamagazine.org/content/dispatches/main-accuser-pope-francis-work.

38. The full text of the conversation in English can be found at https://laciviltacattolica.com/people-creative-conversations-jesuits-chilre-peru/; February 15, 2018 edition.

39. Piqué, *Francis: Life and Revolution*, 28.

40. Elisabetta Piqué was the first to break this news in her book, *Francis: Life and Revolution*, 28.

41. Incredibly, some who don't agree with Pope Francis's leadership and ministry have sought to use this fact to delegitimize him by alleging that his election was invalid, notwithstanding the fact that the voting procedure outlined in the apostolic constitution was properly observed and, moreover, the Vatican's top canon lawyers were among the electors in the conclave.

42. March 20, 2013.

43. March 18, 2013.

44. *Universi Dominici Gregis* 87–89.

45. *Universi Dominici Gregis* 86.

46. Cardinal Comastri, the archpriest of Saint Peter's Basilica, revealed this on Vatican television, with the new pope's permission. Several others have confirmed this too.

47. *Universi Dominici Gregis* 88.

48. *Universi Dominici Gregis* 91.

49. http://w2.vatican.va/content/francesco/en/speeches/2013/march/documents/papa-francesco_20130316_rappresentanti-media.html.

50. March 20, 2013.

51. Cardinal Levada told several people that Rodé made this remark as Francis was leaving the Sistine Chapel, another cardinal told me.

52. *Universi Domenici Gregis* 71.

53. The tradition that the pope wears a white cassock appears to go back to Innocent V in 1276. A member of the Order of Preachers founded by Saint

Dominic, and the first Dominican to be elected pope, he continued to wear his white friar's habit during his pontificate.

54. Interview with Elisabetta Piqué, March 24.

55. Interview with Salt and Light TV, October 2013.

56. Murphy-O'Connor, *An English Spring*, 218.

57. Piqué, *Francis: Life and Revolution*, 33.

58. Murphy-O'Connor, *An English Spring*, 219.

59. Benedict XVI, *Last Testament: In His Own Words*, with Peter Seewald, paperback edition (London: Bloomsbury, 2017), 28.

60. *L'Osservatore Romano*, March 14, 2013 edition, which was published on the evening of March 13, p. 8.

61. Benedict XVI, *Last Testament*, 28–29.

62. Jorge Bergoglio–Abraham Skorka: *Sobre el cielo y la tierra* (Buenos Aires: Editorial Sudamericana, 2010). Translated into English in 2013 under the title: *On Heaven and Earth: Pope Francis on Faith, Family, and the Church in the Twenty-first Century*.

63. Text in *L'Osservatore Romano*, March 16, 2013, p. 1.

PART FOUR

1. Elisabetta Piqué, *Francis: Life and Revolution* (Chicago: Loyola Press, 2015), 36.

2. Francis had inherited the second secretary of Benedict XVI, the Maltese monsignor Alfred Xuereb, but he reassigned him to the Secretariat for the Economy in March 2014.

3. http://w2.vatican.va/content/francesco/en/homilies/2013/documents/papa-francesco_20130314_omelia-cardinali.html.

4. *L'Osservatore Romano*, March 16, p. 7.

5. Piqué, *Francis: Life and Revolution*, 177.

6. Fr. Lombardi told the press, "He is experimenting with this type of living arrangement, which is simple; it allows him to live in community with others."

7. Piqué, *Francis: Life and Revolution*, 36.

8. http://w2.vatican.va/content/francesco/en/speeches/2013/march/documents/papa-francesco_20130315_cardinali.html.

9. Cormac Murphy-O'Connor, *An English Spring* (New York: Bloomsbury Continuum, 2015), 219. When Francis met Cardinal Murphy-O'Connor that morning he joked, "You are the one to blame (*Sei il colpevole*): you told me I would be pope." The cardinal told me this on March 17.

10. Elisabetta Piqué devoted a whole chapter to Bergoglio's relation to the media in her biography: *Francis: Life and Revolution*. She noted that before becoming pope he didn't feel comfortable giving interviews because he was not confident that his words wouldn't be manipulated. On p. 158, she quotes him as saying, "If I give four notes to the journalists—do, re, mi, fa—they might end up composing a wedding march or a funeral march."

11. http://w2.vatican.va/content/francesco/en/speeches/2013/march/documents/papa-francesco_20130316_rappresentanti-media.html.

12. *Avvenire*, March 17, p. 9.

13. Piqué, *Francis: Life and Revolution*, 176.

14. March 17, p. 9.

15. http://w2.vatican.va/content/francesco/en/homilies/2013/documents/papa-francesco_20130317_omelia-santa-anna.html.

16. http://w2.vatican.va/content/francesco/en/angelus/2013/documents/papa-francesco_angelus_20130317.html.

17. *Corriere della Sera*, March 18, p.14.

18. http://w2.vatican.va/content/francesco/en/apost_letters/documents/papa-francesco_ bolla_20150411_misericordiae-vultus.html. See my article: https://www.americamagazine.org/issue/pope-francis-declares-jubilee-year-mercy.

19. See my report on this: https://www.americamagazine.org/.../pope-francis-opens-holy-door-says-we-have-put.

20. The names of the eight members of the Council of Cardinals: Monsengwo (Africa), Gracias (Asia), Marx (Europe), Errázuriz Ossa (Latin America), Pell (Oceania), O'Malley (North America), Bertello (Vatican), Maradiaga (coordinator). A year later, in July 2014, Francis added a ninth member to the council, Cardinal Pietro Parolin, the man he had appointed as secretary of state in August 2013, who had participated in all the meetings up to then.

21. Pope Francis formally established the council with a chirograph signed on September 28, 2013, and published by the Vatican news service on September 30.

22. Fr. James Martin, SJ, published the father general's report in *America* magazine: https://www.americamagazine.org/content/all-things/father-general-his-visit-pope.

23. The informal way of speaking in Italian and Spanish. "*Tu*" is the familiar way of saying "you" in Italian.

24. See http://w2.vatican.va/content/francesco/en/elezione/stemma-papa-francesco.html.

25. "Jesus saw the tax collector and, because *he saw him through the eyes of mercy and chose him*, he said to him: Follow me." (trans. *Liturgy of the Hours* 1975, p. 1418). The original Latin reads: *Vidit ergo Iesus publicanum et quia miserando atque eligendo vidit, ait illi 'Sequere me.'"* (Om. 21; CCL 122, 149–151).

26. Piqué, *Francis: Life and Revolution*, 38.

27. Pope Francis's determination to give priority attention to the poor took an important turn in July 2013 when he appointed a Polish priest, Msgr. Konrad Krajewski, as papal almoner. The priest, then working as a master of ceremonies in the Vatican, was well known for his work with the poor of Rome. I highlight the significance of the appointment in my article in Vatican Insider: www.lastampa.it/2013/08/06/vaticaninsider/pope-tells...almoner-do.../pagina.html. Francis made Msgr. Krajewski a cardinal at the consistory of June 2018.

28 . *Avvenire*, March 20, p. 3.

29 . The tradition appears to go back almost eight hundred years. The fisherman's ring is first mentioned in a letter from Pope Clement IV to his nephew in 1265.

30. The wax cast of the ring was made for Paul VI by Henry Manfrini but "it was never cast into metal and Paul VI never wore it, because he always wore the ring that was commissioned at the time of the Second Vatican Council," Fr.

Lombardi told the press on March 18. He said Paul VI's secretary, Archbishop Pasquale Macchi, kept the cast and on his death had bequeathed to an Italian prelate, Msgr. Ettore Malnati, who had a silver ring with gold plating made from the wax cast, and then gave it to the Vatican for today's ceremony.

31. http://w2.vatican.va/content/francesco/en/homilies/2013/documents/papa-francesco_xx20130319_omelia-inizio-pontificato.html.

32. This would be seen, for example, in his apostolic exhortation *Amoris Laetitia*, written after the two synods on the family in 2014 and 2015. Significantly, he signed the exhortation on March 19, 2016, the feast of Saint Joseph, exactly three years after his inauguration.

33. The encyclical *Laudato Si'* was published on May 24, 2015. The full text in English can be found at: http://w2.vatican.va/content/francesco/en/encyclicals/documents/papa-francesco_20150524_enciclica-laudato-si.html.

34. *Avvenire*, March 20, p. 5.

35. *Avvenire*, March 20, p. 8.

36. Francis made clear to the world that care for migrants and refugees is a top priority of his pontificate by visiting Lampedusa on July 8, 2013, and the Greek island of Lesbos on April 16, 2016. He met migrants in both places, and wept for the twenty thousand who had drowned in the Mediterranean Sea over the past decade. On January 1, 2017, Pope Francis established a special Office for Migrants and Refugees, in the Vatican Dicastery for Integral Human Development, which reports directly to him. The office is managed by Fr. Fabio Baggio, CS, and Fr. Michael Czerny, SJ.

37. Pope Francis had completed the writing of the exhortation by mid-August 2013. The full text in English can be found at: http://w2.vatican.va/content/francesco/en/apost_exhortations/documents/papa-francesco_esortazione-ap_20131124_evangelii-gaudium.html.

INDEX